Symbolists and Symbolism

Symbolists and Symbolism

by Robert L. Delevoy

SKIRA

RIZZOLI
NEW YORK

First published 1978

First paperback edition 1982

Published in the United States of America in 1982 by

RIZZOLI INTERNATIONAL PUBLICATIONS, INC.
712 Fifth Avenue/New York 10019

Translated from the French by Barbara Bray (Introduction and Chapters 3-8),
Elizabeth Wrightson (Chapter 1 and Index) and Bernard C. Swift
(Chapter 2)

Library of Congress Catalog Card Number: 81-86434

ISBN: 0-8478-0430-5

Printed in Switzerland

CONTENTS

WHY is it that Symbolism now appeals, and has been appealing for some years past, so strongly to both the eye and the mind? This new interest is a natural reaction against stereotyped views which have prevailed in the arts and literature for a good half-century or more; during which time the critical intelligence was too exclusively focused on signifiers, too much occupied with artistic and poetic languages as such, with their formal phenomena alone. True, that criticism accomplished much, bringing us through the reversal, the dislocation, of the old grammatological order and attuning us to the sonorities of the twentieth century, at the cost perhaps of an undue emphasis on the purely functional. So matters stood when, in the 1950s and 1960s, a need was felt for a fresh look at another side of the nineteenth century, at its symbols and the desires that shaped them, its dream mystique and longing for intimations of the gods; all this in order to return to a wider range of significations. Then began the overdue re-exploration of the wealth of late nineteenth-century art and poetry in many countries from Vienna to London and beyond; the re-exploration of the neglected world of symbolist imagery and the passions and spiritual aspirations behind it. For both are there in abundance, and neither of them will be found to have lost their urgency today, rooted as they are in the deepest levels of the human psyche irrespective of time, place or frontiers.

Henceforth the essence of nature must be expressed symbolically; a new world of symbols is therefore necessary.

Friedrich Nietzsche, *The Birth of Tragedy*, 1871

William Blake (1757-1827): Satan Smiting Job with Sore Boils, c. 1826-1827. Tempera.

Times on times he divided & measur'd
Space by space in his ninefold darkness,
Unseen, unknown; changes appear'd
Like desolate mountains, rifted furious
By the black winds of perturbation.

William Blake, *The First Book of Urizen*, 1794

INTRODUCTION

Polarity of the symbol

An artistic phenomenon, whatever its nature, can only come to life in the individual consciousness when there exists a social and economic context which, through institutional decrees that are bound to be to some extent precarious, allows the work of art to set itself up as a response to the fleeting solicitations of taste, as an object of active perception, and as a field for emotion: in other words, something specially designed to be at once experienced through an imagination focused by history, perceived through an alerted sensorial system, and read in accordance with acquired codes.

Thus, over and above man's permanent and specific faculty for transforming sensations into symbols, access to a work of art depends not so much on any "mystical unveiling" as on the availability of the sensibility and the situation of the intellect. As Leroi-Gourhan has put it, we may say *a priori* that symbolization as a form of mental integration "is capable of going from the heights to the fundamental depths, and that everything in man can be linked to the processes of aesthetically constructive thought." All the more so since, as Marx has shown, no aesthetic object can exist except by being constituted as such by a subject and designated by a cultural practice, though in the West this practice is imprisoned in concatenations, grids and schemas which all too often open on to a reality which is only rationality—what Michel Serres, the most brilliant renovator of symbolical thought in this latter part of the twentieth century, has called a "mass of cloud."

It may well be that the growing interest in what lies beyond the visible, in discontinuity of meaning, in the rearticulations of mimesis, has its origins in a desire to defend sensibility, feeling and the body against unbridled rationalization, the debunking effect of electronics, the statistical relationships and apocalyptic prospects of the post-industrial age. This would account for the rapid expansion of psychoanalysis and the spread of sub-rational ethnological lore; the fashion for science fiction and the occult sciences; the demand for holidays and escape; the attraction exercised by clairvoyance; the fascination exercised by death. All these are so many deep and radical thrusts in all directions, often historial and always on the look-out for symbols. They thus represent a turning towards fundamental structure: the appeal to symbols as an instrument of knowledge aims at discovering, or rather recovering, some modality of reality hitherto buried in cultural silt. It is as if rational thought, strangled in its own operational field, were trying to make its way towards mythological thought; as if it felt saturated in and by urbanism and the process of industrialization. It is in fact a sudden awakening to the symbolical void produced by electronic civilization, and more particularly to the libidinal disinvestment brought about by the substitution of technical objects for the traditional acts of labour.

Similarly, the functionalist myth has eroded the visceral awareness of our own corporeal perception which we enjoyed in our former pre-industrial, pre-speculative, pre-disciplinary, pre-repressive environment. It is no accident that Baudrillard has observed that "the classic children's drawing of their mother's house, with its doors and windows, symbolizes simultaneously themselves—the human face—and the mother's body." The disequilibrium, the break in continuity between man and Nature, between man's mythological roots and the world of the Logos, began in the middle of the nineteenth century with the gradual disappearance of any consistent distance between the possibilities of action inherent in man's biological status (and the power of adaptation it entails) and the operational area to which life restricts him.

In this connection we may recall the disastrous consequences of the anarchic proliferation of cities (regarded as efficient instruments in terms of the functioning of the social organism); and, on the level of behaviour, the disastrous consequences of the priority given to form, pure visuality, and "objective perception." But Flaubert was already pointing out that there is something more than "straightness of lines and smoothness of surfaces." There is something more than the dividing up of cities into hard and fast zones and arbitrary sectors—just so many devitalized tissues. There is something more than the technocratic dream with its objects either scattered or over-rigidly grouped in the space of the modernist myth. The prevailing tendency to reduce architectural production to "art and technics," together with the parallel tendency to reduce painting to the mere manipulation of plastic space, led in all sectors of artistic activity to the encouragement of a taste for novelty as event, for language as method of creation, for functionalism as religion freed of all historical reference, for production as myth capable of repressing all previous experience.

It is true that as early as the 1920s the masters of "modern" architecture agreed to proceed *from zero*, in accordance with the models recently worked out in the field of painting by Mondrian and Malevitch—a method which protected their functionalist, technological and formal postulates from academic precept. In the 1960s Sibyl Moholy-Nagy said: "The Muse of Gropius, Mies van der Rohe, Le Corbusier, Aalto, Oud and several others permitted no illicit love affairs with history." In 1964 she went on: "The inability of the international style to stimulate the creative imagination of architecture, to satisfy the customer's desire for identification, and to answer the need for historical awareness within the urban environment, was the immediate cause of the resuscitation of the corpse of history. This revival did not originate, as it logically should have done, in the schools of architecture, for these, in America, show a servile subservience to all trends instead of being the promoters of architectural revolutions. The credit for the rediscovery of architectural continuity belongs to practising architects, and contributed to the great success enjoyed by some of them. Saarinen was perhaps the first, with the Lombard-style chapel he built for M.I.T., followed by Johnson, Rudolph, Kahn, Johansen, Yamasaki, and so on. They all attempted a kaleidoscopic combination of historical and contemporary elements, with the object of rediscovering architecture in the interstices left by building technology. The results were rarely successful and often ridiculous."

Since then a strong attempt has been made, on the critical level, to debunk the theoretical attitudes and practices linked with the C.I.A.M. movement (International Congresses on Modern Architecture). This was accompanied by an effort to reintroduce the historical dimension into architectural criticism and, consequently, into architectural practice. A choice of texts by G. C. Argan, R. Venturi, R. Banham, F. Choay, F. Borsi, C. Norberg-Schulz, P. Portoghesi, M. Tafuri, A. Rossi, E. Bonfanti, G. Bekaert, P. Noviant, L. Krier, H. Damish, A. Grumbach, P. Boudon, F. Loyer, R. Bentmann and M. Müller would throw considerable light on the relations established between cultural anthropology, history, the social sciences, psychoanalysis, linguistics, and semiology (J. Lacan 1966, J. Derrida 1967, Bourdieu-Passeron 1970, Radcliffe-Brown 1972, R. Barthes 1971, A. Touraine 1972, J. Baudrillard 1972). These relations were directed towards a general restructuring of knowledge which would provide the basis for fundamental anthropology, the comprehensive science whose elements, scope and method of approach have been defined by Edgar Morin in *Le Paradigme perdu* ("Paradigm Lost"), 1973.

Against an equally wide background must be placed the present transformation of the operational field of art, the break with the ideology of consumption, the ups and downs of sensibility, the emergence from formalism, and the anxious inquiry directed towards the "stupid" and "unspeakably foul" nineteenth century, as Villiers de l'Isle-Adam called it. It should be pointed out, however, that the real

Rodolphe Bresdin (1825-1885): The Comedy of Death (enlarged detail), 1854. Etching.

emergence of this "movement" towards the recent past, strategically supported by the revival of historicist culture, took place between 1955 and 1975, with the enthusiasm which arose throughout the West for Art Nouveau, a baroque, lyrical and symbolist phenomenon which appeared very rich and dense by contrast with the semantic poverty of international architecture, which, to apply J. K. Huysmans' words, could only reflect an "era of mercantilism and haste." Moreover, the interrogation, via Art Nouveau, of nineteenth-century painting came well before the interrogation of architecture. It was inspired by the same fundamental reasons: the need to find a universe of significations again, after having accorded a special position to a line starting with the Impressionists, passing through Cézanne and Paul Klee, and ending in conceptual art, but excluding all works based on traditional figurative processes and/or involving cultural decodage or connotation. Discourse, hitherto exiled, tended to take on new force and vigour and brilliance.

After an over-confidential prelude sponsored in 1958 by André Breton—an exhibition of symbolist drawings at the Bateau-Lavoir Gallery in Paris—the movement got under way in 1961 with the reconstitution at the Louvre of the "enchanter's domain" of Gustave Moreau. But the real launching seems to have taken place in Brussels in 1962, with the astonishing exhibition, *Le Groupe des XX et son temps* (The Group of "The Twenty" and Their Time). The movement spread, and 1969 was a decisive turning point in the history of contemporary taste with the huge, disturbing exhibition, *The Sacred and Profane in Symbolist Art*, held in Turin and then Toronto. The year 1972 saw the show of *French Symbolists* in London and Liverpool, *English Romantic Painting and the Pre-Raphaelites* in Paris, and a Belgian show devoted to *Painters of the Imaginary*.

The road which in André Breton's words had been "blocked for too long by the level crossings of *nothing*" was now open. In 1973, in Paris, came a provocative exhibition of "*pompier*" or academic painters under the title *Equivoques* ("Ambiguities"). An exhibition on a similar theme, called "An Imaginary Salon," had been held in Berlin in 1969. All this was followed in Paris in 1974 by a temporary reconstruction of the collection in the Musée du Luxembourg, Paris, as it was in 1874, the year of the first Impressionist exhibition (the Luxembourg being at that time *the* museum of contemporary art in Paris). This show presented the first results of a concerted attempt to trace throughout France all the hundreds of paintings acquired by the French State at the annual Salons or directly from artists in the course of the nineteenth century. It thus reflected official or academic taste at the time, a choice which some regarded as dictated by an "ideology of slickness": hence the Luxembourg's reputation as a shrine of official art.

This Paris exhibition should be related to one on *The Architecture of the Ecole des Beaux-Arts* held at the Museum of Modern Art in New York in January 1976. Here examination entries by winners of the Grand Prix de Rome were to be seen beside photographs of important works of nineteenth-century French architecture, like Garnier's Opéra, that "worldly cathedral of the Second Empire," and Labrouste's Bibliothèque Sainte-Geneviève, a pioneer work of steel-frame architecture. Even this long series of "retro"-active shows was only a preface to the impact of the fabulous exhibition on *Symbolism in Europe* held in Rotterdam, Brussels, and Paris in 1976, and to the big Puvis de Chavannes exhibition shown in Paris at the end of 1976 and Ottawa in 1977. This latter looked afresh at a kind of painting which the superstition of formalism had long held in contempt. A kind of dress rehearsal had already been seen in Toronto in 1975, in an exhibition entitled *Puvis de Chavannes and the Modern Tradition*, in which the artist's "modernist" posterity included Gauguin, Seurat, Hodler, Matisse, Maillol, and the Americans Prendergast, Glackens and Arthur Davies.

The above-mentioned initiatives, whether concerned with the architecture or with the painting of the nineteenth century, did not aim only at making up for deliberate omissions. They also undertook reappraisals, investigations likely to upset received ideas. They called in question value judgments more or less strongly established. They helped to modify mental constructions conditioned by theoretical, economic and political attitudes. The differences between the angles from which the nineteenth century was examined by architectural criticism on the one hand and art criticism on the other are less important than common attitudes which emerged, together with recognition of the necessity, which had become more and more evident in the 1960s, to restore to theory its power to motivate all practice. Another parallel development was the extraordinary extension of the human sciences. All these attitudes were affected by a factor analogous to that which had fostered the spread of Symbolism in the nineteenth century: i.e. uneasiness at approaching the *"fin de siècle,"* at the thought of the dangerous and possibly fatal transition through the junction of two stretches of time. It was probably a similar notion which aroused so much actual fear at the approach of the year 1000 A.D.

It has been said of Symbolism that it is, above all, *literature*. But this is too facile. We need to extrapolate Heidegger's question and ask—though we know there can be no answer—"What is literature?" But the question is absurd: how can discourse be anything else but symbolist? From Baruchello back to Homer, from Burroughs to the *Vedas*, Dante to Lewis Carroll, the Psalms to Buren, Carpaccio to Jules Verne, a work of art has always been mythology, an uninterrupted movement, a record of the struggle between the body and the imagination, a graph of all the impulses that have appeared on the screens of illusion. It has always been an essential mythography. It is not a question of language or writing, but of language *and* writing, an indissoluble pair in which the combination of all knowledge includes all the formalities implied in the difference between the two: images which are plural, complex, ambiguous; relays, condensations, reductions; changes; metaphorical investments. It includes journeys from perception to memory, from memory to perception; translations, correlations, correspondences, synaesthesias. Verbal, chromatic and aural violence; visual veils; spatial spasms. Scenographic mirages, coincidences, metamorphoses, detonating mixtures, semantic charges, hallucination. We might reverse Goethe's aphorism and say: *Everything that is permanent is symbol.* And this whether what is permanent is fluid, opaque or transparent, and although it always tries to modulate fiction and reality: between vibration and explosion, between life and death.

To some extent, symbol will always be that which leads from the visible to the invisible, and from the invisible to the illusion of appearances as perceived by man at a given moment in his history, in History itself. That being so, it would not be honest to represent Symbolism as an original movement in itself, localized, unified and consistent. As if there could be any relation other than a symbolic relation between the methods of Gauguin and those of Gustave Moreau, between the writing of Huysmans and that of Mallarmé, between the figurative imagi-

nation of Khnopff and that of Klimt, between the poetry of Toorop and that of Redon, between the signs used by Puvis de Chavannes, Segantini, Mucha, Munch, Kubin, Maurice Denis, Walter Crane, Arnold Böcklin, and Jànos Vaszary, except that of belonging to the same cultural area and the same portion of time—the second half of the nineteenth century—and of seeming to stand at an equal distance from the art manufactured for the Salons and from "impressionist" and "post-impressionist" art (Odilon Redon called the first an "edifice whose vaults were rather low"), which were trying, at the same moment, to recast traditional imagery and rejuvenate the approach to poetry, music and the visual arts. The production of the Symbolists was simultaneous with that of Monet, Renoir, Manet, Cézanne, Seurat, parallel even to that of Courbet and Zola. Does that mean it was trying to solve a common problem? And did it possess enough coherence to be called a "movement," a deliberate whole with a deliberate object? Or did it rather follow, via normal paths, the route of the oldest mythography there is?

The answer to this question will emerge in the course of our examination of the development of what is called "symbolism." But one thing is certain already, and that is, in painting, an attachment to the classic processes of mimesis, and an attempt to revive a syntax worn out by more than four centuries of use by investing the dreamed image with iconic substance. It was this that separated the "marginal" Symbolists from "official" art, though they adopted a deliberately idealist approach. They used Greek, Celtic and Judaeo-Christian legend to "culturalize" their work and make it accessible to a particular social class. As Charles Morice said in the 1880s: "Art... is essentially subjective. The appearance of things is only a symbol which it is the artist's task to interpret. Things have no truth except in that; they have only an inner truth." (This is very close to the *inner compulsion* which Rainer Maria Rilke later called the central motive of creative activity, and the condition of its authenticity.) Hence a desire on the part of such artists to differentiate themselves from the prevailing Realism, lest it should be left to the Naturalists "to storm the future" (Castagnary). This attitude overlapped with a deep hostility towards social emancipation (except that of William Morris), and consequently with fear lest the Left should attack the privileges of the ruling classes. In this context the symbolist movement of the period 1870-1900 may be regarded simultaneously as an ideological structure incorporating into pre-existing paradigms information derived from an environment (social and physical) and from history; as a political commitment opposing positivism and historical materialism (an opposition coinciding with the "rise of science" and the spread of the myth of progress); as a semantic field directed towards the annihilation of art and taking its impetus from the anguish, distress and confusion caused by upheavals in the environment, urban inflation, and economic and technological change; as an expression of protest against thermodynamics and its massive production of steam, which "whistles and smokes to get to a destination in which no one believes" (Villiers de l'Isle-Adam). Or it could be seen as a flight, an escape passing via Romanticism, the nearest available mythological lever. A flight forward, drug-scented, towards the "decadence" of *fin-de-siècle* art, arranged concurrently with the erotic festivities—graphic, linear and chromatic—of Art Nouveau, as a symbol covering both the power and the fears of the industrial bourgeoisie. A flight backwards, towards the hallucinations of Blake and the "graceful pantheistic chaos" of Fuseli; towards the irrational violence of Goya; towards the Gardens of Death of Rodolphe Bresdin, of whom Baudelaire said that what he lacked in talent he made up for in genius. So it involved eccentricity, a break with all behaviour dictated by the commonsense which marked the boundaries of the bourgeoisie. But it was also an archipelago of lonely islands, where the machines of desire and the ego feverish with self-love could function all the more freely: Gustave Moreau in Paris, Ensor in Ostend, Munch in Oslo, Rimbaud in Somaliland, Gauguin in Tahiti. Were they exiles? Points of fall? Rather, points of escape where desire could be invented, where the theatre of discourse could exorcise reality. Where the pressure of difference cracked open the vault of dreams: beyond the pleasure principle.

John Henry Fuseli (1741-1825):
△ *Titania, Bottom and the Fairies, 1793-1794. Oil.*
◁ *Self-Portrait, c. 1777. Charcoal and white chalk.*

TITANIA TO BOTTOM:

Come, sit thee down upon this flowery bed,
While I thy amiable cheeks do coy,
And stick musk-roses in thy sleek smooth head,
And kiss thy fair large ears, my gentle joy.

Shakespeare, *A Midsummer Night's Dream*, Act III, Scene 2

Mankind does not live in periods of a year or a decade or a generation, or even in what Focillon has vividly described as "secular
spasms." So apart from the occasional texts which stand like out-
crops in time, we cannot date the first appearance of a superstructure,
a trend in art, or a variation in taste as we can date the rise or fall of an
empire. It would therefore be pointless to try and give the exact date of
the birth of Symbolism, especially as the mythical discourse the word
denotes began to disperse and ramify even before it could be identified.
Nevertheless it is not surprising that André Breton saw a close parallel
between the period (1870-1871) of the Franco-Prussian War, the revolutionary outburst of the Commune and the establishment of republi-
can government, and the period of similar unrest and ferment just after
the First World War, when Surrealism made its appearance in France.
Breton's eagerness to make the connection probably derived from his
discovery at the age of sixteen of the Gustave Moreau Museum in
Paris, which "conditioned for ever his way of loving." He wrote in
1960: "It was there that beauty and love were revealed to me, through
a few feminine faces and poses. The *type* these women belonged to has
probably hidden all other types from me: I was completely spellbound.
Myth, kindled into life again here as nowhere else, must have come
into it. The woman who, almost without changing, was in turn Salome,
Helen, Delilah, the Chimera, or Semele, became the incarnation of
them all. From them she drew her power, and fixed her features in
eternity."

Thus "conditioned" by what he felt as Moreau's power of evocation,
Breton, soon after the war, published a text which is a bridge between
Surrealism and historical Symbolism, a link which is all the more useful
because apart from the brilliant episode of the surrealist review *Mino-
taure* (Paris, 1933-1939), Surrealism in its heyday aroused no great
interest in those whose business it was to recognize the main trends of
the period. "The years 1870 and 1871," wrote Breton in 1922, "witnessed the two great indictments brought against old art by young
men. The elements of one of those indictments are to be found in a
letter by Rimbaud dated 15 May 1871 and published in the *Nouvelle
Revue Française* in October 1912. For the other we must look to the
unreprinted *Poésies* of Isidore Ducasse."

Isidore Ducasse, self-styled Comte de Lautréamont, who had been
living since the beginning of March 1870 at 15 Rue Vivienne, died on
November 24 of the same year. He was just twenty-four years old. At
the time of his death Paris was under siege, and a few copies of a
strange book, hastily bound in a yellow cover, were circulating in
secret. They had been published more or less clandestinely the previous
year by Lacroix and Verboeckhoven, printers, of Brussels. According to
the author himself the book painted life "in over-harsh colours," and
"for fear of the public prosecutor" the printer soon suspended sales of
the *Chants de Maldoror*. Meanwhile the Librairie Gabrie had just published in Paris itself the *Poésies* which Breton refers to: two books inspired by Ducasse's insurmountable urge to drown "the poetic moan-
ings and groanings of this century." To write of boredom, pain, woe,
melancholy, death, darkness and gloom was, he said, "to insist childish-
ly on looking on the wrong side of things. Lamartine, Hugo and Musset
deliberately transformed themselves into old women... Always snivell-
ing! That is why I have completely changed methods..." (Letter to
M. Darasse, 12 March 1870). Ducasse had taken the trouble to write a
preface to his *Poésies*, warning the reader of the many elements of

In the midst of colossal aerial buildings, with neither foundations nor roof-tops, covered with teeming, quivering vegetation, this sacred flora standing out against the dark blues of the starry vaults and the deserts of the sky, the God so often invoked appears in his still veiled splendour... At the foot of the throne, Death and Sorrow form the tragic basis of Human Life, and not far from them, under the aegis of the eagle of Jupiter, the great Pan, symbol of Earth, bows his sorrowful brow, mourning his slavery and exile, while at his feet is piled the sombre phalanx of the monsters of Erebus and Night...

Gustave Moreau, commentary on his *Jupiter and Semele*, Notebooks, 10 October 1897

Gustave Moreau (1826-1898):
◁ *The Persian Poet on a Unicorn, c. 1890. Pencil.*
▷ *Jupiter and Semele, 1894-1895. Oil.*

cruelty, homicidal fantasy and sexual violence in his work, and of the transformations he had imposed on classical and romantic texts (Byron, Poe, Baudelaire, Pascal, Vauvenargues, La Rochefoucauld, etc.). He had toyed with these texts to show that he could treat language as a system of symbolic communication and a means of gaining access to what Julia Kristeva has called "the meaning of fiction."

"Yes, good people," wrote Ducasse, "I tell you to roast on a red-hot shovel, with a pinch of brown sugar, the duck of doubt with its lips of vermouth, which in a melancholy struggle between good and evil sheds tears not from the heart, it has no air-pump, and creates over all a universal void." His was the poetry of revolt, a writing that devoured language as it was until then, a writing freed of the conventions of "art" and made out of the entrails of the verbal system. His texts are taut and savage, full of "poisons" and "deadly emanations." Symbolism, vehicle of the "ironical waters of the ether" and all the images of the "nightmare hiding in the phosphoric corners of darkness," begins when words travel on the tangent of the imagination and, borne forward on the frequencies of the waves, enter the axis of metaphorical condensation. A modern poet, Joseph Noiret, in a poem dated 1974, makes an unexpected contribution to the *Theory of Clouds*:

> I shall live in clouds that look like hoops
> rolling to infinity
> from oak branches in autumn
> slipping in the inertia of mists
> I shall live in brands which blacken the snow
> breaches in the shadow
> through which sifts the water
> of endless siltations
> I shall live in openings in the head
> in falls in the mines of memory
> I shall live in women and their black conflagrations
> while the birds that are my hands
> draw landscapes
> on the brink of birth.

Are these just bold leaps, a haphazard linking of the near and the far? It is always the same drifting, but from the same point of departure. Probably all the texts are linked, but in different degrees. They are linked in that they all proliferate out of a strict verbal procedure, from "verbal spells," from language treated as an aural instrument which produces images, from the disalienated word freed from all the weight of meaning (the meaning booby-trapped by the known order). This liberated word licenses tones and sounds which themselves create metaphors free of all syntactical restraint, and fresh with all the latent symbolism which stretches between light and darkness against a permanent background of universal analogy. Descartes said: "There is more analogy or relationship between colours and sounds than between material objects and God." Perhaps after all it was Aloysius Bertrand who showed Baudelaire how one might think of language as music. But already Rimbaud had stretched the chain of syntax:

> *On voit, roulant comme une digue au-delà de la*
> *route hydraulique motrice,*
> *Monstrueux, s'éclairant, sans fin.*

(We see, rolling along like a causeway beyond the hydraulic driving road, monstrous, brightening, endless.)

Rimbaud, while still a schoolboy in Charleville, was equally eager to publish his first poems and to throw himself into politics. At sixteen he came to Paris via Charleroi with a ticket to Saint-Quentin, but was arrested because he had "no home and no visible means of support." He was in the Mazas Prison in Paris while Félicien Rops and Camille Lemonnier witnessed, with mixed feelings we can easily imagine, the French surrender at Sedan (2 September 1870). (Rops had shown Baudelaire around Namur in 1865: both had a "passion for skeletons.") Meanwhile the Third Republic was proclaimed in Paris, where Gustave Moreau, a volunteer in the National Guard, was detailed to

Etienne Carjat (1828-1906): Photograph of Arthur Rimbaud in 1871, at the age of seventeen.

Shaping of the Symbolist mentality

defend the ramparts; where Puvis de Chavannes "resisted" through painting; where the "government of national defence" was set up. Meanwhile, at Oxford, Ruskin began a series of *Lectures on Art*, and his paranoiac friend Dante Gabriel Rossetti published his first book of poems. Meanwhile Villiers de l'Isle-Adam was living first in Weimar and Munich, then at Tribschen near Lucerne and his idol Wagner. While the German armies were marching on from victory to victory, Wagner had no qualms about writing to his French friends Catulle and Judith Mendès, on 12 August 1870: "See if you can think of one real statesman! That's the only thing that can get France out of its present situation. A statesman of real courage... who above all is capable of explaining to the French people what the German people is and what it wants: for it is the German people, challenged out of both ignorance and complacency, which is now knocking at your door, not the *Prussians*, as people like to think of us so as to deliver us over to hatred and contempt... I imagine myself in your shoes, on the ramparts of Paris. I would say to myself: Supposing this huge capital were to fall in ruins! But there's no supposing about it! It will. The regeneration of the French people will have found its point of departure."

On 22 March 1870 Verlaine had gone to Brussels with Villiers de l'Isle-Adam for the first performance in French of *Lohengrin* at the Théâtre de la Monnaie. A. W. Raitt tells us that Verlaine made a caricature of the occasion, in which one can recognize Villiers, Sivry,

Henri Matisse (1869-1954) : Portrait of Baudelaire, 1932.
Etching, illustration for Mallarmé's poem "Le Tombeau de Charles Baudelaire."

Catulle Mendès and his wife Judith all applauding as hard as they can. What we cannot see in the picture is that Villiers, immediately after Baudelaire set the ball rolling in 1861 with his *Richard Wagner and Tannhäuser in Paris*, was a forerunner in the building up of Wagnerian ecstasies. His campaign on behalf of the author of *Rheingold*, from 1867 on, was passionately intense, especially in the weekly articles he wrote for his own *Revue des Lettres et des Arts*, which also serialized his story *Claire Lenoir*, an elitist fiction in which Wagner appears as the symbol of idealist art and as "a miraculous genius, but accessible only to the initiated intelligence." The idea of initiation was already a feature of the budding symbolist outlook.

It was in a pamphlet written thirteen months after the "uproar" over the failure of the three Paris performances of *Tannhäuser* that Baudelaire went back to *the beginning of the question*. He could no longer endure the diatribes of F. J. Fétis against Wagner in several issues of the *Revue et Gazette musicale de Paris*. In defense of "the towering majesty of this music," Baudelaire tried to show that it was, like his own poetry, based on the emotional ambiguity of images, on a sensorial topology, on the *deep and shadowy unity* of correspondences, a unity which according to Chklovski aims at "increasing the difficulty and duration of perception":

"True music," wrote Baudelaire in *Richard Wagner and Tannhäuser in Paris* (1861), "suggests analogous ideas in different minds. Nor would it be foolish here to argue *a priori*, without analysis or comparison; for what would be surprising would be to find that sound could *not* suggest colour, that colours could *not* evoke the idea of a melody, and that sound and colour were unsuitable for the translation of ideas; things having always been expressed by reciprocal analogy ever since God brought forth the world as a complex and indivisible totality.

> *"La nature est un temple où de vivants piliers*
> *Laissent parfois sortir de confuses paroles;*
> *L'homme y passe à travers des forêts de symboles*
> *Qui l'observent avec des regards familiers.*
>
> *Comme de longs échos qui de loin se confondent*
> *Dans une ténébreuse et profonde unité;*
> *Vaste comme la nuit et comme la clarté,*
> *Les parfums, les couleurs et les sons se répondent."*

(Nature is a temple whose living pillars sometimes let indistinct words come forth; there man passes through forests of symbols that watch him with familiar eyes. Like long-drawn echoes that from afar blend into a deep shadowy unity, vast as darkness and light, scents, colours and sounds answer one another.)

"Let me go on," continues Baudelaire. "I remember that from the very first bars I experienced one of those happy impressions that almost every man of imagination has known in dreams or sleep. I felt myself released from the *bonds of gravity*, and found again in memory the extraordinary *thrill of pleasure* which lives and moves *in high places*. Then I found myself imagining the delightful state of a man deep in reverie, in absolute solitude, but a solitude with a *vast horizon* and a *wide, diffused light*: immensity with no other setting than itself. Soon I had a sensation of brighter *light*, an *intensity of light* growing so rapidly that the subtle distinctions of the dictionary are inadequate to express *that ever-renewed increase of ardour and whiteness*. Then I fully understood the idea of a soul moving about in some luminous setting in an ecstasy *made up of pleasure and knowledge*, and soaring far above the natural world."

Here we have romantic plenitude, the dimensions of infinity, a region where belief in universal analogy strengthens the ideal of "convertibility" on which the symbolist dialectic was to be based, aiming at establishing a network of equivalences. Were they overlappings, reciprocities, or usurpations? Was this the unification or the disintegration of the aesthetic field? A major element in this sector, where art seemed to approximate to religion or even magic and soothsaying, was to be the articulation between the myth of an original language and a longing for lost unity (the striving after the *Gesamtkunstwerk*, the total work of art).

Lohengrin, Tannhäuser, et Parsifal le Chaste,
Dont les pennons de pourpre ondulent avec faste,
Chevauchent aux clameurs des cymbals d'airain!

Ils vont: et, quand s'endort la splendeur de leurs glaives,
Un chœur de harpes sur le seul rythme serein
Remémore l'horreur de l'Idéal des rêves.

Stuart Merrill, poem in the *Revue Wagnérienne*, 1886

(Lohengrin, Tannhäuser, and Parsifal the Chaste whose purple pennons ripple gorgeously, ride on to the clamour of brazen cymbals. On they go: and when the brightness of their swords is stilled, a choir of harps in serener strain recalls the horror of the dream-begotten Ideal.)

Christian Jank (1833-1888): Castle Falkenstein of King Ludwig II of Bavaria. Gouache, 1883.

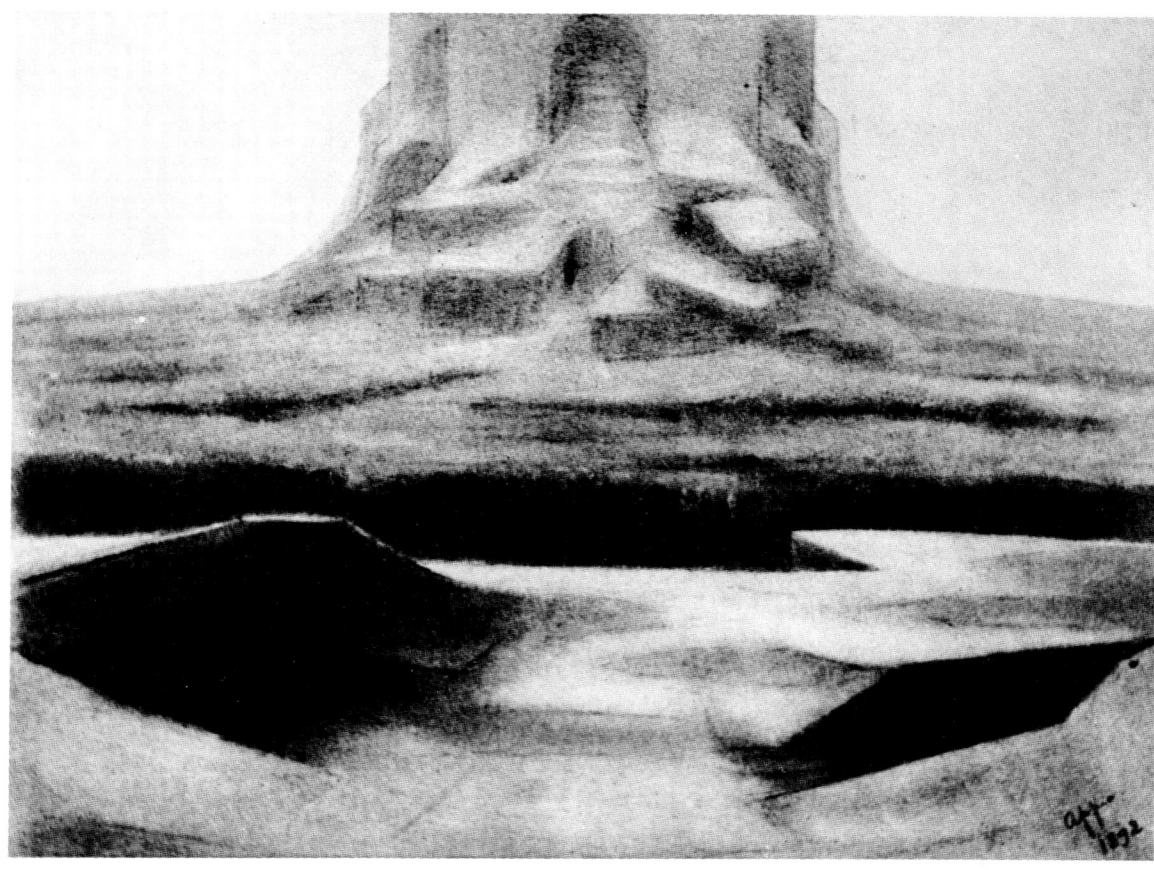

J
ust before the Franco-Prussian War, the names of Puvis de Chavannes and Manet were brought together in the Salon of 1870,
apparently for the first time. Surprisingly, some people compared
them, despite the radical difference between their two attitudes to
painting. Camille Lemonnier wrote (*Salon de Paris*, 1870): "Manet and
Puvis are the two men who come closest to each other at the moment
in terms of the system, and perhaps dislike each other the most, also in
terms of the system. Manet does not practise painting, any more than
Puvis: but they both proclaim that they practise expression. Puvis
refines on the ideal, and Manet refines on reality." Puvis was presenting a recently finished work, the final stage of a composition of which
at least two preparatory versions exist: *The Magdalene in the Desert*. It
was seen at the time as "proof that small canvases do not suit him"
(A. Baignères, *Gazette des Beaux-Arts*, 1881). The critics, imprisoned in
their own theories, were paralyzed. Elie Sorin (*Le Salon de 1870*) wrote:
"Nothing could be colder than this sinner in the midst of a desert
which tries to be scorching but whose very glow is tepid." Camille
Lemonnier was even more damning: "Take some slut à la Jordaens
from a disreputable hovel... If she is genuine she will have more style
than all the expurgated puppets served up by Etruscans [meaning
Puvis!] under the cloak of the ideal." These cavalier judgments were
influenced by the need to be contemporary and to conform to the
ideology of realism. Sources were suspect. Today this strange work is
classed, again too hastily no doubt, as belonging to the realm of Symbolism. But at first glance it has nothing in common with the various
practices of Levy-Dhurmer, Khnopff, Klimt, Mellery, Kubin, or the
disciples of Péladan!

It is, however, an aristocratic product, though outside the prevailing
taste, outside the academic tradition, outside the "decorative" pomp of
the Second Empire and the Third Republic. *The Magdalene in the*
Desert, in fact, is not painted in accordance with the usual standards,
the terms in common use. It departs from them as a logical consequence of the choice which led the painter to undertake great monumental compositions as vehicles for cultural, classical and mythical
discourse on the walls of public and private buildings. The painting of
murals imposes pictorial schemas, generalizing figurative processes,
analogical effects through synthetical arguments in which size and
technique prevail over drawing and tone. The page we read on the
wall functions out of time. It brings condensations designed for dis-
tances close up to the eye. So mimesis departs from its immediate data.
The rock, the sky, the mountain, the tree, the plain, the snake, the
stone are all organized so as to quit reality, to exchange and reduce
their tones, blue and white, white and blue, grey and white, white and
grey, light and dark. And all around one central figure. The indica-
tions are that it is the Magdalene, one of the Holy Women of the New
Testament. An example of ideal humanity, upright, hieratic, proud,
gentle, cylindrical, solitary, a formal classical beauty, close to the pro-
totypes of Rossetti. She is proud, strong, feminine. She is radiant,
haloed, meditating on surrounding death. Chaste? Yes, according to
the texts. Proud of her body, warm, and shrouded in her flowing
golden hair. The casket of the breast uncovered. Like fruit. Talking
with the skull. Eros. Vestige and temptation. Is eternity barren? The
skull, a trophy of love, recalls life, gives value to the microcosm, makes
sacred, by analogy, the sky and the mountain. The painting quietly
weaves its discourse, linking the economy of the libido to the rhetoric of
the image, bringing to the inhabiting of space the illusion of unreality.

A comparison which J. K. Huysmans called "curious" was made at
the time: "The bracketing together, *under the heading of refinement*, of the
names of Puvis de Chavannes and Gustave Moreau." Huysmans went
on: "Puvis de Chavannes is a frequenter of the omnibuses of art, for

Pierre Puvis de Chavannes (1824-1898):
The Magdalene in the Desert (or The Magdalene at the Sainte-Baume), 1869. Oil.

Gustave Moreau (1826-1898):
Thracian Girl Carrying the Head of Orpheus on his Lyre, 1865. Oil.

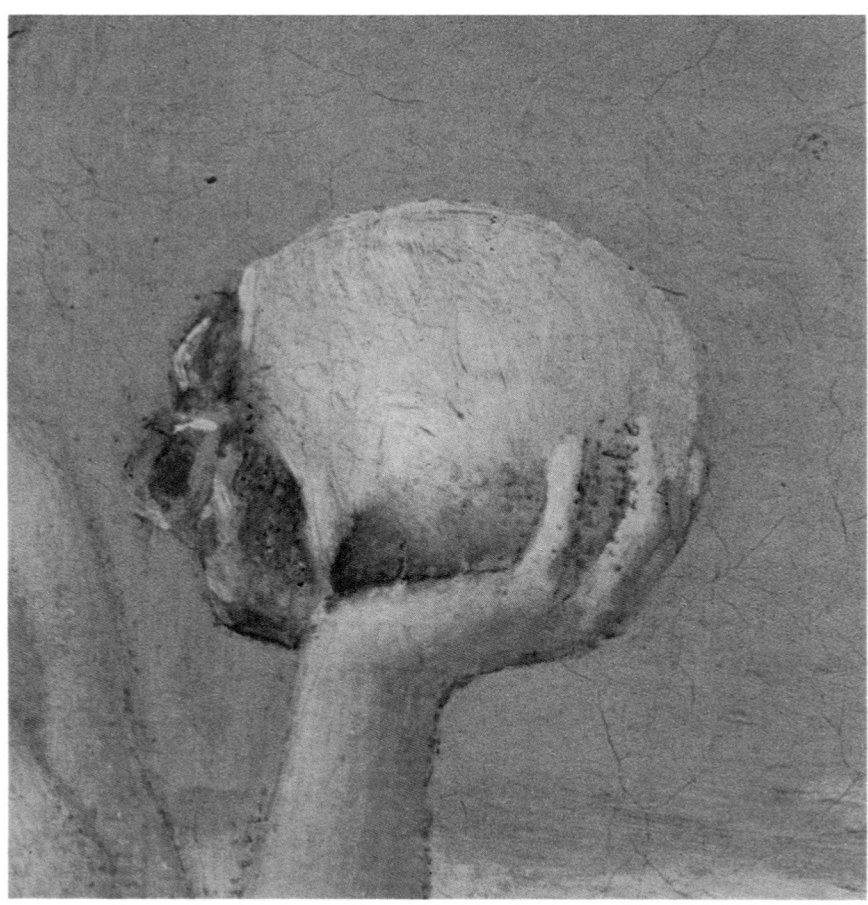

Der Tod ist groß.
Wir sind die Seinen
lachenden Munds.
Wenn wir uns mitten im Leben meinen,
wagt er zu weinen
mitten in uns.

Rainer Maria Rilke, *Das Buch der Bilder*,
Book II, Part 2, 1906

(Death is great. We are in his grip, even in our
mirth. When we seem to taste life to the full, Death
is there within us and dares to weep.)

Pierre Puvis de Chavannes (1824-1898):
The Magdalene in the Desert (detail), 1869.

every year he always instals himself in very bad company at exhibitions. Compared to his fellow passengers, people like Boulanger, Cabanel, Gérôme, Tony-Robert Fleury and Henner, those faithful custodians of ancient formulas, those vigilant curators of human stereotypes, he looks like an extraordinary painter, almost a thunderbolt." But "to compare Puvis de Chavannes and Gustave Moreau, to link them together in the matter of refinement and offer them both the same bouquet of admiration, is truly to commit one of the most obsequious possible heresies. Gustave Moreau has given new freshness to dreary old subjects by a talent both subtle and ample; he has taken myths worn out by the repetitions of centuries and expressed them in a language that is persuasive and lofty, mysterious and new. From disparate elements he has managed to create a form which is henceforward his own... Puvis has not created anything. Unlike Moreau, he has not refrained from academic tricks and venerable frauds; he has pilfered the Italian Primitives, sometimes going so far as downright pastiche. Where the people of the Middle Ages were naive and truly believed, he shows us the aping of faith, the affectation of simplicity. He is really a gourmet who takes us in with pictures of starvation, an old rigadoon trying his hand at a requiem!"

This may seem rather facile now. Until quite recently, all works were read, perceived, discovered, defined according to their relation with the models from which they derived. "Almost all books," wrote Mallarmé, "contain the fusion of some calculated repetition." Almost all books? Almost all texts which have to be recognized as belonging to the modelizing system once they move into what I. Lotman has called "the sphere of the coding system," a semantic system which has to be recognized as being at the heart of social life. While Gustave Moreau and

Puvis de Chavannes both worked basically from the same cultural code, they had different relationships to the archetypal models they transformed. The code cannot disguise either the variety of sources, or the way in which the work of each painter was articulated with reference to the texts involved—so much so that here and there the work of intertextuality tends to condition the use of the code. L. Jenny admits, however, that it may sometimes be "difficult to say whether the intertextual element derives from the use of the code or is the actual substance of the work." In the case of Puvis de Chavannes, brought out by Huysmans' radical reprobation, intertextuality depends less on the formal modifications suggested by the work of Dante Gabriel Rossetti than on the artist's handling of the figurative code, ransacked in order to build up a text whose plastic economy, iconical abbreviations, chromatic inversions, and method of outlining (the figure of the Magdalene may be read as having been prefabricated and applied afterwards to that strange lunar landscape devoid of all illusionist intentions) all combine to produce an image which, looked at as a whole, functions as a montage rather than the all-in-one-piece discourse of Poussin or Balzac.

In this montage of a figure in a landscape there is a continual coming and going, a dialogue between perception and what is perceived. The object is in relationship with itself, the same relationships as in *Thracian Girl carrying the Head of Orpheus*, which was painted in 1865 and is one of the culminating products of Moreau's imagination. (*Alice in Wonderland* belongs to the same year). The *Thracian Girl* was acquired by the State after the 1866 Salon for the sum of 8,000 francs, and exhibited the following year in the Musée du Luxembourg in Paris, after having provoked excitement, dismay, embarrassment, pleasure,

But give them me, the mouth, the eyes,
the brow!
Let them once more absorb me! One look
now
Will lap me round for ever, not to pass
Out of its light, though darkness lie
beyond :
Hold me but safe again within the bond
Of one immortal look! All woe that
was,
Forgotten, and all terror that may be,
Defied,—no past is mine, no future :
look at me!

Robert Browning, *Eurydice to Orpheus*, 1864

Gustave Moreau (1826-1898): Head of Orpheus, detail of
Thracian Girl Carrying the Head of Orpheus on his Lyre, 1865.

puzzlement, fear and enthusiasm in the Champ-de-Mars exhibition in 1867. Ernest Chesneau, the most influential critic of the day, wrote: "Just show me a landscape in the Salon which is more grandiose, a sky more magical than that in Moreau's *Orpheus*, a more harmonious figure than that of the girl and a finer head than that of Eurydice's lover in the same painting." It was soon to become a target for the "symbolist generation," and one of the pictures most admired by Marcel Proust: "We thought the poet dead, we meant to make a pilgrimage to the Luxembourg Museum as one goes and simply stands before a tomb; and like a woman carrying the lifeless head of Orpheus we go and simply stand before the *Woman Carrying the Head of Orpheus*, and we see in that head of Orpheus something looking at us, the mind of Gustave Moreau painted on that canvas which looks at us with fine unseeing eyes in the shape of mind-made colours."

It has recently been observed that Puvis's *Magdalene*, reversed, is almost identical in form to the woman's figure in Moreau's *Thracian Girl Carrying the Head of Orpheus*. Their attitudes are similar, and the lines of force in the background are also comparable. Apart from these formal links, everything seems to separate the two works: Eros and Thanatos, the skull and the decapitated head. But we must listen to the faint hint that brings them together. It does not refer to the immediate, the data of the senses. What are the figures doing in Monet's *Camille in a Green Dress*, Manet's *Fifer*, Renoir's *Lise with a Sunshade*, Corot's *Woman with a Pearl*? Moreau annexes the myth to give body, his body, to the image. What are the origins, what capital is being drawn upon? Is the murder of the primal father being re-lived as the first moment of humanity? Is this a vestige of buried rituals and beliefs? The picture shows a symbolic murder, the image is unctuous, smooth, polished,

shining, scintillating. It is ornate, ornamental, flowery. But there is restrained evidence of anguish, an echo of a celibate's anxiety, in which the Oedipus complex vies with castration complex. Is it by chance that the woman's face reminds one of the portrait of Moreau's mother, as we know it from an old photograph? Ernest Chesneau points out that it also resembles "the Salome of the Scriptures, who contemplated, but with what strange looks, the decapitated head of John the Baptist." The mysteries of mythography are certainly based on the labyrinths of our inner life, of a present which has already happened, of a future which is past. Time disintegrates in the elections of space.

There is now no doubt that Gustave Moreau and Puvis de Chavannes were both in their very different ways affected by the Pre-Raphaelite movement, as revealed in France at the exhibition held at the Paris World's Fair of 1855, and even more at the Galerie Anglaise in the Champ-de-Mars during the Paris World's Fair of 1867. And despite the distance separating the two men as artists (though they were exact contemporaries) and their differences of opinion, character and practice, their closeness is less "curious" if we remember that they were on excellent terms with each other, as we can see from an amusing portrait in black crayon which Puvis did of Moreau between 1865 and 1870 (Musée des Beaux-Arts, Rouen). There are also about thirty unpublished letters from Puvis to Moreau, covering the period from 1865 to 1890. And there is a drawing by Moreau which shows Puvis and Elie Delaunay presenting themselves at his town house in the Rue de La Rochefoucauld (Musée Gustave Moreau, Paris). All this evidence discredits the legend spread by Jules Breton in 1899, soon after the death of the two painters, according to which Moreau hated Puvis's painting.

Pierre Puvis de Chavannes
(1824-1898):
The Carrier Pigeon, 1871.
Oil on canvas, with frame
painted by the artist.

24

1

THE UNREALITY OF THE IMAGE
1870-1876

L'étoile a pleuré rose au cœur de tes oreilles,
L'infini roulé blanc de ta nuque à tes reins
La mer a perlé rousse à tes mammes vermeilles
Et l'Homme saigné noir à ton flanc souverain.

Arthur Rimbaud

(The star wept pink in the heart of your ears, the infinite
rolled white from the nape of your neck to the small of your
back, the sea rippled russet to your rosy nipples and Man
bled black in your sovereign womb.)

IN THE first days of January 1871, while Paris was under bombardment by the German army, Puvis de Chavannes painted *The Carrier Pigeon*. This exceptional picture was a companion piece to another, equally unusual picture, *The Balloon*, which Puvis had painted the previous year to commemorate the exploit of Gambetta, who on 7 October 1870, as French Minister of the Interior, had boldly escaped from besieged Paris in a balloon to organize resistance to the Germans. Balloon and pigeon were readily understandable symbols of a France reduced to the last extremity but determined to elude the grasp of a seemingly all-powerful invader. But they were also more than symbols, for during the long months of encirclement by German armies both served the practical purpose of keeping Paris in touch with the rest of the country. For the besieged city they were the only means of communication left with the outside world and thus all hopes were placed in them. And not in vain, for the Prussian eagle proved powerless. So Puvis depicted the eagle in his painting. Immobilized in mid-air, as if by an occult power, it screams in vain. Its cry of frustration re-echoes over the icy ramparts of the snow-clad city. It is not here, not yet, that the hawk stands ready to be transmuted into the pigeon, herald of the spring. This does not prevent the painter from redoubling the symbolism of his painting. Firstly, by personifying besieged Paris as a graceful feminine figure in mourning garb. Secondly, by bringing home the pictorial message with the help of an inscription written along the broad painted frame of the picture, or rather, of both pictures. Under *The Balloon*, across the lower edge, runs the inscription: "The beleaguered city of Paris confides to the air its appeal to France." The caption on the frame of *The Carrier Pigeon* runs as follows: "Escaped from the enemy's talons the awaited message exalts the heart of the proud city." These were laconic inscriptions, heavy with a weight of meaning felt by every Frenchman in the circumstances of that day. They easily compensate for the *unreality* of the images which they accompany and to which they refer—tellingly enough for the message to come home clearly and forcefully in both visual and emotional terms.

These two symmetrical figure paintings are deliberately treated in monochrome, in a low key. The balloon and the pigeon: whatever the dramatic values they embody and convey, the colour scheme is reduced to a single positive tone, a muted brown which sets these works in sharp contrast to the prevailing imagery of their day. Even the treatment of the figures, opaque and homogeneous, marks a break with visual appearances, setting them effectively apart as invented, arbitrary, disembodied symbols. The abbreviation of the colour answers to an equally radical abbreviation of line and form, thereby lifting the image to the level of *unreality* as a message pregnant with topical meaning, however devoid of reference to the bloodshed and physical suffering of the events to which it refers. Tension, starkness, colourlessness, concision: these were the qualities Puvis sought when he turned from the large-scale murals in which he had hitherto specialized, to the format of the easel painting necessary to his present purpose. And he achieved those qualities so well that, when his picture was reproduced as a lithograph (while the German siege continued), 50,000 copies were sold in Paris in the space of a few days. But the spirit of resistance it inspired was to no avail. The historic capitulation took place on 1 March 1871, and on that day German troops marched down the Champs-Elysées.

Sir John Everett Millais (1829-1896) : Ophelia, 1852. Oil.

"We'll just have to face up to it," wrote the painter Gustave Moreau, "we have been soundly beaten, reduced to nothing by a great nation, one that is noble, brave, able and of great intelligence. It is for us, therefore, to acknowledge the superiority of the German people over the French people in the nineteenth century." This romantic, out-of-touch remark, trying to halt the march of politics, was similar to many that were heard in France between the years 1940 and 1945. At the meeting of these two worlds Gustave Moreau hid within himself, in a sort of limbo, though nonetheless content. The Paris uprising had no effect upon him except that of accentuating his loneliness and isolation. Gustave Flaubert described Moreau as suffering from the same "ill-ness" as he himself, that is to say, "an inability to put up with the mob... a common complaint since our misfortunes, or so it seems." An innocent enough failing. He pretended to be concerned only with the outward manifestations of what was happening, but there was more to it than that. Even before the bourgeoisie found itself confronted with a new social order, a political act, a totally new power—extolled by Marx on 31 May 1871, who saw in the Commune the change from theoretical Socialism to active Socialism—Puvis had already, in 1869, given himself up to that "aristocratic pleasure" which consisted in being "concerned only with a select few," in keeping aloof from "the fickle and indifferent crowd" and taking refuge in "the safe haven of truth and beauty." It was the self-isolation of the idealist, an apparent detachment, so that his work could be imbued with the ruling ideology. According to Théophile Gautier, Gustave Moreau's painting was also "done for the delicate, the refined, the curious." Gautier adds, not without appositeness: "One must have seen many paintings by Mantegna, Botticelli, Verrocchio, and those artists who at the dawn of the Renaissance began to blend the sense of Antiquity with the forms of Gothic art, in order to understand Gustave Moreau's way of painting" (*Le Moniteur universel*, 15 May 1866).

This is a key criticism in the understanding of Moreau's work and can be applied to the work of that other great outsider, Puvis de Chavannes, as it can to some of the contemporary English painters, and in particular to the members of the Pre-Raphaelite Brotherhood, who were so much influenced by early Italian art that they took it as their model. It afforded them a protection against their own artistic environment and was suitably stimulating. Their vision, both alien and yet deeply rooted in the past, was a twofold one: on the one hand it revived both history and myth, while on the other it put great store on contemplation, observation, on the visual analysis of the landscape so as to push the imitation of reality to its utmost limits. In both cases the declared objective was the same: to reveal the "truth" as a moral ideal; to combine ethics and aesthetics. There were seven of them:

1. William Holman Hunt, painter
2. John Everett Millais, painter
3. Dante Gabriel Rossetti, painter and poet
4. Thomas Woolner, sculptor
5. James Collinson, painter
6. Frederic George Stephens, painter at first, critic later
7. William Michael Rossetti, Dante Gabriel's brother, writer on art.

Influenced by the principles set out in Ruskin's *Modern Painters* and by Keats's poetry, these young men got together in 1848 to form the Pre-Raphaelite Brotherhood, the initials P.R.B. appearing on their work both as signature and as a sign of their common aim. It seems that the idea for this pseudo-brotherhood, as well as for the magazine in which their ideas were aired, came from Dante Gabriel Rossetti, who had a lively imagination, an abundance of enthusiasm, and who was attracted by the mysterious. "As the son of a *carbonaro* he had a taste for setting up more or less secret societies" (Jean-Jacques Mayoux). The first issue of their magazine, *The Germ*, was published on 1 January 1850; but only four issues appeared, the last two being

Ophelia

*Sur l'onde calme et noire où dorment les étoiles
La blanche Ophélia flotte comme un grand lys,
Flotte très lentement, couchée en ses longs voiles...
— On entend dans les bois lointains des hallalis.*

*Voici plus de mille ans que la triste Ophélie
Passe, fantôme blanc, sur le long fleuve noir ;
Voici plus de mille ans que sa douce folie
Murmure sa romance à la brise du soir.*

Arthur Rimbaud

(On the calm dark stream where the stars lie sleeping, the white Ophelia floats like a great lily, floats so slowly, lying in her long raiment. In the distant woods the huntsmen can be heard. For a thousand years and more the sad Ophelia passes, a white ghost, on the long dark river; for a thousand years and more her gentle madness murmurs its romance to the evening breeze.)

published under a title which was less crusading and less symbolic, *Art and Poetry*, a title which shows a definite desire to unite art and literature in a common bond. As for the group, its life was short-lived : five years. Nonetheless, the "noble error" which it expounded, carried on by Burne-Jones and William Morris and brilliantly taken up again by Beardsley, made such an impact abroad that it can be considered as one of the most important influences on Symbolism, and therefore on Art Nouveau.

At first sight, the movement seems to have been born from the refusal of a few individuals, eager for novelty, to accept the conventional rules of their time. They wished to rid art, starting from the slightest sketch, of its traditional vocabulary. This was a deliberate choice, which does not, and cannot make sense, unless one takes into account the background to their particular situation, unless one studies the reason, or reasons, behind their choice. It is here that one must understand what lies behind their attitude, for it is not easily seen at first glance and their writings give nothing away. However, for those who know how to read their works, they are alive with signs. The criticism of the time, such as can be read for example in *The Germ* under the signature of F.G. Stephens (No. 2, 1850), was incapable of going beyond what Octavio Paz has aptly called "the uppermost strata of awareness."

"An unprejudiced spectator," wrote Stephens, "of the recent progress and main direction of Art in England will have observed, as a great change in the character of the productions of the modern school, a marked attempt to lead the taste of the public into a new channel by producing pure transcripts and faithful studies from nature, instead of conventionalities and feeble reminiscences from the Old Masters; an entire seeking after originality in a more humble manner than has been practised since the decline of Italian Art in the Middle Ages. This has been most strongly shown by the landscape painters, among whom

Sir John Everett Millais (1829-1896) : The Lady of Shalott, 1854. Ink wash and sepia.

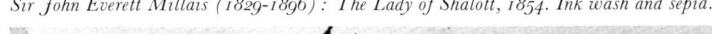

there are many who have raised an entirely new school of natural painting, and whose productions undoubtedly surpass all others in the simple attention to nature in detail as well as in generalities. By this they have succeeded in earning for themselves the reputation of being the finest landscape painters in Europe...

"It has been said that there is presumption in this movement of the modern school, a want of deference to established authorities, a removing of ancient landmarks. This is best answered by the profession that nothing can be more humble than the pretension to the observation of facts alone, and the truthful rendering of them. If we are not to depart from established principles, how are we to advance at all? Are we to remain still? Remember, no thing remains still; that which does not advance falls backward. That this movement is an advance, and that it is of nature herself, is shown by its going nearer to truth in every object produced, and by its being guided by the very principles the ancient painters followed, as soon as they attained the mere power of representing an object faithfully. These principles are now revived, not from them, though through their example, but from nature herself."

All of this, which is based on the religion of conventional ideas, was restated and put into historical perspective by Ruskin in one of his "Lectures on Architecture and Painting," delivered in Edinburgh in November 1853:

"The subject on which I would desire to engage your attention this evening, is the nature and probable result of a certain schism which took place a few years ago among our British artists.

"This schism or rather the heresy which led to it, as you are probably aware, was introduced by a small number of very young men; and consists mainly in the assertion that the principles on which art has been taught for these three hundred years back are essentially wrong, and that the principles which ought to guide us are those which prevailed before the time of Raphael; in adopting which, therefore, as their guides, these young men, as a sort of bond of unity among themselves, took the unfortunate and somewhat ludicrous name of 'Pre-Raphaelite Brethren'...

"It was asserted that the Pre-Raphaelites did not draw well, in the face of the fact, that the principal member of their body [i.e. Millais], from the time he entered the schools of the Academy, had literally encumbered himself with the medals given as prizes for drawing. It was asserted that they did not draw in perspective, by men who themselves knew no more of perspective than they did of astrology; it was asserted that they sinned against the appearance of nature, by men who had never drawn so much as a leaf or a blossom from nature in their lives. And, lastly, when all these calumnies or absurdities would tell no more, and it began to be forced upon men's unwilling belief that the style of the Pre-Raphaelites *was* true and was according to nature, the last forgery invented respecting them is, that they copy photographs. You observe how completely this last piece of malice defeats all the rest. It admits they are true to nature, though only that it may deprive them of all merit in being so. But it may itself be at once refuted by the bold challenge to their opponents to produce a Pre-Raphaelite picture, or anything like one, by themselves copying a photograph.

"Let me at once clear your minds from all these doubts, and at once contradict all these calumnies.

"Pre-Raphaelitism has but one principle, that of absolute, uncompromising truth in all that it does, obtained by working everything, down to the most minute detail, from nature, and from nature only."

This was very apposite, though Ruskin had been too much conditioned by medieval art to fully understand what was happening around him. Suddenly, under the influence of a group of young artists intensely active from 1848 to 1853, painting in England had made, or seemed to make, a leap backwards. It was a similar situation to that which occurred in the 1930s with the Surrealists and the accepted painting of that time. Is this, then, what it means to be modern? In this case, the first impression one gets is that it is a lot of show, particularly in the use of new forms. However, nothing much was made of this by the critics; indeed, Ruskin tried to ignore this side completely, for fear that in attaching too much importance to it the more relevant side of their art

Photograph of Jane Morris, 1865.

William Morris (1834-1896) : Queen Guinevere, 1858. Oil on canvas.
(The model was Jane Morris.)

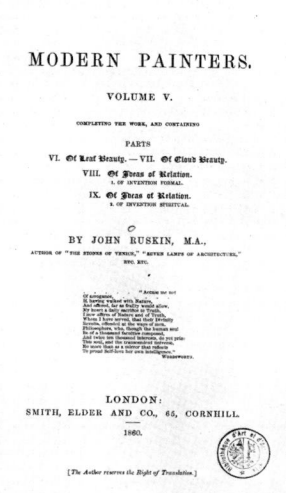

MODERN PAINTERS.

VOLUME V.

COMPLETING THE WORK, AND CONTAINING

PARTS

VI. Of Leaf Beauty. — VII. Of Cloud Beauty.
VIII. Of Ideas of Relation. I. OF INVENTION FORMAL.
IX. Of Ideas of Relation. I. OF INVENTION SPIRITUAL.

BY JOHN RUSKIN, M.A.,

AUTHOR OF "THE STONES OF VENICE," "SEVEN LAMPS OF ARCHITECTURE," ETC. ETC.

LONDON:
SMITH, ELDER AND CO., 65, CORNHILL.
1860.

[The Author reserves the Right of Translation.]

Ancilla Domini

would be hidden. By this he meant the photographic image used by the Pre-Raphaelites as an important support to their work, and not as Delacroix and Courbet did as a mere aid, something which helped them in the beginning and was then completely altered. (In 1862 Thoré-Bürger, one of Courbet's most ardent defenders, accused the Pre-Raphaelites of being too realistic, of using photographic, microscopic, and stereoscopic effects.) However, and this is something which Ruskin did not realize, without the help of photographic techniques the Pre-Raphaelites could never have achieved their effects of hyper-realism or the strange quality which their pictures possess, despite the interest they showed in the Flemish Primitives, observed on the ritual pilgrimages which most of them made to the museums of Belgium.

Does Pre-Raphaelitism, then, represent an arbitrary break in the line of artistic development? The answer is undoubtedly Yes, if you think strictly in terms of formalism, pictorial space and chronological progression; and undoubtedly No, if you admit that art of that time laboured under the same constraints that the Pre-Raphaelites did. The difference was that the Pre-Raphaelites tried to alter the balance between constraint and desire by a return to the "real," the living—that very reality which the Quattrocento painters had abandoned in their painting. It is true, as Lyotard says, that in cultural history "there is no natural organization of visual space, and that Renaissance perspective must have been no less difficult to understand for people who were used to the imagery of International Gothic than Cezanne's way of painting was difficult to understand for the lovers of Pre-Raphaelitism." To understand the art of Millais, Rossetti and their friends one must understand the background. This was made up of all that was forbidden at the time; in other words, the taboos of a Victorian and puritanical England. This forced every artist, whether painter or writer, who wished to flout the rules, to use subterfuge. For everything was not as free as the triumphant Free Trade mentality, economic prosperity, and unimpeded circulation of capital and products would have one believe. This is the reason why Pre-Raphaelitism as a movement turned towards the past—the Primitives, Gothic architecture, Germanic legends, Icelandic sagas, medieval ballads, Dante, Shakespeare—and was forced to deal with the aspects of daily life, conventional scenes, sexuality, desire, non-conformism, Roman Catholicism and Socialism, under the cover of myth, even though the reality thus portrayed was divested of some of its power. Unless, of course, the members of the Pre-Raphaelite Brotherhood believed Gérard de Nerval's saying, according to which "the true is false, at least in art and poetry."

Holman Hunt, who was by temperament passionate and headstrong, but also precise and an ardent man of religion, had a horror of "realist" painting; he thought it "vulgar and ugly". He worked during the summer and autumn of 1851 in the Surrey countryside with Millais,

the one in order to paint the rural background for *The Hireling Shepherd*, the other in order to paint the green, damp, stifling, flowered atmosphere of *Ophelia*. At the 1855 World's Fair in Paris, Hunt exhibited a rather strange picture, *The Light of the World*, of which Théophile Gautier wrote: "Our neo-Gothic painters have never gone so far." By 1875 Hunt was regarded as "the most illustrious representative of the Pre-Raphaelite aesthetic" (this was because he had followed the theoretical model laid down by Ruskin more faithfully than any of the original group, and in so doing he had almost drowned in the Dead Sea in 1854, while painting *The Scapegoat*).

In conjunction with Holman Hunt, John Everett Millais perfected a technique which consisted in painting with pure colours on a damp white ground. In the three pictures which Millais exhibited in Paris in 1855, Théophile Gautier thought he could see "the pious simplicity of Memling, the colour of Van Eyck and the thoroughgoing realism of Holbein." What he did not see, however, was the fact that Millais's *Ophelia* does not fit into any known scheme. He did not see, and did not even try to understand, the ambiguity inherent in the picture, nor did he see the rapport which exists there between dream and reality, between culture and visual perception, between the true and the false, between theatre and life, between the extra bright colours which are supposedly taken from life, and the accuracy of the brushstrokes so markedly evident in the painting.

While Millais was still under the influence of Ruskin, and before he strayed into making comforting anecdotal pictures that would appeal to bourgeois taste, he was one of the most faithful followers of Pre-Raphaelite orthodoxy, whose "unusual handling of the paints" and "strange sentiments" so fascinated the French art critic Ernest Chesneau, who was writing a *History of the Pre-Raphaelite School in England*. Was Hunt right in saying that, in the strict sense of the word, Dante Gabriel Rossetti had never been a Pre-Raphaelite? It is true to say that Rossetti seems to have painted only two pictures in the true spirit of the Brotherhood: *The Childhood of Mary Virgin* in 1849, and *Ecce Ancilla Domini (The Annunciation)* in 1850. It is also true that he refused to exhibit with his colleagues (apparently he only exhibited once, in 1856 at Russell Place), and while he was alive none of his paintings were shown abroad. However, he sold his work easily to his friends Ruskin and William Morris and to a select group of people who appreciated his rather strange pictures. After the break-up of the Pre-Raphaelite Brotherhood he was a member of a group during the early 1860s to

How is it in the unknown land?
Do the dead wander hand in hand?
Do we clasp dead hands, and quiver
With an endless joy for ever?
Is the air filled with the sound
Of spirits circling round and round?
Are there lakes, of endless song,
To rest our tired eyes upon?
Do tall white angels gaze and wend
Along the banks where lilies bend?

Elizabeth E. Siddal, lines from *The Final Poem*, 1862

3

which Swinburne and Whistler belonged. The group was formed to defend art as a phenomenon independent of morality, and to claim the right of creating works which were capable of shocking the public; however, despite this, their subversive aims were largely disguised by metaphor and symbol. Only a few days before his death (he died on Easter Sunday, 9 April 1882), Dante Gabriel Rossetti wrote to Ernest Chesneau that, far from being in any way the leader of the Pre-Raphaelite school, he scarcely felt that he belonged to it at all: for him, he claimed, it had been a matter of comradeship rather than stylistic affinity.

And yet, despite everything that one might say, it is still Rossetti's name which comes to the fore when one reconsiders the ambiguities of Pre-Raphaelitism. It is *his* work, an admirable constellation of word and colour, sound and image, painting and poetry, to which one turns each time that the symbolist vision poses a problem, each time that Pre-Raphaelitism seems to overstep its boundaries. Posterity has in some ways reinvented Pre-Raphaelitism around Rossetti, for it is he who seemed to set the tone of the Pre-Raphaelite imagination and who abandoned the most obvious traces of a style that only *seemed* naïve for those who gave it a cursory glance. Rossetti was the strongest personality, and the least conformist of the initial group, which was why he was forced out on his own. This "great tormented Italian, lost in the inferno of London," as Ruskin called him, had determined to pattern his life on that led in Florence in the sixteenth century. He ruled like a god among his admirers. "It wasn't *his* face that I thought I saw light up," wrote Watts, "but the face of Michelangelo; it wasn't *his* voice, but the voice of Dante, that I thought I heard coming out of the depths of the studio." In the streets of London he was constantly on the look-out for models; he was a Don Juan without a failure to his name (it was said that a disturbing *odor di femmina* hung around him). Whistler, in his spiteful way, said of Rossetti that "he thinks himself capable of doing anything, even of painting," and Ruskin reproached him for doing only *what* he liked, *how* he liked. He was a frequenter of the evening parties given by the admirable, incisive Ford Madox Brown, and in the early 1860s he became a free thinker and shared a house with Swinburne. Rossetti was the man of the disillusioned dream, of slighted passion, of several lovers at a time, of spiritual death. In 1860, after waiting ten years, he married Elizabeth Siddal, the mistress whom he no longer loved, for by this time he was in love with Jane Burden, the model whom William Morris had married several months earlier.

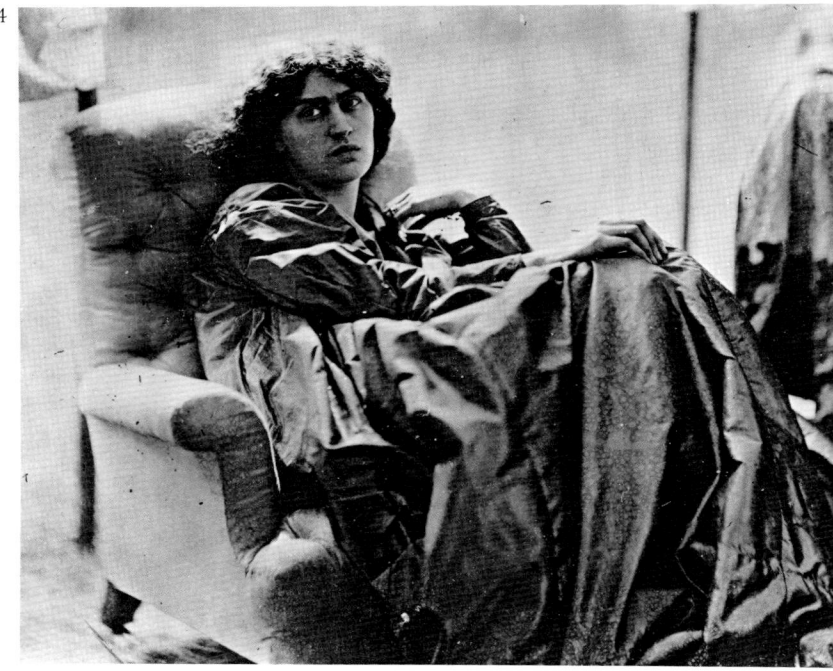

4

1. John Ruskin (1819-1900): Title page and frontispiece after Fra Angelico for the fifth and final volume of "Modern Painters," 1860.

2. Photograph of John Ruskin (left) and Dante Gabriel Rossetti (right), 1863.

3. Dante Gabriel Rossetti (1828-1882): Elizabeth Siddal, 1860. Pencil.

4. Photograph of Jane Morris, 1865.

This then is a portrait of Rossetti. He was a complex mixture of lasciviousness and sensuality, cruelty and venom. He became the model for European Symbolism. As an artist or as a writer he was unchanging. His vision was always the same, a mirror vision, fed by phantasms, all of which shared a common ground which can be identified quite separately from the biographical details. The whole of his oeuvre is marked by overblown forms, all cast in the same mould: a certain image of woman—as though he always used the same model. This was Elizabeth Siddal, the beautiful, delicate shop-girl with a mass of red-gold hair, whom Rossetti discovered in 1850 (Millais used her as his model for *Ophelia*). One sees her in the figures of Alexa Wilding (the daughter of a piano-maker whom Rossetti met in 1865 and who was supposed to be the model for *The Blessed Damozel*), of Fanny Cornforth (whom he met in 1860), of Jane Burden (first discovered in 1857 and used by Edward Burne-Jones and William Morris as the model for the frescoes painted at the Oxford Union under Rossetti's direction). In each picture, whatever the model Rossetti used, the same image appears over and over again: an image of anxiety, an image which follows "the listless steps of death." It is self-contained, but radiant; the model is often in a state of meditation, set in a formal background and surrounded by flowers. The face is oval, with a regular profile and a gentle expression. The painting style is uniform with flowing lines and the clothes are full and loose. The gestures are rounded, and emphasis is placed on lips, hair and flowers. Another point of importance is the fact that the model's beauty is enhanced by a playing-down of Nature, like the touching-up process used by portrait photographers. This makes one think that the photograph takes over, leaving the real model far behind, thus further emphasizing how unreal the picture is.

In 1862 Swinburne saw Rossetti paint one of the most romantic pictures of all, *Beata Beatrix*. In 1862 Elizabeth Siddal had died from an overdose of laudanum, which looked suspiciously like suicide. *Beata Beatrix* was Rossetti's memorial to her. Beatrix in ecstasy is Elizabeth on the eve of her death; dead already, and as beautiful as Beatrice Portinari. Rossetti is Dante. He identified himself with the poet of the *Vita Nuova*, that love song which he so beautifully translated into English. William Blake, some of whose illustrated poems Rossetti possessed (in a now famous manuscript which he picked up in 1847 for ten shillings), had drawn him to Dante; his father had also inspired him with admiration for the great Italian poet, by giving him, as a child, long and detailed explanations of the poems full of politico-masonic

An admirable constellation of words and colours

James McNeill Whistler (1834-1903) : Three Figures in Pink and Grey, 1867-1868. Oil.

interpretations. *Beata Beatrix* is pure symbolism and easily understood. Beatrice is the personification of disillusion, disenchantment, suffering and distress. She is also innocence, fidelity and purity. Evil spells stir her to the very core of her being. Everything is veiled, troubled. Her closed eyelids dismiss the world's gaudy spectacle. She dreams and she becomes that dream: Rossetti's dream, where Elizabeth and Beatrice are one. In the mythical space behind her, two apparitions appear: Dante and Love, while in the harshness of the evening light, or rather of the footlights, the divine bird of Eros is about to place the poppy of eternal sleep between his idol's hands. A morbid lethargy often remarked upon, imbues this work. One is reminded of the words of Gérard de Nerval: "The first moments of sleep are the likeness of death; a cloudy numbness steals over the mind." *Beata Beatrix* is a reflection on love and death, such as one sees in almost all Rossetti's work, a reflection which underlines the contention that poetry and painting come from the same source—that is, writing. Writing was for Rossetti a way of eliminating the difference between speech and image. Writing was one way of setting down the passionate and sensual aspects of a life that had been lived to the utmost. This is why the transfer of sound into colour and vice versa is so frequent in his work, even if this is not immediately recognizable. *The Blessed Damozel*, which was painted in 1875-1879 (slightly different from an initial, larger version which is now at the Fogg Art Museum, Harvard) takes as its theme one of Rossetti's best-known poems, begun in 1847 (when he was nineteen) and published in 1850 in *The Germ*:

The blessed damozel leaned out
    From the gold bar of Heaven;
Her eyes were deeper than the depth
    Of waters stilled at even;
She had three lilies in her hand,
    And the stars in her hair were seven.

Her robe, ungirt from clasp to hem,
    No wrought flowers did adorn,
But a white rose of Mary's gift
    For service meetly worn;
Her hair that lay along her back
    Was yellow like ripe corn...

A modern-day Petrarch? One might easily think so from the metres and themes he chose, and from the strict form of the sonnets in the sequence of *The House of Life*. But Rossetti translated the pre-Petrarchan Italian lyricists of the twelfth and thirteenth centuries: Ciullo d'Alcamo, Cino da Pistoia, Guido Cavalcanti, Guido della Colonna, Dino Frescobaldi, Giacomino Pugliese and Guido Guinizelli, and the expressions of love which fill both the poem and the painting of *The Blessed Damozel* with such a feeling of sensuality—that sensuality which singled him out as the leader of the "fleshly school of poetry"—are surely as much taken from these poets as they are from Dante. Rossetti was the only modern poet of the nineteenth century who was able to turn feeling into imagery—the tender night, her enchanted hair, the ray of light that she spins, the dead years, the sound of a sigh, the wind on the cold iron, the dull resonance and the gold bar of Heaven on which the Blessed Damozel leans. One can see a link here between Edgar Allan Poe's *Raven* and *The Blessed Damozel*. Here are two lovers, whom death has set apart and who dream of meeting one another. It is one long prayer of desire. The picture of *The Blessed Damozel* is surrounded by a heavy frame, like an early Renaissance altarpiece, but with one important difference, for here the frame is no longer a sacred area, but contains, in the lower half, a painting of the lover left behind on earth who gazes up to his lady in Heaven.

Between Rossetti's poetry and his painting there exists the same sort of relationship as that which exists between Apollinaire's poetry and Braque's painting, though in Rossetti's case it is less of a relationship than a change from the visual to the verbal. That is to say, a move from one way of expression to another, in an area ruled by the same rhythms, and though the one is not the absolute equivalent of the other, they mutually help each other. Thus the poem helps us both to understand the picture and make its symbolism clearer. There are two poles of language here, the real and the imaginary. It is therefore not by chance that Claude Debussy composed *La Demoiselle élue* ("The Blessed Damozel") in 1887-1889, during the time when he was an *habitué* of Mallarmé's Tuesday evening gatherings. This cantata was inspired as much by the picture as by the poem. He could either take

As he that loves oft looks on the dear form
    And guesses how it grew to womanhood,
    And gladly would have watched the beauties bud
And the mild fire of precious life wax warm: —

Dante Gabriel Rossetti (1828-1882): Beata Beatrix, c. 1863. Oil.

So I, long bound within the threefold charm
    Of Dante's love sublimed to heavenly mood,
    Had marvelled, touching his Beatitude,
How grew such presence from man's shameful swarm...

Dante Gabriel Rossetti, *Sonnet on the "Vita Nuova" of Dante*, 1852

33

the picture as a mere picture, or could see in it a double meaning: that is to say, the connection between life and death, between the Blessed Damozel in Heaven and her lover on earth. Debussy no doubt got to know Rossetti's work through his friends Paul Bourget and Gabriel Mourey, who had for English art the undiscriminating admiration and fondness of true devotees. Certain people still profess to think that music is in no way connected with painting and literature, which seems to me to be a narrow point of view, though it must be said that Debussy has been compared to the Impressionists rather too often. However, the "fuzziness" and the "haziness" that the composer attributed to sounds shows that he is closer to the Symbolists, he who was a neighbour at Saint-Germain-en-Laye of that well-known Symbolist, Maurice Denis. Debussy made his position clear when he wrote the following: "Really music should be a hermetic science, protected by texts which take so long to interpret and which are so difficult that in this way the crowd of people who take music for granted would be thoroughly put off. Instead of trying to make music more accessible to the public, I propose the setting-up of a 'Society of Musical Esotericism'..." Here, then, clearly set out are the socio-cultural implications of the symbolist viewpoint. Such ideas would have greatly pleased Rossetti, Gustave Moreau and Puvis de Chavannes, and they would have scandalized and horrified William Morris.

In 1872, in Paris, the magazine *La Renaissance* published some fragments from the drama *Axël*, the most intriguing and hermetic work of the French symbolist writer, Villiers de l'Isle-Adam. A few months later, in August 1872, the English poet John Payne, who had already dedicated his *Songs of Life and Death* to Wagner with an inscription to "the king of the new world of fire harmonies," contributed to this short-lived magazine (it ceased publication in 1875) a poem dedicated to Mallarmé, *The Phantom Soul*, which introduced a familiar theme of symbolist poetry, that of the wandering soul in search of another self.

What about Rimbaud? Can he too, between about 1871 and 1875, be assumed to have dipped into the traditional sources of occultism? It is hard to say, and indeed nothing is less certain. The assumption made by Serge Hutin, that while still in his native Charleville Rimbaud may have taken part in Tantric ceremonies, rests on no proof. It is even more rash to suppose, as Philippe Junod has done, that Rimbaud's *Sonnet de voyelles*, his vowel sonnet, "appears to be connected with an out-of-date theory, but one which in fact is still valid." This is the theory of "correspondences" in which there is a link between words and colour, rather as in the *Sonnet de voyelles* each vowel is given its appropriate colour. André Breton, the Surrealist writer, used the theory of correspondences to write his *proses parallèles*, a series of highly coloured prose pieces based on paintings by Miró. For Breton, as for Hegel, poetry could easily be translated into colour. Baudelaire and Mallarmé were equally attached to this idea and it is quite clear that Rimbaud's poems, *Une saison en enfer* and *Les illuminations*, make the same point as Baudelaire's *Fleurs du mal*. In other words, they go beyond the forbidden, beyond taboos and fetishisms; they lay bare the hidden corners of consciousness and break the shackles of hitherto accepted poetics. Words, which up until then had somehow been sacred, are finally released and given their full force; the unconscious is forced to speak out. These were anarchist principles erected on a revolutionary foundation. Rimbaud's letter of 15 May 1871, signed "A Clairvoyant," was the first to shift the emphasis to the third person, the impersonal pronoun "One," instead of the first person, the egoistic "I." This letter of Rimbaud's plays an important part in the history of the Paris Commune. "For I is someone else," it says. "If the trumpet announces that it no longer needs a player to make music but will play on its own, this is not its fault. That much is evident. I look on at the flowering of my thought..." As cultural history, this letter is marginal, but the ideas inherent in it change our way of seeing and knowing. It is a theory which goes beyond the conventional norms. It is an intense plea, a strong analogy, a dialectic of discovery. Without holding back, the letter continues: "I say that one must be *clairvoyant*, make oneself *clairvoyant*. The poet makes himself *clairvoyant* by turning all meaning upside down in a long and reasoned manner..."

The noblest painting is a painted poem.

Dante Gabriel Rossetti

THE LADY OF SHALOTT.

PART I.

I.

On either side the river lie
Long fields of barley and of rye,
That clothe the wold and meet the sky;
And thro' the field the road runs by
 To many-tower'd Camelot;

△ *William Holman Hunt (1827-1910): Illustration for the Moxon edition of Tennyson's "Poems," 1859. Wood engraving.*

▷ *Dante Gabriel Rossetti (1828-1882): The Daydream, 1872-1878. Pastel and black chalk. (The model was Jane Morris.)*

Pierre Puvis de Chavannes (1824-1898) : Hope, 1872. Oil.

This was a new idea, which gave the Symbolists what they needed without having to go so far as the poetic language used by such people as James Joyce and Mallarmé. From the outside, they *seemed* to go as far as the writers, but this was, in fact, not so. They went as far as necessary so as to remain fashionable, but never too far (a sign of this is the portrayal of the idealized, forbidden mother). This point of view was not an isolated one. It affected not only London, Paris, Brussels and Munich, but the whole of Europe in 1875. Bourgeois nationalism goes hand in hand with the cosmopolitanism of "citizens without a country, crossing frontiers and cultures": Mucha, Rops, Masek and Schwabe in Paris, Böcklin in Florence, Burne-Jones' in Rome, Klinger and Toorop in Brussels, Von Marées in Naples, Villiers de l'Isle Adam in Lucerne.

The Europe in which these men lived was at the peak of capitalist development and colonial expansion—the driving force of all those countries at that time—whose corollary was nationalism; that nationalism which Puvis de Chavannes summed up when he painted *Hope*, with the use of Pre-Raphaelite techniques. It was an allusion to the lost war of 1870, with ruins and make-shift cemeteries dotted with wooden crosses abandoned in the depths of the countryside. He portrays an image of peace and rebirth. It is a time-honoured allegory: a young girl seated with an olive branch in her hand. She may be interpreted as an intimation of the future harvest, as the propagator of future generations in opposition to the fields of death and desolation against which her white, luminous figure stands out. This is the promotion of unreality. The overall effect of this strange picture is mat and muted, the colours merge into one another and the light conveys a sense of indefinable abstraction. The prevailing colour is purplish-blue and over the whole picture there hangs a sense of alienation. The formulation of the colour scheme takes precedence over the representation, and the figure does not seem to fit into any known pattern.

Where is one to situate such an *invention* as this, if not outside time and space? The critics, at the time, could make nothing of it, and its political, ideological and sentimental context did not help its reception in any way. The reviewer in *L'Opinion nationale* (7 June 1872) saw in it "a studio lay-figure... draped in a sort of bath towel... sitting on an old chest with a sheet of paper in her hand." "An easy way out," wrote another reviewer, "for a man who can neither draw nor paint." And

Sir Edward Burne-Jones (1833-1898): Two Heads, 1874. Pencil.

The myth beneath the meaning

Love made himself of flesh that perisheth
  A pleasure-house for all the loves his kin;
But on the one side sat a man like death,
  And on the other a woman sat like sin.
So with veiled eyes and sobs between his breath
  Love turned himself and would not enter in . . .

A.C. Swinburne, *Hermaphroditus*, 1862

another: "All this is painted as if on a piece of crockery; it is dry, uncouth and toneless. Why call this sinister figure *Hope?*" So many judgments which show how deep-seated the realist prejudice is, how completely visual habits can blind the viewer when faced with a new, an *unexpected* work.

There is an important link between Puvis de Chavannes, Gustave Moreau and Burne-Jones in their use of mythological and mythical references as well as in their use of symbolism. Of all the painters of his time, Burne-Jones was the most literary. He was the only one to have based all his work on written texts and written legend. However, this does not hide the fact that there still has to be a transposition from the

◁ *Sir Edward Burne-Jones*
(1833-1898):
The Call of Perseus (unfinished),
1877 and 1897-1898. Oil.
The picture represents Athena giving
Perseus a sword with which to slay
Medusa, and a mirror in which he
can observe her without danger to
himself.

▷ *Gustave Moreau (1826-1898):*
Œdipus and the Sphinx, 1864.
Oil.

written word to the image. In that operation it is not only the imagination that counts: it is important to make the models taken from life as real as possible while at the same time endowing them with certain cultural references. (Michelangelo's writings were a particular favourite of Burne-Jones's.) However, the viewer, though he is able to understand the picture with the help of cultural references, often forgets this aspect and concentrates on the erotic elements of the picture. This is, no doubt, the reason why Burne-Jones was censured for several years for having exhibited a small watercolour, *Phyllis and Demophon*, in 1870, which was considered improper because of the nymph's sensual expression. (At the same time, Browning and Tennyson professed themselves

shocked by the sensuality of Rossetti's poems.) From this date onwards, Burne-Jones lived, with his friend William Morris, what he called "the seven best years of work that I've ever known."

It was during this period that he began a series of eight pictures based on the legend of Perseus which shows the complexity of the parental relationship, while at the same time emphasizing the importance of Nature. This series is linked to some illustrations which Burne-Jones had recently done for *The Earthly Paradise*, a long poem or poetic romance by William Morris. The first picture of the cycle, *The Calling of Perseus* (by Athena, his mission being to kill the Gorgon Medusa), was begun in 1877 and was never finished, though Burne-Jones took it up and worked over it again in the last year of his life. Even as it stands, it is a striking achievement, being one of the first pictures to speak the language of sexual mystery (or sexual truth). Death pervades the image, which is heavily symbolic. The style is both harsh and gentle, the light metallic, almost like electric light. The general atmosphere is barbaric and the landscape is desolate. The figures are abstract, sensuous and sombre. These solid presences set in a void are at the same time gentle and aggressive, while the sword and the mirror, which will enable Perseus to kill Medusa, lend a threatening note to the scene. It is a phallic celebration, but at the same time desire is distorted and the essential happens off-stage. An eager crowd, excited by the enthusiasm shown by Swinburne and Henry James, flocked to see the picture when it was exhibited at the Grosvenor Gallery in 1877-1878 in a show, opened by the painter Sir Coutts Lindsay, which was devoted to the paintings refused by the Royal Academy.

So Burne-Jones became the idol of the "Temple of Aesthetes." The adoration paid to him has been compared to that paid to Wagner. In fact he was influenced by Wagner, and this is shown in a picture which was to bring Burne-Jones lasting fame. This was *Laus Veneris*, begun in 1873 and finished in 1875. It is the larger version of a watercolour done in 1861, which no longer exists, and which is thought to have been influenced by a performance of *Tannhäuser* given in Paris in 1860 (the same performance also inspired Swinburne, in 1862 to write his poem *Laus Veneris*). Mannerism and Pre-Raphaelitism are combined in this picture, but it is a different Pre-Raphaelitism from that practised by the original Brotherhood, for here the Gothic element is very much to the fore. In this picture, "pale, haggard Venus" is "tormented and consumed by deception and desire," an over-riding obsession, but the Oedipus myth plays no part.

However, a similar kind of visual stimulus was needed at that time if a painter wished to remain a success in society. At any rate it is true that, in 1864, Gustave Moreau gained a certain notoriety in Paris with his picture *Oedipus and the Sphinx*. This introduced a theme which was to reverberate throughout the world of symbolism. Of course this *début* of Moreau's is relative both in terms of what had gone before, and also because apparently his picture was a challange to Ingres. He traced the theme from its formulation in modern times back to antiquity, while all the while immersing himself in the atmosphere of the fifteenth century, to such an extent that it might easily have been taken at that time as a pastiche of Mantegna. By endowing this work with an excess of eroticism and morbidity full of decorative and composite elements, by mixing reality and imagination so that the "created" object looks quite out of place in its over-"natural" setting, Moreau does more, even though the picture remains an enigma, than reveal the cry of the two sexes face to face. He went beyond both myth and tradition. He quite clearly showed the anguished fulfilment of incestuous desire. He led the way, a way which put abnormality firmly on view. The picture has a certain feeling of super-reality about it, or rather that convincing aspect which dreams give to the unreal. It is undoubtedly for these reasons that the visitors to the 1864 Salon accorded this "model" picture a similar reception to that which was given to Burne-Jones's *Laus Veneris* in London. "M. Gustave Moreau," wrote a Salon critic, "is the hero of this exhibition, and those critics who are usually never satisfied agree that if the 1864 Salon is saved from discredit, it is only thanks to his *Oedipus and the Sphinx*... the work of this unknown painter attracts one's attention and holds it irresistibly, no matter what one does."

Gustave Moreau was the man of the moment. Aloof, independent, solitary, he yet became fashionable in high society and was taken up in masonic and occult circles. His very success lent strength to the opposition which was gathering against the Impressionists (whose first group exhibition was to take place on 15 April 1874, in a studio which had recently belonged to the photographer Nadar, on the second floor of a building on the corner of the Boulevard des Capucines and the Rue Daunou). Degas regarded Gustave Moreau as a mystic, an opportunist, "who swims with the current." The movement which he started is not the confrontation between "naturalists who face the future undeterred" (Castagnary) and "primitives of an important movement of artistic revival" (Duranty). Gustave Moreau was both detached from and uninterested in the world around him. He wished to bury himself in a dream world, in a world peopled with the archetypes of ancient myth, surrounded by the ghosts of desire which assail a bachelor dedicated to protecting the love he feels for his mother (with whom he lived until her death in 1884). His point of view was so radically opposed to that of realism that it could not fail to upset the acknowledged spokesman of social emancipation: Zola. The more the public acclaimed the three pictures which Moreau showed at the 1876 Salon—*Hercules and the Lernean Hydra*, *Salome Before Herod* and a large watercolour also on the Salome theme, *The Apparition*—the more was Zola's fury aroused. He finally expressed his feelings in a long article in *The Messenger of Europe*, a Russian periodical published in Moscow. For the first time, apparently, the notion of Symbolism as a movement beyond the normal currents of the time was set down in no uncertain terms.

"I shall have noted all the curiosities of modern painting when I have dealt with Gustave Moreau, whom I have left to the last as being the most astonishing example of the extravagances into which an artist can fall in the search for originality and the hatred of realism. It was inevitable that contemporary naturalism and the efforts of art to study nature should call forth a reaction and bring forward artists with an idealistic turn of mind. This retrograde movement, in the realms of the imagination, is particularly interesting in the case of Gustave Moreau. He has not taken refuge in Romanticism, as one would have imagined; he scorns the romantic fever, the too-easy use of colour, those haphazard strokes of the brush, which cover the canvas with effects of light and shade until you are quite blinded. No, *Gustave Moreau has plunged into symbolism* (my italics). He paints pictures partly composed of riddles; rediscovers archaic or primitive forms; takes Mantegna as his model; and affords an enormous importance to the minutest details of his pictures. His method becomes understandable if I describe the last two pictures that he has shown this year. The subject of the first is *Hercules and the Lernean Hydra*... His second picture, *Salome*, is even more bizarre. The action takes place in a palace 'of ideal architecture,' according to an enthusiastic critic. In fact, I shall allow myself to borrow the description of the painting from this critic, because, frankly, I must admit that I am not capable of writing anything similar. 'Opposite, Herod is seated on a throne or rather on an altar. Behind him, against a colonnaded background, is the triple god, whose breasts hang down like bunches of grapes and who opens both hands in a symbolic gesture. Herod is deathly pale in his white robes; he is like a ghost and obviously represents the old world about to collapse with him. At the foot of the altar is a slave with a drawn sword in his hand, static, dumb and as pale as his master; on the opposite side one can see Herodias, next to a female musician, who is playing some kind of instrument. The beautiful young girl, Salome, glides forward on tiptoe, her white feet bedecked with rubies and jewels. One arm is stretched out, the other bent, and she holds up something which seems like a pink lotus in front of her face. This then is her dance, and yet how well one understands the madness of the Tetrarch in offering Salome one half of his kingdom.' This description of a Moreau painting by one of his admirers really says it all. His talent consists in taking subjects which have already been dealt with by other artists and altering them, treating them more ingeniously. He paints his dreams, not simple, naïve dreams such as we all have, but sophisticated, complicated, enigmatic dreams which are

Gustave Moreau (1826-1898) : Nude Study for Salome, c. 1876. Pencil.

difficult to understand immediately. What value can such art have in these days? It is a question which I find it difficult to reply to. It seems to me, as I have already said, to be an outright reaction against the modern world. Painting is in no great danger from this movement. One shrugs one's shoulders and passes on, that is all there is to say."

This is an extreme point of view and was held by Zola at the same time that he was hailing Manet as "a modern artist, a realist, a positivist." Manet at least "painted people as he saw them in life, in the street or at home, in their ordinary surroundings, dressed according to present-day fashion, in other words, contemporary." But there is

Gustave Moreau (1826-1898) : The Apparition (Salome and the Head of John the Baptist), c. 1875. Oil.

something else that needs to be said here, and that is the fact that Zola, in the same year, 1876, championed the cause of Puvis de Chavannes, who to him was in no way a symbolist painter: "In our time," observes Zola, again writing in *The Messenger of Europe*, "with the disappearance of classical principles, the state of mural painting has become critical. In the past there were noble heroes, the drawing was uncluttered and the rules made a sort of bas-relief of the picture whose muted colours did not clash with the marble of the churches and palaces. This no longer exists, for we now have Romantic paintings. It seems to me, however, that Puvis de Chavannes has found a way out of this *impasse*. He knows how to be both interesting and lively by simplifying the lines of his drawing and using uniform tones in his compositions...If the truth be told, Puvis de Chavannes is for me just a forerunner of what is to come. It is indispensable that monumental painting should find its subjects in contemporary life. I do not know who will be the painter of genius capable of extracting art from our civilization and I do not know how it will be done, but it is a fact that art depends neither on draperies nor on nudes painted according to the rules of antiquity; art is nourished by humanity and as a result each society must have its own individual idea of beauty..."

The dialectics of unreality

I love my art so much that I shall only be happy when I can practise it for myself alone.

Gustave Moreau

△ *Gustave Moreau (1826-1898): The Rape of Deianira by the Centaur Nessus. Pen and Indian ink.*

▷ *Gustave Moreau (1826-1898): Hercules and the Lernean Hydra, 1876. Oil.*

It was plain that Zola could not accept something which was for him an ideological deviation and which was at the same time both dangerous and negative. Nonetheless, he was intrigued by the complexity of a movement which abandoned every pretence at the portrayal of reality (at least Zola's kind of reality) and which portrayed an unreality which led the painting into the realms of mystery, doubt and fascination. The paintings are at the same time exasperating, full of elements which are added on anyhow like a collage. Moreau's attention to detail in his scriptural compositions, such as *Salome*, is in total opposition to the lines in his drawings which are hesitant; these same blurred outlines are not in accord with his ornamental style. Everyday objects become totally unrecognizable; luxury becomes lewdness in his pictures; the static is shown in contrast to the active; inertia is set against dynamism; the bodies of his models are often decorated with marks like the marks of calligraphy; the real and the imaginary are inextricably entangled with one another, and that which you are meant to see is hidden by the imaginary. Death is triumphant in a festive background. Unreality is a guiding factor in his work, which seems free of outside constraint.

All this is summed up in *Salome* and *The Apparition*. In the first picture, Salome dances before her step-father Herod; in the second, John the Baptist's head appears as an apparition before her. This is a variation on the same theme and is central to Moreau's entire oeuvre. Can we really understand it? "If you tried to enter into the spirit of this mysterious, symbolic and intimate way that I have of portraying things, which is the crux of my talent, unique in its way, you would enjoy subjects painted in this manner." This is Moreau himself addressing a close friend, Henri Rupp.

He continues: "This bored, temperamental, highly sensual woman is given very little pleasure at seeing her enemy laid low, so sick is she of always having her every desire satisfied.

"This woman, walking nonchalantly, bestially, in gardens which have just been stained by that horrible murder, which so horrified even the executioner that he ran off distractedly—you should really enjoy this.

"When I want to portray these nuances, I find them, not in my subject, but in the real nature of woman today, who searches for unhealthy emotions and because she is so stupid, does not understand the horror of the most appalling situations.

"It is one of the aspects of this subject which I have thoroughly dealt with."

This is a basic critique, which demands a certain amount of attention. It talks of the inner secrets which the image is capable of showing. The dregs of passion, "that useless passion," as Sartre would say, which expressed the idea of a sterile, feline beauty, of baleful perfection and feminine triumph over the male. Is this the creation of an unsatisfied libido? Is it because the painter refuses to face reality that he is forced to hide in a world of phantasms? The idol is, as one says, "well executed." She is *Salome*, she is *The Apparition*, identical in the two paintings, one like the reflection of the other. At the 1876 Salon these two pictures drew the crowds. More than 500,000 visitors flocked to see them, drawn by reports in the newspapers. Does this mean that the painter obtains honour, power and love through success, because he is incapable of obtaining them any other way? Up until now Moreau's painting had not gained the favour of the public, which is why *Salome* came to mean so much to him. One could say that art since the Romantic period had been an "attempt at reconciling an unhappy relationship with things and people—a deferred revenge."

Salome and *The Apparition* served as basic texts and privileged models for the generation of Symbolists of the 1880s. The Moreau cult spread, as the ripples on a pond spread when a stone has been thrown in. However, a taste for the morbid and the erotic had already appeared: Baudelaire had introduced the idea of the "cold majesty of the sterile woman" and Mallarmé had written a poem, *Hérodiade*, which was in the same vein.

But, above all, it was J.-K. Huysmans who was Moreau's greatest champion. His novel *A Rebours* ("Against the Grain") came out in 1884 and the middle pages of this outburst are devoted to passionate descrip-

tions of *Salome* and *The Apparition*. They mark an important step in the history of Symbolism and are a witness to the heights of decadence: a change from meaning in painting to meaning in words.

"Envelopped in the odour of depravity, in the overheated atmosphere of this church, Salome, the left arm stretched out in a commanding gesture, the right arm bent, holds a large lotus on a level with her face. She moves forward slowly, on the tips of her toes to the sound of a guitar, whose strings are plucked by a woman who is crouched behind her. With a rapt, solemn, almost majestic expression, she begins the lascivious dance which is aimed at awakening the deadened senses of old Herod; her breasts form two hillocks whose nipples stand up, rubbed by her jangling necklaces; diamonds glisten on her moist skin, while her bracelets, belts and rings throw out sparks of light. Her triumphal dress is sewn with pearls and interwoven with a design of silver and gold, while the breast-plate, product of a goldsmith's art, in which each stitch is a precious stone, seems to flame and become entangled with fire serpents who swarm over her dull flesh and her skin the colour of a tea rose, like glorious insects with marvellous wings, marbled in carmine, crossed with flashes of yellow, speckled with steel-blue and spotted with peacock green..."

In 1876, at the Salon on the Champs Elysées, a festival of symbols summoned the crowd. Without any prior warning they were faced on all sides with a sea of allusions. The ghosts of decadence had already taken up their positions and simple enjoyment was banished. Could this crowd, full of taboos as it was, have understood such a complex phenomenon? Could it have seen in the feline Salome the Great Prostitute of the Apocalypse? Could it have realized that the black panther and the fan of peacock feathers represented lasciviousness? Could it have understood that the Sphinx, holding between its claws the battered body of a masculine victim, was the symbol of depraved domination? Would it have associated the idea of the origin of magic fluid with the immense eye hanging from a bracelet? And would it have given a phallic meaning to all those columns? Undoubtedly, the crowd carried out the semantic adjustments to its understanding which it felt to be necessary, and had no difficulty in seeing in the beauty of this woman her voluptuousness, her death-dealing cruelty. The crowd's curiosity, its interest, even its enthusiasm were necessarily contained within the limits of its imagination. It had no other pretensions. Social convention always demands a certain minimum delay before being able to judge whether the critics have been right or not. Which is why reading the works of "those who know" is not necessarily the best thing to do. Focillon was right to maintain that the real character of a work of art depends on the reception of all its implications, which include the absurd and the incredible.

Henri Fantin-Latour (1836-1904): The First Scene of Wagner's "Rheingold", 1876. Black crayon.

2

THE MAUVE DECADE
1876-1885

Eve am I, who have been summoned to you from those unbounded regions whose pale frontiers can only be glimpsed by Man between certain dreams and certain slumbers.

Auguste Villiers de l'Isle-Adam, *L'Eve future*, 1886

IN THE FRANCE of the late nineteenth century, the dominant intellectual current seemed to be a narrow form of rationalism—the positivism of thinkers such as Taine, Renan and Littré. One of their main opponents was Count Villiers de l'Isle-Adam. He was not a philosopher, any more than many of the advocates of positivism were philosophers, and yet, during the 1880s, he was generally held to be a significant thinker by the idealist minority. He was considered to be the main authority in France on the pessimism of Schopenhauer and the pantheism of Wagner. The idealists looked up to Villiers as the leader of their crusade against rationalism, and indeed he seemed out of place in his own century. He castigated his contemporaries for their easy acceptance of positivism, which flatters the disbelief of the shallow and the arrogant. He regarded the bourgeois—in the intellectual or artistic sense, rather than its now more common political sense—as the purveyors of a dangerous materialism, founded on the belief that "common sense" was an infallible guide to knowledge. Their common sense, he felt, was a negative, derisory faculty, which dealt with trivia in a trivial way and led its victims to make a virtue of the inconsequential and to take pride in the passionate pursuit of banalities. He considered that their belief in progress was a delusion which produced a paralysing atheism, a closing of the mind and a progressive deadening of the sensibilities. Villiers believed that the truths of life lie in its mysteries, and that mysteries are absolutely intractable, and therefore perfectly fascinating. A mystery explained is no mystery: its reality is that it is unintelligible and must by definition remain unintelligible. This idealism, which for a time seemed to owe something to Hegel, accounts for Villiers's interest in Baudelaire and in the mysticism sometimes associated with Swedenborg's theory of universal correspondences, and it helped to draw him towards writers of the macabre, the esoteric and the occult. In his novel *L'Eve future*, which was a pamphlet as much as a work of fiction, he launched a virulent attack against the essentially materialist desires of contemporary society. The conception was Faustian, evoking the traditional figure of an idealizing scientist in an atmosphere of occultism and the fantastic. The scientist is based on the American inventor, Edison. In the novel, Villiers imagines Edison condemning, not reason or the evidence of the senses, but the deification of reason and sensory experience imposed by positivist rationalism. The central idea of the novel is conveyed mainly through the esoteric figure of a beautiful female android, created by the fictitious Edison. She is an ethereal, angelic woman: Hadaly, whose name means the Ideal. The image of idealized woman, which has served many different purposes through the ages, was given a particular visual form by Gustave Moreau, and for the French Symbolists of the late nineteenth century it was a medium for the expression of an extreme form of idealism.

Woman refined and idealized: we find this image in Verhaeren's Helen of Sparta and in Henri de Régnier's Galatea. There are elements of it in Viélé-Griffin, Remy de Gourmont and Jules Laforgue. There were antecedents in Baudelaire and some Romantic writers. It is present in the haunting, intangible figure of Mallarmé's Hérodiade, where the visual image is vague and its magical quality derives from its power of suggestion. This uncertainty of detail was a deliberate technique. According to Symbolist theory, the mystery and sacredness of reality could only be evoked, never stated explicitly. In Mallarmé's terms, it was not the object itself which was to be depicted, but the effect which it produced. This doctrine of suggestion could lead to supernatural effects. The idealized woman appeared cold, distant and frightening, a fleeting, ghostly figure. Although Villiers himself claimed that he did not believe in the frivolity and posturing of the waking dead, and denied the existence of such fantasies, he succeeded in creating an other-worldly ideal: "I will create living woman anew, transfigured according to your most intimate desires! She will hold the harmonies of Hoffmann's Antonia; she will embody the mystery and the passion of Poe's Ligeia; she will be as powerful and alluring as Wagner's Venus!" This concept brought together music, literature and the visual arts. The desire for unity in the arts was characteristic of much late nineteenth-century thinking about the nature of artistic creation and response. Villiers's position was representative of the period, with his combined taste for literature and music. He also realized the ideological potential of idealized characters in literature and the opera. He was filled with enthusiasm for Wagner, and his enthusiasm became an almost religious veneration for the "Temple of the music of the future" when he attended the Bayreuth music festival in August 1876 and witnessed the triumph with which the first complete performance of Wagner's works was received. For Villiers, human innocence seemed to be glorified and artistic truth was re-affirmed and honoured in Wagner's myths and idealizations. Not all responses were so uncritical, however. In September of the same year, for example, Karl Marx wrote to his daughter Jenny that the question on everybody's lips was "What do you think of Wagner?" His own view was that Bayreuth was a circus, with Wagner as juggler, clown and wizard.

Nevertheless, the Wagner cult persisted. In Paris in 1885, two years after Wagner's death, Villiers was closely associated with the foundation and organization of the *Revue Wagnérienne*, which was a literary as much as a music review. Its director, Edouard Dujardin, went so far as

Loys Delteil (1869-1927):
Portrait of
Villiers de l'Isle-Adam
(detail), 1896. Etching.

Jules Bonnet:
Photograph of Richard Wagner
at Tribschen (Lucerne),
detail, autumn 1867.

Hans Thoma (1839-1924): The Rhine Maidens. Watercolour.

Revue Wagnérienne

to claim that Wagner's symphonic and unifying concept of the various arts was an essential source of the French Symbolist movement. *Total art* was seen as an ideal: it was conceived as an attempt to transpose the sense perceptions, to combine sound and colour, to unify the traditionally separate artistic media, to stimulate the mind by complex metaphor, seeing the waves of the ocean in the movement of forest trees, catching in the siren's song the eddies of the wind. Wagnerism involved a belief in individual and collective ecstasy. For the world-weary, it allowed a lyrical escape which enabled the Romantic imagination to drift into a fanciful dream-world. It attracted disciples for many different reasons. For some, Wagnerism was above all a political rallying call, appealing to class consciousness. For others, it stimulated the most diverse idealistic beliefs. It brought together folklore and philosophy, in a confused combination of myths and images. Its music was labyrinthine, hazy and swelling, suggesting sometimes the terrors of pessimism, sometimes the most intense hostility. It carried with it a dazzling eroticism, and the heavy, persistent tolling of death. Such effects were admirably suited to a prevailing taste for the primitive, the colossal, the exotic and the macabre. This late nineteenth-century development of Romanticism gave rise to extravagant transpositions: Baudelaire had helped to lead artistic sensibilities in this direction, and the theory of transpositions was exploited by Böcklin, whom Wagner had wanted for the settings of his Tetralogy. The most fervent disciples of the new cult, writing in the *Revue Wagnérienne*, considered that the theory of the transposition of the arts admitted, and indeed demanded, the concept of "Wagnerian painting." This idea was elaborated by Teodor de Wyzewa in his review of the Paris Salon of 1885:

Henri Fantin-Latour (1836-1904): The Calling Up of Erda ("Siegfried," Act III, Scene 1). Illustration for the "Revue Wagnérienne," 8 May 1885.

"A painting by Monsieur Moreau, the symphonist of refined emotions, or one of the terrifying drawings by Monsieur Redon, or again the exhibition of Old Masters which opened recently at the Louvre— these are Wagnerian events... For Wagnerism is above all the exclusion of slavish exercises, of any work which has not been inspired solely by the artist's hunger for divine, speculative Creation. This year, I have examined several kilometers of painted canvas, in the hope of coming across a few works serious enough to serve as examples of the Wagnerian theory. Almost in vain. Apart from that admirable master of Wagnerism, Monsieur Fantin-Latour, I found only two worthwhile items: a symphony in dark colours (the catalogue calls it a *Portrait*) by Monsieur Whistler, and a marvellous scene by Monsieur Bartholomé, depicting girls playing in a courtyard. These splendid works contrast sharply with the miserable compromises, academic imitations and dishonest vision of the other canvases. Monsieur Fantin-Latour is my consolation among so many derisory offerings. He sets out deliberately to be Wagnerian: he knows, admires and glorifies the Master... In this Exhibition he has again given us two models of the two arts: one of them is a lithograph entitled, I think, *Daughters of the Rhine*. The subject is taken from Wagner: it shows the excited mockery of the water sprites, while Siegfried goes away towards his death. The subject itself is of little importance, however. The precise place, the similarity between this painting and the Bayreuth picture—these are not of the essence. What matters is that Monsieur Fantin-Latour has wished to translate the emotion of the scene into plastic form, and he has succeeded admirably..."

Wyzewa, who was admittedly one of the more naive theorists of Symbolism, maintained in his article on the 1886 Salon that, in addition to Fantin-Latour, Puvis de Chavannes was a Wagnerian artist in his "emotional, symphonic painting." Similarly, Redon must be accounted a Wagnerian, for his "dark landscapes": "Monsieur Odilon

Revue Wagnérienne

Redon attempts to create afresh the empty landscapes of bitterness and fear, and the cruelty of imagery, by which Monsieur Félicien Rops evokes the vicious passions of an age of perversity." Again, the entire works of Henry de Groux were inspired by the Wagnerian cycle: *Sieglinde and Siegmund, Siegmund and the Bird*, the *Death of Siegfried, Mount Salvat, Lohengrin*. Although these are obviously weak, literal imitations, Ensor was indebted to de Groux for the influence which Wagner's opera had upon him, and one of Ensor's most subtle compositions was to be *The Ride of the Valkyries*. It is instructive, however, to return to J.-K. Huysmans, not yet in connection with his famous novel, *A Rebours*, which we shall consider later, but in order to illustrate the impact of Wagnerian Symbolism on the sensibility, imagination and obsessions of the anti-realists of the years 1880-1885. Together with many writers of greater or lesser importance in the evolution of French Symbolism, Huysmans contributed to the *Revue Wagnérienne*. There is in particular a very striking passage by Huysmans, written under the impact of the opening of *Tannhäuser*:

"The orchestra suddenly breaks in on this fluid, fantastic, evocative scene, depicting briefly and decisively the approach of Tannhäuser. The darkness retreats, light floods the scene, wreaths of mist and cloud take on the contorted forms of writhing hips and heaving, throbbing breasts. Avalanches of blue sky are gradually filled with naked shapes. From the orchestra the music rises in shrill cries of unbridled desire, piercing screams of lewd sensuality, outbursts of an eternal, supernatural carnality, and above a sinuous espalier of swooning, satiated nymphs, Venus rises. But this is not the familiar Venus of antiquity, the legendary Aphrodite, the pagan goddess of concupiscence, who

I shall always remember the gaze which, from the depths of his extraordinary blue eyes, Wagner turned upon me.

"But," he answered with a smile, "were it not that I feel in my soul the living light and love of the Christian faith, my works, in which I embody my mind and the span of my life, would be those of a deceiver, an imitator. As it is, all my works testify to that faith."

Auguste Villiers de l'Isle-Adam, *Souvenir*, in the *Revue Wagnérienne*, June 1887

Odilon Redon (1840-1916): Brunnhilde ("Die Götterdämmerung," final scene). Lithograph illustration for the "Revue Wagnérienne," 8 August 1885.

reduced gods and men to whinnying fools. This Venus is terrible and profound, the living embodiment of the Spirit of Evil, the incarnation of Lust, all-powerful and irresistible. This Venus is a magnificent, enthralling She-Devil, forever preying on Christian souls, corrupt and utterly corrupting.

"Wagner's Venus may be seen as a return to the medieval allegories: she is an emblem of our material nature, an allegorical figure of Evil in conflict with Good, a symbol of man's grievous inner struggle between paradise and hell. His Venus is reminiscent of the great allegorical poem by the early Christian poet Prudentius—the living Tannhäuser who spent many years in a life of debauchery, but who finally escaped from the arms of the Temptress and found refuge in penance and the adoration of the Virgin.

"The musician's Venus is like a descendent of the Luxuria of the poet, the white, perfumed tamer of beasts, who overwhelmed her victims by means of enervating flowers. She attracts and captivates like Prudentius's most dangerous goddess—the goddess whose name the Christian poet dared not even write, except in fear and trembling: Sodomita Libido.

"However, although Wagner's Venus has so much in common with the medieval allegorical figures, his concept of the goddess of love contains also a modern element. He has introduced a current of fine intellectual discernment into the savage flood of sensuality. To the naive images inherited from the past, Wagner's Venus brings a heightening of the sensations, and, by glorifying our refined and sharpened senses, suggests that the hero's destruction is completely unavoidable, as he is initiated suddenly into the complex spiritual wantonness of the exhausted times in which we live..."

Mallarmé's response to Wagner was very different. In the *Revue Wagnérienne*, together with Huysmans's sensual and scathing appraisal of Wagner, Dujardin published an important article by Mallarmé entitled *Richard Wagner. Reverie of a French Poet*. Dujardin himself conceded that the ardent disciples of Wagner would have been deeply shocked if they had understood Mallarmé's position, and the gulf which separated his ideal from that of Wagner. By comparing Mallarmé's article with Huysmans's emotional involvement, it is possible to appreciate Mallarmé's intransigence and distant authority. Mallarmé's "furiously intelligent" reaction contrasted sharply with Huysmans's heady decadence. At the same time, the independence of Mallarmé's point of view on the obscure aesthetic polemics of the period becomes clearer. Music, for Mallarmé, was the "vibrating prolongation of all things, of Life itself." He therefore wished to introduce music into literature, while confessing that the origins of music and its essential meaning must remain unknown. He considered that the apparent purpose of Wagner's art was related to his own ideal of literature "only insofar as it entailed a strict observance of complex, self-imposed laws, in order, initially, to express the imprecise intuitively, confusing the colours or lines of the characters with the tones and themes of the music, in the richest imaginable atmosphere of Reverie." Wagner's music evoked a form of deity "costumed in the invisible folds of a tissue of chords." Mallarmé felt that this music always tended towards the theatrical, and that Wagner's art was therefore in conflict with the nature of music itself. By adding the modern orchestra, Wagner had introduced a radical change into the old concept of the theatre. Whereas the characters and settings of the theatre had contained its meanings and created its effects, the musical theatre of Wagner used settings and characters as allegorical figures. In themselves, these allegorical devices were empty, abstract and impersonal; they would have been entirely lacking in reality or persuasive power without the life-giving flow of the music. For Mallarmé, a Symbolist theatre presupposed the abolition of characterization and personification: it would be a theatre of sound, of the voice, a theatre of the Idea. "Does a spiritual evocation—the preparation or development of Symbols—need to be situated in a particular place? The fictive scene created as it were by the converging lines of vision of the audience is a sufficient situation!" The final paragraph of Mallarmé's article on Wagner reveals his modesty, his independence of mind, and the tenacity with which he wished to pursue his own artistic ideal. He acknowledged the enthusiasm of Wagner's uncritical admirers, and expressed regret that he was unable to join them wholeheartedly in their jubilant celebration of Wagner's art. The adepts had the fervour of the converted, their search for an ideal had been finite, and it had therefore been completed successfully. He described Wagner's work as a magnificent Temple, standing halfway up the holy mountain of artistic idealism. For the crowd, it was a place of pilgrimage and salvation. For himself, it was a welcome resting place—delightful, certainly, but only a temporary shelter which allowed some respite from the haunting insistence of his own ideal, from his aspiration towards the "menacing summit of the absolute, hidden high above, imagined beyond the clouds, dazzling, bare, solitary." No one, wrote Mallarmé emphatically, no one seems capable of attaining this ideal.

Mallarmé was not always so intransigent, so seemingly peremptory. The friends who used to visit him when he held his famous Tuesday-evening discussions knew a warm, sympathetic Mallarmé, always ready to pay careful attention to any serious art, no matter how it diverged from his own aims. His home in Paris, at 87 rue de Rome, itself became a place of pilgrimage. Many of the most famous writers and artists of the age came there to discuss literature and the arts, and above all to listen to Mallarmé's discourses: Emile Zola, Villiers de l'Isle-Adam, J.-K. Huysmans, Catulle Mendès, Félicien Rops, Henri de Régnier, Manet, Redon, Munch, Gauguin, Verlaine, Nina de Villard, Eugène Lefébure, Stuart Merrill, Georges Rodenbach, Henri Cazalis, Teodor de Wyzewa, Gabriel Mourey, Elémir Bourges, Robert de Montesquiou, Emmanuel des Essarts, Emile Verhaeren, Gustave Kahn, and many others of greater or lesser importance. On the whole they agreed that Wagnerism was a significant social and cultural phenomenon, though each had of course his own predilections and private interpretations. They observed, and sometimes they joined, the hordes of snobs who left Paris annually, in increasing numbers, to attend the Bayreuth

Paul von Joukowsky (1845-1912): Portrait of Richard Wagner Reading, Venice, 12 February 1883. Pencil drawing in a sketchbook of Cosima Wagner.

"There is no end to the poetry of the beautiful."

Arnold Böcklin, 1849

festival. The French aristocracy—Robert de Montesquiou or the Countess of Beausacq, for example—added their own style to this vogue, and the ladies in particular took advantage of the opportunity to parade themselves. A contemporary chronicler made his point with some asperity: "Very smart, the Bayreuth set. With the latest fashions and their idle ostentation, they defile the sanctuary which was intended to exclude them, in this distant corner of Bavaria." Again, Maurice Barrès wrote in July 1886: "They go to Bayreuth to be seen, to enhance their reputations, to amuse and be amused…"

Mallarmé himself took an interest in women's fashions. Indeed, it is perhaps not too fanciful to see a Wagnerian element of social ostentation and theatrical parade in his "society and family gazette," *The Latest Fashion (La Dernière Mode)*. Mallarmé was responsible for eight numbers of the magazine, in late 1874, under the pseudonym of Marasquin. The enterprise was prompted partly by the need to earn money. In his well-known "autobiographical letter" to Verlaine, written in 1885, he explained the episode in the following terms: "At times of financial difficulty, or in order to purchase expensive books, I had to take on particular tasks… which are best forgotten. But apart from that my concessions to necessity or to pleasure have been infrequent. And yet, for a short period, when I was giving up hope in the despotic Book which I imagined I might write, and when I had peddled a few articles around, I did try to edit the magazine *The Latest Fashion*. I was solely responsible for the articles on dress, jewelry, furnishings, theatres and even cookery menus. When I take down the eight or so numbers which were published and blow away the dust, they still have the power to send me off into long daydreams and imaginings." There can, of course, be no question of interpreting this minor work as a vital element in Mallarmé's complex and often obscure thinking. Nevertheless, the very complexity of his thought prevents us from dismissing *The Latest Fashion* too easily. It could well prove rewarding to situate this lonely enterprise in the context of the concept of total art: the magazine brought together decorative art, music, literature and the theatre, suggesting implicitly a broad art of living which may have some kinship, however remote, with the effects of the cult of Wagner.

Arnold Böcklin (1827-1901): The Isle of the Dead, 1880. Oil.

According to the evidence, it was probably in 1882, in the heightened atmosphere of Mallarmé's Tuesday-evening gatherings, that Huysmans decided to use Mallarmé's visitor, Robert de Montesquiou, an aristocratic aesthete, as the main model for his most notable fictional character: Jean Floressas des Esseintes. Des Esseintes was the central character in Huysmans's novel *A Rebours*, which was published in May 1884. The novel has been translated into English under the title *Against the Grain*. It appeared at the time of the first Salon des Indépendants in Paris, which Redon had helped to found. In February of the same year, the "Group of Twenty" *(Les XX)* had opened their first exhibition in Brussels, with works by Ensor, Khnopf, Rops, Whistler, Rodin, and many others. Huysmans himself had not been associated with the idealist or pre-Symbolist opponents of scientific positivism; he had belonged generally to the Naturalist novelists whose most telling and authoritative representative was Emile Zola. *A Rebours*, a novel of decadence, but written by an allegedly Naturalist author, was therefore quickly recognized as a novel of particular significance in the artistic and literary climate of the late nineteenth century. In 1886, the author was sketched as follows by Félix Fénéon: "Huysmans, Joris-Karl. Spare appearance, piercing deep-set eyes, ogee-shaped nose...In the street, encased in a close-fitting dark-brown jacket, he walks quickly, sensitive and snug. At his home in the rue de Sèvres, walls hung with etchings, charcoal drawings, impressionist watercolours. A fat, yellow, moulting cat sheds fur around your legs. In his novels, he always uses his protagonists as mouthpieces for his likes and dislikes: sudden changes in the weather, alcoholic strength, the pungency of tobacco, the noise of the trams, the stupidity of the girls, the toughness of the beef. Has invented a certain phraseology—direct, virulent, denunciatory, fiercely metaphorical, a literary tattoo, nauseating, suggesting a thick atmosphere of tumultuous venom."

Des Esseintes was a mask, a fictional device which served as an imaginary mirror for the author. Protected by the mask, Huysmans was able, if only unconsciously, to give literary expression to his hidden desires. In this play of mirrors, appearance and reality were virtually indistinguishable. Des Esseintes, with his particular ideas, fetishes and exquisite hypersensitivity, may be seen as a product of Huysmans's innermost being: some commentators have been tempted to interpret this in terms of a sexual narcissism, in which the revelation and contemplation of the self are a sign of both alienation and pleasurable acquiescence. This inward-turned, frenetic self-absorption, with its obvious suggestion of hypochondriasis, may help to explain why des Esseintes was "interested only in works of art which are inflamed and fevered, already wasting away." This melancholy led to the realization of a latent corruption: "Beneath a sullen sky, in the heavy, lifeless atmosphere, the walls of the houses sweat darkly above their rank cellars. Our disgust with life increases; an overwhelming despondency bears down upon us. The seeds of filth contained in every soul begin to grow. The most austere of men are plagued by longings for foul amusements. Men of high esteem begin to see the world through criminal eyes." Des Esseintes created a chemistry of sensations, responding with delight to the powerful urges of sensuality. He turned in upon himself, seeking unique experiences and hallucinations. This self-indulgent pursuit of original, imaginary experience involved a repudiation of the themes and stylistic preferences of the French Naturalist novelists. The following extract is symptomatic of both the style and the intention of the novel. "With his vaporizers, des Esseintes sprayed the room with a blend of ambrosia, lavender, sweet-pea and flowers; it was an essence which, when perfectly distilled, so well deserves the name 'Essence of Meadow-in-Bloom.' Then, to this fragrant meadow, he added a further blend of polianthes, and orange- and almond-blossom. Instantly, artificial lilac-trees sprang up, while the lime blossom faded and trailed its pale perfumes low along the ground... Des Esseintes created this general setting with a few broad strokes, allowing the scene to extend indefinitely within his mind. And then he rained down into it a fine mist of human, almost feline, perfumes—the faintest flavour of the sex, a delicate hint of woman, powdered and painted—stephanotis, eupatorium, opopanax, bergamot, champac and Indian orchid. To these essences he

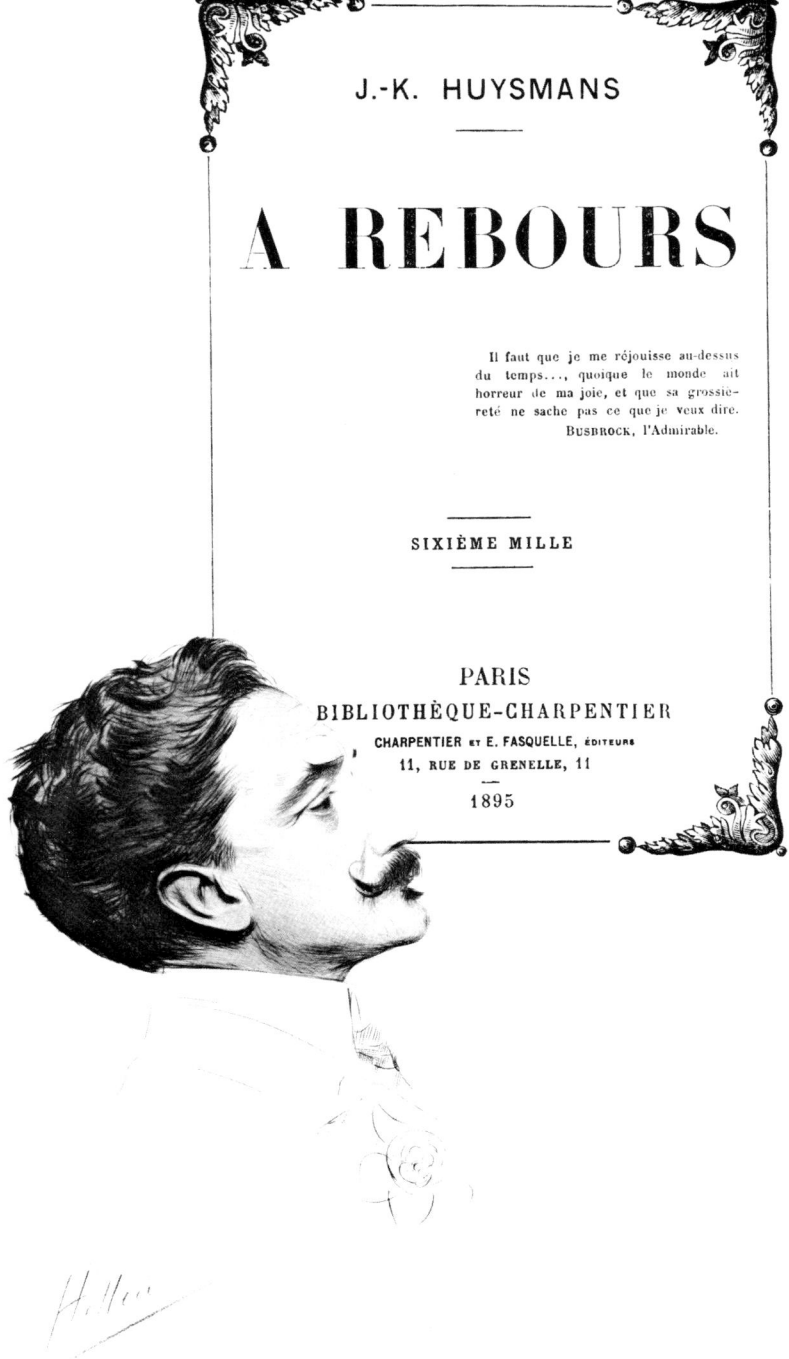

Joris-Karl Huysmans: Cover of "A Rebours," second edition, 1895. Overprinted on it: Portrait of Robert de Montesquiou (1855-1921), drypoint by Paul Helleu.

Here it is, this unique book, which had to be done—and well done it is, by you! and that at no other literary moment but now! Really, as I see it lying closed upon my desk, with all the treasure of its learning locked within it, beneath one's eye, I cannot conceive of its being other than it is, in that hour, you know, of reverie which follows upon one's reading, when almost always a different book takes the place, even of the book one admires. Here no! So it is, nothing is to be found wanting in it, perfumes, music, liquors and old books and all but the books yet to be; and such flowers! the absolute vision of all that, for a man set down before the feast of barbaric or modern delight, may open up the paradise fields of sensation alone...

Letter from Mallarmé to Huysmans, 18 May 1884

added a breath of seringa, so bringing, to the exquisite artifice of their fragrancies, the natural scent of merry, sweating saturnalia in the sun." There is an almost mesmeric concentration upon the idea of sensory experience. This emphasis on the idea at the expense of the reality, together with the florid, sometimes meretricious style, and the general preoccupation with cerebral stimulation, marked a very sharp break with Naturalism. Huysmans had deserted from the Naturalists, in favour of systematic dreaming, over-refinement and morbid affectation. Through des Esseintes, Huysmans had "immersed himself in dreams of antiquity, in the ancient corruption, far removed from the manners and life of our own times." Through literature, he was seeking an exquisite, subtle form of painting. In the Preface to *A Rebours*, written twenty years after the first publication of the novel, Huysmans wrote that by 1884 he had felt stifled by the monotony of Naturalism, with its theories and incessant repetitions of predictable social ideology: "I had a vague desire to escape from this suffocating blind-alley, but I had no particular plan; and *A Rebours*, which freed me from that deadening literature, is a completely unconscious work. I wrote it without any preconceived ideas or future intentions. It is a work of the imagination, based on nothing at all."

Huysmans's apparent modesty was a response to the fame which *A Rebours* had quickly acquired. If the novel was based on nothing at all, this "nothing" included a whole range of factors which, it is generally agreed, contributed to the French intellectual climate of the late nineteenth century. It included Schopenhauer, for whom Huysmans openly professed an excessive admiration. It included the "prodigious opera of Wagner," "the heightened style of Verlaine and Mallarmé," the prose poems of Mallarmé "salvaged from long-dead magazines: *The Demon of Analogy, The Pipe, Poor Pale Child, An Interrupted Show, The Future Phenomenon*, and above all *Autumn Complaint* and *Winter Shivering*, which were Mallarmé's masterpieces." For des Esseintes, it included Villiers de l'Isle-Adam, in whose works he found "hallucination, delicate tenderness, seditious comment, spasmodic vibrations"; it included Tristan Corbière's poems, *Yellow Loves*, and Theo Hannon, the "Brussels Idol, with made-up face and his belly pickled in perfume"; it included Barbey d'Aurevilly's "sensual monstrosities," and the *Satyricon*, the "tale without a plot, depicting the vices of a broken civilization, while the author does not intrude himself even once." It included Gustave Moreau's "desperate, erudite works," Bresdin's *Comedy of Death*, "an inconceivable landscape of woods, copses, clumps of trees, shaped into devils and phantoms, covered with birds with tails like vegetable-pods and heads of rats, while the ground is littered with animal-bones, ribs, skulls..."; and it included Odilon Redon's "unimaginable apparitions, with their especially weird imagery, their fantastic atmosphere of sickness and delirium."

So, when Huysmans wrote that *A Rebours* was based on nothing at all, he was in fact passing over an intellectual climate in which various artists and writers were experimenting with forms which might render or suggest the inexpressible, by a complex appeal to the sensations, emotions and intellect. Huysmans's "nothing" was not the nihilism of outworn ideologies, or the helplessness of a solitary and disorientated writer. It was a figure of speech, no doubt; but it was also the intuition that truth and the source of creativity lay in unknown and possibly unknowable recesses of the mind, which could, at best, only be hinted at by the artist. This view conflicted directly with positivist thought, to which the concept of an unknowable truth was alien. Huysmans's novel touched its readers with the vigour of a manifesto, and helped to bring into focus the latent aspirations of writers who sensed only obscurely the limitations of Naturalism. *A Rebours* was not simply a negative reaction away from Naturalism, it was an active provocation which played its part in the development of the vogue of decadence in France in the 1880s and 1890s. Many of the sources of this decadence were learned: texts, myths, traditions of various kinds. But it was characterized above all by a taste for the contrived, the perverse and the morbid. It was, in fact, closely related to the dandyism which Baudelaire had considered to be a necessary way of life for the independent artist, involving social and psychological detachment, the cultivation of

Odilon Redon (1840-1916): The Smiling Spider, 1881. Charcoal.

hallucination by means of drugs, the attractions of deviance and non-conformity, and a world-weariness which precluded surprise while the writer himself sought to surprise his reader by carefully exploited, artificial shock-tactics. For des Esseintes, artifice was the "distinctive mark of human genius," whereas the natural was out of date: "nature, with the appalling uniformity of her landscapes and skies, has finally wearied the patience of the refined and thoughtful mind." The decadents of the 1880s were the refined minds, delicate, subtle, sophisticated, fragile, desiring novelty, but scarcely willing to acknowledge it. After all, a new experience is instantly overtaken by time. They repudiated political anarchism: they belonged in fact to an already dominant social class. They were in no way affected by the economic depression of 1883-1887, with its widespread unemployment and movements of mass protest. They were unmoved by the famous "Trial of the Sixty-Six," when Prince Kropotkin and a group of anarchists appeared in court in Lyons to answer the charge of being affiliated to the workers' International.

A Rebours had immediate repercussions. In June 1884, Paul Margueritte called it the "manual of the perfect neurasthenic." In an article in *Le Constitutionnel* on 28 July 1884, Barbey d'Aurevilly came to his famous proto-surrealist conclusion: "After writing such a book, the author has nothing left to do except choose between the barrel of a pistol and the foot of the cross." (In the event, Huysmans was to choose conversion.) Huysmans was therefore the "ideal decadent," but he had not invented decadence; it was in the air, a general mood of the times. It had appeared increasingly attractive since the French defeat by Prussia in 1870. In April 1876, Paul Bourget had written of decadence in the following terms: "We accept this terrible word *decadence*, without

*In him were two writers essentially unlike:
the romantic and the ironist... His novel* L'Eve
Future *would seem to represent a blending of
these so very different tendencies, for this book of
withering irony is also a book of love. Villiers
thus fulfilled himself both through dream and
through irony, heaping irony on his dream, when
life made him sick of his dream.*

Remy de Gourmont, *Le Livre des Masques*, 1896

pride and without humility. Why should it be considered so ignoble
and derisory? Why should we be told to destroy any works which are
said to be dishonoured by their decadence? The greatest centuries must
draw to a close, and even if they could last forever their frightening
monotony would pall, and our admiration would turn to disgust."
Bourget had a considerable influence on the young writers of the day.
He wrote with authority, and his writing seemed "advanced." He
formulated a theory of decadence in 1881, taking Baudelaire as the
great precursor in the transposition of sense perceptions and in inversions of taste. This decadence of the 1880s had its roots in the earlier
European Romanticism. Baudelaire represented in many ways the
summit of the Romantic achievement, and he exercised the most far-
reaching influence on both the visionary and the intellectual artists
who succeeded him. In the perspective of ill-assimilated German idealist
philosophies, decadence brought a renewed vitality to the great
Romantic preoccupations: the infinite, the ideal, the unreal, the fantastic, self-identity, nostalgia, disillusionment, death.

Jules Laforgue was a witness to certain artistic manifestations of this
decadent spirit. He was himself a French poet of melancholy, revolt,
delicate perceptions; he had discovered the bitterness and suffering of
slow, early death, and his poems are an immortal cry of anguish. This
sensitive, perceptive young man was in Berlin from 1883 until 1886,
and from time to time he wrote articles for the *Gazette des Beaux-Arts* in
Paris. In August 1883, reporting on the Berlin Salon, he observed
tepidly that Böcklin was "one of those men that we either take or
leave"; for himself, he preferred Gustave Moreau. In October 1886,
however, when he wrote about the centenary exhibition at the Royal
Academy of Berlin, he revealed that Böcklin had now made a strong
impression upon him. Böcklin was "a strange master of the art, belonging to no school of painting, but working alone, with his private vision
of fantasy." One of his works was *The Isle of the Dead*, of which five
versions are known. The first, painted in 1880, is a dream-like picture—dense, sombre, silent—reminiscent of Caspar David Friedrich
and Max Ernst. It is both simple and complex, like a Rothko. We feel
that we must approach the painting cautiously, but we are drawn into

*His magnificent head of a drunken and bantering Mongol
has sniffed the air of many lands, jails, churches, taverns
and steam-packets. Of late he lived in the forest of Arden,
like Rosalind. His lodgings now are in the Place de la
Roquette, where he will doubtless perish, and thereby outdo
even François Villon.*

Félix Fénéon, on Verlaine in
Petit Bottin des Lettres et des Arts, 1886

I can remember the sad disappointment I met with, when, all excited by the wild, impassioned descriptions given by Huysmans in A Rebours, *I finally saw some pictures by Moreau. I could not refrain from telling Huysmans that "they were as grey and dull as a sidewalk."*

Paul Valéry

After looking and looking at Gustave Moreau's pictures, to such a point that you begin to take an interest in them and almost to like them, you leave them with an invincible desire to paint the first slut you meet in the street.

Emile Zola, July 1878

Moreau lives in a transfigured world of the imagination, where history is metamorphosed into legend, where the myths themselves are interpreted in raptures.

Paul de Saint-Victor, in *La Liberté*, 1876

1. *Photograph of Auguste Villiers de l'Isle-Adam (1838-1889), detail.*

2. *Auguste Villiers de l'Isle-Adam: Cover of his "L'Eve Future," 1886.*

3. *Photograph of Stéphane Mallarmé (1842-1898).*

4. *Eugène Carrière (1849-1906): Portrait of Paul Verlaine (1844-1896) in 1890. Oil.*

5. *Gustave Moreau (1826-1898): The Life of Mankind, 1886. Oil on panel.*

Arnold Böcklin (1827-1901):
Flora, c. 1875.
Tempera on panel.

it irresistibly. We are caught by a silence which seems to scream; we are hypnotised by the weight of representation, the enveloping sky, the devastating calm. Our attention is taken by a massive, rocky concentration, strange, flashing and frozen. It is as if we are being drawn on, in the cold, humid darkness, towards some inevitable place of destiny. There is a Wagnerian quality in this sense of impending fate. It is a place of death, inexorable: a cemetery, with graves superimposed, silent vaults of eternity. Viewed in this way, the picture is an intense representation of death, but containing nothing alien to the purely visual medium. However, if we consider the picture further, we find other possible layers of meaning, interpretations which are based on experience other than the visual, on memory and myths, on previous knowledge or perhaps our personal and hidden desires. Further interpretations offer an obvious gain in the meaning of the picture, but they often involve some loss in what might be called the purely pictorial fascination of the work. The dark hue of opaque foliage in the picture is no longer perceived in itself, alone, or even as a cypress tree. To the inquisitive mind its form may become phallic, and the possible interpretations may be extended almost at will. It is the male principle, the tree of life, associated with the genealogical tree of the whole human

race. It is a sign of permanence, and, if we accept the universal, primitive symbolism of conifers, we may be tempted to interpret it as a token of immortality. The cypress has a place in Chinese visionary tradition: the winter frosts, which cannot strip the cypress of its leaves, merely serve to emphasize its strength and resistance. In the Greek and Roman myths, the cypress is the tree of the underworld, associated with Pluto. In this context, it is the tree of the graveyard, a sign of mourning, an emblem of sadness and death, a symbol of silence amongst the tombs. Interpretations such as these obviously rationalize the painting, expanding on the symbolism of death and life.

However, it seems that the title *The Isle of the Dead* was a later invention by an art-dealer. Böcklin himself is said to have referred to it more simply as a "dream picture." This is quite possible. It is also possible that the literary model for the image is to be found in Gottfried Keller. But while the source and meaning of the picture remain obscure, its influence is clear. It was received enthusiastically by Stefan George. Jules Laforgue defended it in advance against the criticisms which have been levelled against it since 1886 ("pseudo-Romantic hotchpotch," "theatrical," "painting taking refuge in literature"). Laforgue expressed particular appreciation of "its consistently dream-

Hans von Marées (1837-1887):
Homage, c. 1883. *Charcoal*.

*Arnold Böcklin (1827-1901): Self-Portrait with Death
Playing the Fiddle (detail), 1872. Oil.*

like quality, its blinding fantasy, the impeccable ease with which it renders the supernatural." In 1906, Giorgio de Chirico discovered works by Böcklin in the Neue Pinakothek and the Schack Gallery in Munich, and acknowledged Böcklin's creative qualities by using his art as the basis for an anti-realist theory of art. Chirico reveals Böcklin's influence in his titan and centaur paintings, and in his later series of *Roman Villas* which derives from the *Villa by the Sea* theme treated by Böcklin several times between 1870 and 1890. Böcklin's influence extended still further: following Chirico's experiments, Salvador Dali turned to Böcklin's surreal, inner fantasies, and Paul Delvaux was inspired in turn by Chirico and Gustave Moreau, who influenced his own essentially symbolic manner.

Although the Franco-Prussian War of 1870 had helped to increase the fervour of already divisive nationalist sentiments in Europe, artists and writers of various nations found themselves drawn together by similar national objectives: Puvis de Chavannes and Hans von Marées, Böcklin and Rossetti, Anselm Feuerbach and Gustave Moreau. Their aim was to preserve the allusive quality and the power of suggestion which had characterized "classical" pictorial imagery, and to resist the social and cultural impact of painters who sought a direct and slavish

reproduction of social conditions. They wished to separate the poetic function of the image from its practical application, and to use their painting both as a means of suggesting the spirit of the nation and as a way of protecting the ascendant social classes to which they belonged. There are evident contradictions in this enterprise, but it was carried out with style and confidence. In Munich, Count Von Schack used his art-dealing as a form of social self-defence, capitalizing, like Maria Berna in Frankfurt, on resplendent social ostentation. In terms of the idealist theories of art, the painters themselves wished to avoid any dependence on immediate visual realism, and to concentrate exclusively on the creative, image-making powers of the mind. They regarded the painting itself as an object derived from the unreal, but also conveying and consisting of the unreal. The idealist painters were deeply indebted to Romanticism, and they were brought together by a common desire to eschew photographic realism, and to break through the barriers of visual appearances. They shared the fashion for Italian culture and for the myths of Greco-Roman antiquity; and like the great Romantics, they indulged in reverie and nostalgia, and tried to renew their perception of nature by exploiting classical techniques of artifice; but these predilections were now to be followed ideally at the expense of any readily recognisable imagery and of any form of imitative realism. Such, at least, were the artists' theories and intentions. If we consider the works produced between 1876 and 1885, we find that space, light and form had indeed given way to the imaginary, and that the painters' rejection of realism seemed to have destroyed the old rationalist dualism. However, it is also evident that the primacy of the dream had restricted the mind's eye to the dreamer himself. The artists were haunted by their own image, and their imagination was dominated by the narcissistic self-absorption characteristic of the period. Despite their aspirations towards the unreal and the purely imaginary, the human body itself became an essential image in their works, the comforting link, even when distorted, between the real and the imagined.

1. *Arnold Böcklin (1827-1901)*:
   Odysseus and Calypso, 1883. Tempera on panel.

2. *Max Klinger (1857-1920): Eve in the Garden of Eden.*
   Preface I, sheet 1 of the set of etchings "Ein Leben" (A Life),
   1883. Etching and drypoint.

3. *Max Klinger (1857-1920): The Judgment of Paris, 1887. Oil.*

In this respect, the works of Max Klinger were exceptional. His complex visual conceptions were based on excesses, contrasts, conflicts. He used the "real" as his starting point, but always went far beyond it. It is as if his images were caught between two poles: Gustave Doré and Puvis de Chavannes. In 1879 Klinger was working with Emile Wauters in Brussels, where he made his first series of prints. He was captivated by the unreal distortions in the pictures by the Belgian national artist Wiertz, and stimulated by his ruptures of scale and his super-dimensionality.

At the same time, Klinger found in Goya socio-critical ideas which profoundly influenced his political beliefs. He evolved a political plan similar to that of Courbet, and was so committed to it that he lived in constant fear of failure. This eager, troubled idealism gave him a sharp sense of being "eternally suspended, paralysed by the gap between our wishes and our powers, between the objects of our desires and what we should reasonably expect to be able to achieve." This seems to account for the defiant project which he eventually undertook. He was a great Wagnerian; his Wagnerism, like that of Odilon Redon, had the intensity of an extreme cult, and he saw in Wagner's musical dramas the "combined manifestation of all the arts." Again, Brahms was a very close friend of Klinger. Yet, at the turn of the century, he carved an immense statue of Beethoven, in polychromatic marble, in the image of the Zeus of antiquity—a grandiloquent compromise between the chryselephantine *Athena* of Phidias and Rodin's *Thinker*. It is an exaggerated and impertinent piece of plastic bombast, a monumental overstatement, in black, white, bronze, ivory, purple, gold and platinum. In 1902 it was the sensation of Vienna, the apotheosis of the idea of total art. To display it, Josef Hoffmann planned a suite of three rooms for meditation, and on the walls were placed, amongst other things, seven Klimt panels inspired by Beethoven's Ninth Symphony. This "heroic symbolism" was above all the grand poetic gesture of an artist who had not found his element.

In 1887 there had already been the sharpest of reactions in Vienna, when Klinger had exhibited an enormous *Judgment of Paris*, in which artifice interfered with representation. In this painting, the light is a blend of morning and evening twilight. The setting is a theatre: the boards, the stage-flats, the back-cloth, the forestage. To increase the illusion of an illusion, the artifice is intensified by careful positioning, and the frame itself acts on the picture as a whole. There is a wide ornamental space, isolating the area in which the symbolic acts of the scene are being unfolded. It is a strange spectacle, sensual and allusive, and entirely removed from the exterior, analytical and carnal mythology often depicted in seventeenth-century paintings. The effect is that of a half-waking dream, in which one's vision is sometimes clear, sometimes curiously impeded. Here and there, the painting resembles a shrill dumb-show, its detail out-of-place. Although it is a kind of waking dream, its themes appear to rely on none of the great myths. Such myths would suggest meanings, clear thematic lines of thought. Here, however, the invention seems to be total, and the artist is entirely open to what may be called the psychic imagination—the imagination which William Blake regarded as the very essence of human life. This form of imagination creates a universe of terror: unexpected, disturbing, fantastic, unaccountable, grotesque, unique. It suggests sensations of the most chilling horror. The aberrant bursts in upon the familiar. Whatever is conventional, ordered or comforting is overthrown: the dependable mirrors of daily life are smashed, and all normality is lost. The laws of the universe are rejected and the result is an art of intense subversion. For Klinger, who took a special interest in prints and print-making, the engraving was the great medium of freedom, the most appropriate means of responding to the impulses of psychic dynamism. In 1883 he wrote that this procedure was "the genuine organ of the imagination in the fine arts."

His work as a whole is dominated by a series of ten etchings on which he worked from 1878 to 1880, *Fantasies on the Finding of a*

Max Klinger (1857-1920): △ *Homage, from the set of etchings "Fantasies on the Finding of a Glove," 1881.*
▽ *Seduction, sheet 4 of the set of etchings "Ein Leben" (A Life), 1883.*

Glove. These are some of the most fascinating works of artistic symbolism. On the strength of these creations alone Klinger must be regarded as one of the most unusual innovators of the nineteenth century. Nevertheless, for many years, he was ignored by the critics who preferred a certain logic of representation: Meier-Graefe, Scheffler, Richard Hamann, Hermann Beenken. Once again it was Chirico who drew the attention of his contemporaries, whose artistic sensibilities were gradually changing, to the telling non-conformity of the artist, and Klinger was quickly recognized by the Surrealists. The glove "story"—the story of a glove, of *the* glove—takes us immediately to the heart of the problem of the relationship between art and hallucination. In it, Klinger creates ten dramatic moments, ten stages of anguish, ten degrees of sexual impatience, arranged in a sequence which is innocent enough: *Place, Action, Desires, Rescue, Triumph, Fears, Homage, Calm, Abduction, Love.* It has been said that the sequence is conceived like a musical suite. It might be a little more accurate to imagine it as a strip of pictures without words, or as a film sequence from the era of the silent cinema, complete with Wagnerian sound effects: a storm, a murmur, a deafening crash, a triumphal climax. The sequence therefore has a temporal dimension. The pictures are not unlike cinema stills, frozen images of a number of consecutive stages. This parallel may be misleading, however, as is the title "glove *story.*" The sequence should be interpreted neither as a narrative, fictitious or real, nor as the logical representation of a story. Rather, it is a succession of independent images, a set of figurative processes, very specialized and arbitrary, which the engraver has devised in order to register his emotion. What, then, does the glove convey? It is soft, supple, long, inert, gigantic, multiple, triumphant. Do these different images have some inner meaning? Should the changing glove be regarded as a disguise, as a special example of the mask so often adopted by Symbolist writers and artists? It is possible to discern some meaning in the glove, in view of the central place it commands within the associated groups and sub-groups which make up the series of hallucinatory substitutions. The development could be conceived in the following way. Klinger is lost in the fashionable Berlin of the Belle Epoque: he is alone, and is looking in vain for pleasure. A lady, in a skating party, drops her glove, a long, white, perfumed glove with six buttons. Klinger hurries forward, picks it up, but then pauses, wondering whether or not he should accept this enticing invitation. He decides to ignore the challenge and keep the glove. As he walks away, his mind begins to wander into a spell-binding dream of experience by proxy. The familiar scene around him gives way to wild, hypnotic fantasies. Having renounced the woman, he

Max Klinger (1857-1920): Abduction of the Glove, from the set of etchings "Fantasies on the Finding of a Glove," 1881.

finds that the self-inflicted deprivation precipitates a passionate desire for fulfilment. His agony increases with his longing. She has been seen, desired, loved, adored, and now she must be possessed. The glove becomes a substitute for her body, an inert and wordless fetish. Then it becomes movement and energy, at first gentle and subdued, but soon swept away by the waves, wrecked in the storm. It is unattainable— unattainable because, with its turbulent, convulsive sexuality, it becomes a prodigious form of life which astounds and mystifies the dreamer. There is, then, no real triumph. The glove is imagined driving a flying chariot above an ocean of receptacle plants, an Art Nouveau water-garden. The apotheosis fails, the nightmare persists, and at the open window of his room the artist stretches out his arms in anguish towards the hideous bat-winged monster which is carrying in its grotesque, snout-like beak the object of his love, against the background of a black, flower-lit sky. When the theme is treated architecturally, the glove is multiplied: the gloves spread out side by side in neat ranks, standing to attention, to form a ceremonial screen, a guard of honour in front of the object, which is now limp and jaded, lying alone on a pedestal-table, in the middle of a disconcerting imaginary space. The scene is arranged as if it were a curtain, and the same grotesque muzzle of a beak is here, raising silence. The images have a flickering ambiguity. They suggest the instability and claustrophobia which often characterize a feverish narcissism, and the cerebral eroticism which becomes an act of self-destruction.

Max Klinger (1857-1920): Triumph, from the set of etchings "Fantasies on the Finding of a Glove," 1881.

Félicien Rops is unknown to the public; but while he may have no reputation, he has fame. Three hundred subtle minds admire and love him, and this approbation of thinkers is all that matters to this master; if a man of the middle classes, one of those for whom popular works are written and who actually read them, should happen to show a liking for one of his works, he would immediately destroy it. As a practician of art, he wishes for no other judges but his peers, and not out of pride. The best token of his modesty is the fact that he is so little known, and that is how he wants it to be, because he knows that Art is a druidic cult which receives into its ranks all minds that rise high enough...

Joséphin Péladan, in *La Plume*, 1896

Rops: Anoints himself with rouge, dyes his hair and wears a blood-red shirt: looks, or so he hopes, like a sarcastic Satan.

Félix Fénéon, *Petit Bottin des Lettres et des Arts*, 1886

Rops has not confined himself, like his predecessors, to rendering the attitudes of bodies swayed by passion, but has elicited from flesh on fire the sorrows of fever-stricken souls and the joys of warped minds; he has painted demonic rapture as others have painted mystical yearnings. Remote from his century, from an age when materialistic art can see nothing but hysterics eaten up by their ovaries or nymphomaniacs whose brains beat in the regions of the belly, he has celebrated not contemporary woman, not the Parisienne, whose simpering graces and dubious finery are not for him, but the essential and timeless Woman, the naked malignant Beast, the handmaid of Darkness, the absolute bondwoman of the Devil.

Joris-Karl Huysmans, in *La Plume*, 1896

Félicien Rops (1833-1898):
1. *Self-Portrait (detail). Pencil.*
2. *The Idol. - 3. The Sacrifice*
   both from the series of
   "Sataniques," 1883.
   Watercolour and gouache.

Odilon Redon (1840-1916) : The Ball. Charcoal.

"Redon, prince of dreams."

Thadée Natanson

"When I dream," says Jorge Luis Borges, "I am not blind." For Borges, all pictures are imaginary: "Realism is the heresy of our times." These could well have been the words of Odilon Redon. He had constructed a dream-world for himself, and his enthusiasm for Wagner throws light on his intense belief in the subjective. He was convinced that the future of the world lay in subjectivism, and in his art he was concerned to seek out the mysterious, "anything which goes beyond the immediate, anything which will extend and amplify it indefinitely." He therefore sought the unsolved and the disturbing. He wished to express the imprecise and the indefinable, to draw out of objects those features which might suggest a troubling, spreading, expansive vision: "My drawings *inspire*. They do not define. They resolve nothing. Like music, they place us in the ambiguous world of the indeterminate." For Redon, dreams and fiction are the stuff of art. He

wrote that the sense of mystery arises from being in a constant state of ambiguity, of uncertain identity, and his works were based entirely on a "docile submission to the *upsurge of the unconscious*." While acknowledging that he belonged to the so-called "rationalist generation," he believed that he had surrendered obediently to what he called "secret laws... which have somehow allowed me to create, within the limitations of my imagination and my abilities, objects into which I have put my whole being." One must, however, treat Redon's words with some caution. His earliest works belong to the period before Freud began his serious investigations, but some of his remarks about himself, written between 1867 and 1915 in the diary entitled *A Soi-même* (To Oneself), followed the development of psychoanalysis. His autobiographical comments have the benefit of hindsight, and so involve some degree of self-congratulation or distortion. Nevertheless, despite this dubious element of self-justification, Redon did indeed put his "whole being" into his works—so far, that is, as it is ever possible to put oneself entirely into a work of art. And yet, Redon's works, with their monstrous and spectral images, must be regarded as an expression of failure. Their persistent message, even when conveyed by the most fascinating of his images, is a message of defeat.

It was in Paris in 1881, at the offices of the review *La Vie Moderne*, that the public first saw the black, broken, blurred effects of Redon's charcoal sketches. Charcoal was admirably suited to his imagery. It was, he wrote, "an indifferent material, with no intrinsic beauty, but invaluable for my experiments in rendering effects of chiaroscuro and suggesting the invisible." Blackening (*nigredo*) was, in the symbolism of the alchemists, the fundamental quality of primary matter, of the universe in its original state of chaos. Huysmans noted Redon's "surprising art" of entropy, and situated it promptly: "If we leave aside Goya, whose works have a spectral quality which is more immediate and more coherent, and if we leave aside also Gustave Moreau... we find that Redon's only precursors are poets, and possibly also musicians. He has succeeded in transposing one art into another. His masters are Baudelaire and Edgar Allan Poe. Above all, Poe. Redon might well have adopted Poe's consoling aphorism: 'The only certainty is in dreams.' Yes, Poe is the true precursor of this original mind. In contemplating Redon's works, we delight in losing touch with reality, in floating away in the dream..."

In another exhibition the following year, Redon supplemented his drawings by two series of lithographs. The first, entitled *In the Dream*, was introduced by the image of a tree—hollow, bare, broken and decaying—symbolizing death. This first series dated from 1879. The second series, completed in 1882, was dedicated *To Edgar Poe*. It consisted of six lithographs inspired from Poe's tales, which Baudelaire himself had translated into French under the title *Histoires extraordinaires*, capturing in his text the intensity of Poe's nightmare imagination. Huysmans again commented on the power of Redon's vision: "We find almost inconceivable hallucinations, skeletons doing battle with one another, the weirdest faces, coneshaped or resembling shrivelled pears, heads with emptied skulls, disappearing chins, low foreheads merging immediately with the nose, enormous eyes, staring madly and starting out of the head, magnified and distorted by the nightmare." The lithographs are very reminiscent of one of Redon's earliest prints, an 1865 etching entitled *The Ford*. To his signature on this etching, Redon had added the words "... pupil of Bresdin," indicating his debt to Rodolphe Bresdin, an excitable and wildly imaginative engraver whose landscapes were, in the words of Théodore de Banville, detailed "to the point of madness." In *A Rebours*, Huysmans confirmed his appreciation of Redon's "incredible spectres" by counting Redon among the artists whose works des Esseintes imagined he had purchased in order to "adorn his solitude." The other works of art included notably Bresdin's *Comedy of Death*, but Redon was particularly to his taste: "These drawings surpassed all the others. For the most part, they went far beyond the normal limits of painting, introducing a unique kind of fantasy, an extravagant delusion of sickness and delirium. Some of the faces, entirely dominated by huge, crazed eyes, and some of the bodies, grotesquely inflated, or deformed and twisted as if

What have I put into my pictures to make them convey so many subtle suggestions? I have put into them a small door opening on the mystery. I have recorded my imaginings. It is up to the pictures to carry them further.

Odilon Redon, in his diary *A Soi-Même*, 1888

The sense of mystery means keeping continually to the equivocal, to the dual and triple aspects of things, the faintest shades of an aspect (pictures within pictures), forms which are about to be or will be according to the viewer's state of mind. All things more than suggestive, since they appear to the eye.

Odilon Redon, in his diary *A Soi-Même*, 1902

they were being viewed through glass decanters, brought back to des Esseintes's mind distant memories of childhood hallucinations, burning nights of typhoid fever, hideously exaggerated and distorted visions." Whatever the terror of the child, his hallucinations had been innocent and unpremeditated, but, as the man who longed for vivid experience recalled these terrors, artifice and the creative imagination intervened, and the memories dissolved silently into the agony of a daytime nightmare.

Mallarmé, too, appreciated the power of suggestion to which Huysmans had responded in Redon's work. In January 1885, Redon followed up a suggestion which Huysmans had made to him, and sent Mallarmé a series of six lithographs dedicated to Goya. The quality of the lithographs was uneven, but the main impression was striking enough: a white light illuminates a scene of disaster and stillness. This marked the beginning of the friendship between Mallarmé and Redon, a friendship which may be thought in some ways to symbolize the similarity of purpose between certain writers and artists at this period. Mallarmé, who had apparently been hoping to receive something by Redon, replied on February 2nd that the lithographs had given him a "most unusual artistic pleasure." "For two days", he went on, "I have been looking again and again at this extraordinary sequence... and such is the sincerity of your vision, and your ability to recreate this sincerity and this vision in others, that I have not yet exhausted the diverse impressions which each one conveys." A severed head, with the face of a clown, dominates this nightmarish scene, hovering, flying and swinging, in a setting of total night. The face, suspended on the flexible stem of an unknown plant, sheds light onto an area of dead water, a thick liquid of night-time terror. Redon called this image *The Flower of the Swamp*. For Mallarmé, this uncanny head had "an indefinable inner meaning which throws into relief the weary tragedy of our daily life, its brightness contrasting with our own pallid indifference."

The image of the severed head governs Redon's entire works. It is a haunting theme, a remorseless nightmare image which recurs in various forms. It is a constant theme, indicating by turns an obsession with castration, the blindness of sexuality, and the blank dread of death. It may also represent the mind surviving after the death of the body, and conscious of the annihilation of sensory enjoyment. In this perspective, captured within the dramatic structure of the picture, it may be an image of Orpheus, tortured by his unsatisfied passion. The image therefore belongs to certain ideological currents of the century, in which idealism was often associated with visual images of disenchantment, individual exile and loss, and a painfully heightened sensibility. It has parallels in Baudelaire and Poe, and in Moreau, Rops, Puvis de Chavannes, Ensor, Toorop and Delville. It may be associated also with the age-old dream of human flight, and with related images of the sphere of the heavens, in which the celestial bodies appear as eyes. It recalls the mystic representations of the Ascension. Whence: "The eye, like a strange balloon, travels towards Infinity" (Plate I, *To Edgar Poe*). Globe: "Sad Ascent" (Plate IX of the series *In the Dream*). Together with the severed head, the eye is a dominant nightmare image in Redon's imagination. The eye suggests the concept of an original, fundamental sphere: "There is perhaps a basic form of sight in the flower" (Plate II in the series entitled *The Origins*, 1883). According to Goethe, the eye is the "organ of totality." It is a bisexual image, which Redon used with many different connotations, according to his various intentions and sources. It could suggest magic, danger, intoxication, clairvoyance, perspicacity, wisdom, fire, life, light, the sun, eternity... The connotations are generally complementary: the eye, or sight, may be envisaged as a property of the heart, the soul, the spirit, the planetary world. These analogies between the eye, the universe and human affections appear to break down when the cosmic imagery becomes spatially too remote. However, the symbolism of the eye is particularly persuasive when it is used to suggest the idea of the continuation of consciousness after death. The image of the eye may express both the philosophical dualisms and the vivid emotional responses or intuitions which defy reason.

3

Odilon Redon (1840-1916) :
1. Vision, from the set of
   lithographs "Dans le Rêve," 1879.
2. The eye, like a strange balloon, travels
   towards Infinity, from the set of
   lithographs "A Edgar Poe," 1882.
3. Head of a Martyr. Charcoal.

The work of Puvis de Chavannes cannot be fully understood unless one sees it from his own point of view, which is this, without any doubt: to model the human figure and trees and all things as if they stood not just in the background, but far in the background. That is the key to his work.

Puvis de Chavannes is long-sighted by abstraction... He has been able to show us his mind unreservedly, to paint his dream, and to produce, in a word, an œuvre which others imitate and which will last: he has found a style.

Odilon Redon, in his diary *A Soi-Même*, 1902

You tell me that the artist straightens things out according to his dream. I should prefer to say that he orders things according to his dream. For I am convinced that the best ordered conception is at the same time the most beautiful. I love order because I love clarity passionately.

Puvis de Chavannes

Pierre Puvis de Chavannes (1824-1898) :
△ *Study for a Head in "Sleep," 1867. Pencil.*
◁ *The Dream, 1883. Oil.*

Nightmare vision does not seem to have troubled the serenity of Puvis de Chavannes. At the same time, he too was fascinated by the dream of flying, a recognized symbol of sexual desire. At the 1883 Salon, he exhibited *The Dream*, which he himself described in the catalogue as the sleeper's vision of Love, Glory and Wealth. The sensual dreamer conjures up three female figures, limpid and graceful. They hover lightly, peacefully and silently, like diaphanous muses of poetry and music in the *Sacred Grove*. They combine the impression of white light with images of slow, graceful movement. Gaston Bachelard has pointed out the artist's substitution: "You, the dreamer," he wrote, "are yourself this slowly moving symmetry and elegance." At the exhibition, the picture contrasted so sharply with conventional productions

that it was variously considered to be "childish," "oversimplified" and "difficult." Despite these dismissive criticisms, the importance of the picture was recognized by Théodore Duret. This well-known critic and art-collector, who did so much to encourage the Impressionist painters, bought *The Dream*, and in 1894 (in the preface to the sale catalogue of his own collection), Duret expressed his admiration for the picture in the following terms: "Those who acknowledge that Puvis de Chavannes has the power of imagination to create forms and scenes of an ideal world, must acknowledge also that *The Dream* is his most forceful imaginative work. It will be seen that *The Dream* is for Puvis de Chavannes what *The Angelus* was for Millet—the perfect expression of his creative powers."

Pierre Puvis de Chavannes (1824-1898) : The Sacred Grove beloved of the Arts and the Muses, c. 1884-1889. Oil.

VAN GOGH ON PUVIS'S "SACRED GROVE":

Seeing the picture and looking at it a long while, one could believe that one is witnessing a complete but kindly rebirth of all the things that one had believed in and desired, a strange and happy meeting of very remote antiquities with crude modernity.

Vincent van Gogh, letter to his sister Wilhelmina, 1890

Paul Gauguin (1848-1903): Girl with a Fox (Study for The Loss of Virginity), 1890-1891. Chalk on paper.

3

THE TIME OF MANIFESTOS AND DEMANDS

1885-1892

Two schools thus remain face to face: the Impressionists and the Symbolists; those who strive to convey on canvas, vividly and crudely, the impression pure and simple, and wholly objective, which one aspect of things has produced on their sensorial imagination; and those who break down that same impression in order to recombine it as they see fit, intent as they are on expressing in their work, not fleeting effects, but enduring things, eternal meanings, representations meant to be definitive.

These two approaches are equally valid and sincere: in practice they join and complete each other, for the Symbolist must draw on a fund of Impressionism, and any Impressionist who should merely seek to capture nuances would be but a barren rifler of landscapes.

Remy de Gourmont, *Les Premiers Salons*, in *Mercure de France*, Paris, May 1892

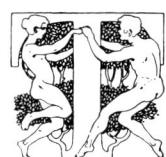 HAT EVENING a group of painters, sculptors and engravers, together with one architect, were arguing with fervour and deep conviction about skill in drawing. Their object was to be able to identify in these terms the presence or absence of vocation in an artist, and to be able to pronounce, in their temporary capacity as a "jury," on the quality of a work of art. Could they arrogate to themselves such a right? As is only too often the case, none of them seemed to realize that the notions on which their arguments were based were so highly codified and integrated that the debate merely produced an exact and arbitrary mental image of their own standards, a reflection of the criteria on which their own opinions rested. It did not occur to them that what they said made sense only to themselves. They seem not to have suspected that to speak of drawing "well" or "badly" is really meaningless, at least once drawing is accepted as coming under the head of "writing"; and this being so it is not a question of following a norm, a model, a system or a culture but, essentially, of uttering *oneself*, of *being* the "writing," and so of appearing with a greater or lesser degree of intensity, force and immediacy in the trace of oneself which is left behind.

Thus the *Girl with a Fox* is one of the places where Gauguin most reveals his own necessity, where the image takes the form of dream— intense, erotic dream, dense, calm and profound, quite different from Redon's dream, Klinger's nightmare, or the visions of Puvis de Chavannes. Gauguin's dream has nothing to do with these, at least in its condensation and graphic transcription. Here the image is partial, fragmentary, even schematic if read with reference to a figurative language which is itself imaginary. But it is strong and coherent and complete when deciphered as something self-sufficient and not as a part or detail of a potential whole; in other words, if it is read without mimetic superstition. The image-making matter is composed of signs which are soft, smooth, flexible, languidly sinuous. Of rough, thick parallels and obliques, of a homogeneous area of darkness, and of reserved silences in the support, which is thick yellow paper. The artist uses segment and synthesis, amplitude and economy to situate his subject macroscopically. The picture is a close-up in which the design is deft, both veiled and veiling.

But this was not how Félix Fénéon saw it when he wrote the catalogue for the Octave Mirbeau sale in 1910. The description he gives is an odd one, limited to the visible, to what can be directly perceived: "Naked, and seen to just below the breasts, a Tahitian girl whose abundant smooth black hair stands out against a dark background carries a dog on her left shoulder: one of its paws rests on the young woman's bosom." But the animal is not a dog: at a sub-figural level it is a fox, a satanic creature regarded in the East as a source of demoniac possession and occurring in many Inca myths as a vehicle of lust, an image of desire, or a crafty seducer. Gauguin introduced the fox into his work as early as 1888, as the "Indian symbol of perversity," he explained in a letter to Emile Bernard in 1889. The fox tempts, suggests, assaults. Nakedness is the flesh. Here we have a transcription of fantasy, a dramatic presentation of desire. Symbolic investment disguises instinctive drive. Gauguin knew all about the workings of ambiguity. When he could he used to attend Mallarmé's Tuesday-evening gatherings, with Charles Morice. He had read Mallarmé's reply to the survey carried out by Jules Huret in 1891 for the *Echo de Paris*. It aroused such reaction and interest that in the same year the Bibliothèque Charpentier brought out a book on it. Gauguin knew that, in painting as in literature, to present "objects directly" was to treat them "in the same way as the old philosophers and the old rhetoricians." "I think," said Mallarmé, "that on the contrary there should be only allusion. Lyricism is the contemplation of objects, the image rising up out of the reveries they arouse. The *Parnassiens* take a thing and show it in its entirety, and so they lack mystery, they deprive the reader's mind of the delight of thinking it is creating. To *name* a thing is to abolish three-quarters of the pleasure of a poem, which consists in gradually guessing. Suggestion is the ideal. It is the perfect use of this mystery which constitutes symbolism: the gradual evocation of an object in order to show a state of mind, or conversely the choice and revelation of a state of mind through a series of decipherings... There should always be an enigma in poetry, and it is the object of literature —there is no other—to *evoke* objects."

The *Girl with a Fox* was painted when Gauguin was in Paris between his return from Brittany in November 1890 and his first departure for Tahiti on 4 April 1891. It illustrates the deliberate abandoning of a certain kind of knowledge—a knowledge reducible to the syntax of reference—and the radical reworking of a certain kind of practice. "This year I have sacrified everything, execution, colour... because I wanted to make myself do something other than what I can do," Gauguin wrote to his friend Schuffenecker as early as October 1888. Precise reference is adapted to a particular purpose. Optical paths are no longer the lines that control the horizon. Density of meaning dispenses with space and geometry. He gives Schuffenecker the following advice: "Don't paint too much from nature. Art is an abstraction, derive it from nature by meditating before nature, and forget about the result... We alone sail on the ghost ship with all our fanciful imperfection... How much more tangible the infinite seems to us in the presence of what is not defined." Elsewhere Gauguin claims "the right to dare everything." Seeing and dreaming are complementary, contiguous. They interpenetrate. Dreaming and seeing overlap and intertwine. "Models, for us artists, are only a kind of printer's

LA PLUME, supplément du 1er Janvier 1891

Paul Gauguin (1848-1903) : "Be a Symbolist," caricature of Jean Moréas, 1890.

type which enables us to express ourselves." The reaction to social and cultural constraints is clear. It involves the erotic sensibility, so eclipsed since the Romantic movement. And it is enough in itself to show how the attitude adopted by Gauguin, who is generally presented as one of the major sources of twentieth-century painting, belongs to the region where "the synthesis of speech and silence" is achieved through allusion; to show how he accompanies revolutionary treatment of the plastic element with myth incorporated into image; and why the troika Cézanne-Gauguin-Van Gogh, a triad constructed by historiographers on the basis of visuality alone, could be replaced by a more complex grouping linking Mallarmé and Puvis de Chavannes and Verlaine and Carrière and Charles Morice and Rodin; or Puvis and Redon and Moreau; or, more simply, Puvis and Gauguin.

During the winter of 1889 some of the poets who were called indiscriminately "Symbolists still or Decadents already" used to meet in a

Paris restaurant called the Côte d'Or, near the Odéon. One of them was Charles Morice, whom, together with Jean Moréas, Mallarmé recognized as one of the few writers to have achieved a "master work, i.e. an original work, independent of anything that has gone before." Morice had just published *La Littérature de tout à l'heure* (Literature Tomorrow), and in 1884 had founded *Lutèce*, the first symbolist review. In the course of one of the gatherings at the Côte d'Or, Morice noticed the arrival of a "new face, a great gaunt massive face with a narrow forehead, a nose neither hooked nor aquiline but as if broken, thin straight lips and heavy languid lids over slightly protruding bluish eyes which rolled round in their sockets to look right or left while the head and shoulders scarcely troubled to move." Gauguin, for it was he, had come to tell this dozen or so poets and artists why "symbolism is necessary in art and poetry," in order to escape "the abominable error of naturalism." This was Gauguin's first encounter with "literary professionals" and it caused some stir. Morice observed that "the attitude of this painter coming to teach us all about art, including the laws and duties of poetry, annoyed some people. And the distinctive personality of the man himself, the breadth of his theories and shoulders, the piercing intuition of his glance, and the racy disregard for grammatical nicety in his speech, with its mixture of sailor's and artist's slang strangely conveying absolutely noble and pure ideas, all these and everything else about him clashed with the mental and visual habits of writers who, despite their sincere desire to restore the art of literature to truth even at the risk of revolution, were still the guardians of immediate tradition, and preserved certain prejudices about external correctness. Gauguin unintentionally took them down a peg, ousted them from the front of the stage. They, no doubt equally unconsciously, tried to get their own back through their special knowledge, which at least in literature was wider and more accurate than his."

Symbolist though they were, Gauguin's ideas were vigorously attacked by the symbolist poet Jean Moréas, who was vain enough to describe himself as "a more colourful Baudelaire" and "the most essentially unlovable mind you could possibly meet." Scornfully, in his fiery, resounding voice, Moréas denounced Gauguin's views, and Gauguin shrugged his shoulders and let the matter drop. "He never again, at our gatherings of artists and poets," says Morice, "adopted the didactic, professorial tone of that first day. He had learned his lesson." Above all he had learned that Moréas was already renouncing the 1886 manifesto which had claimed to define Symbolism, a notion that for a decade provided food for snobbery, for the "aesthetics of fluidity," and for "decadence." Antonin Artaud, carried away by the early poems of Maeterlinck, went so far as to describe it as a "profound new way of feeling."

The manifesto entitled *Symbolism* appeared in *Le Figaro* of Saturday, 18 September 1886, with the following introduction: "For two years now the Paris press has devoted a good deal of attention to a school of poets and prose writers known as 'decadents.' At our special request, M. Jean Moréas, poet of *Les Syrtes* and *Les Cantilènes*, co-author with M. Paul Adam (author of *Soi*) of *Le Thé chez Miranda*, and one of the

UN MANIFESTE LITTÉRAIRE

Depuis deux ans, la presse parisienne s'est beaucoup occupée d'une école de poètes et de prosateurs dits « décadents ». Le conteur du *Thé chez Miranda* (en collaboration avec M. Paul Adam, l'auteur de *Soi*), le poète des *Syrtes* et des *Cantilènes*, M. Jean Moréas, un des plus en vue parmi ces révolutionnaires de lettres, a formulé, sur notre demande, pour les lecteurs du Supplément, les principes fondamentaux de la nouvelle manifestation d'art.

LE SYMBOLISME

Jean Moréas (1856-1910):
"A Literary Manifesto -
Symbolism," published
in Le Figaro, Paris,
18 September 1886.

Félix Vallotton
(1865-1925):
Portrait of Jean Moréas,
c. 1896-1898. Woodcut.

foremost of these literary revolutionaries, has drawn up for the readers of our Supplement the basic principles of this new artistic manifestation."

The manifesto followed:

"Literature, like all the arts, evolves. It does so according to a pattern, with repetitions which are strictly determined and which vary in accordance with changes brought about by the passage of time and social upheaval. There is no need to point out that every new phase in the evolution of art corresponds exactly to the senility and inevitable end of the immediately preceding school... The fact is that every artistic manifestation is bound to become impoverished and exhausted; and then, with one copy after another, one imitation after another, what was once full of vigour and freshness dries up and withers; what was new and spontaneous becomes platitudinous and commonplace.

"... And so some new art was expected, necessary, inevitable. Now, after long incubation, it has come into being. And all the feeble japes of journalists, all the doubts of sober critics, all the irritation of a public shaken out of its sheeplike indifference, only demonstrate more clearly every day the vitality of the present development in French writing, a development which hasty judges have inexplicably misnamed decadence. It should be remembered, however, that decadent literatures have always shown themselves to be fundamentally tough, resistant, timid and servile: all Voltaire's tragedies, for example, are full of these blemishes of decadence. And what may the new school be reproached with? What is it reproached with? With over-luxuriance, strange metaphors, and a new vocabulary which combines harmony with colour and line—all features of every renaissance.

"We have already suggested *Symbolism* as the only name really suitable to describe the present trend of the creative spirit in art. That name may be allowed to stand.

"At the beginning of this article it was stated that art develops according to a cyclical pattern which is highly diversified; and thus, in order to trace the exact descent of the new school, we have to return to certain poems by Alfred de Vigny, to Shakespeare, to the mystics, and back even further. It would take volumes to deal with all these questions; suffice it to say that Charles Baudelaire is to be regarded as the real precursor of the present movement; that M. Stéphane Mallarmé imparted to it a sense of mystery and ineffability; and that in its honour M. Paul Verlaine freed verse from the cruel fetters previously loosened by the eminent hand of M. Théodore de Banville. But the *Supreme Enchantment* has not yet been achieved, and stubborn, vigilant toil awaits the newcomers.

"Symbolic poetry, the enemy of 'instruction, declamation, false sensibility and objective description,' seeks to clothe the Idea in a tangible form which will not be that poetry's object but which, while serving to express the Idea, will remain subordinate. Nor must the Idea itself be seen stripped of the sumptuous robes of external analogy; for the essential characteristic of symbolic art is never to go so far as the conception of the Idea in itself. Thus, in this art, neither scenes from nature nor human actions nor any other physical phenomena can be present in themselves: what we have instead are perceptible appearances designed to represent their esoteric affinities with primordial Ideas.

"Prose—novels, short stories, tales, imaginative flights—follows a development analogous with that of poetry. It includes elements which are apparently heterogeneous: Stendhal contributes his translucent psychology, Balzac his wide-eyed vision, Flaubert his amply flowing cadences, M. Edmond de Goncourt an impressionism which is evocative in the modern manner.

"The symbolic novel may take many different forms. Sometimes one character moves alone through surroundings distorted by his own hallucinations and desires; the only *reality* is contained in this distortion. Vague figures move mechanically around the one genuine character, mere occasions for his sensations and speculations. He himself is a tragic or comic mask, but his humanity is perfect though rational. Sometimes crowds, superficially affected by all the surrounding representations, now jostling one another, now torpid, travel towards acts which remain uncompleted. Every so often individual *wills* emerge, gathering together, joining and spreading out for a purpose which whether attained or not then scatters them back into their original separateness. Sometimes mythical phantasms, from ancient Demogorgon to Belial, from the Kabires to the Nigromans, appear elaborately decked out on Caliban's rock or in Titania's forest, to strains of the mixolydian modes of barbitons and eight-stringed lyres.

"Thus disdainful of the childish method of naturalism—M. Zola, for his part, was saved by his marvellous writer's instinct—the symbolic/impressionist novel will perform its work of *subjective distortion* strong in this belief: that in what is *objective* art can find only a very scanty point of departure."

Paul Gauguin (1848-1903) : The Loss of Virginity, 1890-1891. Oil.

There is no trace in this vague and imitative text, which does not yet distinguish between symbolic and symbolist, of the pessimism, the "spirit of negation and depression" which Paul Bourget noted in 1886 in his *Nouveaux Essais de psychologie contemporaine*. It is as if rivalry between consciences did not already foreshadow the degrading Dreyfus Affair. As if Marxism had not altered the vision of a world seen "as will and representation." As if "sudden acquisitions of wealth, ostentatious luxury, and the excesses of sensuality" could not impart a poet's words the immediacy of history. As if Alsace and Lorraine were not a dark stain on the map of France. As if Adoré Floupette (in the well-known play by Beauclair and Vicaire) had not already been allured by the "delicious corruption, the exquisite derangement of the contemporary soul." Above all as if Mallarmé himself had not, in that very year, 1886, written a foreword for René Ghil's *Traité du Verbe* (Essay on Words) which was the most penetrating thinking that had ever been done on the subject, placing the creation of meaning as close as possible to the miracle of total speech, without actually mentioning symbolism:

"In the age in which I live there is an irrepressible desire to separate, as if to assign them to different purposes, the two aspects of the dual status of words—crude and immediate on the one hand, essential on the other.

"Narration, instruction, or even description is admissible, and while all anyone need do to take part in the exchange of human thought is silently to take a coin from, or put it into, someone else's hand, the elementary use of discourse is subservient to the universal activity of reporting, which is what all contemporary writing is concerned with, literature excepted.

"What use is the marvel of transposing a fact from nature, through the action of words, into its own vibrant quasi-disappearance, except to make it emanate pure notion, without the encumbrance of any actual reminder, whether obvious or subtle?

"I say: a flower! and out of the oblivion into which my voice consigns all shape other than the known calyx, there musically and sweetly arises the idea itself, not to be found in any bouquet.

"Instead of performing a facile, representational, monetary function as people in general force it to do, the spoken word, which is above all dream and song, rediscovers in the poet, whose art is necessarily devoted to fiction, its full potential.

"A line of verse which out of several verbal elements makes a total word, new, foreign to the language and what might be called incantatory, achieves this isolation of the word itself, denying at one lofty stroke the element of chance which still inheres in the terms we use ordinarily, despite our trick of renovating them in sound and meaning alternately. Such a line makes you feel with surprise that you have never really heard some ordinary phrase, and at the same time the remembrance of the object is bathed in a new atmosphere."

Here again there is a complete contrast between on the one hand the symbolism underlying a stratified language based on a system of closely intertwined impulses, and on the other hand the verbal swamp of decadence; between "the song beneath the text" and semic substantialism. According to the starry imagination of Mallarmé, symbol was within. It governs fundamental structure, and concentrates energy where others dissipate it. Decadent discourse gives priority to lexical categories. All this being so, for most of those who at that time fre-

The miracle of total speech

At the beginning of the year 1891, Gauguin, whose artistic peace of mind had been ruffled by prolonged contact with golden-tongued theorists, undertook a large composition which he considered symbolic, and which he had provisionally entitled The Loss of Virginity... In executing it Gauguin was much less concerned with the pictorial side of the work than with embodying in it some literary theories which are hardly compatible with painting, and the considerable efforts which he expended on this picture failed to bear fruit.

Jean de Rotonchamp, *Paul Gauguin*, Paris, 1925

Paul Gauguin (1848-1903) : Stéphane Mallarmé, 1891. Etching.

quented the Café Caron (where J.K. Huysmans and Remy de Gourmont seem to have met in 1889), the Café des Ministères, and the Café Flore in the Boulevard Saint-Germain, symbolism was identified with the opening of the main article in *Le Symboliste* of 7 October 1886: "Beneath the weight of levelled skies, in the strident light of lamp-posts, the houses, monstrous and squinting, stand along the street. To the cloptrot of skewbald mares and geldings carriage wheels glidder along; here pipes skerry the lit-up leaps of tumblers; there misleading lips of smooth-faced mumblers proclaim their trinkets' virtue. Long-tunicked, crook-necked, with chin-whiskers cubits long, or scirrhous, or filthy— gentlemen. With smiles abortive and beaten bushes, wanton women; ancyloglottal on divans and mysouridic in plexuses of shade, wanton women; wanton women bardocuculated in faille..." And so on, each sentence more outlandish than the last.

This was a direct attack on the 1400 words of Racine's vocabulary. The assault was probably provoked by Baudelaire, who according to Gautier created the prototype of decadent style, "the last word in trying to make language express everything, in pushing it to the extreme limit. An ingenious, complicated, learned style, full of nuances and farfetched expressions, borrowing phrases from every kind of technical vocabulary, colours from every palette, notes from every keyboard, endeavouring to convey thought at its most ineffable, form in its vaguest, most elusive shapes." This throws some light on symbolism as manifested in painting, but does not show to what extent the spoken or written word, stripped down and used subversively, might be frustrated at the level of language in general. Despite Mallarmé, excess sometimes dispensed with syntax. One can scarcely speak here of the "sensual love

of words" which intoxicated D'Annunzio in 1888: "Words," wrote the author of the *Laudi*, "are symbols with no possibility of synonym, which offer all their glory only to the artist capable of studying their origins... He knows how to find words which bestow on the mind of the reader or listener a sudden ineffaceable pleasure." Later he said of language that it was a "physical instinct which purifies and exalts the white-hot flame of the intellect"—a moment of sudden illumination in which D'Annunzio and Mallarmé meet. But, in the intervals between the loftiest heights, those typical of the period preferred to give words "the place assigned to them by ideas rather than by grammar." They were even more eager to seek out the "perfectly artistic expression." Thus when Jean Moréas and Paul Adam published *Les Demoiselles Goubert* in 1886, they introduced a poetry of description which, contemporaries said, neither Zola nor the Goncourts could have dreamed of. Here is a sample: "The double row of balconied houses angulated towards the green masses of the Tuileries as far as the equestrian form of the Maid, raising aloft her oriflamme of bronze. Through the soft breeze, through the lurid light, there rustled the cabs with their roofs shining like convex mirrors and their bright lamps. Up above there rose a sky of faded green satin, pierced by the one little lone star, the harbinger." These are fringe words, triangulated words, semic polygons. A mythical amplification of discourse: "Several rockets sniff choke up above? A world of factors/Itching scatter besiege the heights" (Jules Laforgue). Metaphorical overloading, drifting, displacement of sense: "A bed emphatic as a throne of melodrama" (Paul Verlaine); "exasperated perfumes" (Albert Samain); "with darted neck" (Emile Verhaeren); "polar surplice" (Jules Laforgue); "the unfrocked priest of woe"

(Georges Rodenbach); "the hiemal night and its vapours," "the purplish depths of carpet" (Jean Moréas). "From that time the Moon heard the jackals whimpering through wastes of thyme,—and the eclogues in sabots moaning in the orchard. Then, in the forest mauve and budding, Eucharis told me it was spring." This last is an extract from Rimbaud's *Illuminations*, the most explosive work in the whole "fin de siècle," revealed between 13 May and 18 September 1886 in *La Vogue*, a paper edited by Gustave Kahn with the friendly cooperation of Félix Fénéon and Charles Henry.

In Brussels, *L'Art Moderne* of 10 October dealt with this unbridled irruption of the unconscious under the heading "Literary Pathology." It suggested the whole thing might be a hoax: "In these days we need to be constantly on our guard against the desire which sometimes seizes artists to make fun of the wretched public which for the most part will give credit only to mediocrities and fools." These words are among the first signs of the break which has occurred in the West between art and the "public," a rupture made possible by a new use of language annexed by an élite as a class privilege. And this in spite of Mallarmé's precept about "giving a purer meaning to the words of the tribe."

In *La Vogue* of 28 September 1886 Kahn defined and explained the objectives of symbolism: "As minds evolve, so sensations grow more complex; they need terms which are appropriate to themselves, not worn out by having been used in exactly the same way for twenty

Because of Rimbaud's penchant for obscenity, the chief "key" is to be found in Alfred Delvau's *Dictionnaire érotique moderne* (1864). When Rimbaud writes, "I drank, crouching in a patch of heather—surrounded by young hazel copses—in a warm green afternoon haze..." we now know that "drinking" means making love. When we read: "I walked along, awakening fierce warm breaths, and the stones looked on, and wings noiselessly rose," we know that "stones" belongs to a widespread form of symbolism (in slang the series includes "jewels," "swing," the "flag of bliss," etc.); "wings," or the phrase "it's midday," symbolize erection; and "fierce warm breaths" are the "emanations" and "explosions" of the dreamer, the "crimson perfumes of the polar sun." At the same time D'Annunzio was drawing, in *Il Fuoco*, a portrait of Stelio Effrena based on a hard core of sensuality. "From far, far away there came to him this feverish ardour, from his most distant origins, from the primitive bestiality of impromptu unions, from the ancient mystery of sacred delights." In England poetry breathed forth a strange femininity, indeed a form of hermaphroditism; and Swinburne found the faces painted by the Pre-Raphaelite Simeon Solomon expressive of the sly and cruel sensibility of Sade. An important event took place in Turin on 3 December 1886: the success of the first of a series of revivals of plays from the old, traditional Italian repertoire, usually judged too "strong" for "the chaste and modest ears of our contemporaries." Despite the opposition with which the clerical press greeted Machiavelli's

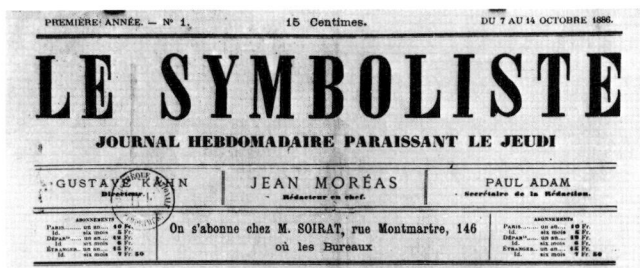

"*Le Symboliste*," literary weekly edited by Jean Moréas,
Paris 7-14 October 1886.

years. Also, the normal expansion of a language through inevitable neologisms and the re-introduction of old words which must occur when imaginations turn back to the epic and the marvellous... As for subject, we are tired of the ordinary, the familiar, and what is nowadays regarded as obligatory, and we should like to be able to place the development of symbol in the setting of some chosen age, or even in dream itself *(dream being indistinguishable from life)*. In place of the struggle between individuals we want to deal with the struggle of sensations and ideas, and for the hackneyed setting of streets and crossroads we want to substitute, as a background to the action, the whole or a part of a brain. The essential aim of our art is to objectivize the subjective (the exteriorization of the Idea) instead of subjectivizing the objective (nature seen through an individual's temperament)." It is not difficult to understand Zola's reaction to such words: "This symbolist movement is the last spasm of the literature of the Ideal." Rimbaud, at any rate, did entirely without such a set of postulates. His writing is free and untamed, and flagrantly breaks the instrument of language. So much so that, out of reach of all prohibitions, he can set aside the chain of representation and, with close access to the truth of the free creator, plough the furrows of his own phantasms and utter his entire self, no matter how much the field has been secretly mined. For in the case of Rimbaud more than in that of any other such enthusiast, words cannot be assimilated to algebraic symbols operating one way only. His entire work, far from being based on "silent analogies," constantly invents meaning derived from words uprooted out of different languages, even slang; and therefore it can only be properly understood by being constantly decoded.

La Mandragola, the theatre was full. According to one account the audience was "cultivated and intelligent." There were few ladies, for none had "taken advantage of the possibility of coming masked." In order to avoid "calling attention to passages better passed over lightly," applause was not allowed. The performance was introduced by the Bologna poet, Enrico Panzacchi: "Every age has its sins: the eighteenth century had obscenity, we have pornography. Obscenity is less to be feared because it is always obvious, superficial and ephermeral, whereas the effects of pornography are insidious; it idealizes vice and often usurps tears."

In Paris, also in 1886, Gustave Moreau, after several years of silence, reappeared at the Galerie Goupil with a series of watercolours. J.K. Huysmans evokes them in *Certains* (1889). He can still see those pictures inhabited by "silent women, naked or decked in fabrics set with emeralds... Motionless Salomes, goddesses riding hippogriffs... idols with tiaras;... women with hair of floss silk, with pale blue eyes, fixed and hard, with flesh chilly white like milk." He recalls the disturbing impression they made: "an impression of repeated spiritual onanism in chaste flesh; the impression of a virgin with a body of solemn grace inhabited by a soul worn out with solitary ideas and secret thoughts; of a woman seated within herself and muttering to herself, in the sacramental forms of obscure prayers, insidious appeals to sacrilege and debauchery, torture and murder."

This is another aspect, glittering, satanic, of decadence. Was it really true that all "ends of centuries are alike. All are uncertain and troubled"? Huysmans thought so when he wrote *Là-Bas*. In 1891. In the land of Satan.

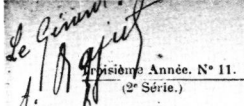

1. *"La Décadence,"* artistic and literary weekly
edited by René Ghil, Paris, 1 October 1886.
3. *"L'Art Moderne,"* artistic and literary weekly,
Brussels, 3 October 1886.
6. *"Le Décadent,"* fortnightly literary review
edited by Anatole Baju, Paris, 15-31 May 1888.
8. *"La Vogue,"* literary review
published in Paris, 4 April 1886.

Félix Vallotton (1865-1925):
2. Portrait of Paul Adam (1862-1920).
5. Portrait of Gustave Kahn (1859-1936).
7. Portrait of René Ghil (1862-1925).

Woodcut illustrations for *"Le Livre des Masques,
Portraits Symbolistes"* by Remy de Gourmont,
Mercure de France, Paris, 1896-1898.

4. First publication of *"Les Illuminations,"*
poem by Arthur Rimbaud, in
"La Vogue," Paris, 13 May 1886.

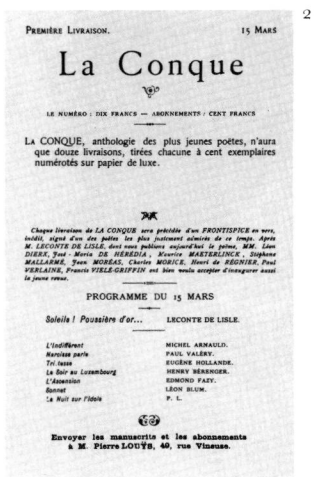

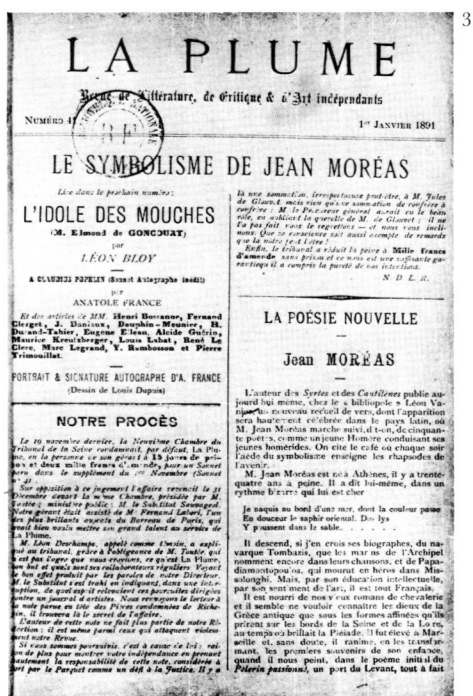

1. *F.A. Cazals (1865-1941): Symbolic composition, illustrating "The Moral Philosophy of Maurice Barrès" in a special issue of "La Plume," Paris, 1 April 1891.*

2. *"La Conque," poetry magazine edited by Pierre Louÿs, Paris, 15 March 1891.*

3. *"La Plume," fortnightly review of literature, criticism and independent art, edited by Léon Deschamps: special issue on "The Symbolism of Jean Moréas," 1 January 1891.*

4. *"La Plume," frontispiece for the first issue of the third year, 1891.*

The area of revolt

Hubert Juin—the closest reader nowadays to a nineteenth century already laid bare by Mario Praz and Pia Pascal—describes Huysmans as "a kind of smuggler illegally importing the most pungent spices." The image is steeped in the underlying idea of decadence. On 10 April 1886 there appeared the first number of a paper founded by an anarchist schoolmaster called Anatole Baju: *Le Décadent* was a name that tried to normalize anomaly, to legitimize a movement aiming at de-civilization. *Le Décadent* immediately linked the challenging of cultural structures to the challenging of social and economic structures. The inaugural address called in question every level of the existing system, advocating *décadisme* in its stead:

"To hide from ourselves the state of decadence we have reached would be the height of senselessness. Religion, morals, justice, everything is decadent, or rather is undergoing an unavoidable transformation. Society is disintegrating, corroded by a deliquescent civilization. Modern man is blasé.

"Refinements of appetite, sensation, luxury and pleasure; neurosis, hysteria, hypnotism, morphinomania, scientific charlatanism, out-and-out Schopenhauerism—such are the premonitory signs of social change.

"It is above all in language that the first symptoms are seen. New needs call forth new ideas, infinitely subtle and full of nuances. Hence the necessity of creating fresh expressions to convey all these complex feelings and physiological sensations. We shall deal with this movement from the point of view of literature only. Political decadence leaves us cold..."

Mallarmé expressed astonishment when Baju told him of the forthcoming publication of *Le Décadent*. Verlaine, though a supporter of the Commune, greeted the move with enthusiasm. Neither of them was regarded by Baju as a leader of the Decadent School: because neither of them, the schoolmaster of Saint-Denis had the audacity to write, "had yet produced the master work we are waiting for, and which is bound to be the ultimate formula of the new art of Writing" (6 November 1886). As for political neutrality, that was a matter of strategy. For it was the "Red Virgin of Montmartre" whom Baju summoned to the bar of *Le Décadent* on 20 November of the same year to address Mallarmé, Moréas, Ghil, de Gourmont, Morice and the rest on the subject of literature. "Our senses are imperfect," said Louise Michel, "but man's thought can capture all sounds, harmonies, forms... The anarchists, like the decadents, desire the annihilation of the old world. The decadents have created anarchy of style." The impossibility of drawing a dividing line between decadents and anarchists, anarchists and symbolists, decadents and symbolists, was emphasized by the confusion which reigned between them in literary circles. This confusion was not necessarily connected with political revolt, since "the motley, brindled soul of anarchism" could apparently only coincide with symbolism when the latter, in complete contrast with tradition, preached radical innovation and the removal of all prohibitions. A sustained analysis of the relations between aesthetic subversion and anarchism is required, as has been shown by Julia Kristeva's work on Lautréamont and Mallarmé, which makes a fundamental contribution to the problem. It studies the convergence between anarchist action and the work of the symbolists over and above the factor of snobism, which is not enough in itself to account for all the psycho-sociological mechanisms behind the spread of any political or intellectual phenomenon. What is needed is an accurate evaluation of the reciprocal action between the nihilist aestheticism of the French aristocracy on the one hand and

The men of the past failed to appreciate me. If I could see them at all, it was only through a dark veil. I blame them for the melancholy and the troubles of my youth. All they could talk about was fine execution, fine arrangement, smooth brushwork. Fine texture, skilled handling, tricks of the trade, conventions. They did not care for me. They had much to say about my failings, and my boldness made them laugh. I was a butt for all the critics' jokes and the fault-finders talked the correct nonsense.

Finally a reaction set in, and some enthusiasts praised the unconforming painter, the unaccountable composer, the writer without rhyme or reason. A special issue of La Plume *appeared: James Ensor, by Lemonnier, Mauclair, Uzanne, Maeterlinck, Verhaeren, Elskamp, Picard, Constantin Meunier, etc., etc.*

Jean Lorrain described my etchings in his novel Monsieur de Phocas, *Edmond Picard in* Psyché, *Eugène Demolder in* Saint-Nicolas. *Maurice des Ombiaux in* Saint-Dodon *roughed out a picture of me pretty sharply. Then came the fine study by the great Verhaeren who got me exactly right, and Gregoire Le Roy came along and followed suit.*

The young men throw themselves into the fray and fight hard, breaking windows and crockery. The young of today find me to their liking, especially the ones who have to fight their way forward. They are touched by my extreme sensibility, my contempt for success tickles their vanity, my composure astonishes them.

James Ensor, 1921

James Ensor (1860-1949):
The Dying Christ or Satan and his Legions
Tormenting the Crucified Christ, 1886.
Pencil and charcoal.

political anarchism on the other—the manipulation of anarchism as an élitist instrument used "against democratic and bourgeois vulgarity." We also need to explain why Huysmans, Mallarmé, de Gourmont and Paul Adam subscribed to Jean Grave's anarchist paper *La Révolte*. Why, in July 1886, did the publication of *Les Paroles d'un Révolté* obtain the reception it did from *L'Art Moderne?* Why, in 1892, did Viélé-Griffin give an anarchist slant to *Entretiens politiques et littéraires?* Why, in May 1893, did *La Plume* devote a whole issue to anarchy? (Mallarmé refused to contribute.) Why, in 1898, could Remy de Gourmont still say, in the *Second Livre des Masques:* "We were all anarchists, thank God! We are still so sufficiently (I hope) to respect in ourselves and in others the development of all intellectual tendencies." It is true that de Gourmont, whose free-thinking cost him his job at the Bibliothèque Nationale, had shown in his essay on idealism in 1893 that decadents "could accept only one type of government—*l'an-archie*." For him, Schopenhauer's "pessimistic idealism ended up in despotism," while "Hegel's optimistic idealism resolved itself into anarchy." That being so, "symbolism, cleansed of the farfetched meanings ascribed to it by the feeble and shortsighted, is translated literally by the word Liberty, and, for the violent, by the word Anarchy." For merely fashionable anarchists, the two things were indistinguishable: such people did not notice, or pretended not to notice, the smell of gunpowder. *Le Gaulois* of 26 March 1892 denounced the innocence affected by armchair intellectuals. The article was simply entitled "Dynamite and the World of Fashion." In 1894 the poet Laurent Tailhade lost an eye in the attack on the Café Foyot organized by his anarchist friends. Who were the people, then, who flocked around the black flag?

Gauguin read the moving appeal of the prisoner of Clervaux, Kropotkin. "You—sculptor, painter, poet or composer—have you not noticed that you lack the sacred fire that inspired your predecessors? That art has become trite, that mediocrity reigns? The joy of having rediscovered antiquity and been steeped once more in the sources of nature, this delight which brought into being the masterpieces of the Renaissance, no longer exists for contemporary art; up till now the revolutionary idea has left it unmoved, and in the absence of other ideas it thinks it has found one in realism, attempting to make colour photographs of a dewdrop on a plant, or to imitate the rump muscles of a cow, the choking filth of a sewer or the boudoir of a kept woman. If the sacred fire you claim to possess is no more than a 'guttering candle' you will go on doing what you have done before, and your art will soon degenerate into mere interior decoration for upstarts' salons, the supplying of librettos for operettas, and the writing of serial stories for the cheap press. Most of you have already embarked on the slippery slope. But if your heart beats in time with that of humanity,... then, confronted by the rising tide of suffering around you, of all the peoples dying of hunger, the corpses heaped up in the mines, the mutilated bodies piled by the barricades, the streams of exiles buried in the snows of Siberia or on tropical islands, the supreme struggle now taking place, the moans of the vanquished and the orgies of the victors, the heroism fighting cowardice, the enthusiasm striving against baseness, you cannot remain neutral. You will come and range yourself on the side of the oppressed, because you know that the beautiful, the sublime, life itself, are on the side of those who fight for light, for humanity, for justice!" Gauguin was not going to remain neutral. Already his once

Leaping over all barriers

Symbolism in Painting: Paul Gauguin

Seen from afar on a fabulous hillside, the ground a glowing vermilion, the Biblical struggle of Jacob with the Angel unfolds.

While these two giants of legend, here transformed by distance into pygmies, pursue their formidable combat, some women look on, interested and naïve, doubtless little understanding what is going on out there, on that fabulous crimson hill. They are peasant women. And by the breadth of their white caps spreading out like seagulls' wings, by the typical motley colours of their shawls and the cut of their dresses and jackets, one can see that they come from Brittany...

Now that in literature naturalism is dying out and an idealistic, even mystical reaction is getting under way, it would be surprising indeed if the visual arts failed to show a tendency to move in a similar direction. Jacob Wrestling with the Angel, *which I have briefly described above, shows clearly enough, I think, that such a tendency exists, and it is understandable that the painters committed to this new path should wish to rid themselves of that absurd label "impressionist," for it implies a programme of action in direct contradiction to theirs.*

Albert Aurier, in *Mercure de France*, Paris, March 1891

1. *Pierre Puvis de Chavannes (1824-1898):*
   The White Rock,
   c. 1869-1872. Oil.

2. *Emile Bernard (1868-1941):*
   Breton Woman with a Cap.
   Pencil drawing.

3. *Paul Gauguin (1848-1903):*
   The Vision After the Sermon
   (Jacob Wrestling with the Angel),
   1888. Oil.

Paul Sérusier (1864-1927): The Talisman (Landscape of the Bois d'Amour at Pont-Aven), 1888. Oil.

It was in the autumn of 1888 that we first heard about Gauguin from Sérusier, who had just come back from Pont-Aven. After making a great mystery about it, Sérusier showed us the lid of a cigar box on which could be distinguished a landscape [The Talisman] which seemed formless because synthetically built up in violet, vermilion, Veronese green and other pure colours, applied just as they come out of the tube, unmixed with white. "How do you see that tree?" Gauguin had asked him as they stood before a patch of the Bois d'Amour. "It's green, you say? Then put on some green, the finest green on your palette. And that shadow: rather blue? Don't be afraid to paint it as blue as possible."

Thus for the first time was presented to us, in paradoxical form, but unforgettably, the fertile concept of "the flat surface covered with colours assembled in a certain order." Thus we were made to realize that every work of art is a transposition, a caricature, the impassioned equivalent of a received sensation. This marked the beginning of a development in which H.-G. Ibels, Pierre Bonnard, Paul Ranson and Maurice Denis all took part immediately.

Maurice Denis, "The Influence of Gauguin,"
in *L'Occident*, Paris, October 1903

Paul Gauguin (1848-1903): Aux Roches noires, 1889. Woodcut illustration in the catalogue of the Café Volpini exhibition, Paris, 1889.

quiet life had been swept away because of a crack in the system—the same which drove Octave Mirbeau to literature and Henri Becque to the theatre. Gauguin was sympathetic to the subversive side of the "symbolist free-for-all." He was exasperated by the oppressiveness of the social and cultural set-up, irked by all its constraints. He was also tired of artifice in all its forms. So he burnt his boats, once and for all, in order to experiment with freedom on several levels at once. He meant to leap over all barriers, and dreamed of escaping "to an island in the South Seas, to live on bliss, and quiet, and art." He had a "terrible itch for the unknown." Twice, before he left for Tahiti, he withdrew to Brittany, away from culture and close to myth. "I find there the wild, the primitive," he wrote to Schuffenecker in February 1888. "When my clogs resound on that stony soil, I hear the dull, muffled powerful tone I am trying to find in painting." It was not, as Charles Morice believed, that he was "running away from the honour of being poor." On the contrary, what he was actually seeking was the language of penury. He wanted to transform his solitude and his utterance into an instrument which could convey his fundamental mysticism and passionate emotions. He wanted to be able to speak to everyone, to the world and of the world. And so he introduced a new type of discourse, a new kind of plastic structure: in it, painting became a semiotic act seen as a process of *transformation*—the transformation of signs and of the relation between signs. The operation was based on a new attitude to significants, and presupposed a change in picture structure. The picture was now addressed as a surface conveying energy instead of civilized "writing," as an arrangement of coloured units, detached, defined, outlined in Prussian blue. This method also presupposed a disjunction, a gap, a difference between the colour offered by appear-

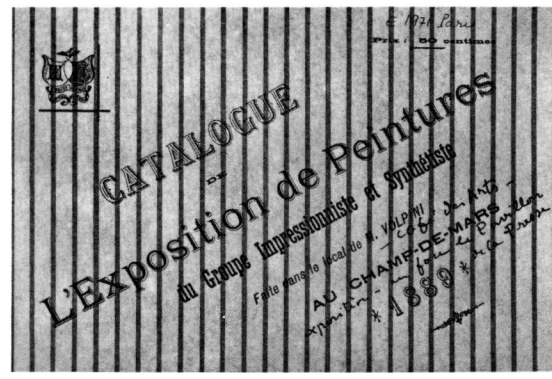

Catalogue of the Exhibition of Paintings by the Impressionist and Synthesist Group at the Café Volpini, Paris, 1889.

ances and so-called arbitrary colour, between colour perceived and colour dreamed, the colour of imitation and the colour of imagination. Baudelaire had called for "meadows dyed red," for "pink hair" and "lilac peasants." With his "disorder of all the senses" Rimbaud saw "blue grass," "orange sands," "green heavens." Gauguin's *Vision after the Sermon* is based on a similar chromatic reverie, just when (in 1888), in the Galeries Georges Petit, at the Society of French Pastellists, Puvis's skies turned yellow and his mountains blue. Was all colour to become "the verbal expression of an Idea," as was Albert Aurier's intention in 1891 when, following Gauguin, he tried to apply a symbolist interpretation to painting? Similarly, in 1892, Saint-Pol Roux saw words "setting sail for sculpturality." At all events, Aurier tried to make his way through the sharp thickets of sensuality: "Musicians experience pleasure through the ear," he said, "but we, with our lusting, insatiable eye, enjoy all pleasures." Image does away with disillusion. It is the imaginary fulfilment of desire. Gauguin felt, knew, that painting links colour to libido. But to the young men who gathered round him in Brittany, first at Pont-Aven and later at Le Pouldu, he

1. *Paul Gauguin (1848-1903): Nirvana, Portrait of Meyer de Haan, c. 1890. Gouache.*

2. *George Minne (1866-1941): Frontispiece for "Serres chaudes" by Maurice Maeterlinck, Paris, 1889.*

3. *Emile Bernard (1868-1941): Madeleine in the Bois d'Amour at Pont-Aven, 1888. Oil.*

Paul Gauguin (1848-1903): The Yellow Christ, 1889. Oil.

So, to sum up and conclude, the work of art, as I have chosen to evoke it in logical terms, will be:

1) idea-ist, *because its sole ideal is the expression of the Idea;*

2) symbolist, *because it expresses this Idea through forms;*

3) synthetic, *because it conveys these forms, these signs, in such a way that they may be generally understood;*

4) subjective, *because in it the object is never considered merely as an object, but as the sign of an idea perceived by the subject;*

5) and (consequently) decorative, *for decorative painting in the proper sense, as understood by the Egyptians and very probably by the Greeks and the Primitives, is nothing else but a manifestation of art which is at once subjective, synthetic, symbolist and idea-ist.*

Albert Aurier, "Symbolism in Painting: Paul Gauguin," in *Mercure de France*, Paris, March 1891

Paul Gauguin (1848-1903): Symbolist Self-Portrait with a Halo, 1889. Oil.

Photograph of Paul Gauguin in 1888.   *Photograph of Albert Aurier in 1890.*

only said: "Don't paint too much from nature. Art is an abstraction, derive it from nature by meditation." In September-October 1888 he gave Van Gogh his own comments on the *Vision after the Sermon*, i.e. Jacob's Struggle with the Angel, in which we see the unexpected irruption of a Gospel theme, a symbolic background to the struggle between heaven and earth, good and evil, the whole strengthened and "coloured" by the fantastic representation of the fallen tree, the wavy lines, the snaky curves. "I think that in the figures I have achieved great simplicity—a rustic and superstitious simplicity. The thing as a whole is severe. For me, the landscape and the struggle in this picture exist only in the imagination of the people praying after the sermon. That is why there is a contrast between the people, who are life-size, and the struggle taking place in a landscape which is disproportionate and not life-size." This is a symbolist approach. Does it mean, as Fénéon skilfully expressed it, that "Gauguin terrorizes reality"? He skirts reality, but at the same time dispenses with and surpasses it, thus reaching the plane on which all the possibilities of unrealism meet. It does not matter if the aesthetic he invokes in order to anchor his theory in symbol was partly suggested to him by Emile Bernard, a young man from Lille who was one of the Pont-Aven group, and who dreamed of a kind of painting which would parallel the poetry of Moréas and Mallarmé. (In 1886 Bernard is said to have introduced a method—line as a flexible contour to a flat area of colour—which was to lead ultimately to *synthesism*.) It does not matter that Cézanne said Gauguin had borrowed "his little sensation" from him.

What is more to the point is to see how Gauguin pondered over the migration of colour and the plastic and chromatic economy in Puvis de Chavannes, whereas he showed little interest in Gustave Moreau ("a

good engraver... far from the heart... who only speaks a language already written by men of letters"). More important still is to learn to discern the influences at work between Gauguin and Puvis, comparable to those between Lautréamont's *Chants de Maldoror* and Byron's *Manfred*. The break between colour and nature and the emergence of synthesis make Puvis's most important work into a kind of archetypal text. The title of a Puvis painting of about 1870, *The White Rock*, was in itself so indicative of a new and visually shocking aim that it was rejected by the then prevailing taste. This picture had to wait nearly fifty years to be deciphered, accepted, bought and sold. It is here too, in the texture of *The White Rock* (and thus well before Puvis's *Broken Amphora* of 1890-1895) that in the last analysis we find the stimulant which Emile Bernard and Gauguin had in common: the linear divisions which both regarded as the foundation of a pictorial method later to impart unity to the approach advocated by the Nabis. This common element disposes of the question once asked by H. H. Hofstätter: Was Emile Bernard Gauguin's master, or his pupil? The watercolour Bernard painted at Pont-Aven in 1886, *Breton Women sitting in a Meadow*, seems much more like a derivation than an inauguration. And the copy which Gauguin is supposed to have made in 1889 of Bernard's *Harvest* of 1888 seems to be both an exchange and part of the taste for intertextuality. This being so, Günter Busch's praise for Bernard as having "led the way" for Gauguin "for a brief moment in the history of art" appears less important than the force of the characteristic touch, the intensity of the method, and the treatment of surface as a site for the vigorous production of the self. This can be seen in 1889 in the *Self Portrait with a Halo*, in which the geometry of dimension is as nothing beside the use of design, drawing and colour as sign, beside the use of space as energy.

Maurice Denis (1870-1943):
1. *Trinitarian Evening, 1891. Oil.*
2. *Frontispiece for "The Blessed Damozel," poem by Dante Gabriel Rossetti, with music by Claude Debussy, 1893.*
3. *Adolphe Retté (1863-1930): "Trinitarian Evening," poem published in "L'Ermitage," 1892.*

1

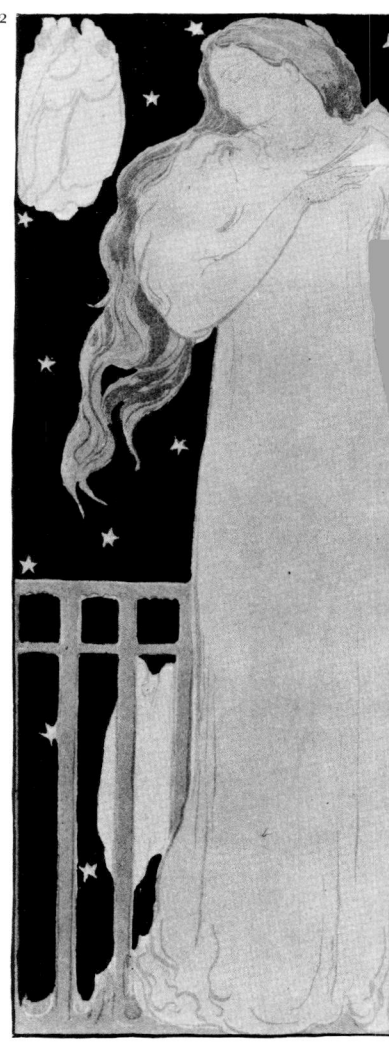

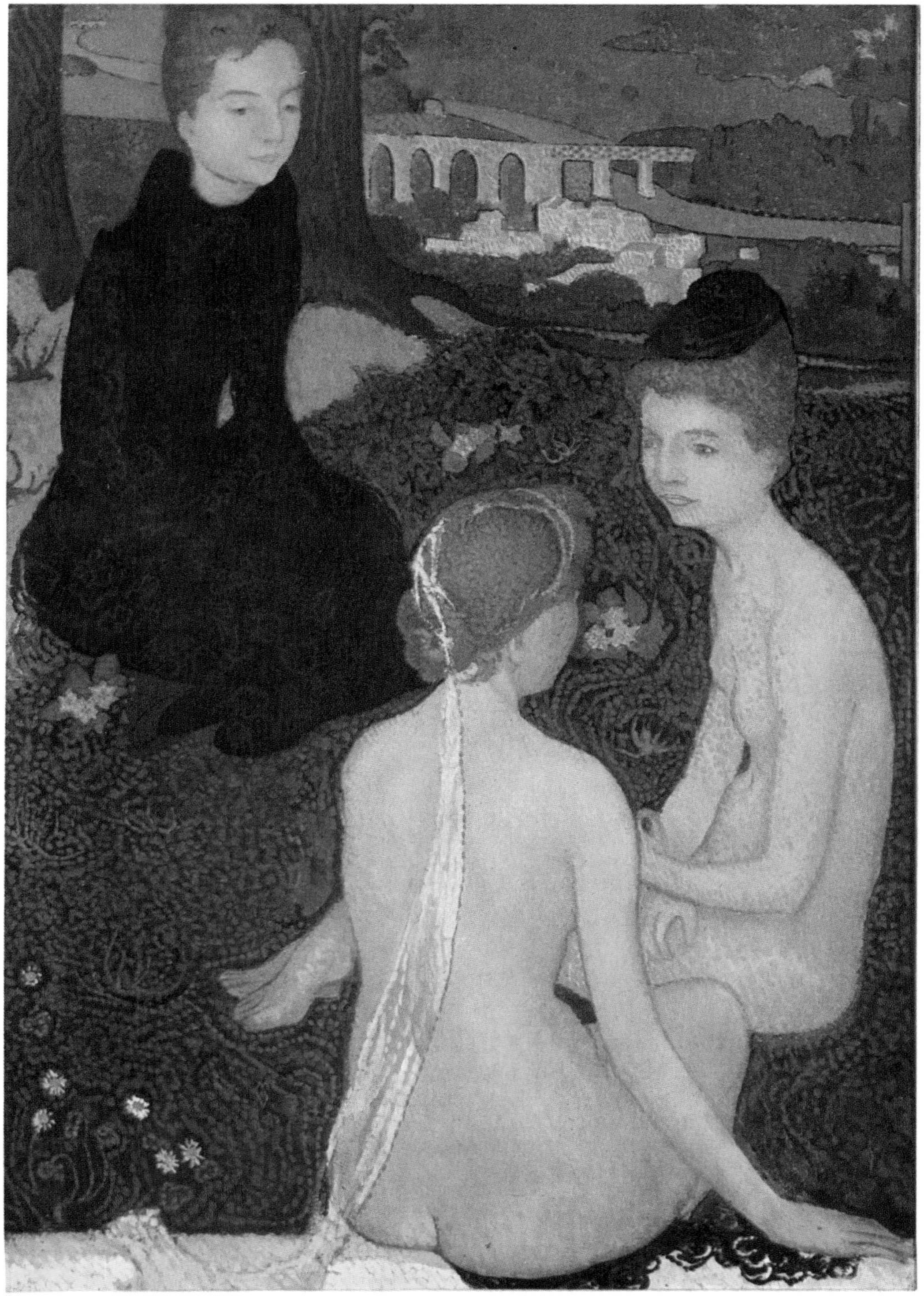

2

3

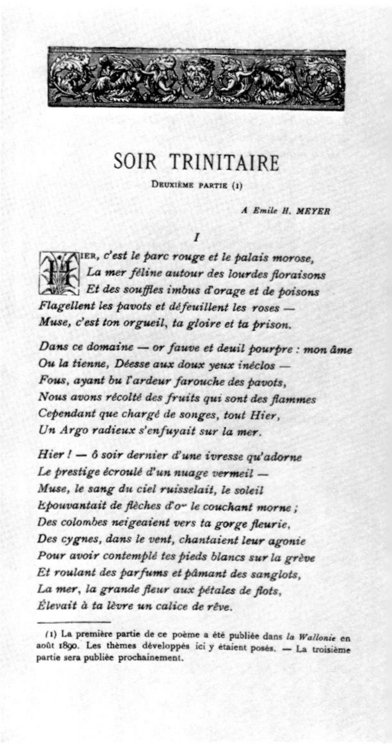

SOIR TRINITAIRE

DEUXIÈME PARTIE (1)

A Emile H. MEYER

I

Hier, c'est le parc rouge et le palais morose,
La mer féline autour des lourdes floraisons
Et des souffles imbus d'orage et de poisons
Flagellent les pavots et défeuillent les roses —
Muse, c'est ton orgueil, ta gloire et ta prison.

Dans ce domaine — or fauve et deuil pourpre : mon âme
Ou la tienne, Déesse aux doux yeux inéclos —
Fous, ayant bu l'ardeur farouche des pavots,
Nous avons récolté des fruits qui sont des flammes
Cependant que chargé de songes, tout Hier,
Un Argo radieux s'enfuyait sur la mer.

Hier! — ô soir dernier d'une ivresse qu'adorne
Le prestige écroulé d'un nuage vermeil —
Muse, le sang du ciel ruisselait, le soleil
Epouvantait de flèches d'or le couchant morne;
Des colombes neigeaient vers ta gorge fleurie,
Des cygnes, dans le vent, chantaient leur agonie
Pour avoir contemplé tes pieds blancs sur la grève
Et roulant des parfums et pâmant des sanglots,
La mer, la grande fleur aux pétales de flots,
Élevait à ta lèvre un calice de rêve.

(1) La première partie de ce poème a été publiée dans *la Wallonie* en août 1890. Les thèmes développés ici y étaient posés. — La troisième partie sera publiée prochainement.

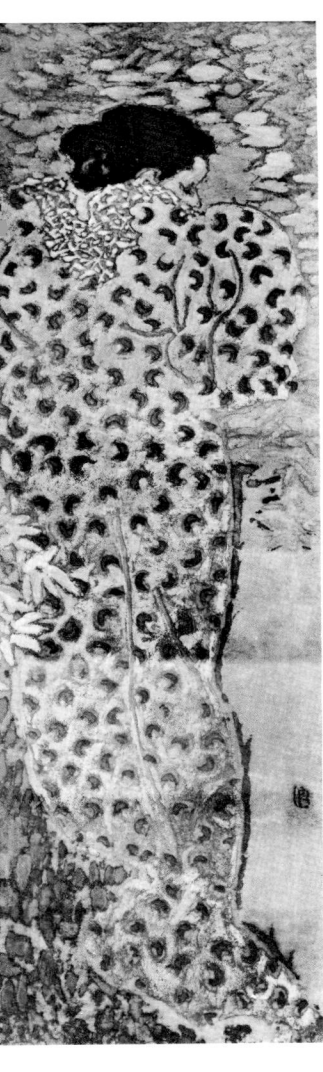

4. *Pierre Bonnard (1867-1947):*
   The Dressing Gown, c. 1890. Oil.

5. *Maurice Denis (1870-1943):*
   The Holy Women at the Tomb, 1894. Oil.

A theory of equivalents

Curves and flats combine to form a stereoscopic image, designed to envelop the spectator like sound, and based on the themes of liberty: liberty of life and thought, liberty to exist and to enjoy. It is an image which at once postulates symbolism and denies it; whence its strength, its ambiguity and its cynicism. There is an equivocal relationship between snake and swan, apple and lily. The painter's disguise, as a "Nabi," a haloed prophet, is obvious. It is also ironic, as is his intention of making fun of the "synthetic philosophy" which the Paris intellectuals constructed around his art.

At the head of these intellectuals was Maurice Denis, by then the author of several works which Félix Fénéon described as "of high culture and ecclesiastic charm." Denis was among the first to analyze Gauguin's method, in 1888-1889, and this study was followed in August 1890 by his manifesto entitled *Definition of Neo-Traditionalism*, one of the key texts of Symbolism. "In this age of decadents," wrote Denis, "who are, I hope, the pioneers in the diligent preparation of something of consequence, those of us who are behindhand are nevertheless the most complete... This is the only form of Art, the true one. When unjustified bias and illogical prejudice have been eliminated, the way is open to painters' imaginations and to the lovers of beautiful appearances. Neo-traditionalism cannot linger over learned and feverish psychologies, or over literary sentimentalities invoking legend, or over anything else that does not belong in its own emotional domain. It arrives at ultimate syntheses. All is contained in the beauty of the work." This text, written at a time when Gauguin kept proclaiming that he was "inclined to the wild and primitive state," opens with a precept which Denis often quoted in his own writings (of which a collection was published in 1913 under the title *Théories*, dedicated to Paul Sérusier "in remembrance of Gauguin") and which acted as a kind of absolute dogma in the criticism of pure visuality in the first half

Fernand Khnopff (1858-1921): The Veil, c. 1890. Charcoal.

Solitude

On dit que des rois morts ont foulé ce sentier
Qui mène au banc de pierre où nous aimons nous asseoir,
Alors que sur la solitude tombe la paix du soir
Et que nos cœurs sont pleins de chants muets, comme des psautiers.

De ce rocher on vit, sous les fanfares de la conquête,
La plaine se hérisser soudain d'épis de fer,
Et des multitudes, revenues des étés et des hivers,
Rouler comme un fleuve rouge vers la grande ville en fête.

Mais ni la chevauchée ensoleillée sous les bannières,
Ni le doux tonnerre des tambours dans le printemps,
Ni le cri des clairons dressés en corolles d'or

Ne valent ce silence où notre fatigue s'endort,
Et la caresse des ombres qu'entremêlent les vents
Et la minute éternelle de notre baiser, cette prière!

Stuart Merrill, from *Les Quatre Saisons*, Paris, 1900

(Dead kings are said to have trodden this path leading to the stone bench where we like to sit, while over the solitude falls the peace of evening and our hearts, like psalm-books, are full of mute songs. From this rock we see the plain, under the fanfares of conquest, suddenly bristling with iron spikes, and multitudes, home from the summers and winters, flowing like a red river towards the great city in holiday mood. But neither the sunny cavalcade beneath banners, nor the soft thunder of drums in spring, nor the cry of bugles upheld like golden corollas are worth this silence in which our fatigue falls asleep, and the caress of shadows mingled with winds and the eternal minute of our kiss, this prayer!)

Aristide Maillol (1861-1944): The Prodigal Son, c. 1890. Oil.

Silence de la chambre assoupie et gagnée
Par de l'ombre qui tend ses toiles d'araignée
Dans les angles, obscurs les premiers, où l'essor
Des rêves va finir son vol de mouches d'or!
Silence où toute l'âme assombrie est encline
A se sentir de plus en plus comme orpheline,
Toute seule parmi le soir endolori
A revoir son passé comme un tombeau fleuri.

Georges Rodenbach, from *Le Règne du Silence*, 1891

(The Reign of Silence: Silence of the hushed room invaded by shadow which weaves its cobwebs in the corners that darken first, where the upsurge of dreams will end its flight of golden flies! Silence in which all the darkened soul is inclined to feel itself more and more an orphan, all alone in the ache of evening, gazing at its past as at a flowered grave.)

Paul Sérusier (1864-1927): Melancholy, c. 1890. Oil.

Je veux un amour plein de sanglots et de pleurs.
Je veux un amour triste ainsi qu'un ciel d'automne,
Un amour qui serait comme un bois planté d'ifs
Où dans la nuit le cor mélancolique sonne;
Je veux un amour triste ainsi qu'un ciel d'automne
Fait de remords très lents et de baisers furtifs.

Jean Moréas

(I want a love full of sobs and tears, I want a love as sad as an autumn sky, a love that is like a yew-planted wood where at night the melancholy horn rings out; I want a love as sad as an autumn sky made of very slow misgivings and stealthy kisses.)

1. *Maurice Denis (1870-1943): Illustration for "Le Voyage d'Urien" by André Gide, Paris, 1893.*

2. *Fernand Khnopff (1858-1921): Illustration done in 1892 for a sonnet by Stéphane Mallarmé published in "Pan," No. 1, Berlin, 1895.*

of the twentieth century: "Remember that a picture—before being a war horse, a nude, or some sort of anecdote—is essentially a flat surface covered with colours assembled in a certain order." In 1895 Denis added: "and for the pleasure of the eye." On the basis of this incantatory formula (inspired by Gauguin's work and its immediate impact, in 1888, on the way Paul Sérusier painted his famous *Talisman*), "we knew," wrote Denis, "that every work of art is a transposition, a caricature, the passionate equivalent of a received sensation." This was the beginning of a revolution in which Denis, Ranson, Ibels, Bonnard, Seguin and Verkade all took part. "The *theory of equivalents* gave us the right to be lyrical... we supplemented the rudimentary teaching of Gauguin by substituting for his over-simplified idea of pure colours the idea of beautiful harmonies, infinitely varied like nature; we adapted all the resources of the palette to all the states of our sensibility; and the sights which caused them became to us so many signs of our own subjectivity. We sought equivalents, but equivalents in beauty!"

There is no doubt that Maurice Denis' manifesto of 1890 is based on the famous "Exhibition of Paintings by the Impressionist and Synthesist Group," held in the Café des Arts as part of the Paris World's Fair of 1889. This exhibition showed for the first time, grouped round some twenty works by Gauguin himself the "synthesists" of Pont-Aven: Emile Bernard, Louis Anquetin, Charles Laval, Emile Schuffenecker, Louis Roy, etc. "The appearance," said Denis, "in an undistinguished setting, of an art then totally new, marked the beginning of the reaction against Impressionism. The symbolist crisis which occurred soon afterwards helped to spread Gauguin's ideas, so that all the applied arts, including decorative painting, objets d'art, posters and even caricature, underwent a renewal." In turn, on this manifesto was based the article-cum-manifesto which Albert Aurier published in the *Revue Encyclopédique* in 1892, a few months before his death. "On all sides," says the poet, "people claim the right to dream, the right to graze in the sky, the right to soar up to the stars of absolute truth. The shortsighted copying of social anecdote, the foolish imitation of nature's warts, flat observation, *trompe-l'œil*, the honour of being as faithfully and tediously

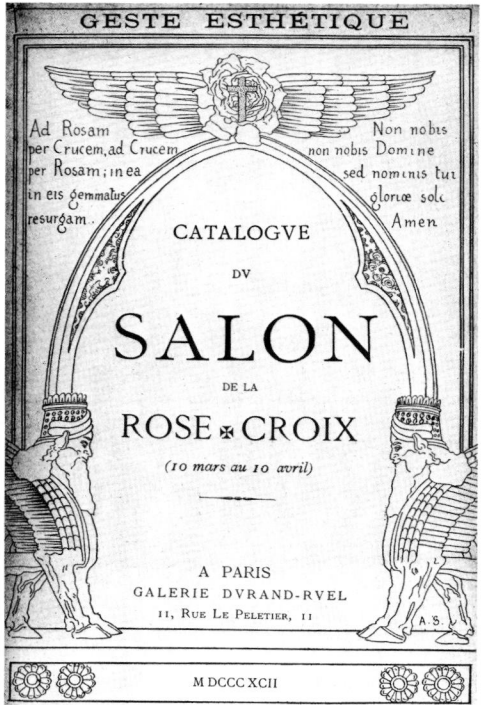

△ Alexandre Séon (1855-1917): Title page for the catalogue of the Salon de la Rose Croix, Paris, 1892.

▷ Carlos Schwabe (1866-1926): Poster for the Salon de la Rose Croix, Paris, 1892.

Carlos Schwabe (1866-1926):
Title page for Emile Zola's novel
"Le Rêve" (The Dream), Paris, 1892.

accurate as a daguerreotype is no longer enough for any painter or sculptor worthy of the name." Here emerges one of the alternative forms of symbolism: "expression through decor, through harmony of forms and colours." At this level the work of art claims to be a "plastic equivalent," a "decorative equivalent" of "all human emotions." For Maurice Denis symbolism was "the expression of human thoughts and emotions through aesthetic correspondences." There was a tendency here to reduce symbolism to surface structure, and this fostered the development of Art Nouveau seen as a formal and visual phenomenon, "ornamental" and "decorative." This was an ostensibly innocent way of setting aside surrounding social and political realities while turning visceral experience into meaning. On the other hand, the material element in the Art Nouveau of the 1890s and early 1900s was to overlap with *hyposymbolism*, as defined by Denis on the basis of his own marked religious awareness, though this never attained the deep sense of the sacred inherent in Gauguin's work.

At a time when anarchist subversion seemed a serious threat, the activities of Maurice Denis and the Christian symbolists he converted to his own aesthetic psychologism helped to protect the established order against libertarian violence. The theory of equivalences, constructed to ward off immediate pressures, implied an attitude of welcome to the sacred which did not entirely conceal the independent influence of religion itself.

Does this mean that at the end of the nineteenth century religion was the only discourse possible? It is disturbing to see anarchist terrorism take on Christian aspects, and, conversely, painters, poets and writers "engaged in a liberation of the individual through language" drawing near to anarchist preoccupations and the struggle against social structures. This situation made it possible for a strange character, who regarded Luther as the first modern anarchist, Wagner as the "only cure for realist poison," and Eliphas Levi as a worthy model, to find a place for himself and try to put an end to the "great Alexandrian schism" in which "religion and occultism despised each other." In June 1890 Joseph Péladan, alias Princess A. Dinska, Miss Sarah, Marquis of Valognes, Merodack, or Joséphin Péladan, member of the Supreme Council of the Cabbalistic Order of the Rosicrucians, left this esoteric order, which he regarded as too anti-Catholic, and organized the Orders of the Rosy Cross, the Temple and the Grail, and assumed the title of Sâr or magus. He thus thought to attach himself to the tradition of a number of secret societies said to have originated in Germany in the early seventeenth century and said to be the heirs of a mythical character called Christian Rosencreutz. At the same time Péladan hoped to find in mystico-ludic activity the answer to a complex sexual situation. For him, art was not only a "theology of expression" and an "ideography of forms" but also—a Freudian idea before its time—"the pure form of pleasure." He regarded aesthetic emotion as "a raised and luminous equivalent of passionate emotion." He proclaimed himself "catholic and competent" (in aesthetics) and "perfectly educated and informed" (in art), for—before Berenson and Malraux—he had "seen and studied the hundred thousand photographs at Braun's in Paris, that Pinakothek made up of all other art galleries." For him the word symbolism "had only a religious or hermetic meaning": he did not understand the word's being applied to "denote some poet without either faith or philosophy." His duty as the head of the "aesthetic" sect of the Rosicrucians was "to honour and serve the Ideal." This was to be done by rediscovering lost "norms" and, having found them, setting up a Salon which would be the expression or rather illustration of *Idealist and Mystical Art* (the title of a book he was writing). If people wanted to overcome decadence they must turn away from "Courbet's ignoble *Burial at Ornans*, renounce the representation of drunkards and scoundrels and peasants, as recounted by Balzac." For "there is no other Reality but God. There is no other Truth but God. There is no other

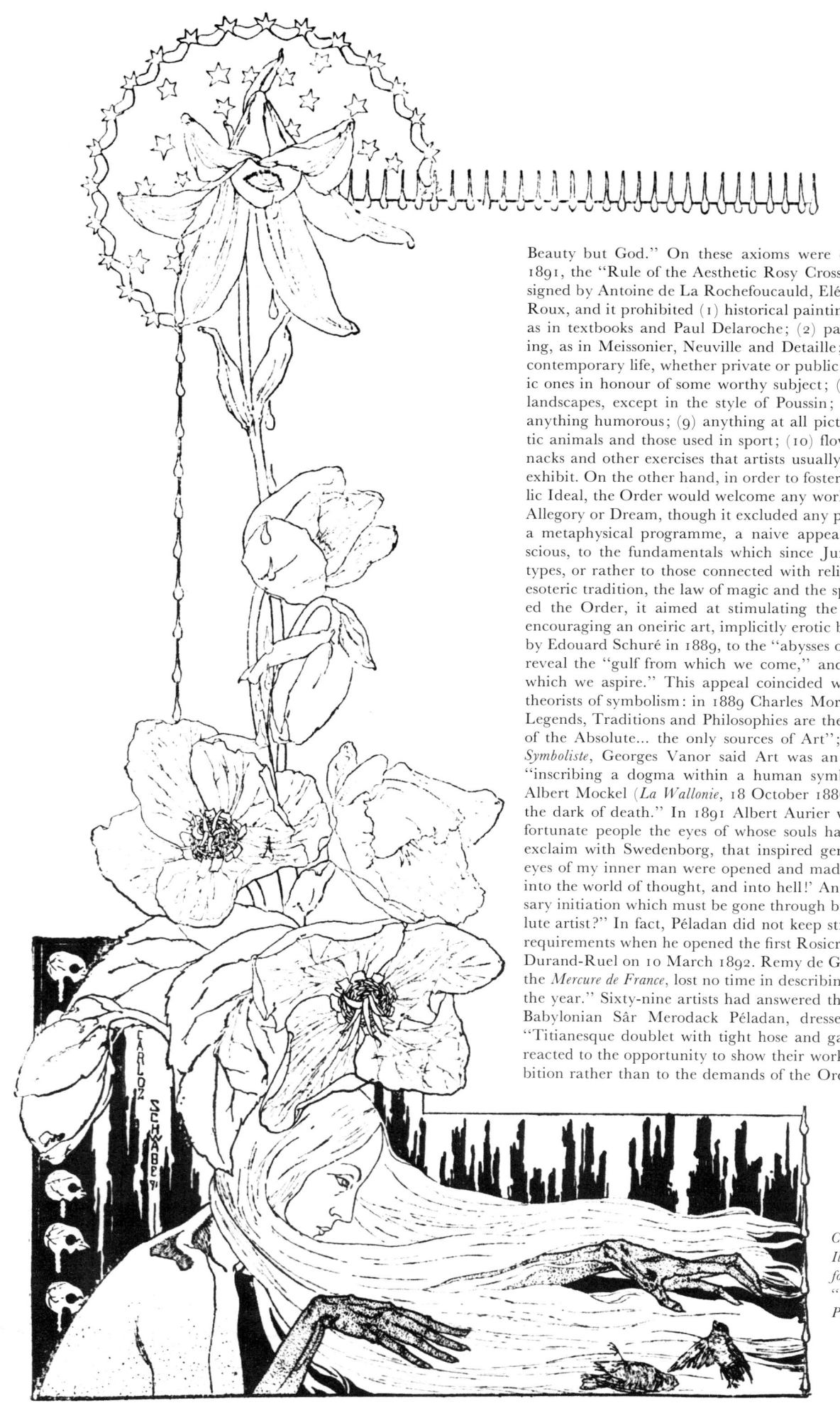

Beauty but God." On these axioms were established, on 23 August 1891, the "Rule of the Aesthetic Rosy Cross." The Rule was countersigned by Antoine de La Rochefoucauld, Elémir Bourges and Saint-Pol Roux, and it prohibited (1) historical painting, prosaic and illustrative, as in textbooks and Paul Delaroche; (2) patriotic and military painting, as in Meissonier, Neuville and Detaille; (3) any representation of contemporary life, whether private or public; (4) portraits except iconic ones in honour of some worthy subject; (5) all rural scenes; (6) all landscapes, except in the style of Poussin; (7) ships and sailors; (8) anything humorous; (9) anything at all picturesque, including domestic animals and those used in sport; (10) flowers, baubles, fruit, knicknacks and other exercises that artists usually have the impertinence to exhibit. On the other hand, in order to foster mysticism and the Catholic Ideal, the Order would welcome any work based on Legend, Myth, Allegory or Dream, though it excluded any paintings by women. It was a metaphysical programme, a naive appeal to the collective unconscious, to the fundamentals which since Jung we have called archetypes, or rather to those connected with religion. Over and above the esoteric tradition, the law of magic and the spiritualism which motivated the Order, it aimed at stimulating the dynamic imagination, at encouraging an oneiric art, implicitly erotic but open, as recommended by Edouard Schuré in 1889, to the "abysses of the Unconscious" which reveal the "gulf from which we come," and to "the dizzy heights to which we aspire." This appeal coincided with the suggestions of the theorists of symbolism: in 1889 Charles Morice wrote that "Religions, Legends, Traditions and Philosophies are the most obvious emanations of the Absolute... the only sources of Art"; in the same year, in *Art Symboliste*, Georges Vanor said Art was an activity which aimed at "inscribing a dogma within a human symbol," the same which for Albert Mockel (*La Wallonie*, 18 October 1886) "shone like a phrase in the dark of death." In 1891 Albert Aurier wrote: "How rare are the fortunate people the eyes of whose souls have opened, and who can exclaim with Swedenborg, that inspired genius: 'This very night the eyes of my inner man were opened and made able to see into heaven, into the world of thought, and into hell!' And yet is not this the necessary initiation which must be gone through by the true artist, the absolute artist?" In fact, Péladan did not keep strictly to his own dogmatic requirements when he opened the first Rosicrucian Salon at the Galerie Durand-Ruel on 10 March 1892. Remy de Gourmont, in his column in the *Mercure de France*, lost no time in describing it as "the great event of the year." Sixty-nine artists had answered the call of the bearded and Babylonian Sâr Merodack Péladan, dressed for the occasion in a "Titianesque doublet with tight hose and gauntlet gloves." They had reacted to the opportunity to show their work at an international exhibition rather than to the demands of the Order. Among the 250 exhi-

Carlos Schwabe (1866-1926):
Illustration dated 1891
for Emile Zola's novel
"Le Rêve" (The Dream),
Paris, 1892.

90

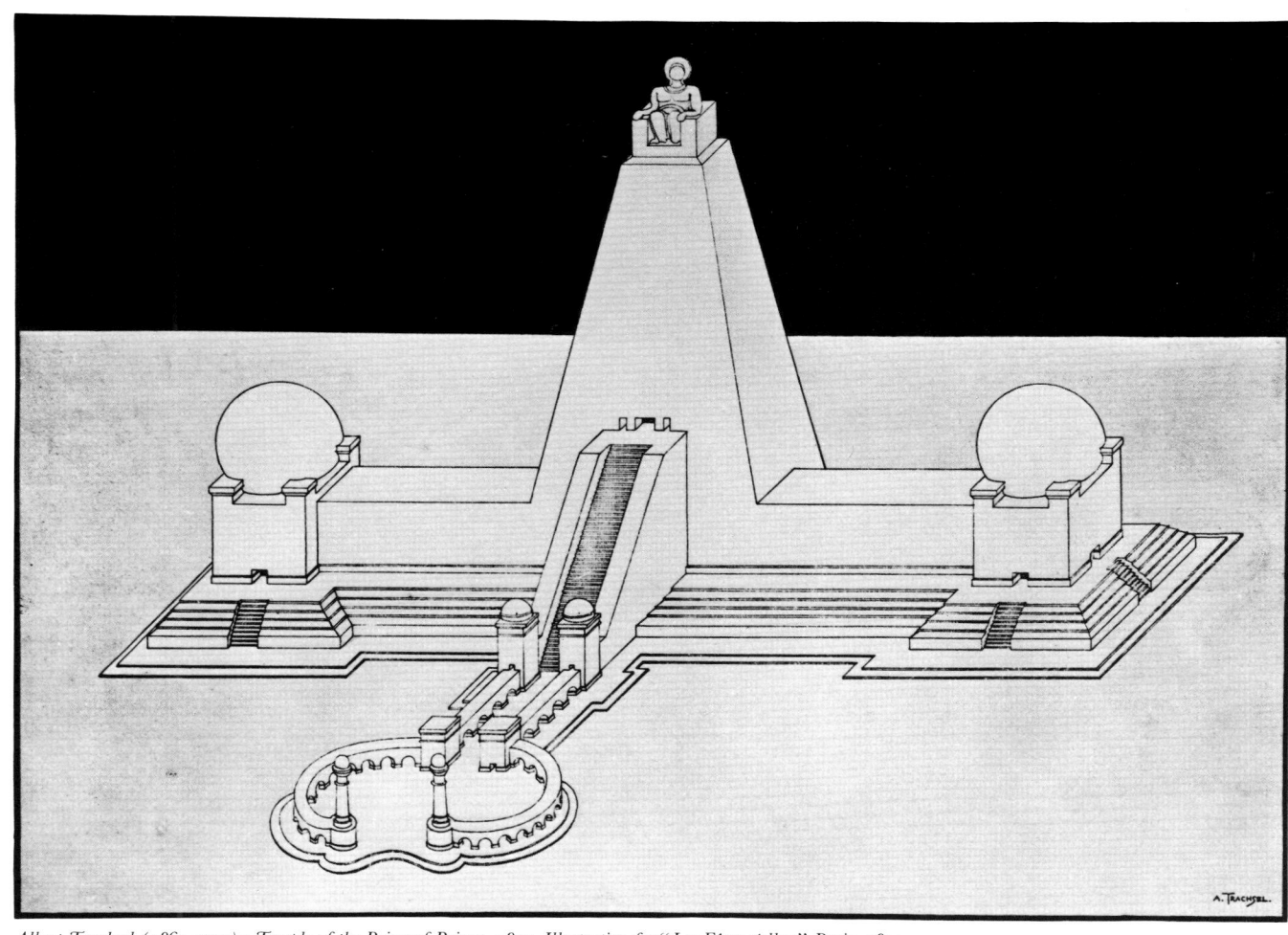

Albert Trachsel (1863-1929): Temple of the Being of Beings, 1894. Illustration for "Les Fêtes réelles," Paris, 1894.

bits in this "temple of occultism" there were sculptures by Bourdelle; a candelabra by Alexandre Charpentier; a "very exquisite Virgo admirabilis" by Pezieux, "embossed with gold and painted mauve, pink and copper blue" (F. Fénéon, *Le Chat noir*, 19 March); wood engravings by Félix Vallotton; watercolours by Eugène Grasset; some very orthodox religious works by Emile Bernard; some "holy pictures" by Filiger "in a Byzantine style humanized by the Quattrocento"; some visionary architectural designs by Albert Trachsel, of "mythico-Chaldean palaces, temples in the shape of human heads, mythical beasts, all highly original, the product of a fine, fearless imagination" (Remy de Gourmont). There was also an "agreeable woman" by Armand Point; a large drawing, "very fine and very incomprehensible," by Georges Minne; a "flosculous ornamentation" by Jan Toorop; some Carlos Schwabes in which the symbolism was "very discreet"; and conversely—Huysmans had just published *Là-bas*—various satanic, ambiguous and multilateral subjects by Jean Delville (later to become Péladan's most faithful Belgian disciple), Hodler, Vallgren and Fernand Khnopff. The latter's contributions seemed to Remy de Gourmont "extremely curious, especially the *Female Sphinx*, which looks as if painted on the glass of a mirror; women are seen in it, their faces at the level of the knees, and by raising themselves a little they can make the image of their foreheads merge with the elusive image of the Sphinx's sexual parts—thus, by a naive instinct, letting their minds come to rest in the appropriate organ." Fénéon, on the other hand, was irritated by the reminiscences, the esoteric aspect, and the symbolist complexity of the exhibition. "M. Fernand Khnopff and many of his fellow-exhibitors will never be brought to understand that a picture should attract first

and foremost through its rhythms; that a painter shows too much humility when he chooses subjects already rich in literary meanings; and that three pears on a tablecloth by Paul Cézanne are moving and sometimes mystical, whereas Wagner's Valhalla is as uninteresting as the Chamber of Deputies, when they paint it." Most of the painters represented there exhibited also in the next five Salons, i.e. every year up to 1897. After that the "Grand Master," wrote Larmandie, historian of the movement, "decreed the entry into hibernation of the knightly and intellectual Order which had so brilliantly achieved a hexade of creation and teaching." The Rosicrucians were not in the habit of challenging the decisions of their leader; they believed in his wisdom and in the reawakening of Brunhilde. The "knight of the ideal barrow," the "sandwich-man of the beyond," had tried to organize a protest against the age, to create a religion of Beauty combined with a cult of mystery. Later Péladan ruefully recognized that he had "gone the wrong way about it." But what had upset him most, at the outset, were the defections of Puvis de Chavannes, who, said Péladan, preferred "presidential honours to the admirable role of painter-preacher"; of Gustave Moreau, "frightened of the Institut's frowns"; of Burne-Jones and Watts, "suddenly unsympathetic and suspicious"; and of Maurice Denis, Odilon Redon and Böcklin. "As for their pupils," said Péladan as early as 1894, "they were afraid of compromising themselves. I had to make do with unrecognized talents who have already partly abandoned me, thinking they have no more need of the Rosicrucian movement; and all, some day, will fly off up to official spheres, as soon as they think they have got from the Order all that can help them in their own careers."

SALON DE LA ROSE✠CROIX

SALON DE LA ROSE✠CROIX   15

DELVILLE (Jean). — *Symbolisation de la Chair et de l'Esprit.*

*Illustrations from the catalogue
of the Salon de la Rose Croix, Paris, 1892:*

1. *Alexandre Séon (1855-1917):
Portrait of Joséphin Péladan.*
2. *Jean Delville (1867-1953):
Symbolization of the Flesh and the Spirit.*
3. *Alexandre Séon (1855-1917):
Frontispiece of "L'Androgyne" (The Hermaphrodite)
by Joséphin Péladan, Part VIII of "L'Ethopée" or
"La Décadence latine," 1891.*
4. *Alphonse Osbert (1857-1939):
Reverie by Moonlight. Charcoal.*
5. *Ferdinand Hodler (1853-1918):
Disillusioned Souls, after Hodler's
canvas of 1892.*

SALON DE LA ROSE✠CROIX

ALEXANDRE SÉON. — *Le Sar Mérodack Joséphin Peladan*
(Étude pour le portrait).

SALON DE LA ROSE✠CROIX   71

SÉON (Alexandre). — *Frontispice pour l'Éthopée VIII: L'Androgyne*

HODLER (Ferdinand). — *Ames déçues.*

Johan Thorn Prikker (1868-1932):
The Bride, 1892-1893. Oil.

Edvard Munch (1863-1944): Attraction I, 1896. Lithograph.

A SPATE OF IMAGES
1892-1896

Men's eyes listen; some there are indeed that speak, and all these eyes solicit above all, they watch, they peer, but none of them look. Modern man no longer believes, and that is the reason for the blank look in his eye.

Jean Lorrain, 1897

Poetry is the food of our souls. It bears within it, like the breeze of summer evenings, a breath of life and death, the presentiment of blossom time, the shiver of corruption, the present, the here and the beyond, an immense beyond. Every perfect poem is at once presentiment and presence, nostalgia and fulfilment.

Hugo von Hofmannsthal

WHEN IT CAME to relationships with society, history had to be buttonholed via the press, the critics and public opinion. On 3 February 1891, at the secret instigation of Jean Moréas, to whom *La Plume* had devoted a special number on 1 January, a banquet was held in Paris at the Hôtel des Sociétés Savantes in honour of Moréas's collection of poems, *Le Pèlerin passioné* (The Passionate Pilgrim). The young Maurice Barrès called it "this masterpiece before whose advent those who sympathized with the 'symbolist' world did not know how to explain themselves to those who were prejudiced against it." Ernest Raynaud wrote that this "magnificent occasion," attended by nearly two hundred artists and poets, had "worldwide repercussions". Raynaud, enthusiastic author of *La Mêlée symboliste* (The Symbolist Free-for-all), went on to express the belief that the gathering "marked the golden age and to a certain extent the apotheosis of symbolism. Moréas was then one of the leaders of the movement, and in acclaiming him people were acclaiming Symbolism itself."

Which people? Redon, Rops, Gauguin, Munch, Seurat, Octave Mirbeau, Edouard Schuré, Catulle Mendès, Maurice Maeterlinck, André Gide, Maurice Barrès, Emile Verhaeren, Henri de Régnier, Georges Rodenbach, Jules Renard, Albert Saint-Paul, Jules Tellier, Alfred Vallette, Anatole France, Francis Vielé-Griffin, Maurice du Plessys, Achille Delaroche and Charles Morice. Others too, but above all those who for some time had already been meeting every Monday evening at the Café Voltaire. Mallarmé, though saluting the "auroral youth" with which he was surrounded, presided at the banquet and was himself the dominating figure. He it was who was acclaimed, who was the oracle, the utterer of profundity's loftiest language, the potential Book, the irresistibly attractive edifice and abyss of symbols. Gauguin did a portrait of him—an image of solitude against a dark background, haunted by the ghost of Poe's *Raven*. But Mallarmé himself was aware of the "fundamental absurdity" of "imitating the example of the literary fraternity and talent." In the *Revue Blanche* of November 1895 he wrote: "To frequent the literary life, apart from the one true kind which consists in awakening inner harmonies and meanings, is only a hindrance.

"Acquaintance with colleagues leads one to the conclusion that everyone, especially and with especial reason anyone of any genius, regards himself as exemplary. This is fundamentally absurd, and also, latently, self-evident. The only reason anyone goes and listens to someone else holding forth, briskly reducing art to his own dimensions and gifts and lauding one particular technique, is that he himself may yield to the sudden desire to suggest that he is really the only one that counts, and to enjoy the polite withdrawal of contradictions concealing the others' stupid despair. One or other of these two things is the only pretext for company and the exchange of opinions: for I cannot suppose that anyone lightly takes pleasure, just for the sake of talking, in revealing the private results of so many failures as against a single success. That one success is enough to create the standing armour of our enigma, which is never to explain or popularize methods for the sake of a fame which is always less than the mystery itself."

The mystery, which in the mythographical tradition is the site of pleasure—and as such necessarily *symbolic*—is, says Julia Kristeva, "the enclave within which genitality, and hence filiation and procreation,

The power of language

I painted the lines and colours that impinged on my inner eye. I painted from memory, adding nothing and omitting the details that I no longer had before my eyes. Hence the simplicity of these paintings, their apparent emptiness.

I painted the impressions of my childhood. The troubled colours of a bygone day...

Edvard Munch, *Saint-Cloud Manifesto*

Edvard Munch (1863-1944):
Puberty, c. 1893. Oil.

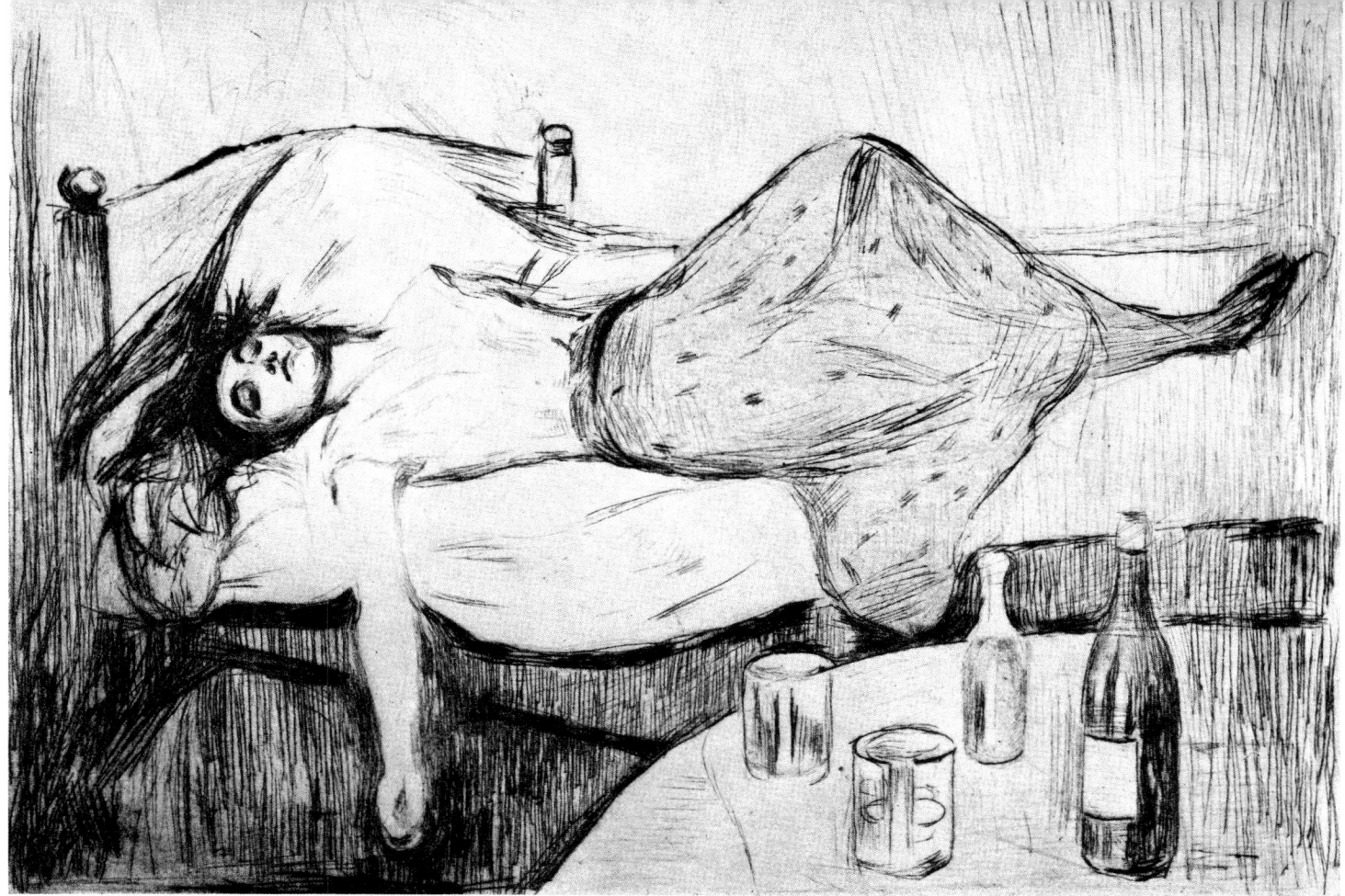

Edvard Munch (1863-1944): The Next Day, 1895. Drypoint.

are reflected." So it is a question of protecting the enigma. "Standing armour." Protecting it through solitude. Though solitude has to be activated, vivified. From without. By, among other things, the Tuesday-evening gatherings in Mallarmé's flat. But there it was only what Mallarmé said that mattered, dominating, flashing, terrorizing, flaming against the still sunset of absolute silence, disconcerting, disconcerted, deathly. The "outer dew" he once required of his friends he seemed to have left behind. Though no one could say he now had less need of "all kinds of stimulants, that of friends who stir one with their voices, that of pictures, of music, of noise, of life." Among other stimulants were those provided by the pictures, the voice, the artistry of Edvard Munch. The relationship was encouraged by Gauguin, and immediately buttressed by certain intimate characteristics which Mallarmé and Munch had in common. Neither of them was moved, then or ever, by "the pride of the creator." Mallarmé called it "a noble sentiment I know nothing of," and was always sceptical about any concrete proofs of fertility.

It was a fascinating plan that Munch followed. As soon as he escaped the seduction of the mirror and, against a background of terror, invented the wave of desire, the trace of nightmare, the intonation of dread, there came a spate of images. To yield to the power of the image was not only to undergo a human experience, but also to let oneself be galvanized by the power, the physical power, of language. The image expressed, as Mallarmé had said of poetry, "a mysterious sense of the aspects of existence," as if plastic art, like literature, revealed the presence of inner harmonies and meanings. Munch might have said, like Mallarmé, that one has to "think with one's whole body." Once he abandoned imitation—i.e. from the Paris years on—all Munch's work forsook history and myth and became a divagation of forces, a rush of the elements, a tension. Colour, volume, line, everything graphic, was

subordinated to the central function of echoing impulse or drive. Munch can be said to have wallowed in the paint rather than laid it on, undermining the traditional units of meaning (this was the converse of what Gustave Moreau did with his calligraphy). Hence the contour in ecstasies, the shuddering line, the fluid exposition, the viscous spasm. It was a violent art, wavering, desiring, vibrating like stringed instruments, warping, buckling. It was a gushing forth, to be compared with elemental fire, and with the "effulgence" which J.P. Richard sees in Mallarmé as an immediate datum of the creative consciousness, a "mad, almost physiological mode" which, like fury, is "the wild impulse of a genius bursting out of himself into the haven of expression."

Mallarmé had discerned the "fury of bravura" in Whistler, and the "fury" which hurled Manet "at the empty canvas, confusedly, as if he had never painted before." There is no doubt that he would have picked out the same instinctual theme in Munch if he had written about him, for there is every indication that the two men were linked by the sympathy which is based on biological imagination, topological subversion, and the cosmic dimension of the body pierced by painful contractions. Thus the figure of the wave in Munch may be compared with the figure of the *pli* or fold in Mallarmé, which J.P. Richard sees as linking the erotic to the concrete: "the fold being at one and the same time sex organ, foliage, mirror, book and grave," all of which things both Munch and Mallarmé bring together in a specific dream of intimacy. Thus a powerful visual condensation is, like a true poem, a mixture of "original subtlety and harmonious fusion." The verse or the colour explodes and evaporates in some rarity. And every text, whatever its content in terms of meaning, has "subtlety floating between the lines" when it generates the motive power of suggestion.

A spate of images is a flood of energies, a crossroads of turbulence. It is something which overflows, outstripping the language of culture as a

Edvard Munch (1863-1944): Ashes, 1894. Oil.

major instrument of pedagogy. It is a scandal which flouts meaning, through the removal of current significants, through the absence of the expected significance, and through the introduction of wild condensations and displacements. The flow of metaphor unbalances the old chain of metonymy, setting up an oscillation between the two which might be said to feed the conflict between fantasies of destruction and fantasies of restoration. If Munch became famous in a few hours in 1892—at least in Germany and the Nordic countries—it was because of the scandal caused by the fifty-five pictures which went on show in Berlin on 5 November of that year: the uproar was such that the exhibition was closed before the public had a chance to see it. This was censorship for the sake of morals, out of conservative instinct. How could anyone dare to outmode in this way the ordinary mechanism of discourse, and replace it with signs which no one yet knew how to control from without? How could the long history of humanism be challenged and denied like this, and the universal language of mathematics undermined? At the moment when thermodynamics was being created, how could he introduce so new and pregnant a paradigm?

Munch's audacity was equal to that of Gauguin, and his innovation so significant that it is still being analyzed after nearly a hundred years. An utterance like a gimlet, floating between lines that were sinuous and insidious. A nightmare of solitude which seemed to some like a primal temptation, a crisis of communication, a refusal of the other person to

satisfy a demand, a state linked to aggressivity and of which the source, according to Melanie Klein, lies in "the fear of destroying the object against which the aggressive impulses are directed": unless, in a world perceived and experienced as a series of absences, anguish serves to bring about a fundamental isolation which establishes us in what Heidegger was to call an "inviolable solitude." Here the message was supported by violently symbolist tests, centred on the relationship between celibacy and creativeness: thus Strindberg described Munch as "the esoteric painter of love, jealousy, death and sadness."

Munch was obsessed by the experience of failure, the central theme of his work, and used his spasmodic line of distress to record the image of the *femme fatale*, magnified by her refusal to procreate. There are three painted versions of *The Madonna* (one executed in 1893, and in the Munch Museum in Oslo; one done in 1894, in the Kunsthalle in Hamburg; and another, belonging to 1894-1895, in the National Gallery in Oslo), as well as various prints. But these, far from being as innocent as the picture interpreted in 1894 by the Polish poet Stanislas Przybyszwski as catching "the moment when the mystery of eternal conception fills the woman's face with glorious ecstasy," are surrounded with spermatozoa and foetuses only to signify the sterility inherent in the trap which woman sets for man. Munch's Madonna is a kind of female Dracula—Bram Stoker's novel was a great success when it was published in 1894—out to suck men's blood like a vampire.

Edvard Munch (1863-1944): Separation, c. 1893. Oil.

Here we encounter the new modern myth of the "bachelor machine," identified in 1954 by Michel Carrouges on the basis of a dream and in an attempt to contrast the "mythological critique of reason" with the "rationalist critique of myth." Carrouges, assuming that the mechanism and the terror hold simultaneous sway, saw the importance of celibacy in the plastic myth of Marcel Duchamp and in the life and work of Kafka, and asked if the two apparatuses, in Kafka's *In the Penal Settlement* and in Duchamps' *Bride*, were not both two great machines based on the myth of celibacy, a dark, mechanical representation of the sexual process implying a very special attitude to eroticism: celibacy, "not as a mere fact but as a characteristic mental attitude, is based on a certain loss of human feeling, an inability to share with and enter into communion with women." The tragedy of the bachelor machine, says Carrouges, "is not that of someone living entirely alone, but that of a creature who can get infinitely close to another creature of the opposite sex and yet be unable to be really with them. It is not a question of chastity, but on the contrary of a conflict between two erotic passions which approach and exacerbate one another but can never reach the point of fusion."

We should also note, though this does not exhaust the many different valencies of the subject, the imaginary function here of the repeated representation of hair: long, rich, flowing, fluid, always wavy, tortuous, trembling, what Mallarmé called a "warm river," dark waves whose erotic blackness probably derives from some Satanic mythology. Hair is a fetish object, winding in great open whorls—arcade, vault, cupola, arabesque. It often encircles and accompanies the big grey-green eyes of the *femme fatale*, bringing out their symbolism, marking the time. And so we ought to stop seeing Munch before he actually existed, as a preamble to expressionism or a prelude to Art Nouveau. That is only to pick out certain elements—architectonic ones—and join them together again at a later level. In a way it is better to approach history as a dialectical phenomenon, a fabric held together by feedback. There is no sense in linking Munch to the Pont-Aven School or the Jugendstil unless we keep these two styles separate in our minds from the artistry in which, as Maurice Blanchot might say, "every phrase is a cosmos, a minutely calculated arrangement in which the terms are all in relationships of extreme tension."

This was clearly seen by Strindberg, who contributed some brief analyses to the *Revue Blanche* of 1 June 1896 on the occasion of Munch's first one-man show in Paris. Munch himself described these pieces as "prose poems":

"It has been said that one would have to set Munch's pictures to music to explain them properly. Perhaps. But until a composer comes along, I shall sing the praises of a few pictures which recall the visions of Swedenborg in the Delights of Wisdom on Conjugal Love and the Pleasures of Madness on Fornication.

"*Kiss*. — The fusion of two beings, the smaller of which is carp-shaped and seems about to swallow the larger, after the fashion of vermin, microbes, vampires and women. Another is a man, creating the illusion which the woman reflects. Man, imploring the favour of being able to give his soul, his blood, his liberty, his peace, his salvation—in exchange for what? In exchange for the happiness of giving his soul, his blood, his liberty, his peace, and his salvation.

"*Red hair*. — Rain of gold falling on the poor wretch kneeling in front of his worst self imploring the favour of being finished off by being stuck with pins. Gilded cords, links with earth and suffering. Rain of blood poured down in torrents on the madman looking for trouble, the divine trouble of being loved, i.e. of loving.

"*Jealousy*. — Jealousy, sacred sense of cleanliness of soul which loathes mingling with another of the same sex through the medium of another. Jealousy, legitimate egoism, born of the instinct to preserve myself and my race. The man who is jealous says to his rival: 'Away with you, fool; you mean to warm yourself at the flames I lit, to inhale my breath from her mouth, to steep yourself in my blood—but you will be my slave because it is my spirit that will rule you through the woman when she has become your master.'

"*Conception*. — Immaculate or otherwise, it comes to the same thing; the red or golden halo crowns the performance of the act, sole *raison d'être* of this creature who has no independent existence.

"*Scream*. — Cry of terror at Nature howling with wrath and about to speak through storm and thunder to the little idiots who think they are being careful without looking like it.

"*Dusk*. — The sun fades, night falls, and dusk transforms mortals into ghosts and corpses; just as they go home to wrap themselves in the shroud of their beds and lose themselves in sleep, there comes that which looks like death but reconstructs life, the ability to suffer which comes from heaven or hell.

"*The Shore*. — The waves have shattered the trunks, but the roots, the underground roots, come alive again and creep through the dry sand to drink at the eternal spring of mother sea! And the moon rises like the dot on an i, putting the finishing touch to sadness and infinite desolation. Venus has emerged from the waves, and Adonis come down from the mountains and villages. They pretend to look at the sea, for fear of drowning in a glance which will destroy their selves and merge them in an embrace in which Venus becomes partly Adonis and Adonis partly Venus."

Munch, who since 1890 had been living at Saint-Cloud with the Danish poet Goldstein, moved to Berlin at the end of 1892. There, up till 1895 (when Vollard had the idea of publishing engravings by artists who were not engravers by profession, and asked Munch to collaborate along with Redon, Whistler, Carrière and Puvis de Chavannes), he was concerned with making contacts in literary rather than in artistic

The signs of distress

Ceux qui ne peuvent plus avoir
D'espoir que dans leur désespoir
Sont descendus de leur silence.

Dites, quoi donc s'entend venir
Sur les chemins de l'avenir,
De si tranquillement terrible?

La haine du monde est dans l'air
Et des poings pour saisir l'éclair
Sont tendus vers les nuées.

C'est l'heure où les hallucinés
Les gueux et les déracinés
Dressent leur orgueil dans la vie.

C'est l'heure — et c'est là-bas que sonne le tocsin;
Des crosses de fusils battent ma porte;
Tuer, être tué! — qu'importe!

C'est l'heure — et c'est là-bas que sonne le tocsin.

Emile Verhaeren, *La Révolte*, from *Les Flambeaux Noirs*, 1890

(Those who can no longer set their hopes on anything but their despair have come down from their silence. Say, what is it then so quietly terrible that is heard approaching along the roads of the future? The world's hatred is in the air and fists to seize the lightning are raised heavenwards. The hour has come for the hallucinated, the beggars and the wanderers to set up their pride in life. The hour has come—and yonder sounds the tocsin; rifle butts are beating at my door; kill or be killed!—what matter! The hour has come—and yonder sounds the tocsin.)

Edvard Munch (1863-1944):
◁ *Madonna, 1895. Drypoint.*
▷ *The Urn, 1896. Lithograph.*

circles. But the decision of the highly conformist *Verein Berliner Künstler* (Berlin Artists' Association) to close down his 1892 exhibition caused, among other repercussions, an immediate reaction on the part of the "advanced" minority. Max Liebermann and Ludwig von Hofmann resigned and set up a dissident Group of XI, whose first act was to advocate the removal of Munch's work to Cologne and Düsseldorf, the big economic and financial centres on the Rhine. Soon after that they were sent to Munich. We now need to re-examine the relationship which was to be established between Munch's work and the ideological imagery of Klinger. We must also try to show what really survives of the early infinity of childhood, once it is absorbed into our uncertainty. We need, too, to look more closely at the anarchist and socialist tendencies of the early days, which will bring us to Munch's immediate interest in *Les Fleurs du mal*. What we are first concerned with here, however, are the repercussions of the row he caused and the chaos he left in his wake. It was above all Munich, that huge bourgeois, commercial, cosmopolitan pulse of Baroque, Catholic Bavaria, which reacted against romantic stereotypes and embraced a whole new attitude to painting.

On 26 November 1892, to emphasize the break, Franz von Stuck, Wilhelm Trübner, Lovis Corinth, Fritz von Uhde, Segantini and Israels founded in Munich a permanent "secession" group, its aim being to engage in avant-garde action and help to organize regular exhibi-

Franz von Stuck (1863-1928) : Innocence, 1889. Oil.

Transformations

Abendlich auf schattenbegleiteten wegen
Über brücken den türmen und mauern entgegen
Wenn leise klänge sich regen :

Auf einem goldenen wagen
Wo perlgraue flügel dich tragen
Und lindenbüsche dich fächeln
Herniedertauche
Mit mildem lächeln
Und linderndem hauche!

Unter den masten auf rüstig furchendem kiele
Über der wasser und strahlen schimmerndem spiele
In glücklicher ferne vom ziele :

Auf einem silbernen wagen
Wo lichtgrüne spiegel dich tragen
Und schaumgewinde dich fächeln
Herniedertauche
Mit frohem lächeln
Und kosendem hauche!

Lang ist nach jauchzendem tode die sonne
*   verschollen.*
Mit den planken die brausenden wogen grollen
Und dumpfe gewitter rollen :

Auf einem stählernen wagen
Wo lavaschollen dich tragen
Und grell lohe wolken dich fächeln
Herniedertauche
Mit wildem lächeln
Und sengendem hauche!

Stefan George, *Verwandlungen*, from *Hymnen*, 1890

(At evening on shadow-attended ways, over bridges, towards towers and walls, when faint sounds are stirring : on a golden car where pearl-grey wings bear you and linden copses fan you, come down with gentle smile and soothing breath! Under the masts on a lustily shearing keel, over the shimmering play of waters and rays in happy remoteness from the destination : on a silver car where pale green mirrors bear you and seaspray fans you, come down with a happy smile and caressing breath! Long after jubilant death is the sun forgotten. The boisterous waves rumble against the planks and muffled thunderstorms roll : on a steel car where lava blocks bear you and lurid clouds fan you, come down with a wild smile and scorching breath!)

Franz von Stuck (1863-1928): Poster for the First International Exhibition of the Munich Secession, Munich, 1893.

O Femme, chair tragique exquisément amère,
Femme, notre mépris sublime et notre dieu,
O gouffre de douceurs et cavale de feu,
Qui galope plus vite encor que la chimère,
Ah! tu la connais bien, Sphinx et avide et moqueur.

Albert Samain, 1891

(O Woman, tragic and exquisitely bitter flesh, Woman, our sublime
disdain and our god, O gulf of sweetness and mare of fire, outgallop-
ing even the chimera. Ah! you know her well, eager and mocking
Sphinx.)

tions to display and support an art that was to be independent of authority and of official criticism. The new group was given the name
Secession by Georg Hirth, a controversial writer influential on the
Münchener Neueste Nachrichten. Franz von Stuck designed the group's
emblem, a helmeted Athena (in Brussels, for the *Pour l'Art* club, Jean
Delville chose a sphinx). Hugo von Tschudi, director of the Berlin
National Gallery, had already fled from the cramping traditional standards and bureaucracy of the new capital of the German Reich and
taken his love for the French Impressionists to Munich, where he col-
lected the nucleus of the modern section of the Bavarian state gallery.
At the same time, Böcklin was staying in Zurich and becoming friendly
with the novelist Gottfried Keller; Maeterlinck's first play, *La Princesse
Maleine,* was performed in July 1892 at a country house near Munich;
another Maeterlinck play, *L'Intruse,* was performed in London; in
Paris, the publication of *Pelléas et Mélisande* in 1892 renewed and prolonged "the interest, the passion" already surrounding Maeterlinck,
the "Belgian Shakespeare," as Octave Mirbeau had called him in a
famous article in the *Figaro*; Maurice Denis's review of the first Salon
de la Rose-Croix in Paris (1892) caused him to quarrel with Emile
Bernard; the circulation of the *Figaro* was said to have shot up suddenly
when it began serializing Georges Rodenbach's novel *Bruges-la-Morte*;
in Amsterdam, Verlaine made a speech at a symbolist exhibition organized by the Arti et Amicitiae Society; in Vienna, Koloman Moser,
Josef Hoffmann, Joseph Olbrich and four other artists founded the
Siebenerclub (Seven Club) to promote book illustration; and Henry de
Groux's huge painting, *Christ aux outrages* (Christ Reviled), exhibited
clandestinely in Paris, aroused the enthusiasm of Puvis de Chavannes,
Redon, Mallarmé, Mirbeau and Carrière.

In Munich the Secession group was temporarily without accommo-
dation, and its first exhibition (1892) had to be held in Berlin, at the
Kunsthalle am Lehrter Bahnhof. Frankfurt and Dresden also offered
hospitality to what was now called the "Association of the homeless,"
but various people came to the rescue, and in the summer of 1893 the
Secession was able to open its first international exhibition on its own
premises in Munich. It was advertised by a poster designed by Franz
von Stuck and dominated by nine canvases by the same artist, including *Innocence* and *Sin.* The group of works by Stuck was symbolic of the
newly acquired celebrity of an artist later to be one of the masters of
Kandinsky, Klee and Albers, and also of the mental outlook of an
avant-garde which was openly hostile to taboos and, in a tradition
started by the Pre-Raphaelites and slanted towards dream by Böcklin,
had boldly adopted an imagery full of extravagance and indirect meaning of the most disturbing kind. Were they trying to astonish the art
world? Perhaps. There was certainly no question of yielding to the
détente brought about by Impressionism, but on the contrary of streng-
thening the pole of immobilization. This produced an agonizing inertia
in which the closed world of the text swelled the realm of illusion, and
the old academic code became a terrorist weapon through the strange
substance it lent to image at every level. Theirs was a programme
based on images, above all on the richest of unconscious archetypes, the
snake. A creature of earth and icy nakedness, of total silence; what
Gaston Bachelard has called "the animal subject of the verb to en-
twine." Provocative, seductive, Satanic, belonging to the primal night
of cold viscosity. Swinburne describes its strong, supple, beautiful body
of clay, covered with poisoned, phosphorescent scabs and cold and
coloured scales, like the scales of leprosy on the skin; its pale green jaws
stretched forth, and its breast fiery as blood; its teeth and claws con-
vulsed by the painful pleasure of pain; its eyelids rent by the dark
flame of desire; and the visible poison of its breath hurled at the face
and eyes of the human soul divine. G. Svenaeus thinks it is possible to
establish a link between the *Serpent-Auréole* (Snake-Halo) engraved by
Odilon Redon in 1890, Munch's *Madonna,* and the theme of *Sin* as
treated by Franz von Stuck. This kind of intertextuality would help to
reduce the gap between symbolists—between those, anyhow, who came
after Gustave Moreau. As for Maldoror, he still continued to shake his
scales tortuously; but neither then nor now did he emerge from the
Book, or from the chalice of St John.

Franz von Stuck (1863-1928) : Sin, 1893. Oil.

Fernand Khnopff (1858-1921) : The Blood of the Medusa, c. 1895. Charcoal.

Meanwhile, as the nineteenth century drew to a close, Brussels became an important place of exchanges, a crossroads of ideas, a centre of social emancipation and a seat of experiment which played a leading role in the spread of Symbolism and the creation of Art Nouveau. In 1881 Octave Maus, a Brussels lawyer, and the poet Emile Verhaeren founded the artistic and literary weekly *L'Art Moderne*, and in 1883 they began to form the Group of XX (The Twenty). It was a neutral and heterogeneous group, apparently without any particular ideology apart from a nostalgia for the old art and craft guilds. It produced a strange mosaic of contradictions and divergences, including as it did, for example, both James Ensor and Fernand Khnopff. On the whole, the Twenty were mainly a sort of backcloth, a prologue, a launching pad, whose intention it was to protect "true originality" in a place "where people are free, not only in fact but above all in thought." Their exhibitions, held every year from 13 February to 13 March, welcomed as guests such men as Félicien Rops, Whistler and Catulle Mendès (who came to give a talk on Wagner) in 1884; Jan Toorop, who was elected a member of the Twenty, in 1885; Odilon Redon and Georges Rodenbach in 1886, the latter invited to give a lecture on the Belgian novelist and art critic Camille Lemonnier; Rodin, in 1887; Xavier Mellery and Villiers de L'Isle-Adam in 1888, the latter reading three of his *Histoires insolites* (Strange Tales); in 1889, Gauguin (who among a dozen other paintings showed the *Vision after the Sermon*), Max Klinger and Teodor de Wyzewa (who gave a talk on "The Origins of Decadent Literature"); in 1890, George Minne and Giovanni Segantini ("up there in his house three thousand metres above sea level," said Octave Maus, "he knew who the Twenty were and replied to their first appeal with letters no less enthusiastic than picturesque. He too joined to the almost documentary aspect of his mountain pictures an element of imagination and transposition. This is how he explains his *Flower of the Alps:* It is a harmony of colours which I found in a marvellous flower standing out

Constant Montald (1862-1944):
Portrait of Emile Verhaeren (detail). Drawing.

The golden age of symbolism

The Group of the XX
("Les Vingt," i.e. The Twenty),
Brussels, 1889.

against the sky and lit up by the sun. I religiously preserved the colours and shape while turning them into an image"); also, in 1890, Stéphane Mallarmé ("a man inhabited by a dream comes here to speak of another, who is dead"—Villiers de L'Isle-Adam); in 1891, Walter Crane, Charles Filiger and Gustave Kahn, the latter come to raise the question of *vers libre*; in 1892, Maurice Denis; and in 1893, Ford Madox Brown, Johan Thorn Prikker, William Degouve de Nuncques, Léon Frédéric, Charles Doudelet, and Verlaine, who came to protest against all schools including his own, the Decadent, and recited poetry by Kahn, Moréas and himself "in a low, muffled voice, without any other movement in his unhealthy face... than an occasional gleam from his dark, deep, mocking eye."

Gustave Moreau and Puvis de Chavannes were invited several times but always obstinately stayed away. Péladan, when asked, said that he would "gladly give the Twenty a free lecture" if ever he came through Brussels on a lecture tour; "otherwise it would have to be lucrative," for lecturing is "only pleasurable when the audience consists entirely of women." His subject would have been "Istar or the Victory of the Self"; but Péladan's lecture tour never took place.

However, the Twenty were chiefly interested in what they called "the bearers of something new": the "charming open-air studies" of Cézanne, the "dazzling symphonies" of Van Gogh, the landscapes of Sisley, Renoir's new compositions, and the work of the Neo-Impressionist group, "whose technique emerges more and more strongly." There are two quite strongly marked currents to be distinguished in the activity of the Brussels group in the 1890s. One, supposed to be "directly inspired by nature," is represented by Cézanne, Van Gogh, Toulouse-Lautrec, Sisley, Signac, Pissarro, Henry van de Velde, Théo van Rysselberghe, Willy Finch and Georges Lemmen. The other tried, according to Octave Maus, "to translate emotions, dreams, symbols and literary reminiscences into the plastic arts: Odilon Redon invented mysterious forms for *Les Fleurs du mal*; Schlobach used lines from Baudelaire or Verhaeren as epigraphs for hieratic figures influenced by the Pre-Raphaelites and often emerging out of a dream vision of London. Most hermetic of all was the Javanese Dutchman, Jan Toorop, an extravagant but sincere artist whose work is difficult to talk of because of its diversity. But whatever the methods used, even the most realist, one element was constant: the search for character, generalization, and soon Symbol as well, beyond contingent forms."

The spread of symbolism, and in particular the increasingly enthusiastic reception given to the work of Fernand Khnopff, the most ambiguous painter Belgium ever produced, preoccupied the commentators in *L'Art Moderne* of 12 January 1890, who took their departure from the political opinions of one of the editors, Edmond Picard. "Art has in our time assumed an aristocratic aspect. It has gradually drawn away from the masses... It exists only for a few who call themselves an élite... A scornful sort of shibboleth has entered into circulation, born of anger at not being understood except by the finer

Catalogue of the exhibition of The Twenty ("Les XX"), Brussels, 1893.

George Morren (1868-1941): Cover of the art magazine "L'Art Moderne," Brussels, 7 January 1894.

spirits: the artist should produce works only for the rare species of the highly cultivated... But our age, in which art is like an abscess formed secretly among the favourites of fortune, is approaching a transformation. What will it be like? One does not need to be very clever to realize that it will accompany the democratic revolution and be influenced by it... When the iniquity of the money monopoly has been destroyed, the iniquity of the art monopoly will have been shattered at the same time. And that at once raises another question: what kind of art is going to replace the one that has been abolished? In a democracy, what form will the art take which now flourishes, a rare and morbid bloom, in an aristocracy?"

A large question, as always, and one which is enough in itself to show how the distance has widened between social reformism and cultural activity. As if democracy necessarily had to go with a normative approach and reassuring images.

On 12 September 1886, again in *L'Art Moderne*, Emile Verhaeren, trying to place the young Khnopff, had written: "Plastic art started off by being symbolic. It had to be, since it represented the Gods, who were symbols themselves. It became complicated with esotericism and rose up sacred. Forms were created, a kind of aesthetic rite which no one challenged. That was a period of frozen art, distant and lofty, hieratical and barbarous. Later it became more human, and as in the past the gods had been lent human form, so now that divinized form was to be given to men; and the Hercules and Jupiters which in the primitive age, coarse and naive though they might be, appeared as formidable and eternal divinities, now became heroic and legendary beings very little different from famous sages, warriors and athletes. Without their accessories one would not be able to identify them. Similarly with Catholic Virgins and Christ and the saints. Once it was Cimabue and Giotto, then Raphael, Titian, Rubens and Rembrandt. After these geniuses came a realist and naturalist art for which they had prepared the way." And what about today? "A tremendous withdrawal of the modern imagination towards the past, a great wave of scientific enquiry, and hitherto unknown passions for a vague and as yet undefined supernatural, have brought us to use a strange symbolism which embodies the contemporary soul just as ancient symbolism once embodied the soul of the past. Only, instead of making it the recipient of our faith and beliefs, we put into it our doubts, our dreads, our troubles, our vices, our despairs, and probably our dying agonies."

Verhaeren goes on: "The master symbolists of our own day, men like Gustave Moreau, Puvis de Chavannes and Félicien Rops, have none of the serenity of the antique masters. None of them praises the gods or fears the devils he sublimizes. They are all tortured by the passions and melancholies of their own time. Look at what love is like in Rops' Venuses, at what wisdom and science are like in the Davids of Gustave Moreau. Only Puvis de Chavannes sometimes dreams peacefully, and does not divinize *femmes fatales* or terrible men."

An outbreak of narcissism

Oh! oh! What is this?... Your hair, your hair is falling down towards me!... All your hair, Mélisande, all your hair has fallen from the tower! I have it in my hands, I have it in my mouth... I have it in my arms, I put it round my neck... I'll open my hands no more tonight.

Maurice Maeterlinck, *Pelléas et Mélisande*, 1892

Don't slant the mirror like that! In it I can see all the weeping willows in the garden; they look as if they were weeping on your face.

Maurice Maeterlinck, *La Princesse Maleine*, 1889

Khnopff had similar preoccupations. He was attracted by the "perversity of certain lilies: Leonora d'Este." And by the "nocturnal and ageless mystery of certain sphinxes: the Pope." But, Verhaeren continues, "now, when subtle minds perceive correspondences with such astonishing clarity, and when our sensations and sentiments not only speak to each other but also move in rhythm and harmony, so that poetry is as pictorial and musical as it is literary, should we not also render in painting the impressions and yearnings which hitherto have been reflected only in music? In literature it has been achieved. I stress this point, firstly because I believe in the mutual penetration of the arts, but also because I think that the symbolist plastic arts can solve the problem. The heart was given violent expression by Romanticism, and a refined, discreet, rarefied expression of this same heart, veiled in dream, must be achieved in its turn. And it will be the sphinxes, the ancient kings and fabulous queens, the legends and the epics, that will help us to make ourselves understood; it will be they because they impose themselves with the despotism of memory and the magnifying effect of time, and because we see ourselves better through the transparency of their myths."

Khnopff strove diligently to reflect the typology of symbolism. Perhaps he did not follow to the letter the Wagnerian programme put forward by Verhaeren. Whether by deliberate strategy or because he got led astray, he surreptitiously infiltrated himself into the argument he was supposed to be propounding. He slipped in in order to construct his own silence, build it on the foundation of his secret aptitude for "orgasms of the Ego," an inclination which ensured, protected and extended his "ability to be alone." It was a plain assumption of narcissism, inside an armour of haughtiness, irony and scorn. One of Khnopff's friends notes that because of his aristocratic origins and his party he had learned how to "perfect his solitude with all the resources of his pride." His proclaimed motto was: "All you have is yourself." Chamfort has said that "one finds happiness in oneself rarely, in others never," and Khnopff might also have agreed with Jacques Rigault in our own day, that "the most beautiful girl in the world can't give me what I have." This was a sign of the pleasure the bachelor machine could give itself, for Khnopff's marriage was only an incident. Celibacy was his natural state, a state said to be encouraged by the inclination he always had for Marguerite, his sister and favourite model.

Rumour aside, the message Khnopff seems to be addressing to the reader, the voyeur, the onlooker, is really always addressed to himself. In this he might be described as idyllic. He also refused to be subjected in any way to what could be named, the better to carry on the war of the senses against significance. The better to enable the rhetorical code he used with such diabolical obstinacy—he worked on the principles of the Flemish Primitives, based on the reinterpretation of the Pre-Raphaelites—to cleanse the image from guilt. His images gave priority to an apparition, a female apparition, an extra-territorial image in that it overflowed the area in which it belonged, was defined, gave itself.

For Khnopff had read everything that had anything to do with his recherché tastes, from Baudelaire to Remy de Gourmont, and including Swinburne and Christina Rossetti. In particular, he had read *Monsieur Vénus*, published in Brussels in 1884, a best-selling novel in which Rachilde, then a girl of twenty, praises the androgynous ideal long before it became the obsession of Péladan and of "decadent" literature as a whole. It was an ideal in which might be seen one of the most relevant forms of the disease of the century, which according to Maurice Barrès, in 1889, was due to "excessive nervous fatigue" and "hitherto unknown pride." Strikingly presented, isolated, framed, and depicted with extreme minuteness, woman as re-presented by Khnopff (except in strictly conventional portraits), was created so that she was simultaneously near to and far from the scrutiny which tried to annex her. Always, and simultaneously, vague and precise. Always and simultaneously single and double. Always and simultaneously sensual and absent, strong and delicate. Always ornamented, sumptuous and blooming with ornaments. Motionless, even when threatened by the serpent. Threatened by it? Its accomplice, rather. The sexuality of the

Music in the Night

Lasse de ce silence nocturne
Dont s'alarmait son amour,
La Princesse à l'âme taciturne
Préluda sur le luth d'amour.

Dans le fouillis des folles étoffes
Ses doigts aux bagues d'argent
Emurent de somnolentes strophes
Sur les cordes d'or et d'argent.

Elle dit les lentes cantilènes
Aux langueurs de souvenir
Où les reines et les châtelaines
Se meurent de se souvenir.

Et par la salle où la lune jaune
Luisait au fil des poignards,
Ce furent, sous les pourpres du trône
Lourdes de l'acier des poignards,

Des frôlements de folles étoffes
Au jeu des bagues d'argent,
Et l'effroi de somnolentes strophes
Sur les cordes d'or et d'argent.

Stuart Merrill, *Musique en la nuit*,
from *Fastes*, 1890

(Weary of that nocturnal silence at which her love took fright, the silent-souled princess played a prelude on her lute of love. In the maze of her wild disarray her silver-ringed fingers called up sleep-inducing strains on the gold and silver strings. She sang the slow cantilenas whose memory-laden languors tell of queens and ladies dying of all that they remember. And through the room where the yellow moon gleamed on the edge of dagger blades, was heard, beneath the crimson of the throne heavy with the daggers' steel, the rustling of her wild disarray at the motion of her silver rings, and the awe of sleep-inducing strains on the gold and silver strings.)

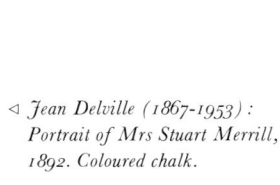
◁ *Jean Delville (1867-1953):*
Portrait of Mrs Stuart Merrill,
1892. Coloured chalk.

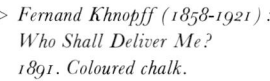
▷ *Fernand Khnopff (1858-1921):*
Who Shall Deliver Me?
1891. Coloured chalk.

· LE SOMMET. ·

Superbe, dans sa forme écrasante et rigide,
Se dresse le Sommet. Aussi fier qu'indolent
Il regarde passer l'Heure: un fleuve si lent
Ou les serpents tordus de la cuirasse Egide.

Devant le ciel rose, devant l'amas turgide
Des blancs nuages ou le midi violent
Devant l'or et le doux sang du Soir opulent
Ou triste, toujours il est demeuré frigide.

Sous le rayonnement des astres fastueux
Dont le cours est sans fin, ses flancs majestueux
S'éclairent un moment, et son albe guipure.

Mais après ce reflet qui disparaît, lassé,
Le roc est aussi sombre et la neige aussi pure.
Ah! pouvoir admirer, impassible et glacé.

snake becomes the sign of lunar androgyny: the sly dimension of what is not said occupies the space of dissimulation. Is she chaste? She has "an alcove in her head." And her eyes? Oh, those eyes, gleaming with "the plaintive emerald of a terrifying lust." Those eyes, as Jean Lorrain was to say, "long, weighed down with incredible lashes, and clear as water." As for the perfumes beloved of Des Esseintes, in Huysmans' *A Rebours*, here they seem to mingle with the dust of the pastel. In another distillation, gold and white predominate, contrasted with whites and beiges and orange. According to a recent theory, blue is supposed to be the area in which phenomenal identity is lost: the perception of blue, the colour of short waves, operates, according to this theory, just within and without the fixed form of the object. That being the case, chromatic experience could be interpreted as being governed by biological memory; as being the subject's memory at an age when he could not yet identify shapes or recognize his own reflection in the mirror. By the same token, symbolist vagueness and fluidity would be the strict counterpart of its own invisible reality. As for gold, wrote Péladan (in *Le Vice Suprême*), it had become "so much a symbol of evil that by some mysterious alchemy it defiles everything it touches."

Before being proclaimed by Péladan an "admirable and immortal master" (at the Second Rose-Croix Salon in 1893—"I regard you as the equal of Gustave Moreau, Burne-Jones, Puvis de Chavannes and Rops"), Khnopff had an exhibition in Paris, as the guest of the Société des Trente-Trois (Thirty-Three Club) in January 1889. The show was reviewed by Félix Fénéon in *La Cravache*. He described what he saw as a "patient art" which aimed at "expressing trouble, perversity, oppressive dreams." Focusing his critical eye on *A Beguiling*, a picture inspired by a line in a Georges Rodenbach poem ("and her hair was all red with my blood"), and already exhibited in 1888 by the Twenty, Fénéon wrote of it as follows: "Out of a stagnant lake of boredom rise pillars that are possibly phallic, vestiges of submerged architecture, from which depends the vague figure of a hanged man, whose blood has served no other purpose than to redden the forehead, belly and hair of a woman standing by." This symbolism seemed to Fénéon to have been "fed on the worst kind of literature." As for the painting technique, it seemed to him "abstract and disappointing... obscure and without strength." This did not prevent Fénéon from saying that pictures like this had "provided the occasion for *Quelques Notes sur l'œuvre de Fernand Khnopff 1881-1887* by Emile Verhaeren, published in Brussels by Mme Veuve Monnom in 1887, which everyone ought to read if they can only get hold of one of the fifty copies which were printed."

Fénéon, revising what had probably been an over-hasty judgement, and being a man of integrity as well as one with reassuring human experience, paid tribute, in an obituary published in the *Bulletin de la Vie Artistique* of 1 December 1921, to "the last representative of the spiritualist and symbolist school which flourished and then vanished thirty years ago. Fernand Khnopff is dead. He was a completely distinguished and charming artist, discreet, aloof, retiring... His work was characterized by refined feeling and careful execution, but his 'literature' was very private and did not try to exert influence even in Belgium. He painted for the initiate. He won the unreserved esteem and affection of those who knew him; he did not seek to stimulate the intellectual world, which takes only impresarios as its guides and not those who live in ivory towers."

The year 1893 was outstanding for more than one reason. It was not only the year in which Khnopff intensified his relations with England (in 1890 he had taken part in an exhibition of "British Pastellists" in London; since 1892 he had been a member of the Society of Portrait Painters; and now he gave talks on the Pre-Raphaelites, and, while his brother Georges was translating Oscar Wilde and Walter Pater, he was developing his friendship with Burne-Jones and preparing to be a regular contributor to *The Studio*). It was also the year which began only a few months after Maeterlinck's play *Les Sept Princesses* had been per-

Fernand Khnopff (1858-1921):
1. *Sleeping Medusa, 1896. Pastel.*
2. *"Le Sommet" (The Peak),*
   sonnet and drawing published
   in "Pan," No. 2, Berlin, 1895-1896.
3. *The Offering, 1890. Drypoint.*

4. *William Degouve de Nuncques*
   (1867-1935):
   Night in Bruges, 1897. Oil.

The interaction of word and line

Psyche looked.
— I can see nothing... Night is falling... it is dark... Khimaera!
— Yes, little Psyche?
— Where is the land of silver light and luminous beings? Where is it? What has become of it?
— Do you not see it?
— No...
— It has vanished then...
— Where?
— Behind us, beneath us...

Roland Holst (1868-1938): The Entry of Helga, 1894. Lithograph.

— Why did you not come down sooner?
— I could not, Psyche, my flight was too rapid.
— You are deceiving me! You could! You did not wish to! Now it is night... darkest night... a starless night... An icy cold wraps us about... Oh, Khimaera, take me home!
He turned with a burst of his great wings. And as he turned the lightning flashed and zigzagged across the sky, the flashes like smooth and glittering swords. The dark atmosphere was shattered by a roll of thunder like clashing cymbals, a storm wind rose, and rain poured down in torrents...
— Oh, Khimaera, take me home!
Psyche nestled against the courser's neck; she buried her head in the warm mane, and while the storm howled, while each hoof fall sent lightning flashing round them, the Khimaera beat the air with his great wings, carrying Psyche homewards, to the Empire of the Past, an ink spot yonder in the inky night...

Louis Couperus, *The Winged Horse*

formed in the house of Councillor Coulon at Passy, by puppets made by the Nabis, with costumes by Maurice Denis and sets by Sérusier and Vuillard. Verkade designed the curtain, and the "princess" dress designed by Maurice Denis was such a success that it was copied, and became the fashionable "hostess dress" par excellence at the turn of the century. 1893 was also the year of the first battle over *Pelléas et Mélisande*, presented by Lugné-Poe at the Théâtre des Bouffes-Parisiens on 17 May. Maeterlinck had "made an ardent study of the Pre-Raphaelites." Some time ago he had discovered the superiority of symbol over comparison and its dramatic resources. The play is constructed on the theme of Mélisande's hair—which is longer than her arms, "longer than I am tall"—and of her eyes—"Do you see those great eyes? They look as if they were proud of being rich... They look as if the angels of heaven were in them, at a perpetual christening... I know those eyes! I have seen them at work." The play could have done without Debussy's music, so sustained was its dramatic intensity. P.-A. Touchard has written: "The prose is in itself one of the most exciting pieces of music a writer's language has ever created. It and *Tristan et Iseult* are perhaps the two most beautiful love songs in French literature." Touchard adds a further remark which is relevant here: "The way Maeterlinck was dispossessed by Debussy of his masterpiece *Pélleas et Mélisande* is a unique case in the history of the theatre. It cannot even be compared with that of *The Barber of Seville*, for although Beaumarchais's charming comedy has lost some of its audience to Rossini's comic opera, its independent career still continues. But *Pélleas* is never performed now without the musical score, and to many people it would be sacrilege if it were."

But 1893 was also the year of the young Dutch artist Thorn Prikker's arrival in Belgium, where he worked for a while, part of the time in the neighbourhood of Visé, after having taken part in March, at the suggestion of his compatriot Toorop, in the tenth and last exhibition of the Twenty. As Octave Maus observes, Thorn Prikker was regarded as "the most hermetic of the artists on show," so vehemently did he "refuse to treat a subject—for example, *The Bride* and *Love*—by means of direct representation. He tries to express it through lines disposed in such a way that they create in the spectator the mental condition (grief, purity, etc.) out of which the picture sprang. At the most, a few symbols in the background may help the mind to interpret the meaning of the lines." A comment in *L'Art Moderne* by the Dutch correspon-

Johan Thorn Prikker (1868-1932): Cherubim, 1892. Pencil and watercolour.

112

Jan Toorop (1858-1928) : Fate, 1893. Crayon.

dent of *De Telegraaf* also evokes Thorn Prikker's position vis-à-vis symbolist method, in which "lines, like sounds in music, like words in poetry, are the means of expressing emotion. Let me explain: the artist who subscribes to this new theory does not convey the sensation he experiences through real images magnified by his own genius; he sets reality aside and creates an imaginary reality from everything he feels in himself: sounds, music, forms and colours. Thus, to represent a human figure for example, the artist thinks of the thoughts, feelings and passions of the person whose image he is reproducing, and tries to express these distractions by means of the primordial lines deriving from or surrounding the image."

It was in 1893 too that Jan Toorop, after showing *The Prowlers* at the Twenty exhibition in Brussels (the picture was inspired by the opium of *Monsieur de Phocas,* a novel by Jean Lorrain), produced one after the other *Fate, The Three Brides, The Song of Our Time,* and *Desire and Satisfaction.* These works, together with those by Thorn Prikker already referred to, were events in late nineteenth-century art. They were radical and disturbing, reflecting a profound change in the practice of painting, standing as they do against the opaque screen of symbolist doctrine and against a literary background in France, Flanders, England, and Holland (where Willem Kloos, Albert Verwey, Frederic van Eeden, Henri Borel and Louis Couperus, the latter thought by some to be the Dutch equivalent of the Huysmans of *A Rebours*, were the leaders of a literary movement known as "the generation of the Eighties"). It was no longer a question, as in the time of Ingres and Delacroix, of wondering which would win, line or colour. It was a matter of giving line language, and simultaneously giving a dream function to colour. Nor did this line have anything in common with the "cloisonnist" line of the "Breton" synthesists. To the divisionism (of colour) Dutch linearism replied with a division of surface such as had never been seen before in Western art. This was indeed an event of importance. It called several codes in question. It forced the eye along winding paths, strewn with creepers. And in the same year, 1893, in Brussels, there appeared the "whiplash line": the Hôtel Tassel, designed by Victor Horta, in the Rue de Turin (now 6 Rue P. E. Janson, and owned by the architect Jean Delhaye). This town house embodied in stone and steel and the three dimensions all the impulses hitherto contained in the field of narcissism, and provided the text, model and trap of Art Nouveau.

*"... the gentle, uncouth soul,
drunk with freedom..."*

*Giuseppe Pellizza da Volpedo (1869-1907):
The Round Dance, c. 1890-1900. Oil.*

Giovanni Segantini (1858-1899): The Angel of Life, 1894. Oil.

For the Death of Giovanni Segantini

*Spenti son gli occhi umili e degni ove s'accolse l'infinita
bellezza, partita è l'anima ove l'ombra e la luce la vita
    e la morte furon come una sola
preghiera, e la melodia del ruscello e il mugghio
    dell'armento e il tuono
della tempesta e il grido dell'aquila e il gemito
    dell'uomo
furon come una sola parola,*

*e tutte le cose furono come una sola cosa
abbracciata per sempre dalla sua silenziosa
potenza come dall'aria.
Partita è su i vènti ebra di libertà l'anima dolce e rude
di colui che cercava una patria nelle altezze più nude
sempre più solitaria.*

*O monti, purità delle cose intatte, forza, mistero
sopra la Terra, ella va e ritorna come un pensiero
immortale sopra la Terra.
O monti, o culmini, il suo dolore fu come la vostra ombra
sopra la Terra. La sua gioia sarà oltre la sua tomba
un palpito della Terra.*

Gabriele D'Annunzio, lines from *Per la Morte di Giovanni Segantini*, in
Elettra (Laudi del cielo del mare della terra e degli eroi, libro secondo), 1904

(Closed are the humble and worthy eyes that welcomed infinite
beauty, gone is the soul in which shadow and light, life and death
were like a single prayer, and the song of the stream and the lowing
of the herd and the roar of the storm and the eagle's cry and the
groaning of man were like one speech, and all things were like a single
thing embraced for ever by his silent power as if by the air. Gone with
the winds is the gentle, uncouth soul, drunk with freedom, of him
who sought an ever more lonely home on the upland wastes. Oh
mountains, purity of untouched things, strength and mystery over
Earth that goes and comes again like an immortal thought over
Earth. Oh mountains, oh peaks, his sorrow was like your shadow over
Earth. His joy, beyond the grave, will be a throbbing of Earth.)

Ferdinand Hodler (1853-1918) : The Chosen One, 1893-1894. Oil and tempera.

To Ferdinand Hodler

Si j'avais dans ma vie une heure, une seule heure,
Où ce cœur, gémissant d'un souffle qui l'effleure,
Eût joui d'un plaisir — si fugace fût-il,
Pour ce furtif instant, pour cette brève joie,
Je reprendrais, moins triste et plus vaillant, ma voie,
Et, puisant de l'espoir en ce bon souvenir,
Je dirais à mon cœur : « Sois fort, tout va finir ! »
Mais j'interroge en vain l'horreur de ma mémoire.
A chaque page, au livre amer de mon histoire,
Un mot s'épanouit comme une rouge fleur :
Malheur — et puis Malheur ! — et puis encore Malheur !

(If I had in my life an hour, but one hour, in which this heart, groaning at the lightest touch of breath, had enjoyed one pleasure, however fleeting, for that furtive moment, for that brief joy, I would go my way again, less sad and more spirited, and drawing hope from this pleasant recollection, I would say to my heart: "Be of good cheer, all will end!" But I question in vain the horror of my memory. At every page, in the bitter book of my history, one word rises up like a red flower: Mischance—and then Mischance!—and again Mischance!)

Louis Duchosal, from *Le Livre de Thulé*, 1891

Gaetano Previati (1852-1920) : Maternity, 1890-1891. Oil.

Pierre Puvis de Chavannes (1824-1898): Death and the Maidens, 1872. Oil.

5

THE AMBIVALENCE
OF DESIRE AND DEATH
1870-1900

Odilon Redon (1840-1916): "Death: I am the one who will make a serious woman of you; come, let us embrace." Lithograph illustration of 1896 for "La Tentation de Saint-Antoine" (The Temptation of St Anthony) by Gustave Flaubert.

The Reign of Silence

Ah! vous êtes mes sœurs, les âmes qui vivez
Dans ce doux nonchaloir des rêves mi-rêvés
Parmi l'isolement léthargique des villes
Qui somnolent au long des rivières débiles ;
Ames dont le silence est une piété,
Ames à qui le bruit fait mal ; dont l'amour n'aime
Que ce qui pouvait être et n'aura pas été ;...

Ames comme des fleurs et comme des sourdines
Autour de qui vont s'enroulant les angélus
Comme autour des rouets la douceur de la laine !

Et vous aussi, mes sœurs, vous qui n'êtes en peine
Que d'un long chapelet bénit à dépêcher
Et un doux béguinage à l'ombre d'un clocher,
Oh! vous, mes Sœurs, — car c'est ce cher nom que l'Eglise
M'enseigne à vous donner, sœurs pleines de douceurs,
Dans ce halo de linge où le front s'angélise,
Oh! Vous qui m'êtes plus que pour d'autres des sœurs
Chastes dans votre robe à plis qui se balance,
O vous mes sœurs en Notre Mère, le Silence !

Georges Rodenbach, from *Le Règne du Silence*, 1891

(Ah! you are my sisters, the souls who live in this sweet aloofness of half-dreamt dreams amid the lethargic isolation of towns slumbering beside feeble rivers; souls whose silence is piety, souls to whom noise does harm; whose love cares only for what could be and will not have been; ... souls like flowers and muted tones round which will come and wind the sounds of ave-bells like the softness of wool round the spinning wheels! And you too, my sisters, you whose only pains are to dispatch a long, consecrated rosary in a pleasant convent in the shade of a bell tower. Oh you, my sisters, —for by this dear name the Church tells me to call you, sisters full of sweetness, in this halo of cloth as round an angel's brow, oh you who for me more than others are chaste sisters in your robe of swaying folds, oh you my sisters in Our Mother, Silence!)

Xavier Mellery (1845-1921) : Beguines Praying, c. 1890. Indian ink.

Uncertain Virgin

Toi qui verses, les nuits tendres, sur tes pieds blancs
Des larmes de statue oubliée et brisée,
Telle une douloureuse et mystique rosée,
Par qui se courbent les doux calices tremblants,

J'irai, ce soir, vers l'eau taciturne où bleuissent
De pâles fleurs, dans la triste mare d'azur,
Cueillir pour tes doigts longs l'iris antique et pur
Que les pleurs amoureux de la fontaine emplissent.

Ainsi je t'aimerai dans ton droit vêtement,
Tes yeux morts dans les miens arrêtés longuement,
Avec ma fleur en tes mains vagues d'innocence;

Nous resterons longtemps muets, d'ombre voilés,
Et je t'adorerai sous ces bois violets
Où de pudiques lys grandissent en silence...

Paul Valéry, *Vierge incertaine*, published in *La Conque*, Paris, 1891

(You who over your white feet, in tender nights, pour the tears of a forgotten and shattered statue, like an aching, mystic dew, beside whom bend the sweet trembling chalices, I shall go tonight to the silent water wherein pale flowers turn blue, and in the sad pool of azure I'll pluck for your long fingers the pure ancient iris which the love tears of the fountain fill. Thus shall I love you in your straight-falling garment, your dead eyes lingering long in mine, with my flower in your hands vague with innocence; we'll long remain silent, veiled in shadow, and I'll worship you under these purple woods where shy lilies grow in silence...)

△ *Fernand Khnopff (1858-1921): Silence, 1890. Pastel.*

▷ *Odilon Redon (1840-1916): Closed Eyes, 1890. Oil.*

1. *Franz von Stuck (1863-1928): Spring, c. 1909. Oil.*

2. *Gaetano Previati (1852-1920): The Funeral of the Virgin. Oil.*

3. *Jan Toorop (1858-1928): The Three Brides, 1893. Pencil, black chalk and colour.*

4. *Jan Toorop (1858-1928): Illustration for "Egedius en de vreemdeling"*
   (Egedius and the Stranger) by W.G. van Nouhuys, Haarlem, 1899.

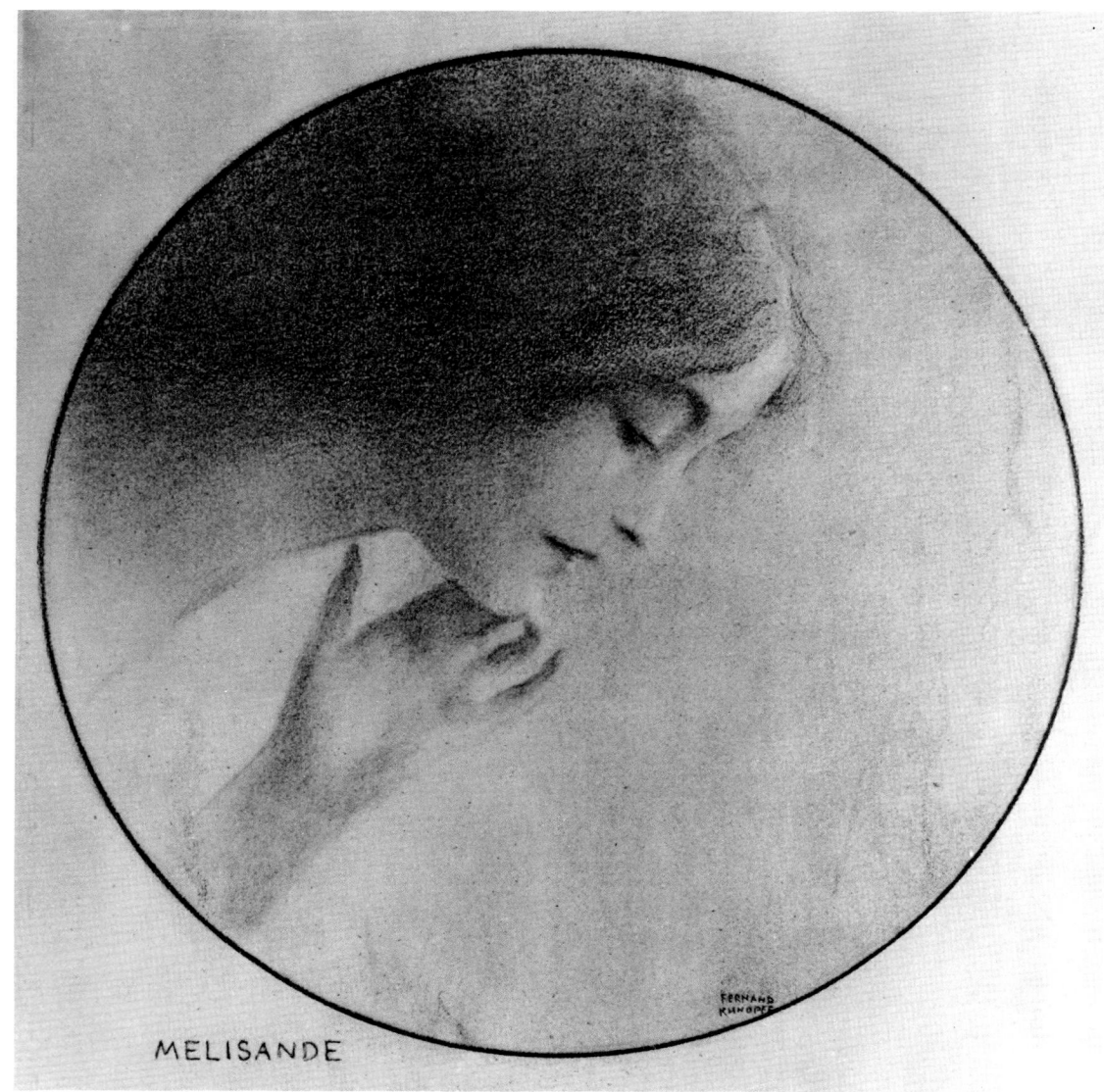

MELISANDE

Fernand Khnopff (1858-1921) : Melisande. Charcoal and coloured crayons.

Song of Mélisande

L'eau qui pleure et l'eau qui rit,
L'eau qui parle et l'eau qui fuit,
L'eau qui tremble dans la nuit...

L'anneau glisse et l'anneau luit,
L'anneau trouble l'eau qui fuit,
L'anneau tombe dans la nuit...

L'anneau tombe et la couronne,
Que les anges nous pardonnent!...
La couronne tombe aussi
Dans l'eau froide et dans la nuit...

Maurice Maeterlinck, *Chanson de Mélisande*,
from *Serres chaudes*, 1889

(The weeping water and the laughing water, the speaking water and the fleeting water, the water trembling in the night... The ring glides and the ring shines, the ring troubles the fleeting water, the ring falls in the night... The ring falls and the crown, may the angels forgive us! The crown falls too in the chill water and in the night...)

Te souviens-tu de ces plumes de paon,
dans un grand vase, auprès de coquillages?...

Viens, viens, ma chère Clara d'Ellébeuse;
aimons-nous encore, si tu existes.
Le vieux jardin a de vieilles tulipes.
Viens toute nue, ô Clara d'Ellébeuse.

(Do you remember those peacock plumes, in a large
vase, beside some seashells?... Come, do come, my
dear Clara of Ellébeuse; let us be loving still, if you
exist. The old garden has some old tulips. Come all
naked to me, oh Clara of Ellébeuse.)

Francis Jammes, *De l'Angélus*
de l'Aube à l'Angélus du soir,
1888-1897.

Odilon Redon (1840-1916):
Woman's Profile with Flowers,
c. 1890-1895. Charcoal.

The Peacock Woman

Des paons légers suivent une femme
    Sur le bleu d'un rêve.
Une blancheur, un épithalame
    De plumes s'élève.

Les paons sont blancs, les plumes sont blanches.
    Elle, est rouge, et nue.
Les paons câlins suivent vers ses hanches
    L'odeur reconnue.

Effleurant l'herbe, allongeant leurs queues
    Ils vont derrière elle
Qui disparaît sous les branches bleues
    Fugitive et frêle

C'est un soupir, c'est une caresse
    Leur démarche ailée.
Ils ont aimé cette chasseresse
    Dans l'ombre étoilée

Ils ont moulé leur col a son ventre
    A son dos leurs plumes
Et doucement se glissent vers l'antre
    Comme un vol de brumes.

Vers l'antre bleu des fleurs nuptiales
    Des fleurs fraternelles
Où s'abandonnent les cheveux pâles
    Mêlés dans les ailes.

Pierre Louÿs, *La femme aux paons*,
published in *La Conque*, Paris, 1891

(Light peacocks follow a woman over the blue of a dream. Up rises a whiteness, an epithalamium of feathers. The peacocks are white, the feathers are white. She is red and naked. The love-sick peacocks follow to her hips the odour they know. Skimming the grass, extending their tails they go along behind her as she vanishes, fleeting and frail, beneath the blue branches. A sigh it is, a caress, their winged walk. They have loved that huntress in the starlit shadow. They have spread their neck over her belly, over her back their plumes, and softly they slip towards the cavern like a drift of haze. Towards the blue cavern of wedding flowers, of brotherly flowers, where the pale hair surrenders, mixed in the wings.)

Edmond Aman-Jean (1859-1936) : Girl with a Peacock, 1895. Oil.

Rose with dark eyes, mirror of your nothingness, rose with dark eyes, make us believe in the mystery, hypocrite flower, flower of silence.

Rose the colour of pure gold, oh safe deposit of the ideal, rose the colour of pure gold, give us the key of your womb, hypocrite flower, flower of silence.

Rose the colour of silver, censer of our dreams, rose the colour of silver, take our heart and turn it into smoke, hypocrite flower, flower of silence.

Remy de Gourmont, *Litanies de la rose* (Litanies of the Rose), 1896

SONNET

Que ta maison soit douce, et qu'en ton jardin mûr
Le noueux espalier s'entre-croise à la treille,
Que Décembre l'argente et que Mai l'ensoleille,
Et que la rose soit plus haute que le mur!

Si le couchant ruisselle en flammes dans l'azur
Ou si l'aube au ciel pâle en souriant s'éveille,
Que ta douce maison qui songe et qui sommeille
S'ouvre aux parfums légers qu'apporte le vent pur.

Que le paon ébloui et la colombe blanche
Qui roue en l'herbe verte ou gémit sur la branche
Franchissent librement la fenêtre et le seuil,

Et, doux de neige tiède ou froid de pierreries,
Que l'oiseau de l'Amour ou l'oiseau de l'Orgueil
Entrent y voir dormir l'Espoir aux mains fleuries.

HENRI DE RÉGNIER.

Sonnet by Henri de Régnier
published in "L'Image," Paris, April 1897.

William Degouve de Nuncques (1867-1935): Angels in the Night, 1894. Oil.

Maurice Denis (1870-1943): Threefold Portrait of Yvonne Lerolle, 1897. Oil.

Apparition

La lune s'attristait. Des séraphins en pleurs
Rêvant, l'archet aux doigts, dans le calme des fleurs
Vaporeuses, tiraient de mourantes violes
De blancs sanglots glissant sur l'azur des corolles
— C'était le jour béni de ton premier baiser.
Ma songerie aimant à me martyriser
S'enivrait savamment du parfum de tristesse
Que même sans regret et sans déboire laisse
La cueillaison d'un Rêve au cœur qui l'a cueilli.
J'errais donc, l'œil rivé sur le pavé vieilli
Quand avec du soleil aux cheveux, dans la rue
Et dans le soir, tu m'es en riant apparue
Et j'ai cru voir la fée au chapeau de clarté
Qui jadis sur mes beaux sommeils d'enfant gâté
Passait, laissant toujours de ses mains mal fermées
Neiger de blancs bouquets d'étoiles parfumées.

Stéphane Mallarmé

(The moon grew sad. Seraphs in tears dreaming, the bow in their fingers, in the calm of vaporous flowers, drew from dying viols white sobs gliding over the blue of corollas.—It was the blessed day of your first kiss. My daydreams loving to torment me revelled knowingly in the perfume of sadness that even without regret or disappointment the plucking of a Dream leaves in the heart of the plucker. So I wandered, my eye riveted to the aged paving, when with sun in your hair, at evening in the street, you appeared before me laughing and I thought I saw the fairy with the hat of light who once passed through the happy slumbers of my pampered childhood, forever snowing down from her unclenched hands white bouquets of fragrant stars.)

Lucien Lévy-Dhurmer (1865-1953): The Gust of Wind, 1896. Oil.

Les Petites Faunesses

Deux faunesses, parmi l'ombre et les herbes bleues,
Se poursuivent au clair de lune, vers la source.
Leurs croupes lestes que bouleverse la course
Font danser les poils ronds de leurs petites queues.

Elles galopent, et leurs sveltes pieds de chèvres
Vont, déchirant les fleurs et sautant les racines.
Elles ont aux cheveux, étant un peu cousines,
Mêmes cornes, et même intense flamme aux lèvres.

Mais voici l'eau, qui sort d'une caverne noire...
Elles grimpent aux rocs, se culbutent pour boire,
Trempent leurs seins aigus entre les hautes pierres,

Se cambrent, battent l'air de leurs pieds, que prolongent
Les ombres, et, pressant leurs mains sur leurs paupières,
Du sommet des rochers dans la cascade plongent.

Pierre Loüys.

"Les Petites Faunesses" (The Little Girl-Fauns), poem
by Pierre Loüys published in "L'Image," Paris, January 1896.

...As for the women in these stories,
why should they not be
Diabolical? Do they not have
enough of the she-devil in them
to deserve this nice name? The Diabolical!
Not one of them here
but is diabolical in some degree.
There is not one of them to whom
you could seriously apply
the word *Angel* without exaggerating.
Like the Devil, who was once an angel too,
but came a cropper,
if they are angels, they are angels like him:
head downwards and their crupper in the air!

Jules Barbey d'Aurevilly,
preface to *Les Diaboliques*, 1874

Félicien Rops (1833-1898):
△ *Pornocrates, 1896. Etching and aquatint.*
◁ *Illustration for the story "Le Rideau cramoisi"*
(The Crimson Curtain) in "Les Diaboliques" by
Jules Barbey d'Aurevilly. Drawing, 1879.

In the failure of nerve that unmanned me, the insane and atrocious idea of throwing the body of this beautiful girl, my mistress for six months past! out of the window flashed across my mind. Despise me if you will! I opened the window... I parted that curtain you see there... I gazed into the pit of shadow at the bottom of which lay the street, for it was a very dark night...

Jules Barbey d'Aurevilly, *Le Rideau Cramoisi*, in *Les Diaboliques*, 1874

Walter Crane (1845-1915) : Neptune's Horses, 1893. Oil.

The Waves

Gustav Klimt (1862-1918) : Moving Waters, 1898. Oil.

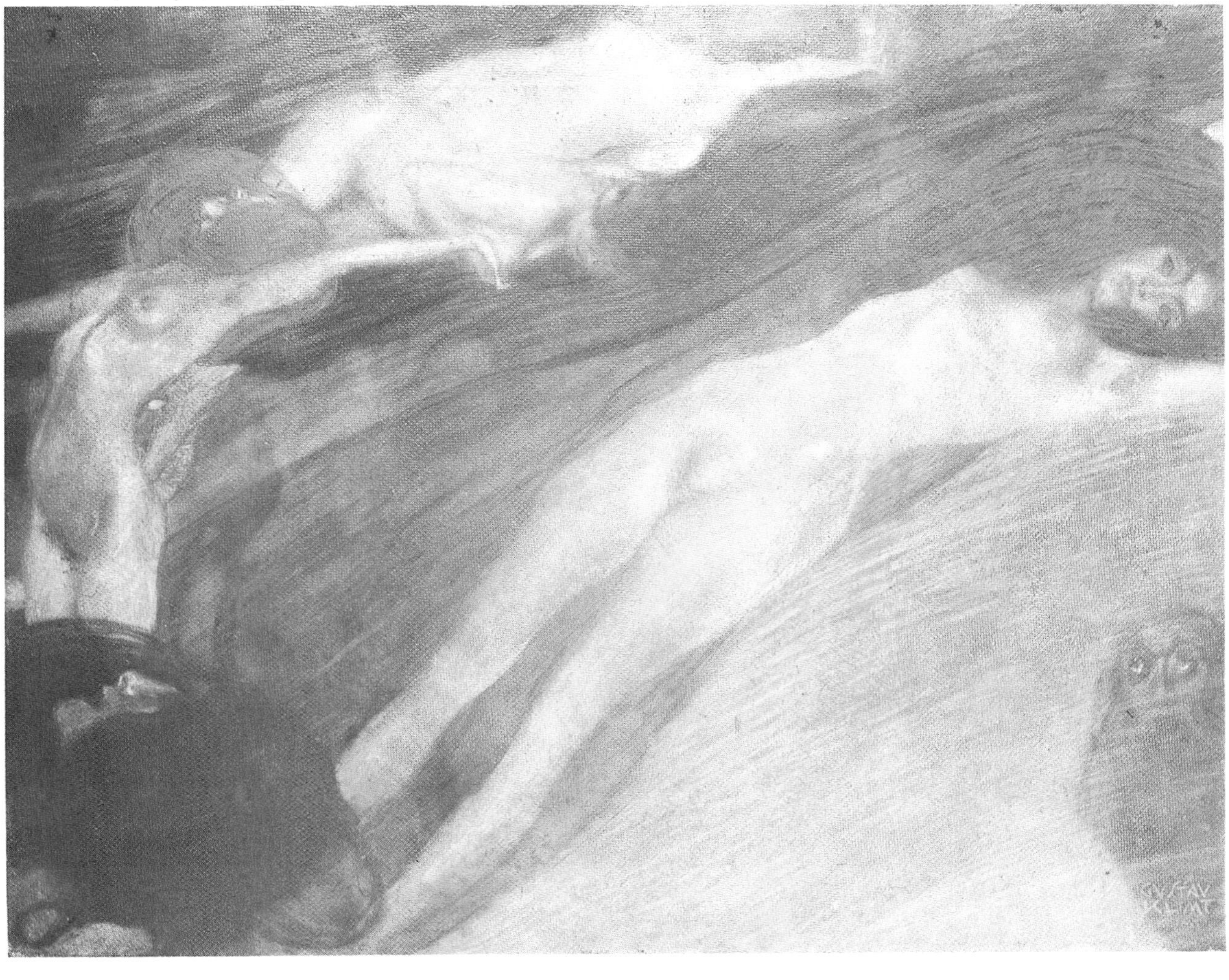

Consider the sea's listless chime:
　　Time's self it is, made audible,—
　　The murmur of the earth's own shell.
Secret continuance sublime
　　Is the sea's end: our sight may pass
　　No furlong further. Since time was,
This sound hath told the lapse of time.

No quiet, which is death's,—it hath
　　The mournfulness of ancient life,
　　Enduring always at dull strife.
As the world's heart of rest and wrath,
　　Its painful pulse is in the sands.
　　Last utterly, the whole sky stands,
Grey and not known, along its path.

Listen alone beside the sea,
　　Listen alone among the woods;
　　Those voices of twin solitudes
Shall have one sound alike to thee:
　　Hark where the murmurs of thronged men
　　Surge and sink back and surge again,—
Still the one voice of wave and tree.

Gather a shell from the strown beach
　　And listen at its lips: they sigh
　　The same desire and mystery,
The echo of the whole sea's speech.
　　And all mankind is thus at heart
　　Not anything but what thou art:
And Earth, Sea, Man, are all in each.

Dante Gabriel Rossetti,
The Sea-Limits, from *Poems*, 1870

Auguste Rodin (1840-1917): The Wave, before 1887. Marble.

Max Klinger (1857-1920) : Forsaken, 1883. Etching and aquatint from the set "Ein Leben" (A Life).

Giovanni Segantini (1858-1899) : The Evil Mothers, 1894. Oil.

The Sirens

Come to the land where none grows old,
And none is rash or over-bold,
Nor any noise there is or war,
Or rumour from wild lands afar,
Or plagues, or birth and death of kings;
No vain desire of unknown things
Shall vex you there, no hope or fear
Of that which never draweth near;
But in that lovely land and still
Ye may remember what ye will,
And what ye will, forget for aye.

So while the kingdoms pass away,
Ye sea-beat hardened toilers erst,
Unresting, for vain fame athirst,
Shall be at peace for evermore,
With hearts fulfilled of Godlike lore,
And calm, unwavering Godlike love,
No lapse of time can turn or move.
There, ages after your fair Fleece
Is clean forgotten, yea, and Greece
Is no more counted glorious,
Alone with us, alone with us,
Alone with us, dwell happily,
Beneath our trembling roof of sea.

William Morris, the Sirens to the Argonauts,
from *The Life and Death of Jason*, 1867

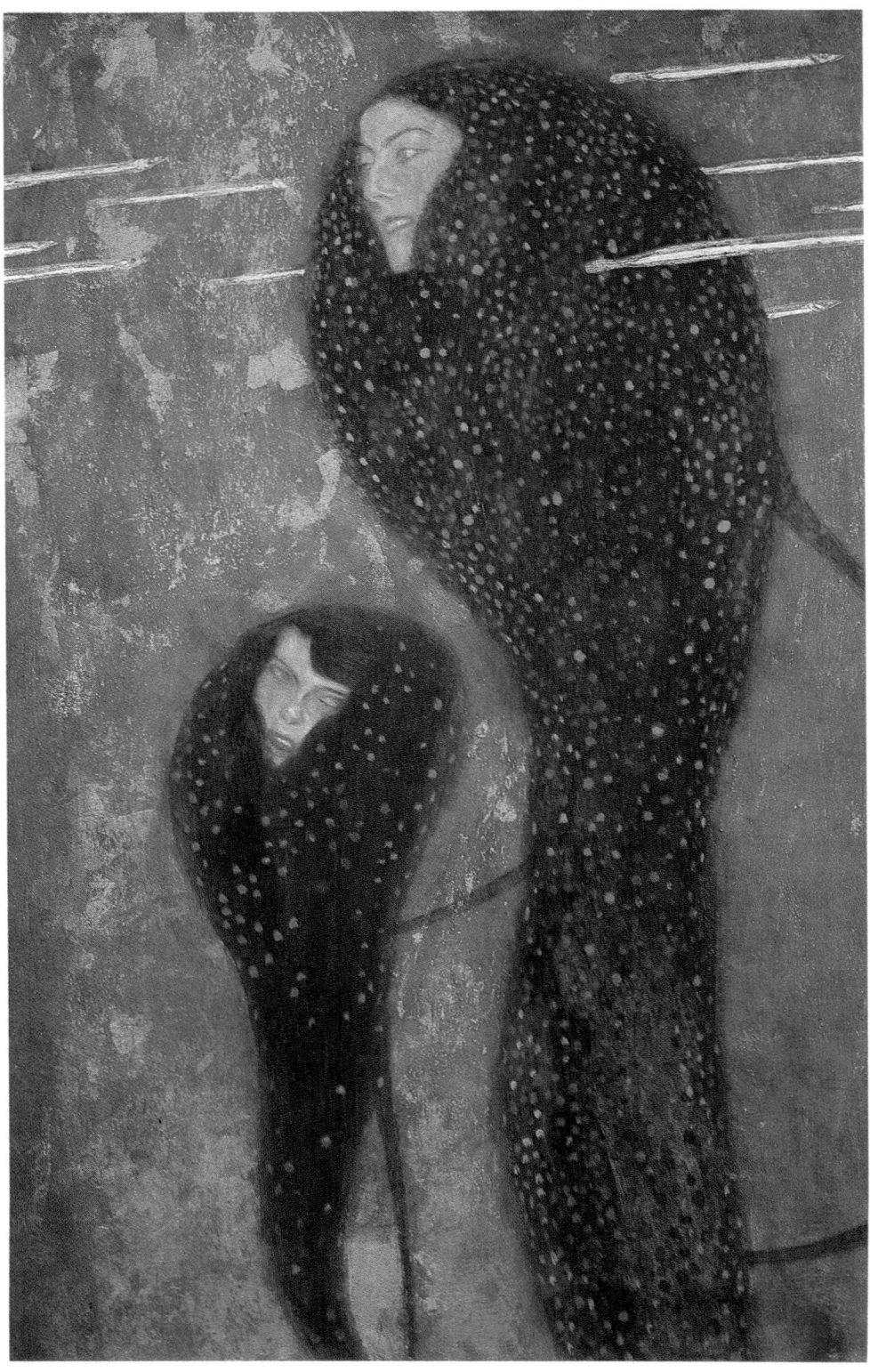

Gustav Klimt (1862-1918): The Sirens, c. 1889. Oil.

Jean Delville (1867-1953): The Idol of Perversity, 1891. Drawing.

The Shudder of the Sphinx

Félicien Rops (1833-1898):
Frontispiece for "Les Diaboliques"
(The Diabolical) by Jules Barbey d'Aurevilly.
Drawing, 1879.

Au pays des Huros, Rhamsès et Sésostris,
mais au temps des Latins et quand la rouge Rome
dressait de bronze et d'or ses empereurs flétris,
c'est l'heure où l'infini pénètre au cœur de l'homme.

Pareille à l'orbe élu des grands nimbes sacrés
dont la tête des saints futurs doit être ceinte,
la lune en fleur sourit ses rêves éthérés
dans l'encens sidéral frôlant la terre sainte.

Au loin des sables bleus du biblique désert,
couché dans son secret et sa béatitude,
le monstre égyptien, de son œil entr'ouvert,
fixe l'éternité parmi la solitude.

Nul souffle dans la nuit. Mais, parfois, obstiné,
le hurlement lointain d'un vieux fauve qui rôde
et renifle à longs traits, ver l'horizon tourné,
les tragiques relents du grand crime d'Hérode.

Jean Delville, *Le frisson du Sphinx*, 1897

(In the land of Huros, Ramesses and Sesostris, but in the time of
the Latins and when ruddy Rome upraised in bronze and gold
her wasted emperors, this is the hour when the infinite penetrates
the heart of man. Like the elected orb of the great sacred haloes
with which the head of future saints should be encircled, the moon
in blossom smiles her ethereal dreams in sidereal incense brushing
against the holy land. Far in the blue sands of the biblical desert,
reclining in her secrecy and beatitude, the Egyptian monster, with
her half-open eye, gazes at eternity amid the solitude. Not a breath
in the night. But, at times, persistently, the distant howling of an
old beast that roams and with long-drawn snuffling, turned hori-
zonwards, scents the tragic exhalations of Herod's great crime.)

Franz von Stuck (1863-1928):
Salome, 1906. Oil.

Fernand Khnopff (1858-1921): Art (The Caresses or The Sphinx), 1896. Oil.

133

Lucien Lévy-Dhurmer (1865-1953): Salome Embracing the Severed Head of John the Baptist, 1896. Pastel.

Ill-starred Prayers

Que ta bouche soit bénie, car elle est adultère!
Elle a le goût des roses nouvelles et le goût de la vieille terre,
Elle a sucé les sucs obscurs des fleurs et des roseaux;
Quand elle parle on entend comme un bruit perfide de roseaux,
Et ce rubis cruel tout sanglant et tout froid,
C'est la dernière blessure de Jésus sur la croix.

Que ton âme soit bénie, car elle est corrompue!
Fière émeraude tombée sur le pavé des rues,
Son orgueil s'est mêlé aux odeurs de la boue,
Et je viens d'écraser dans la glorieuse boue,
Sur le pavé des rues, qui est un chemin de croix,
La dernière pensée de Jésus sur la croix.

(May your mouth be blessed, for it is adulterous! It has the taste of new roses and the taste of old earth, it has sucked in the dim pith of flowers and reeds; when it speaks, what one hears is like a treacherous rustle of reeds, and this cruel ruby all blood-stained and cold is the last wound of Jesus on the cross. May your soul be blessed, for it is corrupt! A proud emerald fallen on the paving of the streets, its haughtiness has blended with the smells of the mud, and I have just crushed in the glorious mud, on the paving of the streets, which is a way of the cross, the last thought of Jesus on the cross.)

Remy de Gourmont, *Oraisons mauvaises,* 1900

The Vampire

Toi qui, comme un coup de couteau,
Dans mon cœur plaintif es entrée;
Toi qui, forte comme un troupeau
De démons, vins, folle et parée,

De mon esprit humilié
Faire ton lit et ton domaine;
— Infâme à qui je suis lié
Comme le forçat à la chaîne,

Comme au jeu le joueur têtu,
Comme à la bouteille l'ivrogne,
Comme aux vermines la charogne,
— Maudite, maudite sois-tu!

J'ai prié le glaive rapide
De conquérir ma liberté,
Et j'ai dit au poison perfide
De secourir ma lâcheté.

Hélas! le poison et le glaive
M'ont pris en dédain et m'ont dit:
« Tu n'es pas digne qu'on t'enlève
A ton esclavage maudit,

Imbécile! — de son empire
Si nos efforts te délivraient,
Tes baisers ressusciteraient
Le cadavre de ton vampire! »

Charles Baudelaire, *Les Fleurs du Mal*, 1857

(Woman who, like the stab of a knife, have entered my doleful heart; you who came, wild and gaudy, strong as a pack of demons, and made your bed and your domain of my humbled mind;—vile woman to whom I'm bound like the convict to the chain, like the stubborn gambler to the game, like the drunkard to the bottle, like the carrion to the vermin,—a curse, a curse upon you! I've begged the quick sword-blade to win my freedom for me, and I've asked the perfidious poison to succour my cowardice. Alas! the poison and the sword held me up to scorn and said: "You do not deserve to be released from your accursed thraldom, you fool—even if our efforts delivered you from her sway, your kisses would resuscitate the corpse of your vampire!")

Aubrey Beardsley (1872-1898): The Dancer's Reward (Salome with the Head of John the Baptist). Illustration for Oscar Wilde's "Salome," London, 1894.

Edvard Munch (1863-1944):
Vampire, c. 1893. Oil.

135

Remember

Remember me when I am gone away,
  Gone far away into the silent land;
  When you can no more hold me by the hand
Nor I half turn to go yet turning stay.
Remember me when no more day by day
  You tell me of our future that you plann'd:
  Only remember me; you understand
It will be late to counsel then or pray.
Yet if you should forget me for a while
  And afterwards remember, do not grieve:
  For if the darkness and corruption leave
A vestige of the thoughts that once I had,
Better by far you should forget and smile
  Than that you should remember and be sad.

Christina Rossetti

Max Klinger (1857-1920):
Dead Mother, 1890. Etching from the
set "Vom Tode" (On Death), part two.

Edvard Munch (1863-1944):
Lovers in the Waves, 1896.
Lithograph.

136

Death and Life

Last night returning from my twilight walk
I met the grey mist Death, whose eyeless brow
Was bent on me, and from his hand of chalk
He reached me flowers as from a withered bough:
O Death, what bitter nosegays givest thou!

Death said, I gather, and pursued his way.
Another stood by me, a shape in stone,
Sword-hacked and iron-stained, with breasts of clay,
And metal veins that sometimes fiery shone:
O Life, how naked and how hard when known!

Life said, As thou hast carved me, such am I.
Then memory, like the nightjar on the pine,
And sightless hope, a woodlark in night sky,
Joined notes of Death and Life till night's decline.
Of Death, of Life, those inwound notes are mine.

George Meredith, *A Ballad of Past Meridian*, 1876

Odilon Redon (1840-1916):
"Death: my irony surpasses all others."
Lithograph illustration of 1889 for "La
Tentation de Saint-Antoine" (The
Temptation of St Anthony)
by Gustave Flaubert.

Paul Gauguin (1848-1903):
"Madame la Mort" (Lady Death), 1891.
Illustration for a play by Rachilde.
Charcoal and wash drawing.

Lovers' Talk

Dans le vieux parc solitaire et glacé,
Deux formes ont tout à l'heure passé.

Leurs yeux sont morts et leurs lèvres sont molles,
Et l'on entend à peine leurs paroles.

Dans le vieux parc solitaire et glacé
Deux spectres ont évoqué le passé.

—Te souvient-il de notre extase ancienne?
— Pourquoi voulez-vous donc qu'il m'en souvienne?

Paul Verlaine, *Fêtes galantes*, 1869

(In the old park lonely and cold as ice, two figures have passed just now. Their eyes are dead and their lips are limp, and their words can scarcely be heard. In the old park lonely and cold as ice, two ghosts have evoked the past.—Do you remember our rapture of old?—Why should you expect me to remember it still?)

Alfred Kubin (1877-1959): The Bride of Death,
c. 1900. Ink wash drawing.

Edvard Munch (1863-1944): Death and the Maiden, c. 1893. Tempera (?).

Félicien Rops (1833-1898): Death Spreading Confusion. Soft-ground etching.

Aubrey Beardsley (1872-1898): The Fourth Tableau of "Das Rheingold".
Cover design for "The Savoy," No. 6, London, 1896.

6

SIGNS IN THEIR PROPER PLACE

1894-1896

Cold eyelids that hide like a jewel
  Hard eyes that grow soft for an hour;
The heavy white limbs, and the cruel
  Red mouth like a venomous flower;
When these are gone by with their glories,
  What shall rest of thee then, what remain,
O mystic and sombre Dolores,
  Our Lady of Pain?

Seven sorrows the priests give their Virgin;
  But thy sins, which are seventy times seven,
Seven ages would fail thee to purge in,
  And then they would haunt thee in heaven:
Fierce midnights and famishing morrows,
  And the loves that complete and control
All the joys of the flesh, all the sorrows
  That wear out the soul.

O garment not golden but gilded,
  O garden where all men may dwell,
O tower not of ivory, but builded
  By hands that reach heaven from hell;
O mystical rose of the mire,
  O house not of gold but of gain,
O house of unquenchable fire,
  Our Lady of Pain! ·

A. C. Swinburne, *Dolores*, from *Poems and Ballads*, 1866

 NOTHER account of our subject which cannot be omitted by anyone who wishes to cover the main evidence was that of the cautious Ferdinand Brunetière, who in 1893 took Symbolism as his theme in the last of a series of lectures he gave at the Sorbonne on "The Evolution of Lyric Poetry in the Nineteenth Century." It was published in the *Revue Bleue* of 17 June. Academic recognition had been on the way ever since, on 1 April 1891, Brunetière had published, in the extremely conformist *Revue des Deux Mondes*, an essay which Jacques Lethève has rightly described as "a kind of revolution." Brunetière, the most highly qualified representative of official criticism, wrote as follows: "It is amazing that the mere words 'Symbolism' and 'Symbol' rarely call forth anything around them but scornful laughter, while all around us everything is symbol and nothing else... Generally speaking, since there is nothing in the world which cannot if necessary express, signify or suggest something more than itself, there is nothing which is not or might not in some way become a symbol. Let us learn this if we did not know it already, but if we do know it already, let us not mock and pretend to be astonished when we are confronted by symbolism. If we do, it is us people ought to be laughing at."

At the same time the incorruptible Catulle Mendès—who had not been misled by Wagnerism—presiding over a group of aesthetes in the Napolitain, "the tiny cream and gold boulevard café with red plush seats, a sort of low-ceilinged corridor," told that intermittent Parisian Oscar Wilde, in a "pale yellow and pink," imperious phrase recorded by Ernest Raynaud, who would never say anything that could not be checked for accuracy: "The symbolists make one laugh. They haven't invented a thing. Symbols have existed since the world began. And to whom do they appeal as their authority? To Baudelaire, an elegiac Satan. The French writers they claim as their masters are just Parnassians gone wrong. Verlaine is a Desbordes-Valmore in trousers. Mallarmé, as Charles Cros used to say, is a broken Baudelaire who couldn't be put together again. What is Rimbaud but a belated romantic, and what is Tristan Corbière but an unsuccessful parody of Pierre Dupont? Jules Laforgue made a certain stir. But he's just a sketch of God knows what, a stammering attempt. His loud, childish verses were a surprise rather than a success. Tomorrow they'll be forgotten. Nor have the symbolists produced any formal innovations. The real initiator of *vers libre* and symbolist technique was a Peruvian from Lima, artillery lieutenant della Rocca de Vergalo who introduced into prosody the 'Nicarene stanza' and all the liberties the new poets avail themselves of. He ignored unsounded syllables, did away with capital letters at the beginning of lines, dropped the alternation of masculine and feminine rhymes, and ultimately arrived at a kind of rhythmic prose. And that's what *vers libres* are. The Peruvian poet said himself, 'I'll start a fashion because my poetry is a revolution.'"

Without any other reaction than that Catulle Mendès was a devil of a fellow and terribly amusing, Wilde took his friend Raynaud off to look at luxury shops and jewellers' windows. He adored jewels, Wilde said, like all pointless and beautiful things whose uselessness made them expensive. It was contemplating jewellery which inspired him to write *Salome*: the idea came to him, wearing a helmet of gold, in a shower of precious stones. What Wilde, that "play-actor of genius," omitted to mention was that he was also remembering *A Rebours*. Also Moreau,

141

Flaubert, Laforgue, Mallarmé, perhaps Heine too. Maeterlinck, anyway, because it was from him that Wilde borrowed the technique and the ambiguity of *La Princesse Maleine*. He wrote his *Salome* directly in French, in Paris in 1891; one legend has it that it was written for Sarah Bernhardt, another that the main image was suggested by a wax model of a decapitated head which Wilde saw on a tray at Jean Lorrain's house. First published in 1893 by *L'Art Indépendant*, the play was banned from performance until 1896, when it was produced, with a moderate degree of success, by Lugné-Poe and his Compagnie de l'Œuvre at the Comédie Parisienne, with Lina Munte as Salome and Lugné-Poe himself as Herod.

Meanwhile the play had been published in English in London in 1894, translated by Lord Alfred Douglas, the young friend with whom Wilde had a relationship which earned him two years in jail. But perhaps the most striking thing about the publication was the set of sixteen "illustrations," more symbolic, voluptuous and deviant than the slim volume itself. They were by Aubrey Beardsley, an ardent young Wagnerian believed to be one of the "Green Carnation" set of intellectual snobs and said to have had an incestuous attachment to his elder sister Mabel. Beardsley had "the fatal swiftness of those doomed to die young," and "ended a long career in the arms of the Church"—at the age of twenty-six. He had a high opinion of himself and lived in constant hopes of winning immediate and resounding success. In 1892 Puvis de Chavannes had already described him as "a young English artist who does astonishing things." They were more than astonishing—they were diabolical. Small drawings executed in Indian ink, insubstantial, fleshless, a language of the void, a space of terrifying fascination. Incisions, coils, whorls, flames lassoed and embraced the white, striped the black, measuring the surface and fragmenting it. Here were signs in their proper place, in the very act of transmission. Writing made its entrance, and set up a numerical relationship with the image. Was it mere transcription of words? "I am Salome, daughter of Herodias, Princess of Judaea." "How beautiful is the Princess Salome tonight!" "Why does she look at me with her yellow eyes?" "I shall kiss thy mouth, Jokanaan. I shall kiss thy mouth." "Is that the queen, she who wears a black head-dress sewn with pearls?" "Salome, come sit near me. I will give thee the throne of thy mother." "As queen thou wilt be very lovely, Salome." "Your little feet will be like... little white flowers that dance upon a tree." "I will dance for you, Tetrarch." "I ask for the head of Jokanaan on a silver charger." "It is said that love has a bitter taste... but what matters it?"

Every illustration is a hallucination induced by words. Each time, the verbal text is invaded by a dream writing in which all is said anew, the dreamer inventing his own graphic grammar. The points at which signifiers touch are slight, the distance between things signified full of tension and violence. This is because, between the two, all the sexual material borne along by dream has entered into action, powered by the energy which circulates between the unconscious and the conscious. According to Freud, when writing consists in "making liquid flow from a pen on to a blank sheet of paper" it takes on "the symbolic significance of copulation." Probably Beardsley's work should all be linked to this notion of metaphorical cathexis in which the imagery expresses a fundamental substitution. This substitution was so inspired that the "illustrations" of Wilde's text surpass with ease their original. This is true of all the "images" which Beardsley took from the silence of the word and made echo through space. This was especially the case whenever the icon or image referred only to himself.

Beardsley put between himself and the writer he was supposed to be representing, illustrating, or commenting upon, a distance sufficient to guarantee the necessary inwardness as well as the excess which enabled him to cross the realm of everyday discontinuity, the neutral zone of the "workaday" world which is defined only by its prohibitions, and to reach the challenging summit of taut, condensed, indelible signs. These were the heights that might contain an abbreviation by Callot, a vibration by Seurat, a grapheme by Rubens, a track left by Daumier, a trace by Leonardo, or a path followed by Uccello. A level of transposition—or, as it used to be called, invention—opening on to the absolute

Aubrey Beardsley (1872-1898):

◁ *Three illustrations for "Le Morte d'Arthur" by Sir Thomas Malory, published by Den[...] London, 1893:*
1. How Sir Bedivere cast the sword Excalib[...] into the water, Book XXI, chapter V.
2. How King Arthur saw the Questing Bea[...] and thereof had great marvel, Book I, chapter XIX.
3. How Queen Guenever made her a nun [...] Almesbury, Book XXI, chapter VII.

▽ *Atalanta. Design (not used) for "The Yello[...] Book," London, April 1895.*

All is symbol

Aubrey Beardsley (1872-1898):
Design for the frontispiece to
"Virgilius the Sorcerer," 1893.

of the irreversible, of permanent communication, whenever the signs may happen to be read. Apart from the pages where amphibian curves led him to his greatest heights—I am thinking of *The Dancer's Reward, The Climax, The Platonic Lament, The Toilette of Salome*—his scope is still limited by listening to others. It is clear that Beardsley, before he really found himself, illustrating Malory's *Morte d'Arthur*, was still involved with topographical, and thus linguistic, preoccupations inherited from the Pre-Raphaelites. But equally clear is the plastic economy of Japanese prints which helped him to break free of the poetics of Burne-Jones; and the influence of the two-dimensional nature of Greek vase painting on Beardsley's development of the flamboyant signs which traverse, in some space out of space, those icy regions, infernal pallors, and black gulfs full of smooth yet ravaged variations, where symbols alone survive. Blood and bonds, peacocks and lilies. Roland Barthes reminds us that Freud saw plaited locks as "the work of a woman plaiting her pubic hair to make the penis she lacks." Whether the textile is graphic or verbal—text, tissue or tress, they are all the same—it cannot be reduced to just a passing meaning. An unambiguous reading is just a partial reading, a truncated interpretation, the cutting off of a lock of hair, an attempt at castration.

Beardsley was in Paris in 1893 and met Puvis de Chavannes, Wilde, Jean Moréas, Stuart Merrill, Jean Lorrain, Whistler and others, deliberately exhibiting himself in grey silk gloves and grey kid shoes. He created a sensation at the dinners held at the Côte d'Or, a fashionable restaurant at the corner of the Rue Médicis and the Rue Vaugirard. He was soon an actual reflection of himself, and his gift for parody, which disconcerted even his nearest and dearest, led him, in the established English tradition of the poet-cum-artist, to write the novel *Under the Hill*. Part of it was published in the first two numbers of *The Savoy* in 1896; an expurgated edition was issued posthumously in 1904. A contemporary then commented upon the sensitive yet cruel precision with which a man "without passion" observed, for preference, things which were perversely artistic, full of fantastic detail, things both unlikely and possible, brought together from the four quarters of the universe. Thus, in perfect "decadent" style, tricked out with the most voluptuous, subtle and perverse ornaments, together with suitable illustrations, the exquisite Abbé Fanfreluche (who had started as the Abbé Aubrey) hid his inability to live in the morbid depths of furs and fabrics, in a place trembling with strange flowers and heavy with repulsive perfumes, full of gloomy nameless weeds not to be found in Mentzelius; huge butterflies with storied wings, as if they had supped their fill on regal tapestries, slept on the pillars that flanked the door. In Beardsley's *Ballad of a Barber*, also published in *The Savoy*, in July 1896, there were more signs of perversity: Carrousel, the barber, stimulated by the youthful freshness of a thirteen-year-old princess, cuts her throat with a broken flask of eau de Cologne. Then:

> "He left her softly as a dream
> That leaves a sleeper to his sleep."

This is not the place to analyze the reasons for the instant success of Beardsley's work, but one factor, independent of its morbidity, should be noted. Although, unlike Walter Crane, Beardsley never actually worked as an engraver, he was so well aware of the limits of engraving and of printing technique that his work lent itself perfectly to reproduction in every possible form—books, reviews, posters, book-jackets, book-plates, and so on. He was a graphic designer before his time, one of the first and greatest—if not the greatest—of experts in mass-produced images. He had a very keen sense of graphic communication. In an article published in July 1894 and entitled "The Art of the Hoarding," Beardsley wrote: "Advertisement is an absolute necessity of modern life, and if it can be made beautiful as well as obvious, so much the better for the makers of soap and the public who are likely to wash... Still there is a general feeling that the artist who puts his art into the poster is *déclassé*—on the streets—and consequently of light character. The critics can discover no brush work to prate of, the painter looks askance upon a thing that achieves publicity without a frame, and beauty without modelling, and the public find it hard to

Infernal pallors

Walter Crane (1845-1915): Woodcut illustration for Edmund Spenser's "Faerie Queene," published by George Allen, London, 1894-1897.

Will H. Bradley (1868-1962): Frontispiece and title page for "Fringilla or Tales in Verse" by Richard Doddridge Blackmore, published by The Burrows Brothers Company, Cleveland, 1895.

Walter Crane (1845-1915): Double-page illustration on the endpapers of "The Yellow Dwarf," one of "Walter Crane's Picture Books, Large Series," published by Edmund Evans, London, 1875.

take seriously a poor printed thing left to the mercy of sunshine, soot, and shower, like any old fresco over an Italian church door. What view the bill-sticker and sandwich man take of the subject I have yet to learn. The first is, at least, no bad substitute for a hanging committee... London will soon be resplendent with advertisements, and against a leaden sky skysigns will trace their formal arabesque. Beauty has laid siege to the city, and telegraph wires shall no longer be the sole joy of our aesthetic perceptions."

Beardsley's mission as a graphic designer was greatly encouraged by William Morris. Morris had been a friend of Burne-Jones at Oxford. Himself a poet of medievalist leanings to begin with, he is said to have introduced Rossetti to Arthurian legend. In 1859 Morris married Jane Burden, the beautiful brunette whom Rossetti had tried in vain not to love and who was the model for Queen Guinevere in the one picture Morris is known to have painted, in 1858. "I cannot paint you," he told her, "but I love you." So he set her among the motionless models he surrounded himself with in the Pre-Raphaelite manner, to produce a Gothic canvas which leaned heavily on the work which had won Rossetti the admiration of his contemporaries. But already social preoccupations were beginning to beckon Morris, who believed art should have, or rediscover, a communal meaning and function; that it should be an integral part of the daily life of the masses. These ideas had been defended by Ruskin and Carlyle. Morris meant to give them substance and reality. In 1861, together with Ford Madox Brown, Rossetti and Arthur Hughes, he started a workshop of artists and artisans which was the starting-point of the Arts and Crafts Movement, which produced some of the basic arguments underlying Art Nouveau. The main points of Morris's teaching are to be found in a lecture entitled "The Society of the Future," delivered to the Hammersmith section of the Socialist League on 13 November 1887.

"It is a society which does not know the meaning of the words rich and poor, or the rights of property, or law or legality, or nationality: a society which has no consciousness of being governed; in which equality of condition is a matter of course, and in which no man is rewarded for having served the community by having the power given him to injure it.

"It is a society conscious of a wish to keep life simple, to forgo some of the power over nature won by past ages in order to be more human and less mechanical, and willing to sacrifice something to this end. It would be divided into small communities varying much within the limits allowed by due social ethics, but without rivalry between each other, looking with abhorrence at the idea of a holy race.

Aubrey Beardsley (1872-1898): The Peacock Skirt. Illustration for Oscar Wilde's "Salome," London, 1894.

A medievalizing poet

William Morris (1834-1896): Opening page of the Prologue to "The Canterbury Tales" in "The Works of Geoffrey Chaucer," Kelmscott Press, 1896. Woodcut illustration by Burne-Jones, border decorations and initials by William Morris.

"Being determined to be free, and therefore contented with a life not only simpler but even rougher than the life of slave-owners, division of labour would be habitually limited: men (and women too, of course) would do their work and take their pleasure in their own persons, and not vicariously: the social bond would be habitually and instinctively felt, so that there would be no need to be always asserting it by set forms: the family of blood-relationship would melt into that of the community and of humanity. The pleasures of such a society would be founded on the free exercise of the senses and passions of a healthy human animal, so far as this did not injure the other individuals of the community and so offend against social unity: no one would be ashamed of humanity or ask for anything better than its due development..."

"Men would follow knowledge and the creation of beauty for their own sakes, and not for the enslavement of their fellows, and they would be rewarded by finding their most necessary work grow interesting and beautiful under their hands without their being conscious of it... Being no longer driven to death by anxiety and fear, we should have time to avoid disgracing the earth with filth and squalor, and accidental ugliness would disappear along with that which was the mere birth of fantastic perversity..."

This reads like an extract from a Utopian novel, in the line of Rousseau, Owen, Fourier and Ruskin. But it has a cruel immediacy nowadays, though some people will always decry it as merely affected or naive. To anathematize mechanical civilization and industrial capitalism, to denounce structures based on the emulation and competition which Morris saw as the chief tools of the "great power of modern Europe," will always be to swim against the tide. Barthes has said that

The Chaucer Type

ABCDEFGHIJKLMNOPQRSTUVWXYZ
abcdefghijklmnopqrstuvwxyz
æœ&fffifflffifflffl!?('.,;:-/
1234567890

William Morris (1834-1896): The Chaucer Type, 1893. One of the three typefaces designed by Morris for the Kelmscott Press.

"there is *no discourse* with which money is compatible," and so it was all the more absurd that Ruskin's books were very expensive to buy. The publisher, George Allen, had them printed "far away from unsightly factories, amidst fields of flowers." It is even said that, since nothing ugly was to be involved in their distribution, they were never transported by rail. Nevertheless, between the aims of the aestheticians and those of the aesthetes there were unexpected resemblances, which sometimes produced unforeseen results. Ruskin and Morris, having preached that art belongs to every level of life, saw young ladies walking about London in broad daylight wearing medieval costume; at evening parties, they would appear in dresses copied from old pictures and wearing lilies in their hair. Behind all this there were also the eccentricities of Oscar Wilde, who claimed he could not write except on "yellow satin," and who had campaigned for dress reform wearing a velvet coat with silver buttons, white breeches and stockings, and a symbolical sunflower.

Such Pre-Raphaelite ardours both exasperated Morris and inspired him to direct his social and creative effort towards books. It was a formidable ambition. How was his aesthetic socialism to be reconciled with his "hatred of modern civilization" and his desire to offer the worker a life in which the apprehension of beauty, i.e. the enjoyment of true pleasure, would seem as necessary as daily bread? How was he to reconcile his hostility towards machines with his faith in the Middle Ages and an attempt to revive their virtues? There are certain contradictions which have to be accepted if one wishes to think and to create at the same time. So the first thing Morris did was to give books back their calligraphic origin, their fundamental architecture. The motto of *The Germ* had been "Thoughts towards Nature in Poetry, Literature and Art." Typographical space was therefore to be a field of homogeneous signs acting as a window on a simulated nature: a dense, written nature, consisting of thick webs of acanthus leaves, vine leaves, bunches of grapes, stretching between curves and counter-curves of tracery

E T s'il revenait un jour
Que faut-il lui dire?
— Dites-lui qu'on l'attendit
Jusqu'à s'en mourir . . .

Et s'il m'interroge encore
Sans me reconnaître?
— Parlez-lui comme une sœur,
Il souffre peut-être . . .

Et s'il demande où vous êtes
Que faut-il répondre?
— Donnez-lui mon anneau d'or
Sans rien lui répondre . . .

Et s'il veut savoir pourquoi
La salle est déserte?
— Montrez-lui la lampe éteinte
Et la porte ouverte . . .

Et s'il m'interroge alors
Sur la dernière heure?
— Dites-lui que j'ai souri
De peur qu'il ne pleure . . .

Charles Doudelet (1861-1938): Illustration for Maurice Maeterlinck's poem "Et s'il revenait un jour" (And should he return one day), published in "Pan," Berlin, 1895.

without beginning or end, framing and enclosing a faultless set of characters. Superfluity was supreme. Not economy, but overflowing energy, meant to be consumed, and consumed on the spot. But despite the extraordinary skill with which masses were balanced one against the other, this was not the main point. Taste apart, the main point lay in the fact that Morris, having founded his own Kelmscott Press in 1891, set about designing and making his own type faces, legible, pleasant to the eye, and of simple and natural design. His task was both unusual and exacting. How many alphabets have really been invented since? To achieve his end he selected a superb model. As we have known since 1959, he used photographic enlargements of the *Historia Fiorentina* printed in Venice in 1476 with a fount by Jacobus Rubeus. The result was the famous Golden Type. Later, moving still further away from Roman, Morris imitated Gothic to produce his Troy Type which, reduced by a third, gave the form known as Chaucer. A fourth fount inspired by the German typographers Sweynheim and Pannartz, who settled in Italy in 1463, remained unfinished, but was taken up by others in 1902 and became the Subiaco Type. Before founding the Kelmscott Press, Morris had much "written and rhymed." He had done wood engraving, produced wrought iron, woven woollen fabrics, embroidered on linen, made stained glass, designed wallpaper, practised calligraphy and illuminated manuscripts, translated Icelandic legends into English, translated Greek and Latin poetry, and designed the oak chair which still bears his name. He was more than a model artist-craftsman, for he surpassed all the combinations that had ever been imagined since Ruskin. Was he swimming against the tide? He was both a devotee of the past and a prophet, a man both Utopian and practical, the symbol of a society that did not wish to die. But perhaps his name should be linked above all with the rebirth of the book. Of the book as something constructed, as a harmony between positive and negative areas, as a sequence of pages and safe repository of signs—a

repository which Mallarmé shattered in 1897 when *Cosmopolis* published *Un coup de dés* (A Throw of the Dice). According to this, the whole effect resides in what Mallarmé calls "pagination" —the arrangement of the characters on the empty page. "A certain word in capital letters requires a page to itself," he wrote to André Gide. "In accordance with strict laws, and in so far as it is possible with a printed text, the constellation so created will inevitably take on the pace of a constellation. The ship gives a list from the top of one page to the bottom of the next... the rhythm of a phrase dealing with an action or even an object has meaning only if it imitates them and, imaged on the paper, with letters repeating the original pattern, manages somehow to convey something of them." To Paul Valéry, to whom he had insisted on sending the corrected proofs of the *Cosmopolis* article, he said, "with a wonderful smile": "Don't you think it's an act of madness?" Valéry did not answer: he saw Mallarmé's venture as an attempt "to raise a page at last to the power of the starry sky." The opposite of the area which Morris had undertaken to circumscribe so rigorously.

Symbolism was in a state of expansion, and 1894 was an important phase in the process. Not so much because Alfred Jarry, who for some months, with Remy de Gourmont, had been editing the *Ymagier*, published his first book, *Minutes de Sable Mémorial*, in the metonymic style already made familiar by Laforgue and Mallarmé. Nor because Gustave Moreau, now sixty, brought symbolist polyvalence to its highest point in *Jupiter and Semele*, incorporating the haziest contemporary mythagogy and leaving the beholder incapable of decoding its mixture of ideolect and pictorial uproar. Nor was 1894 important because in that year *Pelléas* was published in English in New York and in Polish in Warsaw; because Mackintosh published his first drawings in *The Magazine*; or because Redon, in a first exhibition of paintings at Durand-Ruel's, revealed an uncertainty not yet erected into a principle, and achieved through the unreality of appearances the "marvellous real,"

1. Cover design for "The Studio," London, 1893, submitted in a competition.

2. Cover of "Art et Décoration," monthly review of modern art, Paris, November 1897.

3. Aubrey Beardsley (1872-1898): Prospectus for "The Yellow Book," London, 1894.

4. Théo van Rysselberghe (1862-1926): Catalogue for the fourth exhibition of "La Libre Esthétique," Brussels, 1897.

5. Alphonse Mucha (1860-1939): Cover for "L'Image," artistic and literary monthly, Paris, December 1896.

6. Cover of the art magazine "L'Œuvre," Valence on the Rhône, 1897

i.e. reality at its most vital because characterized, "in relation to scientific reality, by its train of fantasy." (It was at this time that Redon, back in his native Gironde, wrote to his friend Bonger, a Dutchman who owned the largest collection of his works: "The same evening I left Paris, tired with too long a stay in town. No one will ever know how hard I've tried, during the last thirty years, to live in the city far away from trees and unconscious nature! In all the places I've lived I have managed to have a view from the window of some meagre branch or twig of greenery, to keep a trace of illusion alive in my mind. But in the end I had to bestir myself socially, and no doubt there's some good to be said about Paris. We speak ill of it, but it does enable the artist to direct his efforts and analyze his ego.") Nor was the significance of the year due to the fact that Beardsley decided that John Lane's new literary magazine should have a cover which would make it *The Yellow Book*. The main thing about 1894, for our purposes, is that in Brussels it saw the Twenty ("Les XX") replaced by the "Libre Esthétique" group, with an exhibition on a scale only to be seen nowadays in Cassel or Venice. It was probably on a somewhat smaller scale than these, and it was organized by one man. Its intention was to give an up-to-date account of things, but not once every two years, nor even every four, but every single year. "An annual Salon which will bring together all expressions of Art: painting, sculpture, graphic arts, applied arts. Concerts and conferences," announced Octave Maus. The Twenty had been a club or federation of artists. The Libre Esthétique, "in order to avoid factional rivalry and group exclusiveness," included no artists. Maus alone decided who was to be invited to exhibit. Twenty-four years later he smilingly said: "Anarchy and autocracy—experience has taught me that these are the only two forms of government for running a Salon. I say so with all the more certainty because I myself applied each system alternately, with identical results."

The Libre Esthétique's first Salon opened in Brussels at the Musée d'Art Moderne on 17 February 1894. It was a great cultural and social event, and crowds of people thronged there. Among them were Eugène Carrière, Ernest Chausson, Berthe Morisot and her daughter (whose beauty caused a sensation), Gauguin, Ensor, Toorop, Francis Jourdain, Félix Vallotton, Fritz Thaulow, Gustave Geffroy, Toulouse-Lautrec, Signac, Khnopff, Degouve de Nuncques, Pierre Louÿs, Henri de Régnier, and Emile Verhaeren. Octave Maus observed: "It was the time of an aestheticism which had survived from the Pre-Raphaelites. There was no stranger sight than one of our openings, where fashionable women in carefully thought-out garbs—tunics of green velvet or mauve silk, peplums of orange gauze, ferronnières, reticules, and lilies which they sometimes bore like candles—tried to match their Ruskinian get-ups with the modern setting in which they found themselves."

Gustave Geffroy at once perceived the importance of the Salon: "This is not just an exhibition of Belgian art, but a beginning of European Art in Belgium; a rendezvous, in a great city, for all the different forms of thought which are current in the civilized world and whose course might be followed like that of rivers and streams joining and flowing together towards the sea." The aim of the Libre Esthétique was not to break down art, or rather painting, into the two previously examined trends, which might be symbolically represented by Seurat on the one hand and Khnopff on the other, but to extend the idea of major plastic creation so as to include the things which make up the ordinary environment, whether public or private. William Morris, making the transition from theory to practice, had for several years been setting an example. Rossetti and Burne-Jones turned from painting to crafts at the same time as Morris. Their political view led them, together with Walter Crane, their most brilliant disciple, to try to offer a consistent answer to the problem of art's social function. The attempt was doomed from the start, at least from the ideological point of view,

7. Special issue of "La Plume" devoted to Henry de Groux, Paris, 1899.

8. Special issue of "L'Art Décoratif," devoted to Henry van de Velde, Paris, 1898.

9. Fritz Erler (1868-1940): Cover of the magazine "Jugend," Munich, 1896.

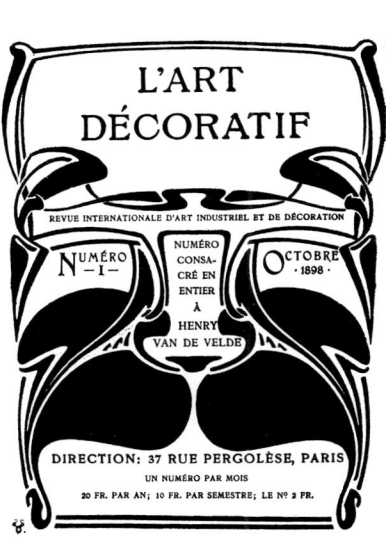

Henry van de Velde (1863-1957): Design for the journal "Van Nu en Straks," Brussels, 1892.

because it was conceived of in terms of class, and, in particular, in terms which were bourgeois. A first consequence of this was that all the things designed to bring art within the reach of everyone derived their vocabulary, motifs, forms and settings from symbolist painting, which proved an ideal source for Art Nouveau to draw upon. The promotion of objects through fashionable exhibitions is a very instructive phenomenon, despite the attempts made after the event to suggest that there was a particular attitude, process, technique or even "philosophy" of ornament. (Gustave Serrurier, in Liège, seems to have been the only artist who, at the time, actually created furniture based on social considerations.) As early as 1891 Khnopff designed the poster for the eighth exhibition of the Twenty: this show itself included posters by Chéret, ceramics by Willy Finch, two large vases by Gauguin and, by the same artist, a statue in enamelled stoneware and two polychrome wood bas-reliefs, *Soyez amoureuses* and *Soyez mystérieuses* (Be amorous, Be mysterious). In the 1893 Salon two whole rooms were devoted to the "decorative arts" and included a screen in size painting by Emile Bernard, some designs for stained-glass windows by Albert Besnard, some ornamental objects by Alexander Charpentier, posters by Toulouse-Lautrec, a tea-table by Finch, and a large ornamental embroidery by Henry van der Velde. This work, intended as a wall hanging and now in the Kunstgewerbemuseum in Zurich, was executed "in fine pieces of cloth fixed one after the other against a background of canvas by means of outlines of silk," and was strongly influenced by Gauguin's *Vision After the Sermon*. In 1894 the Libre Esthétique ventured even further. It showed goldsmith's work by Ashbee, furniture by Niederkorn, panels by Ranson, stoneware by Delaherche, Dalpayrat and Lesbros, wood engravings by Vallotton, pictures by Christopher Whall, Selwyn Image, Heywood Summer and Eugène Grasset, and an embroidery by Maillol. The Comte de Montesquiou had sent a clock, insisting that it should be shown behind glass. When this proved impossible the Comte expressed his dissatisfaction with "those who had inflicted such a serious loss of prestige upon the clock." Beardsley showed fourteen pen and ink drawings which he had just completed for Wilde's *Salome*. Puvis de Chavannes showed *The Prodigal Son* and G. F. Watts his *Portrait of the Marquis of Granby*. While there were paintings by Redon, Maurice Denis, Degouve de Nuncques, Gauguin, Carrière, Khnopff, Mellery, Toorop, Ensor, Sisley, Pissarro, Signac, Renoir and many others, a prominent place was also accorded to books: as well as fine bindings by Charles Meunier and Marius Michel there were also bindings, type faces, ornamental letters and decorations produced by William Morris at the Kelmscott Press: these were judged "noble and attractive." Octave Maus described as "more fantastic and extremely

elegant" the books published in London by Elkin Mathews and John Lane, with illustrations by Ricketts, Laurence Housman and Beardsley.

This was the Libre Esthétique's way of showing that everything was interconnected, and that solidarity between different techniques tended to lead to a "modern" unity of style. Although it was not shown in the 1894 exhibition, there was another publication which was much talked of in connection with the renaissance of the book. This was *Van Nu en Straks*, a review which circulated secretly in these French-speaking circles, and which was strongly committed to the great topical problems of communal art, anarchy, individual revolt and Marxism. The first number appeared on 1 April 1893, and its originator was Auguste Vermeylen, a young Flemish poet and future art historian. It was a dazzling début, distinguished by the quality of the typography, lay-out, titles, ornamental letters and tail-pieces specially designed by Henry van de Velde. It was different from everything else that was being done in Belgium at the time. Striking features were the structure of the review; the way the lines were justified, recalling Plantin; the originality of the wood engravings, clearly influenced by Gauguin; and the general presentation, based on the work of William Morris and Walter Crane. The review itself contradicted one of the aims expressed by its editor, which was to exclude any naturalist "inspiration" from the plastic arts. As if nature, and the nature of art itself, could be so sternly censored! But the mutilation was only verbal, and the castration theoretical. The review itself sufficiently shows the feelings of the writer, and the irrelevance of any theory not based upon experience. Examined carefully, the "decoration" is pleasantly flowery in both the literal and the metaphorical sense. It is attractive through the authority of its style of drawing, the quality of its signs, and the sudden sureness of its invention (hitherto, in painting, Van de Velde had tended to follow Van Gogh and Seurat). It was made up of motifs which were flexible, ample, full and free, punctuated with plump tears and large commas, suggesting the natural growth of plants and flowers, seeming to echo dynamic growth: and beneath this rich, expressive, sensual form there lurked abstraction. The little wood engraving which contained the device of *Van Nu en Straks* only barely recalls its origin, which was a sail swelled by the wind. As Julius Meier-Graefe said in 1899, "All that is left is the expressive direction of the lines, the forward movement perfectly symbolizing the boldly progressive nature of the brave little journal." In the same field the architects and book illustrators of Holland—G. W. Dijsselhof, C. A. Lion Cachet, T. Nieuwenhuis, T. van Hoytema and L.W.R. Wenckebach—following the symbolist painting of their compatriots Derkinderen and Roland Holst, also based their compositions on flowers and plants and animals.

Franz von Stuck (1863-1928): Cover for "Pan," Berlin,
April-May 1895.

Max Klinger (1857-1920): Narcissus and Echo, from the set of etchings "Rettungen ovidischer Opfer" (Deliverances of
Sacrificial Victims in Ovid's Metamorphoses), 1879.

Otto Eckmann (1865-1902): Design framing a
poem by Christian Morgenstern, published in "Pan,"
Berlin, 1896.

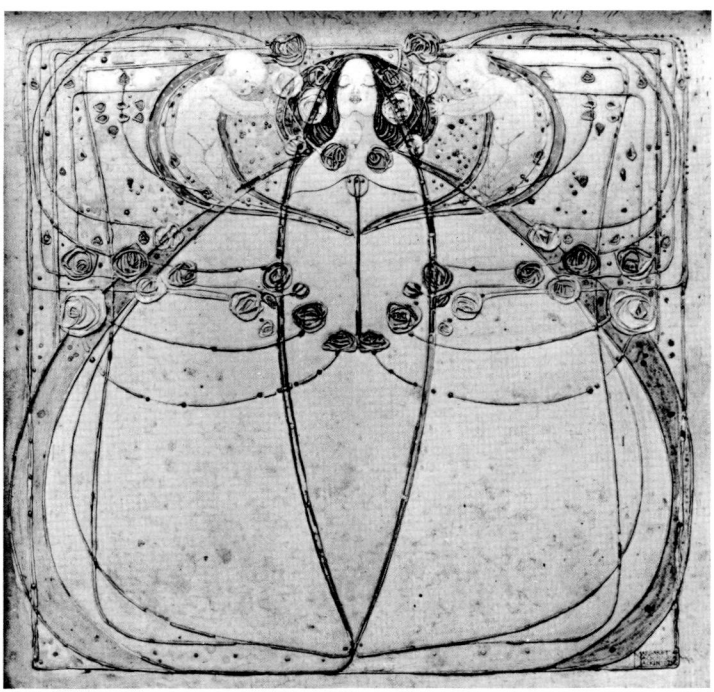

Margaret Macdonald Mackintosh (1865-1933): Relief panel for a writing desk, 1901. Silver and stucco on wood.

W hile the Arts and Crafts Movement, around Morris, and the Aesthetic Movement, around Beardsley, were using sources which belonged to the past, there appeared in Scotland a complete independent, Charles Rennie Mackintosh. By tradition he belongs to the history of architecture, where he is classed as one of the precursors of the rational architecture of the twentieth century. But the interest aroused in recent years by Symbolism has led to his discovery as one of the most subtle, astonishing and elegant painters of his day. He was a creative artist who used watercolour to convey the taut, divided, shared, severed and yet strongly united spaces of which his architecture was composed. Each of his images, which were always unfinished (i.e. complete and limitless), is a whole universe, open on its own spatiality, fluid, sinuous, traversed by transparences, linear spasms, or discreet and fragile lines. All these are instruments of a discourse deriving from Celtic depths or Japanese culture. It does not matter which. Mackintosh invented his own geometry, concepts and materials. He invented his own chromatic derivation, his current, tensions, flow, curves and parallels. Daedalus against Eupalinus? Patches of colour stray, lines form frontiers and they combine to speak of *The Tree of Influence* or *The Sun of Cowardice*. At this point only does deciphering begin. The chemistry of sensation should be allowed to come before that of ideas. No need to define the flux behind these apparent improvisations. Hence they require no translation, and hence their striking importance. To concentrate the eye better they needed to be framed, enclosed, and so they are, but gently, almost absently, marginally. By symbolist boxes.

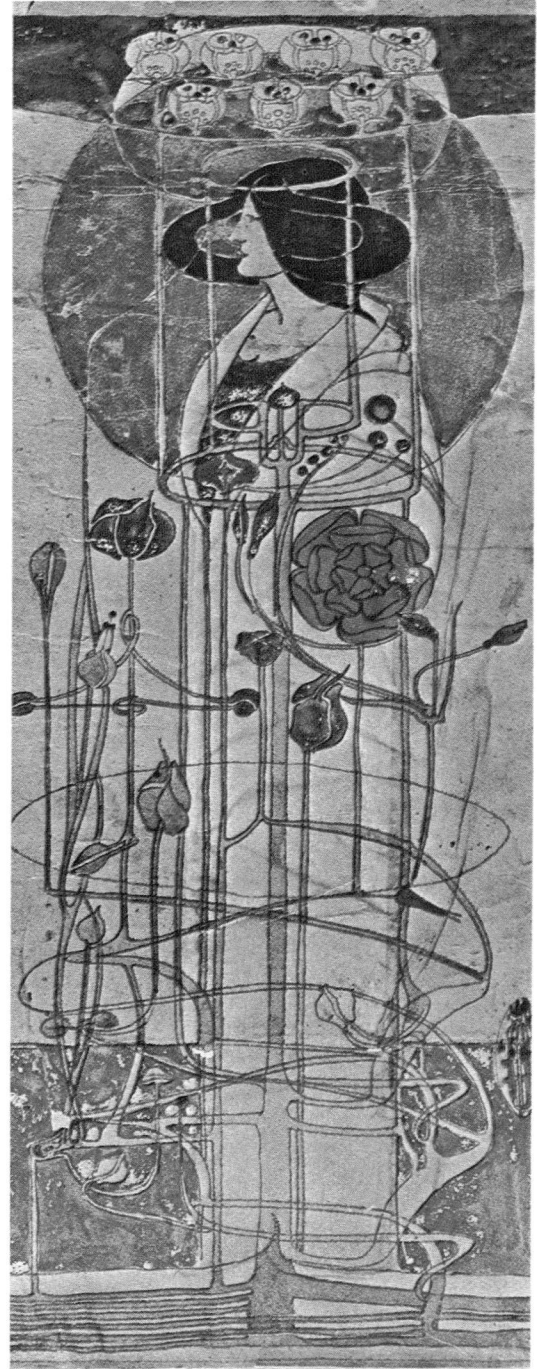

Charles Rennie Mackintosh (1868-1928): Preliminary design for a mural decoration in Miss Cranston's Buchanan Street Tearooms, Glasgow. Watercolour over pencil, 1896-1897.

The charm of the frame

For several years something strange had been going on in the Palazzo Bianco in Genoa: in order to renovate, "modernize," and "spring-clean" the museum, the pictures were being undressed and stripped of their frames, whether these were original or added later. The visitor thus saw them—and sees them still—standing out clearly against a bright or toned-down wall, or hung in a space which no longer imposes limits: instead of being presented on an easel, which might recall their method of execution, they are set in elegant steel supports rising from a solid plinth of stone or concrete. It was a revolution in museum presentation, and also in the theoretical attitude to museums. Whole museums were completely transformed. But no one thought to assess the damage done until Meyer Schapiro called attention to it recently. Hitherto, pictures had been protected. In the West, as soon as the image left its native surroundings on a wall or in a book, it was treated, and continued to be treated, as a picture-cum-object, existing within the limits of a frame specially designed to shelter and protect it and help it to be properly seen. The frame had, since the beginning of easel painting, contributed to the bringing out of its visual function. This became more marked during and after the Renaissance, that point in history when paintings finally became objects, articles of value among others in a commercial system. The new attitude towards the image reinforced the creation of illusion, and a picture became, in Alberti's famous phrase, "a window opening on to nature": *una fenestra aperta per donde io miri quello que quivi sarà dipinto.* But one cannot think of a window without some surround, some frame. According to Manet, "the area selected as the size of a picture... lends the frame the pure and charming arbitrariness of a limitation." These chosen dimensions also determine "the relations between subject and surrounding

Above:
Jan Toorop (1858-1928): The Song of Time, 1893. Pastel and black chalk.

Page 154:
Ludwig von Hofmann (1861-1945): Idyllic Landscape, c. 1900. Oil.

Page 155:
Edgar Maxence (1871-1954): Girl with a Peacock, before 1896.
Pastel and gouache.

atmosphere.'' Mallarmé, however, writing specifically of Manet in 1896, gave it as his own opinion that the art of "limiting the canvas in such a way as to produce the illusion of perspective has never been fully exploited.'' He went on: "The whole charm of a frame consists in its being a limit, and not really a fanciful one, as if the scene can be taken in at a glance, or if not all the scene, at least that which makes it worth preserving. The picture is that, and the function of the frame is to isolate it, even though I know this runs counter to all our prejudices... A spectator who is used to isolating, in nature or in the midst of other people, the thing which pleases him... should find in a work of art all his customary pleasures and, though he knows he is standing in front of a picture, should have the illusion of looking at a mirage of some natural spectacle.'' But in 1922 Félix Fénéon wrote: "It is a long time since there was a definite relation between picture and frame, and when we photograph one we are no longer obliged to photograph the other.'' He was aware of the fact, though, that in the last years of his life Seurat painted his frames in tones and colours complementary to those in the picture, which were enhanced by the contrast. He also knew the trouble Whistler took to choose frames that were curved and fine-drawn. No doubt he was also aware of the care with which Puvis de Chavannes surrounded certain of his easel paintings with "decorative borders,'' which have been said to denote his "transition from the reality of mural painting to the illusion of the image.'' This trend is of a piece with the taste for artifice, and with the intensified love of precious objects which influenced and characterized symbolist "society'': and which also helped to define its particular kind of snobism. The delimitation which is the characteristic feature of any text is rendered uncertain, or at the least ambiguous. The principle of inclusion or exclusion is stretched and confused. Limitation, formerly signal of the end of a text, becomes something vague. The "position of strength'' which I. Lotman attributes to limitation, which indicates to the reader that he is dealing with a text and "reminds him of the whole system of corresponding artistic codes,'' is structurally weakened. The frame, become the instrument of the prevailing irrealism, acts as a prolongation of dream. It has an incestuous relationship with the image. Maxence presents it as doing so in his *Girl with a Peacock.* Toorop leads the "sound line'' of Abel's song out past the frontier of the frame, which is also overflowed by the network of wavy parallels symbolizing forces and perfumes. Queralt uses the frame as ground for a poem, and limits the sphere of the sign itself as though by a theatre curtain. Ludwig von Hofmann carried illusionism to extremes around 1900 with his famous *Idyllic Landscape,* in which the scene within the scene doubles the erotic effect. Rossetti, Klimt, Munch, Moreau, Klinger, Mellery, Redon, Segantini, Schwabe, Riemerschmid, Stuck, Lechter, Vroubel, Janos Vaszary and Willumsen—all were concerned with the dialectic between frame and image. But not all went through the red light at the same speed. The study of different relationships between frame and field has not yet begun. When it does, it will no doubt reveal how and why the image, as text of a text, super-text or sub-ensemble, whether in Morris, Crane, Bradley, Holst, Doudelet, Henricus, Simberg, Rops or other experts in "illustration,'' was always set up with solemnity; and why, at a time when a new approach was tending to shatter Alberti's window, the image sought to increase the attractions of illusion behind the protection of a simulated frame. But the pretence reassures the spectator, because it belongs to his own space, and in their proper place signs always operate in favour of illusion.

Chapitre XII

Le Conteur achève son récit

Il me fallut revenir en France. Des

... me rappelaient.

... terre

... beauté !

... de quelques

... arrivée et

... uvages ont

... lisé", bien

... de

... moment

... rnière

... urant

... et triste

toujours, mais calme, elle s'était assise sur
la pierre, les jambes pendantes effleurant
de ses deux pieds larges et solides l'eau salée,

Paul Gauguin (1848-1903) : Illustrated manuscript page from "Noa Noa," 1897.

7

THE WRITING OF THE RIDDLE
1896-1900

From and For Paul Gauguin

A l'horizon par les brouillards,
Les tintamarres des hasards,
Vagues, nous armons nos démons
Dans l'entre-deux sournois des monts.

Au rivage que nous fermons
Dome un géant sur les limons.
Nous rampons à ses pieds, lézards.
Lui, sur son char tel un César

Ou sur un piédestal de marbre,
Taille une barque en un tronc d'arbre
Pour debout dessus nous poursuivre

Jusqu'à la fin verte des lieues.
Du rivage ses bras de cuivre
Lèvent au ciel la hache bleue.

Alfred Jarry, *D'après et pour Paul Gauguin,*
in *Les Minutes de Sable Mémorial,* 1894

(On the horizon in foggy weather, the hubbub of vague chances, we arm our demons in the sly interspace of the mountains. On the shore that we close dome a giant on the silt. We crawl at its feet, lizards. He, on his chariot like a Caesar or on a marble pedestal, carves a boat in a tree-trunk to pursue us standing thereon as far as the green end of the leagues. From the shore his copper arms raise to heaven the blue axe.)

 HERE did the illusion come from that the symbolization of thought was something new? In 1896 Remy de Gourmont answered the question to his own satisfaction in his introduction to the *Livre des Masques* (Book of Masks), a swiftly sketched gallery of "portraits" that were generous, flattering, facile and fashionable. By now de Gourmont was regarded as an authority: his articles in the *Mercure de France* were a success, as were those in the *Revue Blanche, Ermitage* and *Entretiens,* despite the fact that it was a time of "brotherly blackguardism and timid enthusiasm." The literary "world" had accepted him as *the* theorist of symbolism ever since the death of Aurier and the defection of Moréas. And also despite the appearance in 1892 of *Idéoréalisme,* Saint-Pol Roux's verbal slough, "rightful refuge of genius, home of boldness and daring, where only Prometheuses may flourish," not to mention, in 1894, another verbal episode in the form of Maurice Pujo's *Idéalisme intégral* (All About Idealism). G. Michaud does not mention Pujo in his inventory of symbolist theorists, though P. Junod does so in his discussion of transparency and opacity. Pujo also tried to set up an "independent aesthetic" based on the same confusion of feeling and thought. Thus Remy de Gourmont wrote: "In the last few years we have seen a serious experiment in literature based on contempt for ideas and scorn of symbols. The theory is well known and reminiscent of cookery: Take a slice of life... and so on. Monsieur Zola, having invented the recipe, omitted to make use of it. His 'slices of life' are dull poems full of murky and turbulent lyricism, popular romanticism and democratic symbolism, but always overflowing with some idea or some allegorical meaning, whether in *Germinal, La Mine, La Foule* or *La Grève.* Idealist revolt will therefore not be against the products of naturalism, except perhaps its less worthy works, but against its theory, or rather its claims. For the would-be innovators, appealing to the ultimate and eternal necessities of art, thought they were proclaiming new and even astonishing truths when they expressed their determination to bring ideas back into literature. But in fact they were only rekindling the torch and lighting lots of little candles around it.

"And yet a new truth has recently entered into literature and art. It is entirely metaphysical and (ostensibly) *a priori*; it is quite young—only a hundred years old; and it is genuinely new, because it had not hitherto been used in relation to aesthetics. This evangelical, marvellous, liberating and rejuvenating truth is *the principle of the ideality of the world.* Man is a thinking subject, and the universe, everything outside the self, exists only in terms of man's idea of it. We know only phenomena, we reason only from appearances. Any truth in itself eludes us, essence is unattainable. Schopenhauer popularized the notion in the simple formula: The world is my own representation. I do not see what is; what is is what I see. For every thinking person there is another, perhaps a different, world. This notion, which Kant abandoned in order to go to the rescue of thought, is so attractive and flexible that it has been transposed without loss of logic from theory to even the most demanding practice; it is a universal principle of emancipation for every man capable of understanding. It has revolutionized other things besides aesthetics; but here we are concerned only with aesthetics... A writer's work should be not merely a reflection but a magnified reflection of his own personality. The only excuse a man can

◁ *Pierre Puvis de Chavannes (1824-1898):*
The Shepherd's Song, 1891. Oil.

▷ *Paul Gauguin (1848-1903):*
Whence come we? What are we? Whither go we? 1897. Oil.

have for writing is to write himself, to reveal to others the sort of world that is mirrored in his own individuality. His only excuse is to be original; he must say things that have never been said before, and say them in a way that is new. He must create his own aesthetic, and we must accept that there are as many aesthetics as there are original minds, and judge them for what they are and not for what they are not. Let us therefore admit that symbolism, though it may be excessive, though it may be inconvenient, though it may be pretentious, is the expression of individualism in art."

All this was based on a flattened and watered-down interpretation of Schopenhauer. The idea diversified in all directions, shifting from symbolism to ideism, idealism, symbolic idealism, a whole semantic jungle. (It was not a moment too soon that Bréal founded the "science of meanings" in 1897.) Some commentators, starting from the false dilemma between the imitation of nature and the depicting of ideas, have seen the *fin-de-siècle* aesthetic as based on a "spiritualistic or intellectualist realism" which they have tried to link with the "(materialistic) realism of Naturalism." This might be described as the disease of idealititis, from which Albert Mockel, the most coherent of the thinker poets who followed Mallarmé, was fortunately immune. According to him the Ideal was "the point of intersection between all our infinite and limitless possibilities." Was this hankering after the infinite a romantic survival, something that ought to be forbidden? No, for it affected Ideality at the level of feeling, and could be translated as "that which is undefined, the images which vaguely suggest to us a dream that surpasses themselves." This was a subtle nuance adapting sense to current mental space in a way that was at once skilful, ingenious and moderate. As for Remy de Gourmont, he later had no hesitation in writing: "Idealism is a hopeless and immoral doctrine, anti-social and anti-human." He did not fear the "meddlers who try to compare what I used to think with

what I think now." There were extenuating circumstances. André Hallays remarked of such reversals in the *Revue de Paris* of 1 May 1896: "No other age has seen such unstable and confused opinions." Everyone wanted to be in the swim: "Longhaired blonde youths wrap their necks in satin and their ribs in long frock-coats, and, to beguile the idle years until they are claimed by matrimony and the law, celebrate beneficent anarchy and read Multatuli, in between performances of the *Mass of Pope Marcellus*. For everyone is now an admirer of Palestrina, though this does not prevent it from being proper to like the songs of Aristide Bruant and to follow the counsels of magicians. And the unfortunate wretches, already anarchists, Palestrinians and occultists, must also flock to productions of Ibsen." But in December 1896 the "young Botticellists, Benozzo Gozzolists and Pre-Raphaelites" found themselves disconcerted by *Ubu Roi*. At the same time the American dancer Loïe Fuller, "the dream which comes after reality," took Paris by storm, and Maeterlinck, typically exclusive, gave a cautious welcome to the guests at Georgette Leblanc's literary salon at Poissy: the Sâr Peladan, Jean Lorrain, Georges Rodenbach, Maurice Rollinat, Henry de Groux and Gabriel Fauré. (Here, as previously at Ghent, Maeterlinck surrounded himself with reproductions of works by Rossetti and Burne-Jones. Later, when he entrusted the sets of his play *Joyzelle* to Charles Doudelet, he sent him a book of drawings by Walter Crane, expressing the hope that "the general style and the architectural motifs would be in this vein.")

In 1897 the *Paris-Parisien* almanac, in its portrait of a "snob," said he must "be able to talk about Nietzsche, Ibsen, Darwin and Schopenhauer. Make fun of the music our parents liked, admire César Franck, thrill to Wagner, and try to be capable of understanding Beethoven. Be able to talk about primitive painting. Have been to Bayreuth, or mean to go there next year. Read the reviews designed for the younger gener-

Here, near my hut, in utter silence, I dream of violent harmonies in the natural fragrances that exhilarate me. A pleasure heightened by an indefinable sacred awe which I divine towards the immemorial. In bygone days, an odour of joy that I breathe in the present. Animal figures in statuesque rigidity: something inexpressibly old, august, religious in the rhythm of their gesture, in their rare immobility. In dreaming eyes, the cloudy surface of an unfathomable enigma. And here is nightfall—everything is at rest. My eyes close in order to *see without understanding* the dream in the infinite space that recedes before me, and I have a sense of the doleful march of my hopes.

Paul Gauguin, letter to André Fontainas from Tahiti, March 1899

ation. Be familiar with the symbolist poets." This was a description of a class dialect rather than of a set culture, a dialect made passive, pointless and superficial by its own excess. "The women of those days," says Laurent Tailhade, "wore their hair like spaniel's ears. Aesthetes wore theirs like figures out of Ghiberti or Donatello, and wound Florentine scarves over their shirts so that it was hard to tell whether the black edge round the neck was due to the satin of the cravat or the dirt of the skin." The fauve shapes of Gallé and Lalique were much sought after because they were thought to appear "corroded with poison." There was a sort of fetishism of form. It was fashionable to have Morris furniture, to buy Liberty "drapes of pea-green crepon printed with huge chrysanthemums," or Bing "cretonnes designed by Walter Crane," while waiting for the first opportunity to go to Bayreuth. Redon admits: "Yes indeed, Wagner, with his cycles, and all the people he excites, and the ink he causes to flow, was really someone. But we mustn't judge all that yet. His writings make me think..." As for "artists of the soul" such as Alexandre Séon, Armand Point and Alphonse Osbert, they had to give way before Utamaro, whose pictures were now almost as expensive to buy as those of Moreau. Young snobs were interested in Gauguin, for "Monet and Renoir are already old." Were the snobs ahead of the establishment then? The Musée du Luxembourg in Paris declined Gauguin's gift of a *Virgin and Child*. "What a horrible society," he exclaimed, "where the petty triumph at the expense of the great." After over two years away, it made him afraid of "losing in three weeks in Paris" all the stock he had accumulated of "South Sea youth." He had gone out to find a culture of which he knew nothing, to find myths whose absence he had perceived. To find whiteness. The reason he broke with the "old world" was not, as Marina Scriabin has suggested, because in order to do his work he needed "a certain range of colours, a certain light, a certain environment." Nor did he go into exile in or-

der to find "conditions that would facilitate the technical development of his painting." The essential part of his technical exploits had been attempted and achieved before he left Europe, as we realize if we recall the *Vision After the Sermon* and the *Yellow Christ*. What he was responding to was the heartrending appeal of his *Moi mythique* (Mythical Self)—at least if we pursue the idea put forward by Boris de Schloezer in his *Introduction to J.-S. Bach*, a work which despite its modest title makes an important contribution to aesthetics, an addition to the Gestalt theory which deserves to be better known. Gauguin was also answering the appeal of his own body, his own past. The technical transcription was not lateral; it "produced" its author, in his work. The transcription did not parallel the work; it contained and was inseparable from the act which set it down. And Gauguin is only "primitive," as he has often been called, in comparison with some so-called state of "civilization." In both Le Pouldu and the Marquesas he always used the same technical codes, except in the case of the strange *Noa Noa*, a piquant duel on two levels which Charles Morice and Gauguin decided to produce together in 1893. It was to include both drawings and poems. Morice saw it as "partly stories, by Gauguin, partly poems, by me." Gauguin lost no time in writing notes from which Morice worked up the chapters in which "the Storyteller speaks." Gauguin's own contribution proceeded more slowly. Meanwhile he introduced a striking plan: a combination of iconic and linguistic writing, a simultaneous ordering of word and image. It was in this form that the *Revue Blanche* published the work in 1897, though Gauguin was the sole author. It described the genesis of a process in which image dashes itself against word and word lurks beneath image. A superb interaction in which orgiastic colour encounters patient script, each code mingling with the other in a new solidarity, defying "commonsense." So much for Gauguin's "primitiveness." His real position was outside everything, in

contrast to the "civilized" man who is imprisoned by all the limits he delights in collecting. Gauguin must have made changes in the original work, as conceived by Morice. According to the poet himself, Gauguin "ended up believing that it was he who thought of the original idea," which was intended to "show the superiority of the rough, naive savage over the civilized decadent." The difference of opinion between the two contributors is shown by a letter Gauguin wrote to Madame Morice in February 1899, just when Morice was trying to find a publisher. "Another thing: the book, *Noa Noa*. Please do give me credit for a little experience and for the instinct of the sort of civilized savage that I am. The storyteller mustn't be eclipsed by the poet. A book is what it is—incomplete, perhaps. But if by means of a few stories one says all one has to say or to suggest, one has done a good deal. I know Morice is expected to produce verses, but if there are a lot of them in this book the storyteller's naivety disappears completely and *Noa Noa* loses its pungency from the outset. And aren't you afraid that those who await the book in a carping rather than a friendly spirit may say, Yes, Morice has talent, but he lacks creative power, and without Gauguin he wouldn't have any ideas? And I'm sure that's what people will say if there is a lot of poetry. Whereas it will take very little to sort things out and make way for the successful outcome which as you know is ready and waiting among his papers." Gauguin's lucidity was terrible; the steps he took in support of it, shattering. "Shared painting" was put off to the future (nowadays, its peak is represented by the Alechinsky-Dotremont duet). Implicit in all this is the contrast between the awakening of cultural symbolism and the fundamental symbolism which Gauguin discovered, experienced and confronted. The gulf he set between himself and Paris, seen as a symbol of Western discourse, deepened. When Maurice Denis asked him to take part in an exhibition at Durand-Ruel's, he answered: "True, it will be interesting to see the Cafe Volpini group of painters brought together again after ten years, together with the young artists whom I admire. But my personality of ten years ago is of no more interest today. In those days I wanted to dare everything, to liberate the younger generation in some way, and then to work at acquiring a bit of talent. The first part of my plan bore some fruit: nowadays you can do anything you like, and what's more it won't surprise anybody." With a certain proud melancholy, he went on: "My Papuan work would lose its point beside the... symbolists and ideists. I am sure your exhibition will be a great success. Nearly all of you have money, a lot of customers, and influential friends, so it would be very surprising if every one of you could not reap the rightful reward of your talents and innovations. I am slightly apprehensive on your account lest the Rosicrucians excite ridicule, for though their presence is marvellous publicity, I don't think art has any place in the Péladan set-up..." The exhibition, duly held at Durand-Ruel's, was grouped around Redon, and in March 1899 Maurice Denis described "certain characteristics which distinguish our various kinds of painting":

"The Vuillard, Bonnard and Vallotton group:

"(1) Paintings are small; (2) they are dark; (3) they are done from life; (4) they are done from memory, without models; (5) figures are not prominent, nor therefore is drawing; (6) should look better in a small dim apartment than in a studio or exhibition; (7) complicated subjects, Jewish style. To this group add Valtat (disregarding points 2 and 6) and Redon (disregarding points 3 and 5).

"The group consisting of Sérusier, myself and Ranson:

"(1) Paintings are large; (2) done with a few pure, more or less dark colours; (3) they are symbolic; (4) use of documents, geometric measures, or models; (5) prominence of the human figure; (6) must have been painted in the studio; (7) very plain and simple subjects, Latin style. Article by Geffroy commending another feature of the first group: (8) modern subjects."

The statistics are disturbing and the typology sketchy. Denis's cross-section is hardly exhaustive. But this *Journal* of short notes goes on, in the same vein: "Small pictures must be colourful (initial overall studies), use lake pigments in impasto (Piot), varnish. Do the big picture of Christ with children in black and green, the pink of the cheeks purple. In big pictures, contrive to reduce the number of basic colours... To avoid dullness, add a thin coat of zinc white mixed with turpentine... Lunched with the curé of Sainte-Clotilde; Monsignor Pujol was there." As for Gauguin, his object was to make "the pictures convey their story, my story, there, without the actual narratives aiming to do anything but lift the edges of infinity joining the episodes together, so as to lead [the spectator] along the corridor of space and time, through the memories in which the total dream melts into constituent circumstance." Uneasy, tortured, contemplating death, Gauguin, amidst a culture which never ceases to invade, astonish and attract him, asks the supreme question: *Whence come we? What are we? Whither go we?* Meanwhile, Maurice Denis remarks "that one gets used to even the worst emotions, and that this is an immense help in life." He adds, in August 1897, in the same *Journal*: "Probably three stages in life: one of wholly intellectual and emotional tension, provoking the enthusiasms and despairs fairly easily supported by a youthful organism. Another, after the great sufferings and disappointments, which finds its ideal in well-being, balanced functions, moral health, skill in one's art; and then physical suffering. The third: resignation and a return to the early tension, but now made rational and material (ambition, etc.). I suffer at the thought of amusing myself, at the thought that one has to pass the time, distract oneself. I should like to have a worthwhile goal." At the same time, far away from "the old routines of Europe," Gauguin, overwhelmed by the unknown in the "mysterious world of being of the All Light," uttered the anguished question. He felt mutilated by living in another world, outside Maori words and deeds; doomed to poverty in the midst of wealth. So, in a trance of despair, without a pause, in

the single month from November to December 1897, he asked that anguished question, starting, continuing and completing "this great canvas four and a half metres long." He made no preliminary studies. Perhaps, he wrote, "the lack of deliberation is compensated for by some element inexplicable to anyone who has not known extreme suffering." Moreover, "explanatory factors—known symbols—would fix the picture in a dreary reality, and the problem it poses would no longer be a poem." That is why the figurative has a latent meaning. The trajectory between signifiers and signified bristles with obstacles: where there is enigma, there is room for endless question. This is true even when the narrative fabric, though broken and discontinuous, is clear, and runs from left to right, chronologically, from birth to death. Here the reading is unambiguous, excluding plurality if only by its use of the universal archetypes of the earthly and celestial cycles. Trees, flowers, fruits—plant symbolism must influence any meditation on time and growing old. Earthy tones dominate, to signify the mother, the earth-mother who gives life and who takes it away. This might be the beginning of the whole symbolic mentality. Whence, amid the measureless luxuriance of tropical scents, the absolute union of man and nature, at once desire and memory of a state which existed before love.

As for Gauguin's aloofness towards Puvis de Chavannes at this period, that was more of a stratagem than anything, and could not destroy the fundamental connection between them. According to Gauguin, "Puvis expounds his idea but doesn't paint it. He is a Greek whereas I am a savage, a collarless wolf in the forest. If Puvis called a painting *Purity* he would explain it by painting a young virgin with a lily in her hand—a well-known symbol; so everyone would understand. Gauguin, for the same title, would paint a landscape with clear waters, without any stain from civilized man, perhaps without any people at all. Without going into detail, there is a whole universe between Puvis and me. Puvis, as a painter, is a cultivated man but not an author, whereas I am not cultivated but I may be an author." He was the

Daring everything

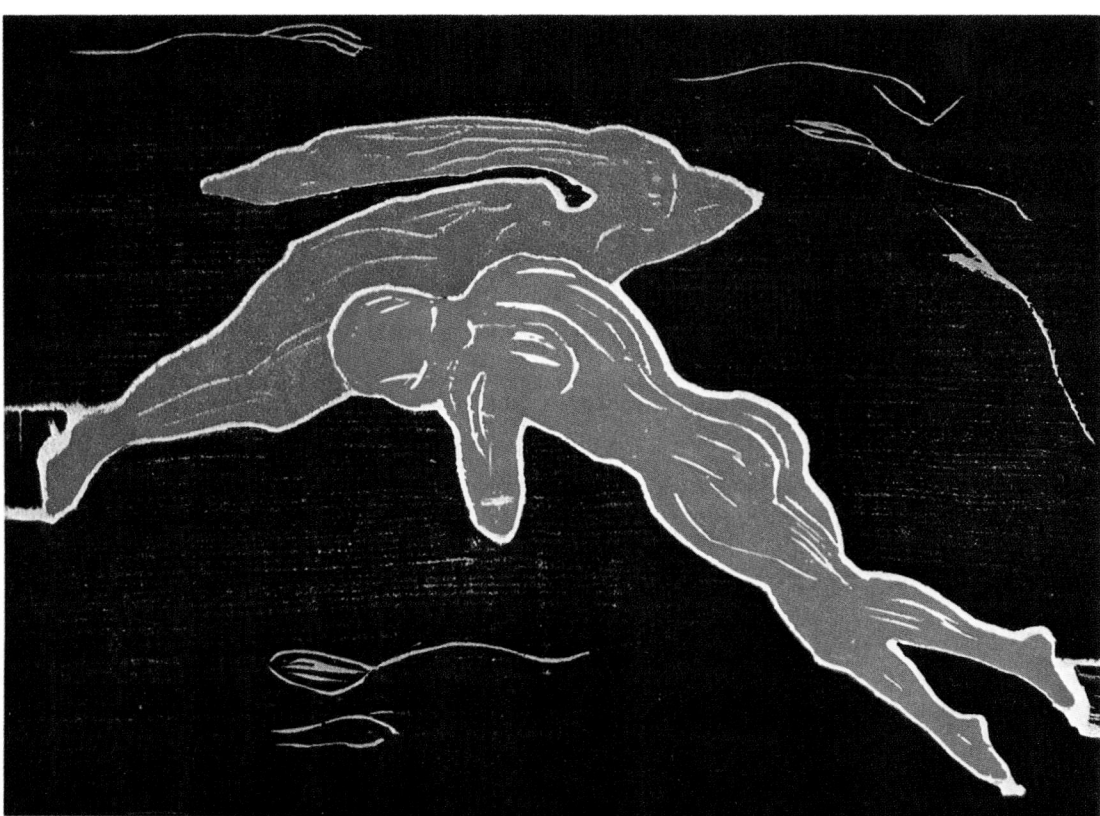

◁ *Paul Gauguin (1848-1903):*
What are we? 1897 (?).
Wood carving.

▷ *Edvard Munch (1863-1944):*
Meeting in Infinity, 1899.
Woodcut.

author of rare, violent, unprecedented texts which still have yet to be deciphered.

But Puvis managed to overwhelm both supporters and opponents by means of a remarkably independent gesture, and to create a unanimity which would have seemed suspicious if it had not gone beyond Maurice Denis's description of him as the "great professor of Order and Clarity." The banquet organized by Rodin to celebrate Puvis's seventieth birthday was an important event. Rodin got together, in January 1895, five hundred and fifty genuine or ad hoc "admirers," everyone who was anyone in Paris, official or semi-official. They included Zola, Anatole de Baudot, Emile Bernard, Rops, Jean Dolent, Catulle Mendès, Boudin, Pissarro, Carrière, Monet, Signac, Robert de Montesquiou and Carolus-Duran. Gauguin was also present, a last concession to the world before his final exile. But the younger generation stayed away en masse, as a protest against Brunetière's being invited to make a speech. For, as *La Plume* said in a special issue on Puvis de Chavannes, "there is not one new idea or noble thought which has found favour with the pedant who tyrannizes over the *Revue des Deux Mondes*. And so he was hissed and booed and interrupted by a terrific uproar." Even then he

As Hugo von Hofmannsthal observed as early as 1895, in an essay on mime, "people are tired of listening to speeches. They are filled with a deep aversion to words. For words are put before things, and hearsay has swallowed up the world." This fairly common attitude explained the fashion for mime, and for the subject of silence in general. Unspoken language was "the language of the body." And wherever the tendency was towards silence, eloquence became suspect, the implication being that what was well said was "not felt." In the last years of the century, all Vienna seemed to share this point of view. In 1891 Hermann Bahr wrote in his *Russische Reise*: "Language is old and worn out. We know the expression for every feeling before we experience the feeling itself." Language made us "the hostages of a dead world." Bahr went on:

"Words are not in the power of men: men are in the power of words... Every time we open our mouths ten thousand dead men speak through us." This implied the interiorization of death, a cessation of the ambivalence between death and life which is a feature of so many cultures, and the investment of death by desire. This came from the unconscious, the roots of our roots, the immemorial past, the age of the

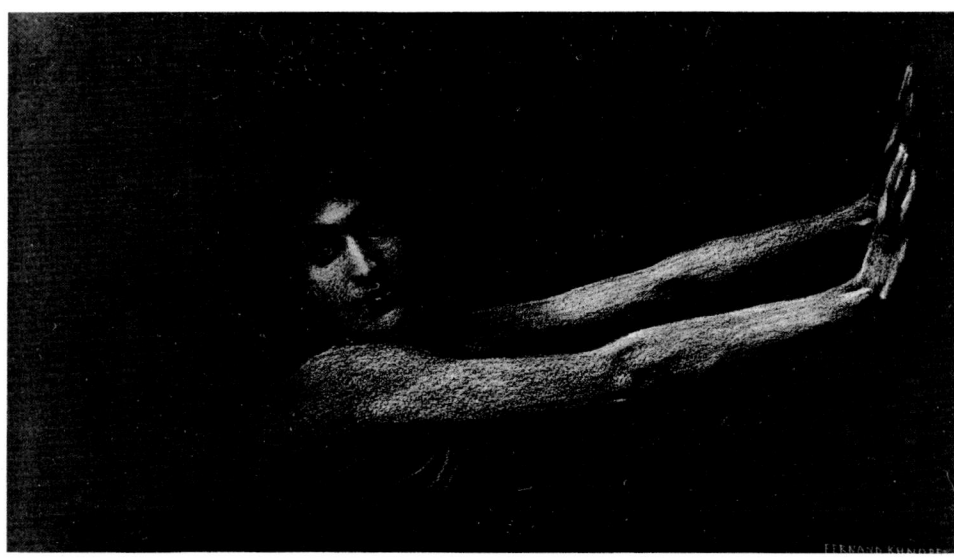

Eros and Thanatos

Fernand Khnopff (1858-1921):
Ygraine at the Gate, 1898.
Pastel illustration for
Maurice Maeterlinck's
puppet play "La Mort de Tintagiles."

persisted in dogmatizing: "So above all I want not to praise or congratulate you, but to thank you for having let light and air into painting... It had become somewhat prosaic by the middle of the present century; some influence or other seemed to have caused it to renounce its noblest aims. The imitation of nature, its indispensable beginning, seemed to have become not merely the end, but the whole. You did not protest against the narrowness of this interpretation: such is not your way; and your modesty showed itself equal to your genius. Instead you asked nature for the secret of the magic harmonies she composes out of elements which may sometimes be rough; you made yourself the master of them, and when you had done so you reduced nature to the role of interpreter of the ideal you found within yourself... Nature merely supplied you with a subject or an occasion; you yourself did the rest; and was not the rest all that we call by the name of poetry? By which I mean the power of summoning up visions which rejoice and purify the eyes of men; and through these visions, the power of suggesting dreams which fulfil themselves in thought; and, on the wings of this thought, the power to raise us above the cares of the present and out of our concern with reality..." This is a typical sample of the dreary platitudes from which Puvis de Chavannes had in fact tried to escape.

first myths, the age before religion. It was based on the duality of the two rival drives, Eros and Thanatos, a pair irreducibly linked to the separateness of good and evil and of the instincts of life and death. As Freud was already saying, "Drives are mythical beings, grandiose in their indeterminateness." It was upon them that Gauguin based what he had to say. And all that he did not say. It was on them that Munch rested his *Frieze of Life*, on the languid swell of death. It was on them that Klimt relied, to enter daily into the plenitude of a present "which transforms everything into a rich text of resources and life." Gauguin, Munch and Klimt, the three great figureheads of cultural symbolism. With Khnopff hovering in the background. Klimt pressed him to go to Vienna in 1898 to take part in the inaugural exhibition of the "Wienner Secession" group. Khnopff showed some twenty works, including *The Sphinx*, also entitled *Art*, and also called *Caresses*. This indeterminateness was provocative. The image was a plural one, moist, warm, and wrapped in dubious denseness. It has the strange grace and appeal of a riddle containing riddles. Painted in 1896, it seems to have been inspired by Péladan's praise of androgyny. (As early as 1884, Khnopff had invented an equally ambiguous image to serve as the frontispiece to *Le Vice Suprême*.) Eros wears a drift of masks. Since Oedipus's incestuous fate, the winged lioness with a woman's head has become a woman-leopard, rampant, snake-like yet feline too, with a perverse smile and half-shut eyes. She caresses, envelopes and seduces a youth, who is motionless, dreamy, consenting. He carries a double sceptre which has been identified with a Rosicrucian symbol in one of Khnopff's own drawings. Behind the two closely conniving faces lies a wood, symbol of the union of the sexes. In 1896, when it first appeared in *La Libre Esthétique*, the critics recognized this image as "a very interesting symbol of the struggle between the desire for earthly domination and the desire for voluptuous abandon." But who is it who is speaking here, and who is it who listens? It is of course the painter himself, speaking in the first person, and marvellously inventing himself each time he writes. This text, so detailed and slow and accurate, this part-image, part-pediment (it might, as its shape suggests, have existed in cut-out form to begin with), should it speak of the impossible fulfilment, would fix it as dazzlingly as in the line by René Char: "A poem is the fulfilled love of desire that remains desire."

In the Vienna of the *belle époque*, "the decorative city par excellence"; the city where, according to Karl Kraus, "all the streets were paved with culture when everywhere else they had turned to asphalt"; the happy hunting ground of an international bourgeoisie famous for its splendours, its deviations, its liberties, its luxurious feasts, and what Hermann Broch called "its imbecile gaiety"—in this reputedly decadent capital so full of new things, this place for which Freud felt "a personal hatred," Klimt for twenty-seven years maintained a relationship with the owner of a fashionable boutique, though he never had any desire to marry her. Thus he could preserve the illusion of liberty, and paint and possess as he pleased. According to one of his women friends, who claimed she never yielded to his desires, Klimt "had affairs with dozens of women, with children, with sisters who became enemies through love of him." In his *Commentary for a Non-existent Self-Portrait* Klimt says: "There is no self-portrait of me in existence. I am not interested in myself as an 'object of representation.' I am interested in beings, especially feminine ones, and, even more, in other apparitions." But of course every one of his works, every sentence he wrote, was a kind of self-utterance. His whole output, and each element in it, spoke like a self-portrait. This was because, before being "representations" of some object, they were traces, prints, trajectories, graphs and graphemes. They were based on a process of notation and recording which involved simultaneously "the physical act of inscribing and that activity's inner essence." This has been the definition of "writing," ever since J. Derrida, overturning traditional knowledge, separated the notion of writing from the classical conception of the representation of thought by means of conventional characters in such a way that language and writing may merge. Derrida writes: "It is as if the Western concept of language... were now revealed as the disguise of a primordial writing, a writing more fundamental than that which Rousseau regarded as a mere 'supplement of the spoken word.'" Graphs and graphemes thus became, in painting, elements of writing which might be roughly compared to the elements in geometry: discrete and autonomous units, independent of any representation. Dots, lines, angles, curves, circles, strokes and so on are not units of recognition, nor conventional graphic artifices, but elements whose combination and concatenation may appear as contributing signs making up a pictorial text. Apprehended at the level of sensual pleasure, they are also aesthetic signs, a symbolic projection of man. Thus, through the basic network of the writing, the painter may make himself present in us, the receivers. He may be felt and perceived in his own actuality, in the space where he realizes himself as fulfilment of desire, where the signs of original violence are formed. This brings us back to the words of Mallarmé: "Writing? An ancient and very vague but jealous practice whose meaning lies in the mystery of the heart." This meaning beyond meaning is to be found in the writing of Klimt. It is not always sensual, but it is always strikingly interior. Hence both its obscurity and its lucidity. For the man who is writing, painting or drawing always imparts to the graph or trace what he does not always impart to the object he pretends to be reproducing. Herein lies the difference between Klimt's images and those of Gauguin

Gustav Klimt (1862-1918): Nuda Veritas, 1899. Oil. The quotation from Schiller reads: "If you cannot please everyone with your work, try to satisfy the few. To please the many is bad."

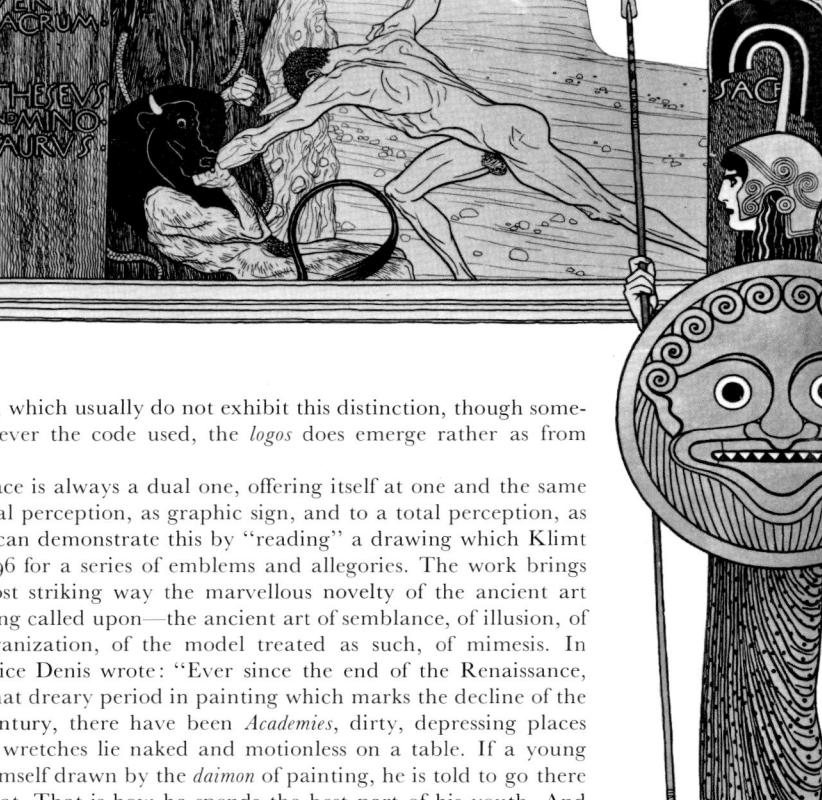

and Munch, which usually do not exhibit this distinction, though sometimes, whatever the code used, the *logos* does emerge rather as from dream.

So the trace is always a dual one, offering itself at one and the same time to visual perception, as graphic sign, and to a total perception, as image. We can demonstrate this by "reading" a drawing which Klimt made in 1896 for a series of emblems and allegories. The work brings out in a most striking way the marvellous novelty of the ancient art which is being called upon—the ancient art of semblance, of illusion, of cultural organization, of the model treated as such, of mimesis. In 1895, Maurice Denis wrote: "Ever since the end of the Renaissance, ever since that dreary period in painting which marks the decline of the sixteenth century, there have been *Academies*, dirty, depressing places where poor wretches lie naked and motionless on a table. If a young man feels himself drawn by the *daimon* of painting, he is told to go there and copy that. That is how he spends the best part of his youth. And the most deplorable thing about it is not that he thus loses his instinct for real life, and the flower of his fresh imagination. It is that gradually, but for ever, the idea is fixed in his head that Art is a copy of something.

"The young Symbolists had to have the audacity to rediscover everything for themselves in order to react against this kind of education, to join up again with tradition, and this at a time when all principles are vague and all rules ill-defined, through having been badly taught, badly fought against, and badly defended! At their age, people usually can only draw or model a torso. They scarcely bother about such things. And yet several of them have been through the Ecole [des Beaux-Arts]! They possess the fruits of many experiments in the arrangement of lines, the play of colours, and the physical laws of expression. They can tell the difference between a study and a picture. Perhaps one day they will get as far as Nature..."

How was it, then, that the methods condemned by the French symbolists through the lips of Maurice Denis, methods enshrined in and by academic tradition, came to be used in such a way that they produced an iconic spectacle which both cast away old roots and established new? To begin with, it was the end of inhibition. Also, it meant the immersion of convention in the nonconventional, in nonconformity, in the unexpected, in a figurative amalgam which could not be reduced to realist paradigm. This amalgam was a carefully calculated arrangement, in a series of superimposed phases, situated on some plane bereft of scale in which present merged with past, and time with space. The mechanisms were those of irreality, to be read at the level of the trace, the writing, propagated like waves, by radiation, in drawing at once open and closed, light and tenacious, strong and supple, free and rigorous. On another level it might be read as an allegory of sculpture, in which trace mingles with what is intelligible, and with what is hidden. Dante is a voyeur. Athena protects. The sphinx questions. Who? What? An apparition, one of those the painter speaks of in his *Commentary*. Is it Eve? What she offers, proffers, is not an apple. It is herself. There in the flesh on the photographer's plinth. But who is it? A model? No, this is not an academic pose. For Klimt it is the nude,

1. *Gustav Klimt (1862-1918):
Theseus and the Minotaur (above)
and Athena with Spear and Shield (right).
Poster for the first exhibition of the
Vienna Secession (March-June 1898) and
cover of "Ver Sacrum," Vienna, May-
June 1898.*

2. *Joseph Maria Olbrich (1867-1908):
Exhibition Hall of the Vienna Secession,
1898-1899, with stained-glass window by
Koloman Moser.*

Gustav Klimt (1862-1918): Pallas Athene, 1898. Oil.

The double trace

femininity, love, the trap. But she is so elegant and charming! Yes, but surrounded by infernos. Her texture, face, her very type (the kind that enchants the painter) is the same as in the image Klimt drew for the review *Ver Sacrum*, founded in 1898 to support the artists of the Secession and their activities. It symbolized the *femme fatale* under the ostensibly innocent title of *Nuda Veritas*. In the review, it is placed close to an image that was familiar in the world of Khnopff: *The Red Lips*. But at the bottom of the "page" we have just "read," at Eve's feet, there is a head, represented full face. Its luxuriant hair, carefully and symmetrically arranged, is crowned with laurels: is she the muse of modern sculpture? Perhaps. But more relevant is the fact that she looks as if she had been drawn by Khnopff. So here is evidence of the link that existed between the two painters. The link was so strong that Klimt symboli-

cally dedicated this work to Khnopff as a token of friendship: the pencil strokes were heightened with gold. The picture is also evidence of how influential Khnopff's presence was in Vienna. At the second Secession show, he exhibited another nine paintings.

On 3 April 1897 a group of painters, engravers, architects, graphic artists and typographers, in an attempt to free themselves from the conservatism of the Künstlerhaus (a professional extension of the Vienna Academy of Fine Arts), broke their corporatist connections with that institution. The Künstlerhaus, to protect tradition, systematically excluded young artists from the most important exhibitions of Austrian painting abroad. The rebels thus brought about a split in the established order. They founded the "Wiener Secession," based on the group started in Munich a few years earlier. On 11 November 1897

"All art is erotic"

1. *Alfred Roller (1864-1935): Cover of the first issue of "Ver Sacrum," journal of the Austrian Artists' Association, Vienna, January 1898.*

2. *Koloman Moser (1868-1918): Two Oriental Dancers, 1903. Illustration for "Ver Sacrum," Vienna, 1903.*

3. *Fernand Khnopff (1858-1921): Red Lips. Chalk drawing published in "Ver Sacrum," Vienna, December 1898.*

It was a delirious vision: her flesh had jade-like transparencies; but from her brow encircled with emeralds fluttered and flowed a veil of black gauze, a vapour of crepe, which concealed her sex and coiled over her thighs and clung like a shackle to her two ankles, deepening the mystery of this pale apparition.

Jean Lorrain. 1899

4. *Gustav Klimt (1862-1918): Allegory of Sculpture (Eve with the Apple in front of a Greek Altar), 1896. Pencil and charcoal with white chalk and gold highlights.*

5. *Alphonse Mucha (1860-1939): Cover design for "Ver Sacrum," Vienna, November 1898.*

Klimt was elected president of the new group by Johann Krämer, Joseph Olbrich, Koloman Moser, Carl Moll, Rudolf Bacher, Rudolf von Ottenfeld, Hans Tichy, Anton Nowak, Julius Mayreder, Edmund von Hellmer, Felician von Myrbach, Josef Hoffmann, Max Kurzweil, Max Lenz and Wilhelm List. The programme was vast but vague. In the first place it had, in accordance with Wagnerian ideology, a soft spot for the "total work of art." It aimed at close collaboration between all disciplines, and at involving all forms of art within the framework of architecture. There is no doubt that Rossetti, Morris and Walter Crane exercised an influence here. Their work had been imported on to the Continent by Henry van de Velde, whose review *L'Art Moderne* published *La Première Prédication d'Art* (The First Art Sermon) on 31 December 1893. (It referred to the political dimension of the question as follows: "The evolution of ideas and the circumstances of social life are no longer fully satisfied by pictures and statues *alone*. It is foolish to rely on them alone to provide for our physical existence, just as it is foolish to believe blindly that they supply all the artistic needs of our age... The artist's profession, as hitherto understood, has become impossible, and we must make the best of it.") The Secession group also aimed at promoting national art. They proposed to invite to Vienna the most "advanced" European artists, and to organize influential international exhibitions. They started a review to back up their policies: the first issue of *Ver Sacrum* appeared in January 1898. It was an outstanding event, even if some people did regard it as a mere counterpart of *Jugend*, which had been appearing in Munich since 1896, promoting and orienting the activities of the Munich Secession group. *Ver Sacrum* was published monthly (until the end of 1903), and concentrated especially on working out, largely through Koloman Moser, a graphic style radically opposed to that of *Van Nu en Straks*: letters as such became as important as images, which tended to be reproductions of works belonging to the aesthetic trend imparted by Klimt to the Secession movement, or ornamental compositions echoing the floral geometry of the belated Viennese Jugendstil. Here "decoration" was seen, developed and understood as "content," a kind of emanation from the depths which was the central theme of the "Modern Style," where surface was an epidermis in which dream and fantasy were bodied forth. Adolf Loos found such allusiveness intolerable, and said so at once in the columns of the *Neue Freie Presse*, opposing the linguistic, scriptural and aesthetic innovations of Klimt, Olbrich and Hoffmann. Drives ought to be repressed. "All art is erotic. The first known ornament, the cross, is erotic in origin. The first work of art, the first act by which the first artist gave free rein to his exuberance by scribbling on a wall, was erotic. A horizontal line is a woman reclining; a vertical line is a man penetrating her... But anyone nowadays who is impelled by some inner urge to cover walls with erotic symbols or obscene graffiti—he's a criminal or a delinquent." For all these reasons, and contrary to the

167

Alphonse Mucha (1860-1939):
Drawings for Jewelry Designs, 1902. Lithograph.
"Youth goes with the passing wind." Design for a fan, 1899. Lithograph. ▷

tions which was to give a Central European echo to the Brussels exhibitions of the Libre Esthétique. Henceforth, every year, both Vienna and Brussels were to try to pinpoint the most recent aspects of current art. On this first occasion, in addition to works by Austrian members of the Secession, and the bold and striking contributions of Khnopff and Rodin, there were works by Puvis de Chavannes (including a triptych, *The Childhood of St Geneviève*), Segantini (*The Evil Mothers*, among others), Besnard, Klinger, Böcklin, Stuck, Whistler, Mucha, Grasset and Crane. During the years that followed, the exhibitors would include Aman-Jean, Carrière, Hodler, von Hofmann, Mackintosh, George Minne, Schwabe, Hans Thoma, Toorop, Gauguin, Redon and Maurice Denis, all in 1903. Munch and Thorn Prikker were invited in 1904. Thus, much more openminded than its counterparts in Munich and Berlin, the Vienna Secession laid definite stress on "painters of feeling," "artists of dream," "painters of the soul," complex painting, plural discourse. The latter warned that "all those who move on the surface are in danger," "all those who try to guess the symbol are in peril." It was a discourse which might have contributed to the research and discoveries of Freud, if Freud had not limited the decoration of his apartment at No. 19 Bergasse to Egyptian and Roman antiquities (statuettes, figurines, urns—mostly funerary objects). But why that reproduction of the Sphinx of Giza in his study? Perhaps it was instrumental

theories of the advocates of Jugendstil, "ornamentation is now no longer organically linked to civilization." So it is not now "an expression of our civilization." It is unworthy of our culture, and should be repulsed, rejected, ignored. A work stripped of ornament reflects thoughts which are clear, pure and profound. "Good form" derives its necessity, and hence its beauty, from the degree of usefulness it expresses. And if there is no art but erotic art, then "good form" is erotic too! Unless, that is, it is regarded as "good" because it has been repressed by reason. Rationalism is always repressive. Culture and civilization are not necessarily the same. Civilization may be the destroyer of culture. Behind this idea is the glittering duality of the human and the divine, colouring the transition from ambiguity to "the harsh contrariety opposing one term to another." Maurice Blanchot has written: "One may live indifferently, or like a sleepwalker, between day and night, but as soon as the stern difference between the two becomes immediate the tragic choice begins: the choice between waking and sleep, the choice between the gods of light and the nocturnal powers, a choice that is always tragic because the pros and cons cancel each other out. One of Heraclitus's answers was: one must choose Difference itself, not that which is different."

And so there opened in Vienna, on 28 May 1898, with a poster designed by Klimt and in ad hoc premises lent by the Horticultural Society and fitted up by Hoffmann and Olbrich, the first of the exhibi-

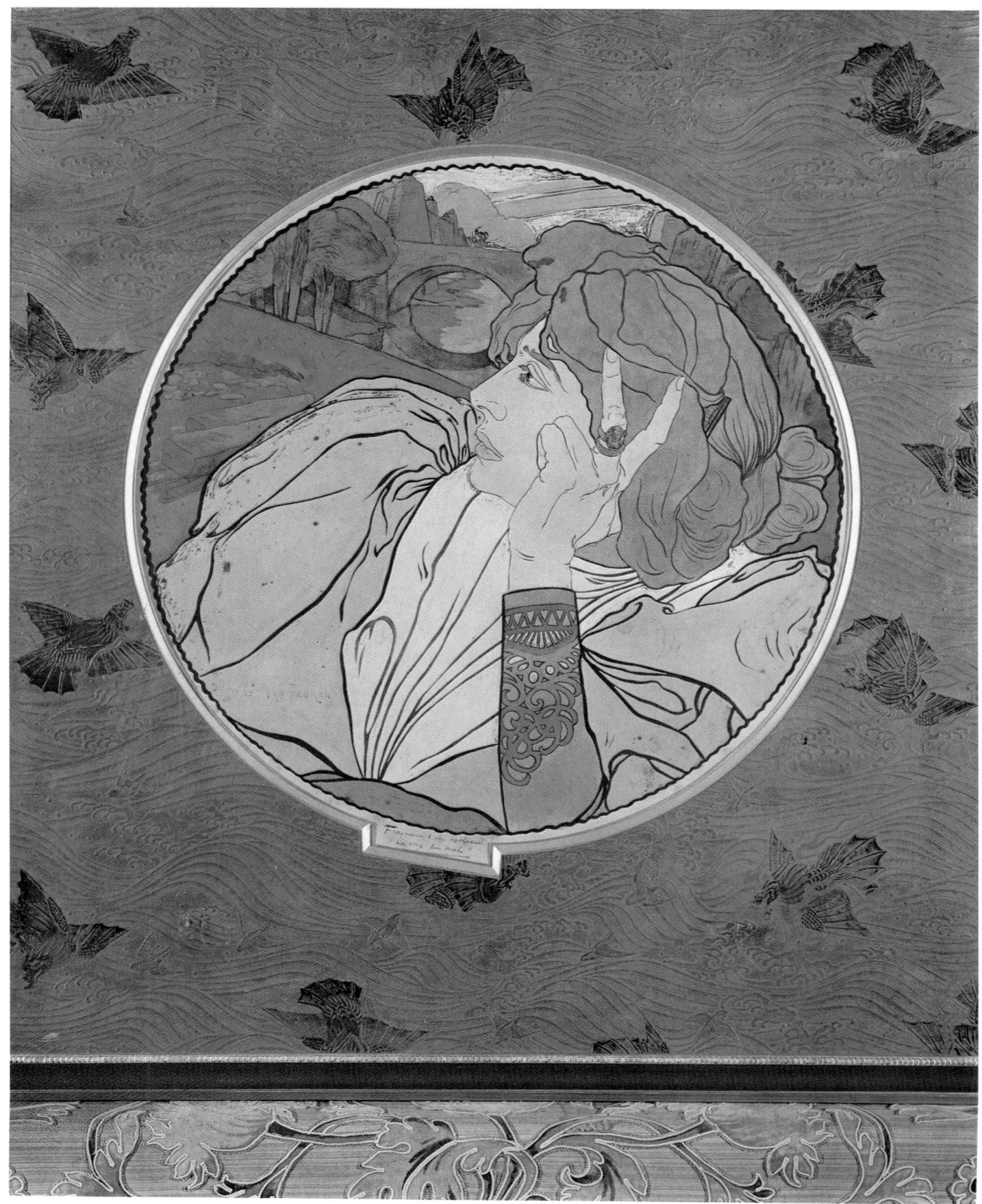

Georges de Feure (1868-1928): The Voice of Evil or Melancholy, c. 1895. Gouache.

Xavier Mellery (1845-1921): The Staircase. Black chalk.

▷ *George Minne (1866-1941): Illustration
for Maurice Maeterlinck's "Sœur Béatrice,"
published in "Die Insel," Berlin, March 1900.*

▷▷ *Léon Spillaert (1881-1946): Lithograph illustration inspired by
Maurice Maeterlinck's volume of verse "Serres Chaudes," c. 1900.*

The dense presence of the past

Quand son époux l'a mise à mort
Elle a poussé trois cris d'effroi.

Au premier cri qu'elle a poussé
Elle a dit le nom de son frère:
Il se réveille et voit passer
Trois colombes aux ailes brisées.
Au second cri qu'elle a poussé
Elle a dit le nom de son père:
Ouvre sa fenêtre à l'instant
Et voit voler trois cygnes en sang.

Au dernier cri qu'elle a poussé
Elle appelle enfin son amant:
Ouvre la porte de son château
Et voit fuir au loin trois corbeaux.

Maurice Maeterlinck, 1893

(When her husband put her to death, she uttered three cries of fright. At the first cry she uttered, she spoke her brother's name: he wakes and sees three doves with broken wings go by. At the second cry she uttered, she spoke her father's name: opens his window at once and sees three bleeding swans fly by. At the last cry she uttered, she finally calls her lover: opens the door of his castle and sees three ravens flee into the distance.)

in the studies which led, in 1905, to the *Three Essays on the Theory of Sexuality. The Interpretation of Dreams*, which inaugurated psychoanalysis, appeared in 1899 but passed unnoticed. In March 1900 Freud, depressed, wrote to Fliess that the reception the book had received and the way he himself was ignored had "again destroyed the relationships which were beginning to grow up between myself and the people about me."

One of his patients, "an outstanding woman," left him in May 1900. As a parting present she gave him Böcklin's *Isle of the Dead*. Though we do not know whether Freud tried to decipher that central passage of historical symbolism. But without Freud's work we should not understand Stuck's *Self-Portrait of the Artist in his Studio with his Wife Mary*. If Stuck, that "formidable contemporary of Klimt," depicts himself in evening dress, it is not so much to demonstrate his self-assurance as to dream the more freely of nakedness. And when Xavier Mellery, between Redon and Seurat, reminds us of Khnopff, and tries from 1890 on to restore what he called "the life of things"; when this strange playwright of chiaroscuro introduces a staircase into his work; then the passive, objective, analytical "reader" sees a staircase with light coming through the banisters. The romantic reader sees a strange corridor where family reminiscences seem to be slumbering. A dreamer sees a vestibule faintly lit by a lamp which casts strange shadows on the dim walls and ceiling. And Mellery answers all this by saying, "Everything is alive, even if it does not move." Because everything, all that is constructed by man, is charged with the dimension imparted by the dense

presence of the past, and added to what is living. That being so, the staircase is no longer just an episode: image emerges from image, comes towards us, comes to us, and tells us it is something else—the bearer of riches derived from the most ancient ways of the human psyche; the trace of a primal symbolism, classical inasmuch as the staircase "depicts plastically the break in level which makes possible transition from one mode of being to another." Inasmuch as, on the cosmological plane, it "makes possible communication between Heaven, Earth and Hell." Inasmuch as the climb it suggests to the imagination shows "the way to absolute reality," the ascent to knowledge. Inasmuch as the movement it suggests evokes sexual union. Since Freud, all these things have been incorporated in the image, even if Mellery's acceptance of Péladan's litanies and his participation in the Rosicrucian Salons suggest that he was initiated into esoteric doctrines. If so, the staircase would represent black magic, and symbolize descent. Even if this were the case the image itself would remain intact, at once the product of original repression and of aesthetic sublimation.

Alphonse Mucha (1860-1939):

1. *Photograph of a model posing for "Documents décoratifs" in the artist's Paris studio, c. 1900.*
2. *Summer, 1896. Lithograph.*
3. *Photograph of Maruska in the artist's Paris studio, 1904.*

Khnopff too, as we know, was closely connected with Péladan and the Salon de la Rose Croix. Does this mean that the strangest aspect of his work derived from contact with the esoteric? Probably not. If his images are often fascinating; if the people they represent are seen as strangers in this world; if they seem detached, unreal, absent, existing in an implacable immobility; if they seem to go beyond, and do go beyond, any aesthetic principle of realism—all this is because they derive from an artifice, because they are the result of a détour, the détour which the Pre-Raphaelites practised so skilfully: photography. Photography used as an intermediary, as a model. The question has already been referred to, and we must return to it now. The image ensnared by the camera is much more arbitrary than we usually continue to think: it is the result of a procedure which works in such a way that a so-called "objective" photograph is always what a certain way of seeing has decreed that it should be—i.e. an image implying a knowledge long invested by a code deeply rooted in Western culture and now contaminated by all the East. But Khnopff does not use this image as Courbet did or as Robert Bechtle does. Nor as Victor Hugo used it, or Richard Estes uses it now, as "always the first stage of the work." Nor, again, like Degas or Ben Schonzeit, who each in their way go beyond what is specifically photographic.

Khnopff undoubtedly knew that Delacroix considered the correct and skilful use of the daguerreotype, "by a man of genius," to be capable of raising it "to heights unknown to us." He also knew that for Millet photography had been an aid "similar to plaster casts." He saw clearly, too, that Ensor regarded it as an icon of transition and source of information, as it might be nowadays for Goings, Kacere and Gnoli. But Khnopff's own way of using photography as a model was altogether out of the ordinary. It inclined towards so close and rigorous a homology and literalness that mimesis, which involves a relationship of resemblance between two existing things, becomes a relationship between two *products*: one which incites the photographic analogy, and another which manifests itself in the act of painting, on the basis of, and in order to confound, analogy. The whole secret is there, in the attack which disguises the rhetoric of reality, and attempts, in the face of all logic, to reinforce a system of signs. This is the origin of the inertia characteristic of Khnopff's poetic. This inertia, while it carries disguise as far as possible, derives also from Khnopff's placing, disorientation and framing, and from the layout he imposed on duplicated objects long prepared and finally brought into play for this purpose. Thus the painter's sister willingly poses for him: to contribute to the mystery of *The Secret*. So also she posed to become the playing figures who move through the void in *Memories*. This is an attack by which the painter defies the imagination, trying to lead astray any real attempt at intertextuality in order to protect his own "professional secrets." No one else could know that photographs were for him essential and fundamental material. And no one ever knew that he practised photography himself. In secret. It was only after his death, when his studio was put up for sale on 27 November 1922, that his friends saw with surprise that his effects included a Steinheil camera, with tripod, six double slides, and all the corresponding equipment! The discovery was all the more disturbing because not only had Khnopff, while alive, kept people in ignorance about it, but he had even (we realize now that it was only to

Fernand Khnopff (1858-1921):
1. & 3. Photographs of the artist's
sister Marguerite posing for "Memories." 2. Memories, 1889.
Pastel.

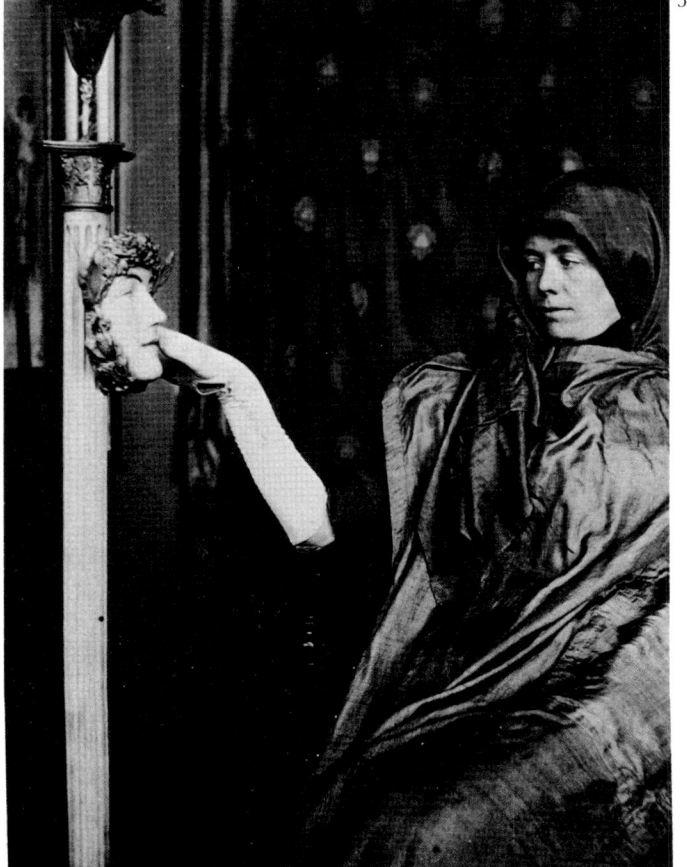

Challenging the imaginary

6

Fernand Khnopff (1858-1921):
4. The Secret and the Reflection, c. 1910. Pastel and drawing.
5. Photograph of the artist's sister Marguerite posing for "The Secret and the Reflection."
6. Photograph of the artist's sister Marguerite posing in his studio.

throw people off the scent) taken the trouble to contribute a paper to the Royal Academy of Belgium, on 8 June 1916, on *The So-called Art of Photography*. In it he condemned photography as no more than "an agreeable pastime for an idler." According to him, "an artist creates; he is the master of his work in the fullest sense of the word: it is his creature; he can do what he likes with it, and modify every part of it as he chooses right up to the last moment. A photographer, on the other hand, has in the subject he borrows from Nature a highly independent collaborator whose artistic contribution is far greater than his own. All the art photographer can do is freeze his models into tableaux vivants, and then, when making the print, alter the lights and shades, mixing up all their relations, destroying the model and coarsening the whole effect. This is clearly shown by the prints, before and after the gum dichromate process, which have been exhibited, proudly or furiously, by certain practitioners. But however hard the most skilful art photographer tries, he can never rise above the form and light imposed upon him by his model; he is its slave to the last. He is like the soldier who shouted to his captain that he had taken a prisoner. 'Bring him here, then,' said the captain. 'I can't,' said the man. 'He won't let go of me'." Khnopff stresses the different natures of art and photography: "For photography, the characteristic feature is realism, with its superficial aspects of life in action. For art, it is *idealism*, with its *personal interpretation of deepest dreams*." He concedes that "the photographer may help the artist with documentation." The painter may even "help to refine the photographer's taste"! But Khnopff is eager to assure us that he is ignorant of "the technical side of photography." Charles de Maeyer has spoken of the painter's "insincerity," but it might be better to see Khnopff's attitude as a stratagem designed to protect a unique territory—an autotext that no one would ever try to annex in any way.

The year 1898 saw a great change, in the deaths of Puvis de Chavannes, Gustave Moreau, Burne-Jones, and Mallarmé. Silence was about to fall on a great generation. A few months before Mallarmé died, Rachilde sent him her latest novel, *L'Animale*. She had invented the man-object in 1884, in *Monsieur Vénus*, symbolizing all the "decadent" obsessions. To her he said now, with his crystalline restraint and unique urbanity, always on the brink of the unexpected: "*The Female Animal*, and also the divine animal, I said to myself as I put down your book, which, in addition to lending it your usual acuity, you have made meditative, superb and exact. An original draught of what is so inadequately called sensuality, containing, at moments, all human aspiration, emanates from your heroine and from your pages. Here, intelligently and with a fine frank scrutiny, and perceived as latent and superior, is the state of loving in absolute form..." Such perspicuity parallels the beginnings of Freud's researches.

Redon, living in retirement in the Gironde, said he was overwhelmed and "almost depressed" to hear of Mallarmé's death. He was being harassed by André Mellerio, who wanted to make a *catalogue raisonné* of all his engravings. Redon was not yet sixty, and already the critics were trying to set bounds to his great experiment! Would not the very need to express himself be threatened? Would he still be able to dream, under this pressure from his impending, though hypothetical, end?

Redon was vexed: "Of what interest can it be to you if I stand before my easel or my stone with preconceived ideas of a subject? People have been asking me the same question for thirty years." And he had never answered. "What is the use of revealing anything else but the result?" But he gave in, and spoke of "following the unpredictable paths of fancy." He went on: "Fancy—fantasy—is a queen who suddenly offers us magnificent and astonishing charms, and makes us her slave... She is also the messenger of that lofty and mysterious stranger, the 'unconscious'." "That," he pointed out, with all the restraint of anguished inactivity, "should make you understand how difficult it is to answer whys and wherefores. For in the fateful crucible where a work of art is formed, everything is subject to the precious whim of that unknown stranger."

Gustav Klimt (1862-1918) : Expectation, c. 1905-1909. Tempera, watercolour, gold and silver leaf, chalk, pencil and gouache.

8

THE SPACE
OF DREAM
1900...

Wenn du der Träumer bist, bin ich dein Traum.
Doch wenn du wachen willst, bin ich dein Wille
und werde mächtig aller Herrlichkeit
und ründe mich wie eine Sternenstille
über der wunderlichen Stadt der Zeit.

Rainer Maria Rilke, from *Das Stunden-Buch,*
Book I, *Das Buch vom mönchischen Leben,* 1899

(If you are the dreamer, I am your dream. But if you
would wake, I am your will and become lord of all
magnificence and grow round like a starry silence over the
wonderful city of time.)

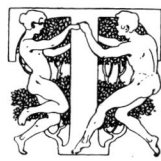

HE TWENTIETH CENTURY had begun. Without apocalypse, without a break in continuity. Gauguin was thinking of moving on to the Marquesas. It was becoming more and more difficult to find models in Tahiti, where "imagination was beginning to cool." He thought it necessary, too, in order to impress the public, to give it a shock. And he had a strategy of communication he intended to follow. For he was afraid of repetition, even if it was only imaginary. "The world is so stupid that when one shows it pictures containing things which are new and terrible, Tahiti will become comprehensible and charming. My Brittany pictures have become rosewater because of Tahiti; Tahiti will become eau de Cologne because of the Marquesas." But he admitted that "the plastic arts are not easy to understand; to make them speak one has to question them ceaselessly, and question oneself at the same time." He did question himself, and in so doing undermined the myth of mimesis. "One wonders why Velazquez's Infanta has something wrong with its shoulders and why the head does not fit on to them properly. And why this is satisfactory, whereas a head by Bonnat does fit properly on to shoulders which have nothing the matter with them, but is not satisfactory! Velazquez remains unscathed, even when Carolus-Duran corrects him." After Gauguin had been in Fatuiva for several months, he recalled: "Some twenty years ago Puvis de Chavannes's *Poor Fisherman* and *Prodigal Son* were mouldering at Durand-Ruel's in the Rue de la Paix, not finding any buyers even at quite modest prices. The head was too big, there were no muscles, the trousers were empty. The woman was ridiculous, the child a mere foetus, and the whole thing looked as if it was bathed in gooseberry fool. The wise Monsieur Brunetière said nothing..." Gauguin also remembered what had happened just after 1870: "The resumption of the Salon was terrific, as far as numbers went. There were soldiers full of hatred because of their defeat by Prussia, and proud of their disgusting reprisals against the Commune. The great Bonnat was the painter of the little Thiers, quite calmly, without shame. After Thiers it was MacMahon, the slayer of cuirassiers, who reviewed the private show. Salute, French painters, your leader is shouting: 'Attention! Forward march!' And everyone fell into line. Behind him, Meissonier, a colonel in the national guard, also shouted: 'Forward march!'—Meissonier, the painter of the hordes of steel, where everything was made of steel except the cuirasses. Everyone joined in, including the State, with all its meretricious luxury, its decorations and its purchases. The dream of pictures hung on the line. Including also the press and the big banks: speculation. Also most artists, and feminine influence. Not everyone can be a pimp." Lately Remy de Gourmont had discovered in the work of Burne-Jones, Redon and Moreau "an exquisite putrefaction that is almost sumptuous." In January 1900 Jean Lorrain saw Moreau as a "symbolic and divine thinker, whose legendary and mythological evocations make him the real father of people like Leconte de Lisle, Gustave Flaubert and Richard Wagner."

Moreau died on 18 April 1898. To guarantee and protect his own survival he had turned his big town-house in the Rue de La Rochefoucauld into a museum. He had bequeathed it, "with all it contains—paintings, drawings, sketches, etc., etc., the work of fifty years, together with the contents of the old apartments in the said house, once occupied by my father and mother—to the State, or failing that to the Ecole des Beaux-Arts, or failing that to the Institut de France (Académie des Beaux-Arts), on the express condition that, in accordance with my dearest wish, they shall always, or at least as long as possible, maintain the integrity of the collection so as to demonstrate the accumulated work and efforts of the artist's whole lifetime." It was the apotheosis of narcissism. In January 1900 Redon visited this shrine. "The Moreau museum," he wrote to his "excellent friend" Mme de Holstein, "left me with an inclination for such sumptuosity as is found in the setting of *The Triumph of Alexander*. This picture is a unique

As for Redon himself, he said in a letter to his friend Bonger on 17 January 1901 that he was "happy in the independent position I occupy, still producing the work I like for a constant number of connoisseurs. People tell me this is an enviable lot. But there are swarms of official artists who have been doing badly, especially since the Centennial. At present they are conducting a campaign against us, but it scarcely affects the market. You know how Cézannes have gone up, and the successes of Renoir; how times change! The new team of youngsters, who are my friends and surround me with affection, are doing nicely too. In short, there is now an art outside the official framework

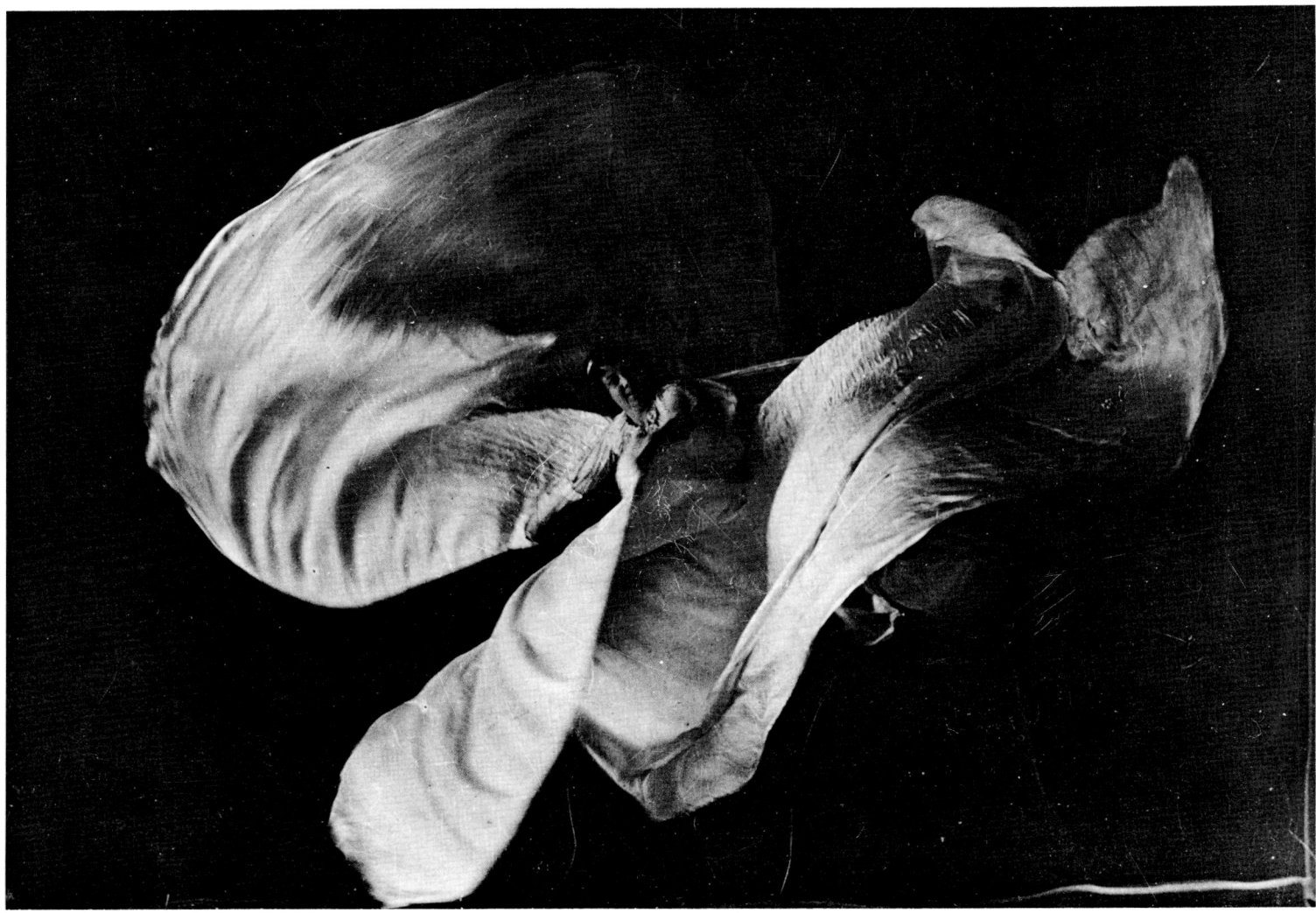

Photograph of the American dancer Loie Fuller (1862-1928), with her "butterfly veils."

example of Moreau. It has something in it of India, only with less sweetness and light—the India of grandiose appearances rather than the India of the *Sakuntala*. The mystic milk does not flow through it; the radiant and sacred fusion deep in the heart of life, in what it contains of before and after, is not there. If I were to contemplate it every day, Moreau's art would lead me now to fashionable elegance. And might not this lead me to *regal* elegance, while I was about it? It seems to me there is too much jewellery." Redon later makes an observation we have no difficulty in understanding today: "In fact, Moreau, a bachelor, produced the work of an elegant bachelor, strictly sealed up against the shocks of life; his work is the fruit of it, it is art and nothing but art, and that is saying a good deal."

which is taken seriously by a public which judges for itself. This public buys, collects, even speculates. And since as in any game there has to be an element of the unknown, these people tend to bet on artists without official recognition. How things have altered since I started out—a long while ago, it's true. What is undeniable is that everything I have loved and admired, all the painting that has given me a thrill ever since I was young, was for long rejected and despised, and it is this art, which once could find no purchasers, that now is sought after and bought at high prices. I am told that the Bernheims are preparing a Van Gogh show for this winter. It's a good sign. And we can be sure of the final result for him, as for the others, can we not? They're taking their time about Gauguin, I think; but they'll get around to him."

Redon, having seen Moreau's *Oedipus and the Sphinx* again in the Rue de La Rochefoucauld, "without being unduly affected," relates how when he was young he had been carried away by it, and long retained that first impression. "Perhaps it had the power to give me strength to follow a solitary path close to its own—perhaps because of the evocative elements dear to lovers of literature." In the middle of the 1890s he had told Edmond Picard of his plan, his hope, "of giving his dreams more exteriority if possible."

For Freud these were the great creative years. Those, to be precise, between 1885 and 1902. While Bergson in France was introducing a

tion it met with. Freud was accused of "lapsing into total mysticism" and "the chaos of arbitrariness." His "artistic imagination" was said to have "got the better of his thought as a scientific researcher." But as he said to Fliess on 7 May 1900: "No critic can see more clearly than I do myself the disproportion between the problems and the solutions I offer, and for my sins none of the unexplored psychic regions which I have been the first human being to enter will bear my name or be subject to my laws." He seems to have had no idea, suspicion or hope that there would be such a thing as Freudianism. Later, when surrounded by a group of followers, he was able to say: "Whoever awakens, as I have

Koloman Moser (1868-1918): The Dancer Loie Fuller. Watercolour and ink.

new mode of knowledge—intuition as an immediate datum of awareness, distinguishing succession from simultaneity (succession being understood as duration, and simultaneity as "measurable time" and "space *qua* homogeneity")—Freud in Vienna discovered the great "secret" of our psychological life: the unconscious. He wrote in March 1894 that he had "the distinct impression of having approached one of the great secrets of nature." It was a secret so great that it is still being unravelled, despite the differences between rival schools. The last chapter of *Die Traumdeutung* (The Interpretation of Dreams) was sent to the publisher in September 1899. At the end of October, his friend Fliess received a copy of the book, and it was on sale by November 4 (though bearing the date 1900). We have already mentioned the kind of recep-

done in order to fight them, the worst untamed demons in the depths of the human soul, must not expect to emerge unscathed from the battle." He was presented with a medal in 1906, on the occasion of his fiftieth birthday. On it were engraved the last words of Sophocles' *Oedipus Rex*: "Who divined the famed riddle and was a man most mighty." He was very moved, and told how as a student at the Vienna School of Medicine he had gazed at the busts of the professors on the façade, and dreamed of having his own place among them, with the same inscription as was now written on the medal. As V.N. Smirnoff has remarked, the discovery of the unconscious "evidently had its own secret history."

Although he felt he had not yet entirely mastered the subject, in 1901 Freud brought together the main ideas of *Die Traumdeutung* in a

Auguste Rodin (1840-1917): The Kiss, 1886. Marble.

succinct exposition, *Über den Traum.* This work contains all the fundamental concepts of Freud's dream theory, and the ideas which have since become the working instruments of psychoanalysis, though they have subsequently been refined, extended and more thoroughly examined. By a strange coincidence, in 1899 a Viennese physicist, Josef Popper-Lynkeus, published a book called *Die Phantasien eines Realisten* (Phantasies of a Realist), though he knew nothing at all about Freud's researches. He spoke of a "man who had the strange characteristic of never dreaming anything absurd," and who wondered why a dreamer is usually unable to interpret his own dreams. "It seems," replies Popper-Lynkeus, "that there must be something hidden in your dreams, some peculiar lewdness, some dissimulation hard for your usual self to imagine. That is why your dreams so often appear meaningless, or even outright nonsense. But basically this is not so. It cannot but be otherwise, for it is always the same man we are concerned with, whether

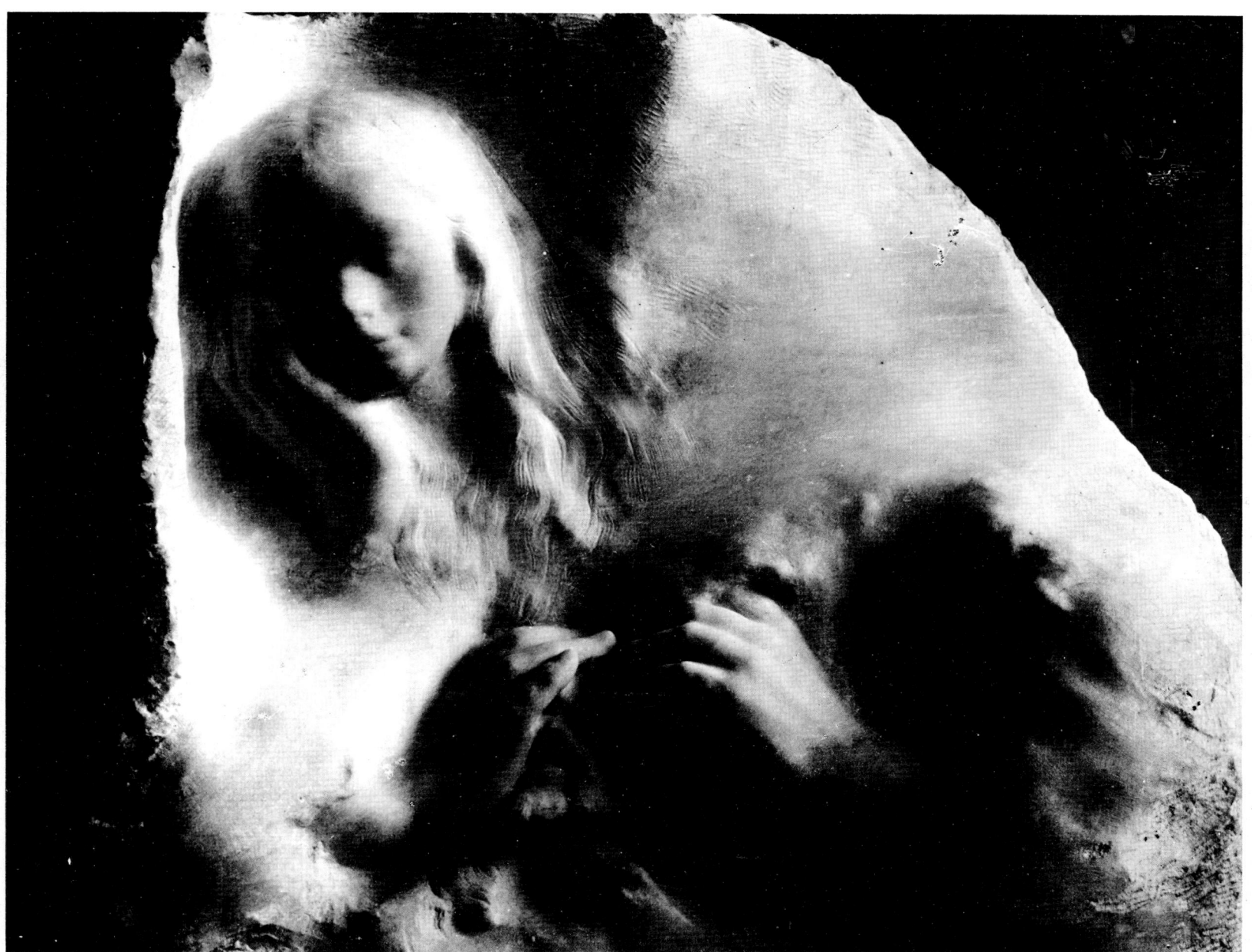

Auguste Rodin (1840-1917): Last Vision or Last Thought, 1902. Marble.

There is nothing in Nature which has more character than the human body. In its strength or grace it evokes the most varied images. At times it resembles a flower: the bending of the torso imitates the stem, the smile of the breasts and head and the lustre of the hair answer to the full bloom of a corolla. At times it recalls a supple liana, a shrub of bold and delicate curvature... At other times, the human body bending backwards is like a spring, like a beautiful bow on which Eros aims his invisible arrows.

Auguste Rodin, *L'Art*

asleep or awake." Meanwhile, at the same time as Klimt was painting *Hope*, one of his most highly sexed works (after the provocative *Moving Waters*, *Pallas Athene*, *Nuda Veritas* and *Judith*), a young Viennese philosopher, Otto Weininger, in 1903 published *Geschlecht und Charakter* (Sex and Character), a violently anti-conformist and even heretical work based on the idea of bisexuality. (All cultural creativeness, however, was attributed to the male principle.) Fliess believed the bisexuality theme had been leaked to Weininger via a manuscript of his own which he had entrusted to Freud.

But why pay so much attention to Freud in a book on Symbolism? Far be it from me to try to establish overhastily a relationship between two different orders of events. But the fact is that Symbolism—an attitude and approach which dynamically affected literature and the plastic arts, music and architecture—attempted, for reasons we have already examined, to establish a codified discourse based on what has

come to be called our phylogenic heritage: the distant past, archaic language, myths of origin. As we have seen, political opposition to reality causes this discourse to interrogate the imagination. The imagination, after operating in its own sphere, reflects on to the image, through the senses, one or more of the cultures lying dormant. Then the signifying imagination produces signs, while the painter, the poet, the creator, endeavours to give direction to the meaning.

Thus, in 1900, historical symbolism and psychoanalysis met in a kind of anthropology of the imagination. Probably this was because the long labour of identification involved in Freud's exploration of dreams resulted in a "collection" of symbols, mostly of sexual origin, which corresponded to information already acquired, and since increased, by such sciences as anthropology, ethnography, mythography and linguistics. No doubt it was also due to the fact that the symbolists adopted the question of culture, and went beneath the surface in search of mythical thought—the thought which "moves in the orbit of symbols"—passing through dream on the way. The most important passages in Gustave Moreau, Puvis de Chavannes, Redon, Khnopff, Munch, Klinger and Klimt only seem to imitate dream in so far as they avoid the appearances of reality. True, Blake, at the beginning of the nineteenth century, had spoken of the great task of opening up eternal worlds, opening the immortal eyes of men to the inner world of thought and of eternity. As regards inner man, Freud had been led to designate as "unconscious" all that which seems concealed in dream, inaccessible to the consciousness of the dreamer: something dissimulated, disguised, censored, and yet essential. Among these hidden things is the shocking desire to commit incest or murder—"which every grown-up man has forgotten and which everywhere links him for ever to his past." The universal meaning of the Oedipus tragedy was revealed for the first time in 1900: "His fate moves us," wrote Freud, "because it might have been our own, because at our birth the oracle pronounced the same curse on us. We have all felt our first sexual drive in relation to our mother, and our first hatred in relation to our father; our dreams bear witness to it. Oedipus, who kills his father and marries his mother, only realizes our childhood wish. But we, more fortunate than he, have been able, unless we are neuropaths, to detach our sexual desires from our mother and forget our jealousy of our father. We regard with horror the man who accomplished our childhood wish, and our horror has all the force of the repression that was imposed on those desires. Like Oedipus, we are unconscious of the desires which offend against morality yet which are forced upon us by nature. When they are revealed to us, we prefer to avert our eyes from the scenes of our childhood."

This key passage from *Die Traumdeutung*, though so well-known, is worth recalling here because the Oedipus complex was a major feature of Symbolism from Moreau to Lévy-Dhurmer. It produced a wealth of images, each more unreal than the last. Unreal? Where does reality actually begin? Nowadays it is easier for us to understand André Breton's enthusiasm for the symbolists, of whom "it will be futile, until further orders, to speak in terms of *reason*. They systematically resumed," wrote Breton, "a *quest* which the nineteenth century put above all other so-called poetic preoccupations, beginning with Novalis and Hölderlin in Germany, Blake and Coleridge in England, and Nerval and Baudelaire in France, and which was to become truly obligatory perhaps with Mallarmé, and certainly with Lautréamont and Rimbaud. Passions remain as unbridled as ever on this subject. It is inevitable that the ambition—the Promethean ambition, as it has been called—which impels the above-mentioned poets to force the gates of mystery and advance boldly into the unknown despite all prohibitions causes the greatest possible offence to all those who have comfortably withdrawn behind the existing barriers, and we all know that their numbers are legion. Their wrath is all the greater nowadays because the history of ideas cannot be halted, and to go backward is as impossible in this matter as in all others. For over a century poetic activity has been first inclined and then actually directed towards the recovery of the mind's original powers, and nothing can now make it resume a subordinate role" *(Entretiens, 1913-1952)*.

◁ *Auguste Rodin (1840-1917): Paolo and Francesca in Clouds, 1894. Marble.*

▽ *Gustav Klimt (1862-1918): Nude in Side View, c. 1902. Black chalk study for "The Enemy Powers."*

Louis Welden Hawkins (1849-1910):
Fan on a Gold Ground, May 1905.
Gouache mounted on gilt paper.

Page 185:
Fernand Khnopff (1858-1921):
The Silver Tiara, c. 1900. Pastel.

Thus Freud, in 1900, stood between two cultural events: historical Symbolism and Surrealism. The science of dreams lent art a potential for liberty which Breton saluted in the *Surrealist Manifesto* of 1924: "On the pretext of civilization and progress, they have succeeded in banishing from the mind everything which rightly or wrongly might be called chimera; in proscribing every kind of search for truth which does not conform to custom. Apparently it is only by the merest chance that there has recently been brought to light part of the intellectual world, in my view the most important part, which people pretended not to care about any more. For this we must thank Freud. On the basis of his discoveries there is developing at last a current of opinion which will allow the explorer of humanity to extend his explorations further."

Symbolism and Surrealism are brought together by a certain mental attitude and a certain style of living. They also share common themes: death, clairvoyance, total art, disorientation, women. The image of the "symbolist woman" as seen by artists from Moreau to Klimt, and that of the "surrealist woman" as treated through the ideological or sexual fantasies underlying the works of Ernst, Dali, Magritte, Bellmer, Labisse and Delvaux, need to be compared and contrasted as emblems of the two cultural adventures between which there are so many analogies and so many differences.

Perhaps, of all the realms through which man passes, in which he sojourns, and from which he departs again, that of symbol is the most vast, and the most complex. It is so because it is the realm of allusion, of sedimentation, all superimposed one upon another, repressed through a series of forgettings, rejections, inhibitions. It is a realm where cultures intersect and overlap, disperse and disappear. But it is an illusion to think they are swallowed up like cities engulfed by the sea. They are the primal nuclei of myth, religion, language and art. Ernst Cassirer has shown quite clearly how the products of art, like those of knowledge, law, language and technology, are indissolubly linked to the origin of myth. All the fundamental forms of a culture, of whatever kind, have their origins in the mythical consciousness in which symbols are created, so many and so various according to their motivations. Psychoanalysis too endeavours to uncover, discover, elucidate them, making libido a major theme, and attributing a major role in the formation of images to the conflict brought about by what are called "advanced" cultures between drives and social repression.

Gaston Bachelard incorporated into this quest an "imagination of matter," intended to stimulate the unreality function to compete with the reality function: "*dreaming well,* dreaming in such a way as to remain faithful to the dream quality of the archetypes rooted in the unconscious" should be more important than the *seeing well* which is the "basis of realist culture." For imagined images are more condensations of archetypes than "reproductions of reality." But Freud, trying to discover the symbolism of dream, admits that the notion of symbol is itself not "clearly defined." It often merges with the notion of substitution or representation. It even approaches that of allusion. A symbol is also often a comparison. But it never actually resembles the thing it symbolizes and summons up. There may be an analogy, either perceived or presumed; there may even be a partial identity, either fictitious or real. For H. Lefebvre, comparison, analogy and identity all enter into the "consciousness of symbol." Seen in this way, symbolism "always presupposes two terms, condensed into one by a trope (ellipse, metaphor)." This is a classical approach. Does it reach the heart of symbolism? Lefebvre does not think so, although symbol does seem to subtend "social imagination" as distinct from individual imagination. It gives rise to signs, sets of signs, fields or "sub-systems." It thus enters into social structures and ideologies. It acts as a ground for emblems or fetishes. Moreover it is a central sun for all the satellites which derive their light (imaginary or real) not from themselves but from it. In some way or another it suggests, recalls, stimulates. It condenses, starts a chain reaction. It is the word of absence, a word that is oblique. It has been called "that which is, without being" (T. Todorov). It is the word of the unspoken, a riddle, a secret, either cultural or innocent. In the highly cultural space of the period from the 1870s to the early 1900s, it became either the result of liberty won over territory acquired by the victorious bourgeoisie (in which case the guardians of the temple said things were going to the dogs, as they always do whenever men discover themselves and speak familiarly to one another, phantasm to phantasm); or it became an image within a system where themes of replacement were codified so as to form a symbolism: as when the cross of Judeo-Christian tradition becomes an emblem of faith.

It was undoubtedly within these limits, within this reserve, that Maurice Denis always operated. For that reason we cannot but include here a text he published in *L'Art et la Vie* in October 1896. This article had an influence, direct or indirect, on the third wave of Symbolism which began between 1890 and 1895, with Georges de Feure, Degouve de Nuncques, Borissov-Moussatov, Hugo Simberg, Alberto Martini, Gallen-Kallela, Pellizza da Volpedo, Carl Strathmann, Mehoffer, Enckell, Egedius, Brull Vinoles, Guirand de Scévola, Kousnetsov and Witold Wojtkiewicz. Working in the same spirit was the Franco-American poet Viélé-Griffin, though he always stood "aloof from the din, safe from honours," and André Breton saw him as "the antidote to someone like Henri de Régnier." Maurice Denis, then, wrote: "I have always attached great importance to the symbolist idea. It was really a revelation to those weary of naturalism and yet at the same time too devoted to painting to give themselves over to idealist dreams. Once more, and belated though it may be, I insist that this famous movement has been underestimated. It certainly was no idealist theory. It was the immediate result of the then fashionable positivist philosophies and of the inductive methods we thought so highly of, and as such was the most strictly scientific of art movements. Those who began it were painters of landscapes and still lifes, and not at all 'painters of the soul.' They were men passionate for truth, living in communion with nature, and, I believe, without a metaphysic. If they 'distorted' things, made up things, invented strange formulas, it was because they wanted to submit to the laws of harmony which govern colour relationships and the handling of line... but it was also to give more sincerity to the rendering of their sensations. Given the structure and physiology of the eye, the mechanisms of association and the laws of sensibility (in so far as we yet know them), they derived from them the laws governing a work of art, and by obeying these at once attained more intense expression. That being so, instead of trying, always in vain, to reconstruct their sensations, they endeavoured to replace them with equivalents. There was thus a close correspondence between form and emotion. Phenomena signified states of mind, and that is symbolism. Matter had become expressive, the flesh was made word. Taine and Spencer showed us the way, and now we have arrived at a genuine Alexandrian philosophy... Symbolism thus rests entirely on one of those very simple truths confirmed since earliest times by both tradition and experience. The ancient artist races of India and Egypt were well aware of the mysterious correspondences between beautiful forms and beautiful feelings. Christianity, taking over the ancient mode of expression and renovating and exalting it, was only linking up with oriental tradition. But it lent this tradition a new and extraordinary vitality which was manifested, at

▷ *Gustav Klimt (1862-1918):*
Judith I (Judith with the Head
of Holofernes), 1901. Oil.

◁ *Alfred Kubin (1877-1959):*
Marsh Plants, 1903-1906.
Ink wash and watercolour.

Alfred Kubin (1877-1959):
▽ *The Dancer, c. 1900. Ink wash.*
▷ *Bat and Graveyard Wall, 1900-1903. Ink wash.*

In a long "dream series" on which I worked for many years, I began by setting down in my drawing some immediate fragments of dreams... In the end I accustomed myself completely to this ghostly reality of dream... and I succeeded in executing compositions of this kind by focusing my subject on the waking dream, like a photographer.

Alfred Kubin, *Die andere Seite*, 1909

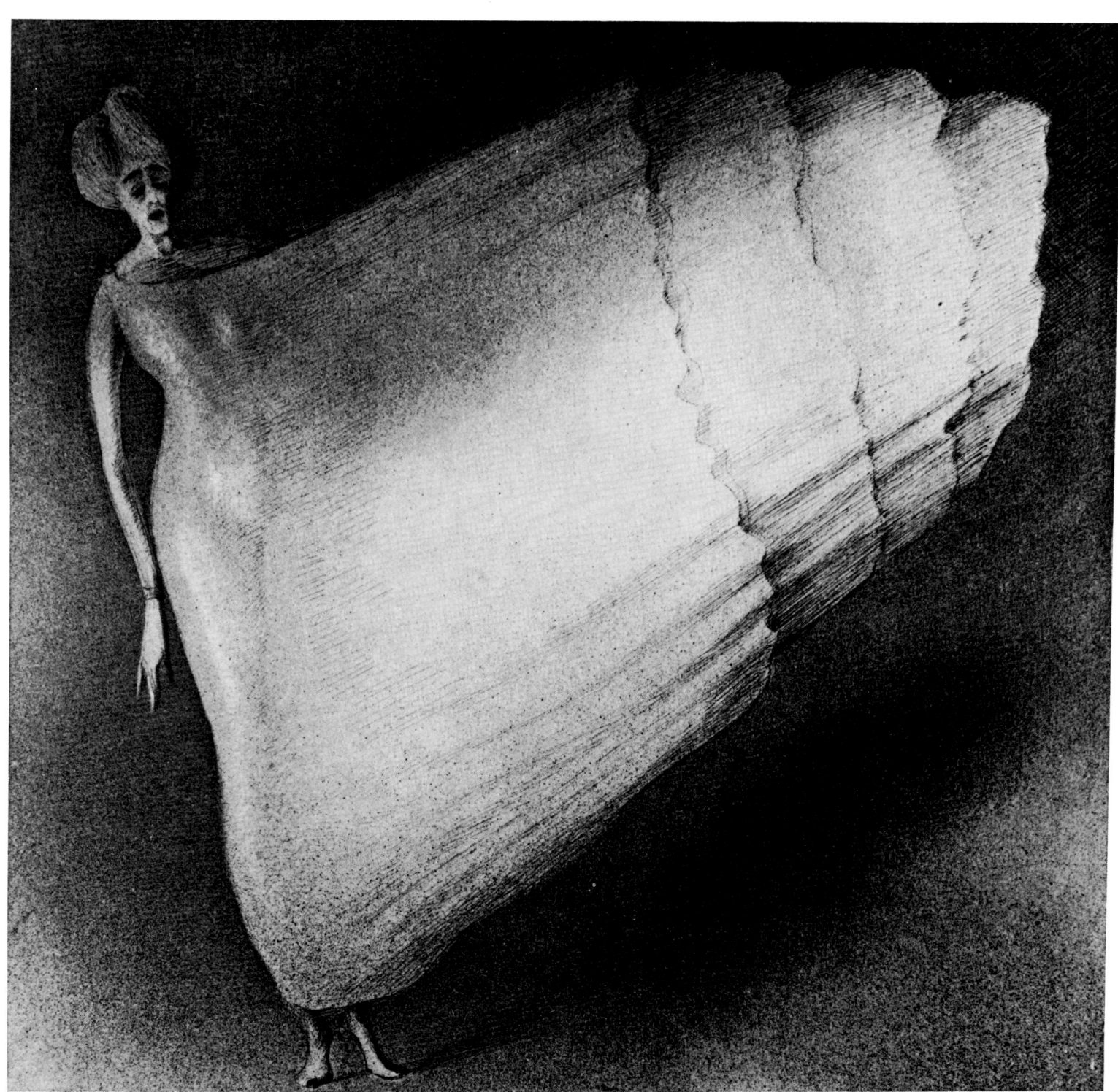

that moment of apogee, in a special development of the art of painting. Thenceforward and for many centuries the history of painting was linked with the history of the Church. A strange example of oriental influence at the beginning of Christian painting is the frequent use of haloes. A halo is a circle around the human head, a perfect expression of the glory of the human mind which is its centre. It is a visible radiation of the abstract, of the immortal, of the absolute. It was an aesthetic highly favourable to Christian dogma, a great help in depicting the supernatural. It is easy to see why in that period of refined naturalism (see the various representations of Antinous during the decadence, and the busts of the emperors), and later, to suit the simplistic imaginations of the Barbarians, the Church adopted this eastern symbolism as profound as it was simple."

Here, even more than above, we see the confusion from which derives the notion of symbol understood as the equivalent of sensation, and the limits which such an interpretation imposed on Symbolism. We see too how dogmatic Symbolism got bogged down in an attempt to surpass itself, an attempt in which mysticism and materialism collided head-on; how the notion even of nature may be ambiguous; and how the use of other than European civilizations involved a subconscious annexation of myth. In fact, and it is here that the historical Symbolism of the last decades of the nineteenth century assumes its true form, "awareness of symbol," in order to counter positivist realism and "naturalism," signified, paradoxically enough, a return to a state of nature, to the man in whom primal experience survived into individual experience.

Golden birds, golden swans, golden bowls, golden flowers; dead lakes, dead days, dead autumns—they were everywhere. When symbols are mass-produced in this way they become mere empty artefacts. It is not hard to see why André Breton was impatient. With Henri de Régnier, symbolism became a convention. This is how Régnier saw it in 1900 ("he lived in an old Italian palace with emblems and figures all over the walls"): "Symbol is the culmination of a series of intellectual operations beginning with the word itself, going on through image and metaphor, and including emblem and allegory. What the poets of today are attempting, and sometimes succeed in achieving, is the most perfect and complete figurative expression of Idea through Symbol. This lofty and difficult artistic desire does them credit. It links them to what is most essential in poetry." In practice, however, "all symbolism involves a certain unavoidable obscurity. Whatever trouble one takes to make it so, no poem conceived of in this way is ever easily and immediately accessible." Why? Because a symbol is "a comparison and an identification going from abstract to concrete, a comparison in which one of the terms remains unexpressed. There is a relationship which is only suggested, and for which the link has to be restored." As for myth, it is seen from the outside, as decoration, vehicle, instrument.

André Breton claimed to appreciate both "subversively" and "also in the most distant manner" the works René Ghil published just before 1900, giving them such strange titles as *Dire des sangs* (Utterance of blood), *Dire du mieux* (Utterance of the best), etc. They had a strange power of plunging Breton "into a sort of verbal darkness, punctuated by rare sparks," which at the same time "disturbed" and "attracted" him. "If the words 'obscure' and 'abstruse' have ever truly applied to any language, they apply to his. And yet, when Ghil's poems floated out over the auditorium (during one of the 'poetry matinées' that used to be held in those days), their musical amplitude would predominate over all the rest. Ghil was then, perhaps with Saint-Pol Roux, the most decried poet in the symbolist movement. But while the critics kept hurling sarcasms and insults at him, I found it touching that despite everything he clung, as he said, to his desire for 'a difficult and sacred art'."

At this time Verhaeren was committing himself politically to the same cause as his friend Emile Vandervelde. He sympathized with the socialist movement, which had become influential in Belgium. He abandoned Catholicism, and resolved to support scientific progress and social emancipation even if it led to "another redemption."

In Paris, Paul Adam expressed the belief that "in the near future, art and symbol will be synonymous." On 17 May 1900, speaking in Nancy after having just been elected as a member of the Académie Stanislas, Emile Gallé declared that "the masters of the word, the poets, are also the masters of decoration," and proceeded to eulogize "symbolist décor." But what was that décor? We have already spoken of it. It was foam in the darkness, a withdrawing wave. In 1900 it was in evidence at the Paris World's Fair, but it was withdrawing from the laboratory. In the Salon of the Libre Esthétique in Brussels it was by now an accepted thing, and for better or worse its commercial spin-off had entered into circulation. As Octave Maus remarked, "Taste is no longer to be cultivated at art exhibitions, except on rare occasions when there is some choice knick-knack." (In 1893, at the last exhibition of the Twenty, two whole rooms had been devoted to the "decorative arts.") This seventh Salon of the Libre Esthétique in 1900 was dominated by a tribute to Henri Evenepoel, one of Gustave Moreau's most brilliant pupils, who had died of typhus at twenty-seven in Paris in December 1899. This time Jean Delville, regarded as "leader of symbolist painting in Belgium," formed part of the same group as Ensor. He exhibited *The Love of Souls*. Léon Frédéric, George Morren and Jan Toorop were also there. Bourdelle exhibited, among other works, a terra cotta called *Violets and Roses*. All together again.

And now silence begins to come down. Over it there seems to be a veil—to protect dream, reverie, nightmare even. As Jean-Jacques Rousseau might say, let us not "throw light on acts which no mortal will ever decipher."

Odilon Redon (1840-1916): Silence, c. 1911. Oil on gesso.

DICTIONARY-INDEX

L'Almanach des Poètes. Cover design by Auguste Donnay, 1898.

Entered the Ecole des Beaux-Arts in Paris in 1880 where he met Seurat with whom he shared a studio for seven years. He was a pupil of Puvis de Chavannes and helped the latter on his large decorative painting, *The Sacred Grove*. In 1885 he won a scholarship to study in Rome and when he returned to Paris he exhibited at the Salon and then at the Salon de la Société Nationale. He

Aman-Jean in his Paris studio, 1896.

moved in the literary circles of the Symbolist movement and took part in all the Salons de la Rose Croix, designing the poster for the Salon of 1893. He also painted some large decorative works, *The Secret* and *Expectation*, for the 1900 room of the Musée des Arts Décoratifs in Paris.

Aman-Jean was a successful painter throughout his life and received many official commissions, in particular a large panel for the Sorbonne, *The Four Elements*. After the turn of the century his art became less symbolist in spirit.

Art Nouveau pavilion at the 1900 Paris World's Fair designed by Georges de Feure.

8th **Banquet** of "La Plume," with Verlaine and Mallarmé, Paris, 1896.

Portrait of Maurice **Barrès** in 1890 by Jacques-Emile Blanche.

B

"The Fra Angelico of Satanism" (as Roger Fry called him), Beardsley made his career as a designer-illustrator. Born in Brighton, he went to school, first in Epsom, and then in 1884 to Brighton Grammar school. He first showed a talent for drawing at the age of fifteen when he illustrated his favourite books, *Madame Bovary* and *Manon Lescaut*. In 1888 he went to London to earn his living and had various jobs including one for an insurance company from 1889 to 1892. Thanks to the friendship and encouragement of Burne-Jones, he started to study art, going in the evening to Westminster Art School. In 1892 he was asked by the publisher J.W. Dent to illustrate Malory's *Le Morte d'Arthur*; this meant that he had to do more than 500 drawings in India ink which were then reproduced in facsimile by a new photographic procedure. After this, orders came thick and fast the most famous of which was a commission to illustrate the first English edition of Oscar Wilde's *Salome*. Shortly after, Beardsley had a brief, though prestigious career as art editor and illustrator of *The Yellow Book*. After having worked there for a year, in which he produced four issues, he was dismissed from the post because of a scandal about his private life. He did a few jobs as an illustrator before being taken on by a publisher of erotic literature, Leonard Smithers.

From 1896-1897 he worked on the illustrations and occasionally on the text of the magazine *The Savoy*, launched by Smithers. He began to draw more and more of those scenes which up until then had been disapproved of by Victorian morality; this can be seen in his illustrations of *Lysistrata, The Rape of the Lock, Volpone, Mademoiselle de Maupin*, etc. In 1897, as a result of poor health (he had had tuberculosis from the time he was seven), he was forced to leave England and settle in France. He went first to Paris, then to Menton. At the end of his life he was converted to Catholicism and he died repentant, calling for the destruction of his "bad drawings."

Emile **Bernard:** Self-portrait, dedicated to Van Gogh, with a picture of Gauguin on the wall, Pont-Aven, 1888.

Born in Lille of a family of shopkeepers, at the age of eighteen Emile Bernard began work in Cormon's studio in Paris, where he became friends with Toulouse-Lautrec and began to paint in a pointillist style. At Asnières (a suburb of Paris) where he had gone to live, he got to know Signac and painted with Van Gogh. In 1888 he met Albert Aurier, who was impressed by the first efforts of this young painter, and soon afterwards he went to live in Pont-Aven, a village on the coast of Brittany where he met Gauguin. The two artists worked together closely, and began a fervent exchange of ideas which resulted in a new direction for painting which they called "synthetist and cloisonniste"; Bernard claimed later that it was he who had made the "discovery." In 1889 he exhibited more than twenty-three paintings at the Café Volpini together with the Pont-Aven group of painters.

After 1890 his lack of success in earning his living by designing fabrics, an unhappy love affair, the suicide of Van Gogh, whom he had greatly admired, and Gauguin's departure for Tahiti combined to make him change course. He went through a deep mystical crisis and afterwards turned towards medieval art: "I intoxicate myself with incense, organ music, prayers, old stained-glass windows and hieratic tapestries," he said. Roger Marx called him "the father of French Symbolism." He himself was to write later: "I dreamed of a painting which corresponded to the poetry of Moréas and Mallarmé..." However, his interests became diversified and later he was to quarrel with Gauguin.

In 1892 he organized a Van Gogh exhibition at the Le Barc de Bouteville Gallery and exhibited his own pictures at the Salon de la Rose Croix. Between 1894 and 1914 he made several trips to Italy and spent long periods in Egypt and Spain. His painting became more and more academic, full of Renaissance and Oriental tendencies. In 1905 he edited a periodical, *Rénovation esthéthique*, in which he argued for a return to a classical ideal. Throughout his life he published theoretical works which are still of interest today; for instance, the article in *Occident* in 1904 where he presented Cézanne's ideas is still relevant, as is his correspondence, particularly with Van Gogh.

Born in Basel, Böcklin studied drawing while attending school there. He then went on to the Academy of Fine Arts in Düsseldorf and studied under J.W. Schirmer, a well-known landscape painter; he also took courses in architectural design, perspective and descriptive geometry. He became friends with the Swiss painter Rudolf Koller, with whom he made a trip to Belgium, and after a short time at Calame's school in Geneva he went to Paris and stayed there until the revolution of 1848. He returned to Basel and in 1850, on the advice of the art historian Jakob Burckhardt, left for Italy, where he discovered Renaissance art and the Roman landscape. He went back to Basel for just over a year and then returned to Rome in 1852 staying there for five years. Until then Böcklin had been essentially a landscape painter; now he began to introduce mythology into his pictures; suddenly his canvases were full of centaurs, pans and satyrs, not to mention all kinds of other weird creatures. His stay in Rome was important for the thematic evolution of his work. In order to earn his living, he painted views of Rome for the tourist market. In 1857 he left Italy and the following year painted a mural on the theme of man and fire in the Wedeking house in Hanover. He then went to Munich and in 1860 to Weimar where he taught for two years at the art school. In 1862 he went back to Italy, first to Rome, then to Naples and paid his first visit to Pompeii. It was at this time that he painted one of his first works with a symbolic theme: the *Villa by the Sea* (first version 1864), a work full of mystery and German sentimentality. From 1868-1870 he worked on a series of frescoes for the staircase of the Basel museum, while during the same period he received several portrait commissions. In 1871 he was at Munich where he painted the *Battle of the Centaurs*, a mythological composition where he let his imagination have full rein, and in 1874 he set out once again for Italy, this time for Florence. There he got to know a small circle of German artists, in particular Adolf von Hildebrand and Hans von Marées. It was in Florence that he painted a work which was to make him famous throughout Europe; this was *Triton and Nereid* (1875) where he portrayed a world of illusion and fantasy with great realism. In 1877, for the first time, a picture dealer showed an interest in his work and the following year he received his first official commission from Germany, *The Elysian Fields*. This was the period when he produced several masterpieces: *The Isle of the Dead, Storm at Sea* and *Ruins by the Sea*, where the magical night landscape is full of supernatural and cosmic effects. After this he painted *Prometheus* and then *The Shrine of Herakles* (1884) in which he went beyond the legend of antiquity and presented the theme of passion allegorically. In 1885 Böcklin became friends with the poet Gottfried Keller and in 1889 he was made an honorary citizen of Zurich, and later, honorary professor at the Federal Polytechnic School *(Eidgenössische Technische Hochschule)*. In 1892 he left Switzerland as his health was declining and settled permanently in a villa which he had bought in Fiesole, just outside Florence. The last years of his life were uneventful.

erous-hearted man with socialist leanings, but he is
mainly remembered as a fashionable portrait painter.
Albert Aurier, who had "discovered" Van Gogh and
Gauguin, waxed lyrical over an important exhibition of
Carrière's work in 1891: "He makes every effort to hide
his overwhelming reality from us, to bathe it in mystery,
though no doubt his tender poet's heart has often suffered from it. He keeps nature and the sordid, banal and
wicked life away from us quite purposefully, and we
should congratulate him for it," wrote Aurier in the *Mercure de France*. While Félix Fénéon, who was more caustic
and less "decadent," and in this particular case more
clairvoyant, wrote the same year in *Le Chat Noir*: "So
often repeated, the gracious, doleful, touching smile of
his painting becomes just like a simpering commercial
trademark... The mists from which the figures emerge
help the spectators to dream. It amuses them to involve
themselves in this 'kind of work..." He finished his article
by calling Carrière "a painter for literary men." The
artist was in fact very close to the literary world; an
habitué of Mallarmé's Tuesday parties, the latter admired
him greatly. His portraits of Verlaine, Gauguin, Edmond de Goncourt (which included one of him on his
death bed) and Anatole France, to cite only a few, are
still famous. Despite the fact that, nonetheless, they conform to his usual "blueprint" for portraits, they often
reveal more of the taste of the period than they do of the
sitter's character. It was because he was considered a
"painter of the soul" that his work was so appreciated
outside France.

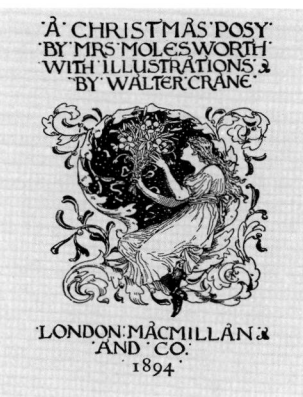

Title page design by Walter **Crane**, 1894.

CRANE Walter (1845-1915) 12, 107, 128, 144, 145, 149, 150, 154, 158, 159, 167, 168;
Faerie Queene, illustrations 144;
Neptune's Horses 128;
The Yellow Dwarf 145.

Born in Liverpool, son of a portrait painter and miniaturist, he early showed a talent for drawing and in 1858 began by illustrating works by Scott, Bloomfield, Cowper, and Tennyson for his own amusement. In 1859 he was apprenticed to W. J. Linton, one of the best wood-engravers in London. In 1862 he did some illustrations for magazines and from 1863 worked for the publisher Edmund Evans, illustrating a series of sixpenny toy-books of nursery rhymes, fairy stories and folktales. These made his reputation. While doing engraving, by which he earned his living, Crane began painting, which was his passion. His subjects were taken from contemporary English literature (Tennyson and Keats), the classics, and after a trip to Italy (1871-1873) from Greco-Roman mythology. Later on his painting became more and more a mirror of his philosophy of existence and of his reflections on human destiny. Among his metaphorical works are *The Roll of Fate* (1882), *The Bridge of Life* (1884), *The Chariot of the Hours* (1886-1887), *The Mower* (1901). However, his painting is of secondary importance, for Crane was above all a designer. After 1874, when he returned from Italy, he joined William Morris and took an active part in the revolutionary movement which was trying to reinvigorate the decorative arts. He designed such everyday objects as ceramics, textiles, mosaics, glassware, and above all wallpaper. His designs for fabrics and wallpapers were based on a naturalism which was at the same time decorative, linear and stylized—a precursor of Art Nouveau. Under Morris's influence, and in accordance with his theories on the democratization of art, Crane became interested in Socialism, and from now on, until the end of his life, he placed his art at the service of political propaganda by

Portrait of Walter **Crane** by William Rothenstein, published in "Pan," Berlin, 1897.

designing pamphlets and posters. In 1891 a large exhibition of his work in many mediums was held at the Fine Art Society's galleries in Bond Street; taken over to the United States in the same year by the artist himself, it was afterwards shown in Germany, Austria and Scandinavia. This exhibition aroused great interest and made Crane's work widely known; his ideas on art were set forth in two books, *The Bases of Design* (1898) and *Line and Form* (1900).

CROS Charles (1842-1888) 141.

DALI Salvador (1904) 55, 185.
DALPAYRAT Pierre Adrien (1844-1910) 150.
DAMISH Hubert 10.
DANIEL Georges 80.
D'ANNUNZIO Gabriele (1863-1938) 73, 74, 114;
Laudi 73, 114;
Il Fuoco 74.
DANTE ALIGHIERI (1265-1321) 12, 30-33, 164;
Vita Nuova 32, 33.
DARWIN Charles (1809-1882) 158.
DAUMIER Honoré (1808-1879) 142.
DAVIES Arthur B. (1862-1928) 11.
Dead Sea (Palestine) 30.
DEBUSSY Claude (1862-1918) 33, 34, 84, 112;
La Demoiselle élue 33, 84;
Pelléas et Mélisande 34, 112.

Group photograph with **Debussy** (seated), 1893.

DEGAS Edgar (1834-1917) 40, 173.
DEGOUVE DE NUNCQUES William (1867-1935) 107, 111, 125, 148, 150, 186;
Angels in the Night 125;
Night in Bruges 111.

He came of an old family of the French aristocracy who settled in Brussels at the time of the Franco-Prussian war. From his family, particularly his father, a man of strong personality, he inherited a passion for things spiritual and when still very young he showed a tendency to indulge in spleen, reverie and contemplation, instead of action. He enrolled at the Brussels Academy, but found the teaching little to his liking. His meeting in 1883 with the Dutch painter Jan Toorop was decisive for the development of his art; the two became fast friends and shared the same studio. Toorop has left us a portrait of his friend, remarkable for the tense, almost haggard expression in his clear eyes. Another meeting destined to influence him greatly was that with the painter Henry de Groux; they worked in the same studio for a time. These two very different influences led him to develop a vision in which the outwardly classical landscape bathes in a

strange atmosphere; his pictures are the forerunners of Surrealism, full of weird apparitions.

In 1894 he married a young painter who was the poet Verhaeren's sister-in-law and thus came in contact with the world of poets and writers, particularly those connected with the Brussels literary review *La Jeune Belgique*. In Paris he was much admired by Puvis de Chavannes and Maurice Denis and exhibited frequently from 1890 onwards. He was an enthusiastic traveller and made many trips to Italy, Austria and Switzerland. For two years (1900-1902) he lived on Majorca and then at the outbreak of the First World War settled in Holland. After the death of his first wife, which left him desperately unhappy and ill for a long time, he went back to live in Belgium at Stavelot. He remained a Symbolist until about 1900.

Henry **de Groux**: Frontispiece for Remy de Gourmont's "Le Fantôme," Paris, 1893.

DE GROUX Henry (1867-1930) 47, 103, 106, 149, 158;
Christ Reviled 103;
Wagnerian works 47.

Born in Brussels, son of a well-known painter. After having studied at the Académie des Beaux-Arts, de Groux joined the L'Essor group in 1886 at the same time as Delville and was later elected a member of The Twenty. At twenty-one he painted his *Christ Reviled*, which was very successful and which, after being exhibited in Brussels, was shown in Paris in 1892. The picture was seen and admired by both artists and writers. Throughout his life, de Groux painted his vision of a hallucinated world peopled by a mass of bewildered and contorted figures. He was a difficult man, temperamental and beset by persecution complexes; one of those *artistes maudits* who, though rebellious and unhappy, are firmly convinced of the importance of both their mission and their genius.

DELACROIX Eugène (1798-1863) 30, 113, 173.
DELAHERCHE Auguste (1857-1940) 150.
DELAROCHE Achille 95.
DELAROCHE Paul (1797-1856) 90.
DELAUNAY Élie (1828-1891) 23.
DELHAYE Jean 113.
DELTEIL Loys (1869-1927), *Portrait of Villiers de L'Isle-Adam* 46.
DELVAU Alfred (1825-1867), *Dictionnaire érotique moderne* 74.
DELVAUX Paul (1897) 55, 185.
DELVILLE Jean (1867-1953) 63, 91, 92, 103, 108, 109, 132, 190;
Le Frisson du Sphinx 132;
The Idol of Perversity 132;
Love of Souls 190;
Portrait of Mrs Stuart Merrill 108;
Symbolization of Flesh and Spirit 92.

Born in Louvain, Delville was a poet as well as a painter. He exhibited for the first time in 1885 in Brussels with the L'Essor group. In 1892 he was one of the founders of the Salon pour l'Art, and when this came to

Jean **Delville**.

an end he founded the Salon d'Art Idéaliste which was a direct outcome, so Delville maintained, of the ideas of Péladan, his meeting with whom was of vital importance to the artist. Inspired by the latter's ideas, Delville settled in Paris and showed regularly at the Salons de la Rose Croix. "Understood in its metaphysical sense, Beauty is one of the manifestations of the Absolute Being. Emanating from the harmonious rays of the Divine plan, it crosses the intellectual plane to shine once again across the natural plane, where it darkens into matter," he wrote in 1899. He was drawn towards occultism, idealism, and esoterism. Feeling himself to be invested with a mission, he wanted to give back to the world the awareness of mystery, and to this end he studied the Cabbala, magic and hermetic philosophy, in reaction against the scepticism of the age.

In 1900 he was appointed professor at the Glasgow School of Art and later became its director. On returning to Brussels in 1905, he obtained a post at the Académie des Beaux-Arts, where he taught until 1937.

Born in Granville (Normandy), his father being a railway official and his mother a milliner. Soon after his birth, his parents settled near Paris at St Germain-en-Laye. Denis returned to live here after his marriage in

Maurice **Denis**: Self-Portrait, 1896.

1893 and it remained his home for the rest of his life. At the age of eighteen he enrolled at the Académie Julian, Paris, where he met Sérusier who, that same year (1888) after a visit to Brittany, brought him "the good news about Gauguin's ideas" and who showed him the landscape painting *The Talisman*, which was to become the pictorial manifesto of Synthetism. The Nabis were then founded (Denis becoming the "Nabi of the beautiful icons") with Bonnard, Ibels, Ranson and, a little later, Roussel and Vuillard. In 1889 he met Redon and that same year saw Gauguin's work for the first time at the Café Volpini exhibition, which made a lasting impression on him. In 1890 he published the manifesto of the Nabi movement in *Art et Critique*, where he formulated the famous definition: "Remember that a picture, before being a war horse, a nude or some sort of anecdote, is essentially a flat surface covered with colours assembled in a certain order." From 1891 on he participated in the Nabi exhibitions at the Le Barc de Bouteville gallery and became friends with the Dutchman, Jan Verkade, who had come to Paris that year and had been one of the painters closest to Gauguin during his Breton period. Verkade's conversion to Catholicism (he later became a monk) made a great impression on the Nabis. Denis designed sets and costumes for the Théâtre de l'Œuvre which his friend Lugné-Poe had recently founded. In 1892 he exhibited at the Salon of the Brussels group, The Twenty, which also showed a large Seurat retrospective. The pictures shown by Denis, which were as much religious as poetical or decorative, impress one by their atmosphere of calm spirituality. Now too he exhibited at the Salon des Indépendants in Paris, published articles in *Art et Critique* and *La Revue Blanche*, illustrated books and designed stage sets. He also designed the programme for Maeterlinck's *Pelléas et Mélisande*, performed on 17 May 1893 at the Théâtre de l'Œuvre with music by Debussy.

Maurice **Denis**: Lithograph for Mallarmé's "Apparition," 1894.

In 1895 he wrote the preface to the exhibition of Impressionists and Symbolists at the Le Barc de Bouteville Gallery and that autumn left for Italy with Sérusier where they did a bicycle tour of Tuscany and Umbria. Two years later he paid a long visit to the composer Ernest Chausson in Florence; then on to Rome where he went sightseeing with Gide and they discussed "methods and classical art." In 1899 he received his first commission for a religious picture. For the rest of his long life, easel paintings in an intimist vein alternated with large religious or secular compositions: the Sainte-Croix chapel at Le Vésinet, 1899; the Théâtre des Champs-Elysées, 1912; the cupola of the Petit-Palais, 1924-1925; the church of Saint-Louis, Vincennes, 1927; the ceiling of the Senate, 1929; the Théâtre de Chaillot and the Lycée Claude Bernard, 1938; the League of Nations building in Geneva, 1939. In 1900 he painted his famous *Homage to Cézanne*. Very soon he began to be known and his work was much admired in Germany, particularly by the critic Julius Meier-Graefe. In 1903, together

with Sérusier, he went to visit Verkade in his monastery at Beuron, in South Germany. In 1908 Denis began teaching at the Académie Ranson in Paris. He continued to make frequent trips to Italy in the years to come.

He also made several long journeys overseas, to the United States, Canada and the Holy Land. In 1919 together with Georges Desvallières he founded the Ateliers d'Art Sacré whose aim was to revive religious art. In 1932 he was elected to the Académie des Beaux-Arts and died in 1943 in Paris, in a traffic accident. He left, apart from his numerous works of art, a considerable body of theoretical writings.

Doudelet studied music and sculpture in Ghent, then went to Paris and Florence on a scholarship. He was persuaded to take up painting by Constantin Meunier. A member of the Brussels group, The Twenty, he also exhibited in Paris. In 1900 the Belgian government commissioned him to make a study of printing and in order to do so he went to Italy where he lived, mainly in Tuscany, until 1925. His study of printing, published in 1912, was entitled *La Beauté du Livre*. To the Brussels Exhibition of 1910 he contributed a painting called *Spanish Dance*.

He illustrated many books and is chiefly remembered for his Maeterlinck illustrations: drawings full of a refined symbolism, whose graphic disposition was always sustained by an original rhythm. He also designed the scenery and costumes for Maeterlinck's plays, *Joyzelle* (1904) and *The Bluebird* (1906).

Fantin-Latour was born in Grenoble but soon after his birth the family moved to Paris. There he studied in the drawing school of Lecoq de Boisbaudran, then at the Ecole des Beaux-Arts under Couture. While copying in the Louvre he made the acquaintance of Whistler (whose portrait he was to paint later, dressed in a kimono and entitled *The Toast*). With him, in 1859, Fantin went to London where he was much impressed by the Pre-Raphaelites; this was the first of many subsequent visits to England. In 1860, together with other students at the Ecole des Beaux-Arts, he petitioned Courbet to open a studio. In 1861 he had a picture accepted by the Salon where he exhibited regularly until 1886. From 1863 he saw much of Manet and in the future his name was to be linked with the Impressionists: he figures in Manet's *Music in the Tuileries Gardens*; it was he who introduced Manet to Berthe Morisot; and he also frequented the Café Guerbois where Manet and the Impressionists met in the evenings. Apart from this, his famous *Homage to Delacroix* (1864) and *The Batignolles Studio* (1870) undoubtedly show Manet's influence. However, Fantin-Latour is important for his own sake and for his impassioned studies of Wagner's music.

Wagnerian subjects abound in his work from 1862 on. In 1902 he painted *Prelude to Lohengrin*. He also did numerous pastels and lithographs inspired by Wagner's operas, some of which appeared in the *Revue Wagnérienne*. Though the critics often disapproved of this attachment, the hazy, elusive, highly imaginative atmosphere of the works stemming from his Wagnerian inspiration was important for the development of his symbolist vision.

This Dutch painter, whose father was an important architect in Holland, used the name Georges de Feure as a pseudonym in the 1890s when he first settled in Paris. After having worked for the poster designer Chéret, he tried his hand at almost all the applied arts. Until about 1910 he was well known in Paris for his dress designs, furniture designs, ceramics, illustrations and posters. In his paintings he employed a certain literary symbolism which explains the ambiguous charm of his compositions: *The Abyss* (c. 1894), *Heading for the Abyss* (1894), *The Voice of Evil* (1895). The theme he used most frequently was woman, in whom he saw the sinuous line of a flower. Woman as an incarnation of evil seemed to haunt him, thus showing the influence exerted upon him by Baudelaire and by the then fashionable Belgian poet Georges Rodenbach, whose *Petits Nocturnes de Bruges* he illustrated in woodcuts (published in *L'Image* in 1897). In 1893 and 1894 he exhibited at the Salon de la Rose Croix and the same year at the Galerie des Artistes Modernes, where the catalogue was prefaced by the Symbolist critic Paul Adam. He later exhibited at the very official Société Nationale des Beaux-Arts. In 1896 he took part in the Munich Secession and published, together with the critic Octave Uzanne, the album *Feminies*. He designed a pavilion for the art dealer Samuel Bing at the Paris World's Fair of 1900 and at the turn of the century was named professor at the Ecole des Beaux-Arts, Paris. He was also invited to participate in the Turin Exhibition in 1902 which was extremely important for the development of the applied arts. In 1903 the Galerie Bing organized an important retrospective of his work. After a long stay in England he returned to France in the 1920s.

Poster for the Theatre **Loie Fuller**. World's Fair, Paris, 1900.

Born in Paris, where his father was a journalist on *Le National*; his mother was of Peruvian origin. After the *coup d'état* in France in 1851 the family went to live for four years in Lima; later he was to confess with pride to being "a savage from Peru". On their return to France he went to school in Orleans, and from 1865 to 1871 he served as a seaman in the French merchant marine. In 1871, thanks to his guardian Gustave Arosa, who was an art collector, particularly of Pissarros, he got a job with the Paris stockbroking firm of Bertin, where he was most successful. Two years later he married a Danish girl with whom he was deeply in love, and as a young, enlightened business man began to build up a collection of modern paintings which were chosen with good taste and an understanding of the aims and concerns of the younger artists. He himself also began to paint, at first as an amateur, but very soon it became a passion with him. In 1876 he sent one of his canvases to the Salon, where it was accepted, and soon afterwards he met Pissarro who encouraged and supported him in his work with both friendship and advice. Until 1882 he exhibited with the Impressionists. In 1883 he threw up his job at the Stock Exchange and began painting full time with Pissarro. Soon his financial situation was such that he was forced to seek refuge together with his wife and children in Copenhagen. There he succeeded in putting on an exhibition of his work, which was closed on the orders of the Academy, being judged as scandalous. Repudiated by his wife's family, which could not sympathize with his ambitions as an artist, he returned alone to Paris where he experienced real poverty.

In 1886 he went to Brittany for the first time, settling at Pont-Aven, and then at Le Pouldu. There he could live cheaply and concentrate on painting, gradually working out his aesthetic ideas with a young generation of artists, and finding himself. His meeting with the young Emile Bernard saw the birth of Synthetism and Cloisonnism. In 1888 he went to Arles to stay with Van Gogh, a visit which terminated in the tragic madness of the latter. A year later, during the Paris World's Fair of 1889, the Impressionist and Synthetist group headed by Gauguin organized their own show at the Café Volpini; the public paid it little attention, but the young Nabis were very impressed. His third and longest stay in Brittany (April 1889-November 1890, broken by brief visits to Paris) was extremely important for the evolution of Synthetism. At Le Pouldu Gauguin was surrounded by his friends, Séguin, Filiger and Meyer de Haan; in Paris he went frequently to the Café Voltaire, where each week he met Symbolist writers and artists (Natanson, Aurier, Morice, Redon, Carrière, Mirbeau, Moréas). He was greatly admired by Mallarmé, and Charles Morice saw him as "the most important Symbolist painter." In 1889 (and in 1891) he was invited to exhibit with the Belgian group, Les Vingt, which had been founded in Brussels in 1884; he also found several buyers for his paintings in Belgium. But his precarious financial situation and his disgust with the art world of Paris, so inimical to his aspirations, made him decide to leave for Tahiti. Mallarmé, who was asked to preside at the banquet organized by La Plume just before Gauguin's departure, spoke of what he saw as the reasons behind the artist's decision to leave: "in order to flee civilization... so as to understand oneself better and to be able to hear one's inner voices," adding that he remained at home "dreaming of the wisdom of the plan."

On 4 April 1891 Gauguin left for the "charmed land, the perfumed land," or so he hoped. His stay in Tahiti lasted two years; disillusioned with the French colony at Papeete, he went and settled with the natives at Mataiea. He worked hard, but ill and unhappy he was forced to return to France in August 1893. That same year Durand-Ruel organized an important exhibition of his work; the financial return was nil, but the impression it made on other painters was very significant. He stayed in Europe for two years, revisiting his wife and children in Copenhagen, a reunion which only confirmed their mutual incomprehension; and he spent some time in Le Pouldu. In 1895 he had a second sale at the Hôtel Drouot (catalogue preface written by Strindberg) but the sale was a complete failure.

He returned in July 1895 to Tahiti and settled on the west coast in the Pounouaouïa district. There he was to paint some of his most masterly works, in spite of loneliness, poverty, ill health and constant pain. In 1897 he produced his most famous pictures, *Nevermore* and *Whence Come We?...*; and *La Revue Blanche* published his manuscript *Noa Noa*. In 1898 he tried to commit suicide. He was continually in trouble with the local authorities. He

contributed to the paper *Les guêpes* and published *Sourire*. "I am leaving for the Marquesas Islands at last," he wrote in 1901, and settled on the island of St Dominic. In March 1903 his ideas as well as his defense of the natives of the island brought him up against the Church, the police, and the French administration—which resulted in a three-month prison sentence and a 1000 franc fine. Gauguin did not have enough money to appeal to Tahiti and died on 8 May 1903.

Book cover designed by **Grasset**, 1883.

Born in Lausanne, son of a cabinetmaker. After having studied architecture Grasset paid a long visit to Egypt where he was much taken by the Oriental atmosphere; however, he fell into such dire financial straits that he had to be repatriated. After a short stay in Switzerland he went and settled permanently in Paris in 1871, working as a designer of wallpaper and fabrics. He was influenced by Gustave Doré's illustrations, Viollet-le-Duc's interpretations of medieval architecture, and the albums of Japanese prints then so popular in Paris.

In 1883 he published an illustrated version of the medieval romance *Histoire des quatre fils Aymon*, which was very successful; this was the first time that Art Nouveau had been seen in book illustration. Grasset showed his talent as an innovator in different art forms: furniture design, stained glass (most of which was of religious inspiration) and ceramics. In 1880-1885 he designed the interior decoration of Louis Gillot's photographic studio. But he is known above all for his poster designs: *Jeanne d'Arc* (1890), *Salon des Cents* (1894), *Librairie Romantique* (1890), *Harpers* (1892). He also invented the famous Larousse dictionary symbol. In 1892 he exhibited at the Salon de la Rose Croix and was invited several times to exhibit at the Libre Esthétique in Brussels. He was director of the Ecole de Dessin in Paris and also an expert botanist: in 1897 he published *La Plante et ses applications ornementales* and in 1905 his *Méthode de composition ornementale*. In 1900 *La Plume* brought out a special issue devoted to his work in which the editor deplored the fact that, despite everything, Grasset was virtually unknown to the general public.

H

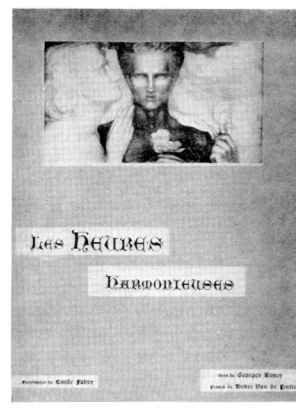

Emile Fabry: Frontispiece for "Les **Heures Harmonieuses**," Paris, 1897.

Born in Berne, Hodler began work as an assistant in his stepfather's commercial art studio while still a schoolboy. In 1868 he was apprenticed to a German view painter in Thun and worked with him until 1871 when he left for Geneva, an important cultural centre where two famous landscape painters, Diday and Calame, had lived. There he spent six years at the School of Fine Arts studying under Barthélemy Menn, a painter who had been at the Beaux-Arts in Paris. Hodler travelled throughout Switzerland and was much influenced by Holbein and Dürer; on a year-long visit to Spain (1878-1879) he saw the works of the Spanish masters as well as paintings by Raphael. Little by little he broke away from his naturalistic realism and developed a style of his own. In Geneva, which was to be his home from now on, he received generally hostile criticism to begin with and for several years his financial situation was extremely precarious. He painted many landscapes, particularly during the summers which he spent in the Canton of Berne and in German Switzerland; he also painted portraits. His first submission to the Paris Salon in 1881 was a self-portrait of which he did a great number throughout his life. Between 1891 and 1900 his first important symbolic work, *Night*, was exhibited in Paris, Munich and Venice. This painting gained him the international renown which he was to enjoy from then on. It illustrates a metaphysical vision where love, sleep and death are joined in harmony. This personal view of human existence is seen in several later works, for example: *The Life-Weary* (1892), *The Day* (1904-1906), *Truth* (1903), *Love* (1903). In 1894-1895 Hodler applied the principle of parallelism to his painting *Eurhythmy*: a system of repetitive, symmetrical and axial patterning calculated to evoke certain sentiments. The succession of hieratic figures are painted linearly in a way which is close to Art Nouveau. Hodler also introduced parallelism in his Swiss landscapes. Here ordered Nature takes on a monumental, architectural character, accentuated by the cloisonnist outlines, where the strokes encircle the forms. His later works showed a more diffuse vision, full of colour and light. Hodler also produced a certain amount of monumental art: painting a mural for the Schweizerisches Landesmuseum in Zurich, *The Retreat from Marignano* (1897-1900) and *Unanimity* (1911) for the Town Hall in Hanover. He was one of the few Swiss painters of the nineteenth century to attain international fame, being a member of the Société Nationale des Artistes Français, the Rose Croix, and the Swiss Society of Painters, Sculptors and Architects (of which he was elected president in 1908), as well as participating in the Vienna, Berlin and Munich Secessions and being a member of the German Society of Artists. Towards the end of his life Hodler received both honours and rewards; he was made an officer of the Légion d'Honneur in France, honorary professor of the Beaux-Arts in Geneva as well as an honorary citizen of that town.

Born in Darmstadt, Hofmann studied art first in Dresden with his uncle, then in Munich, and finally at Karlsruhe. In 1889 he went to Paris where he enrolled at the Académie Julian. In Paris he came under the influence of both Puvis de Chavannes and Albert Besnard. He returned to Germany, to Berlin, where in 1890 he got to know Klinger and Liebermann. From 1891 to 1894 he lived in Rome. In 1892 he came into contact with the work of Hans von Marées which encouraged him to continue in the style he had already begun.

His paintings depict an idealized world, tinged with nostalgia for a lost paradise; keeping to a narrow range of themes (mythological scenes and Arcadian land-scapes), he treated them in a bucolic, elegiac spirit. He tried to achieve formal beauty in a decorative setting. In 1903 he was made professor at the Weimar Academy of Fine Arts and later received important commissions such as the decoration of the Theatre Royal and the Museum in Weimar.

Holst studied under A. Allebé at the Academy of Fine Arts in Amsterdam, then came under the influence of the Dutch Impressionist Anton Breitner. He soon tired of the purely formal and stylistic approach of the Impressionists and went through a Symbolist phase. Between 1891 and 1895 he produced drawings and lithographs in a decorative linear style. He was in close contact with the Dutch literary movement of the time and married a well-known poet, Henrietta van der Schalk. He was never a member of The Twenty but was very close to two artists of the group, Georges Lemmen and Henry van de Velde. He gradually drew away from Symbolism and his art from 1900 onwards was monumental and decorative. He was one of the founders of monumental art in Holland.

Born in London, son of the manager of a City warehouse, Hunt was brought up in an austere Protestant home. His father encouraged his artistic tastes as an amusement but not as a profession and placed him at the age of twelve in an estate agent's office. By perseverance and hard work, however, Hunt got his way and entered the Royal Academy schools in 1844. There he met Millais, his lifelong friend. He very soon rejected the traditional academic technique and began copying nature as Ruskin's theories enjoined him to do. He applied his new principles in *The Flight of Madeline and Porphyro* (from Keats's "Eve of St Agnes"), which was well received at the Academy in 1848. Rossetti soon followed his lead. Under Ruskin's influence, breaking once and for all with academic rules, they formed what they called the Pre-Raphaelite Brotherhood (1848), taking as their models nature and the early Italian painters. In 1849 Hunt showed *Rienzi* at the Academy and in 1850 *A Converted British Family Sheltering a Christian Priest from the Persecution of the Druids*. Both these paintings were condemned by the critics (but praised by Ruskin), while the drawings and engravings which he made in the style of the Italian Primitives only served to discredit him in the eyes of the other members of the Academy. However, encouraged by his friends, Hunt was not deterred from his chosen course. Like Millais, he tried to perfect his techniques so as to obtain brighter, more brilliant colours, by the application of successive coats of glaze and varnish. He was also intent on the problem of painting light. Between 1851 and 1854 he produced three works which excited great interest: *The Hireling Shepherd* and two religious subjects, *The Light of the World* and *The Awakening Conscience*. From now on his main interest lay in sacred painting. In 1854 he went to Palestine to visit the Holy Places and brought back numerous drawings and two pictures. Between 1855 and 1860 some of his works were published as engravings, which helped to make his name better known. He gained a reputation for himself largely outside the Academy, for example by organizing his own exhibitions from 1864-1865. In 1869 he returned to Palestine and when he came back to England in 1872 he brought with him two canvases which very much appealed to the contemporary taste: *The Shadow of Death* and *The Triumph of the Innocents*, which he completed on his third visit to the Holy Land (1875-1878). He returned once again to Palestine in 1892 during the course of an extensive tour through Italy, Greece and the Middle East. During the 1880s the Pre-Raphaelites were at the peak of their success, consecrated by frequent exhibitions. In 1905 Hunt published his authoritative history of the movement: *Pre-Raphaelitism and the Pre-Raphaelite Brotherhood*. By this time he suffered from an eye complaint which made painting difficult and he relied more and more on his assistants. His two last masterpieces showed a return to the sources of his inspiration: *The Lady of Shalott*, based on Tennyson's poem (the Pre-Raphaelites' favourite poet) and a second version of *The Light of the World*. Hunt's reputation was based on the fact that he knew how to link his religious subjects with the moral concerns of the Victorian society in which he lived.

I

Henrik **Ibsen**, about 1900.

Calendar by Grasset for the Paris department store "La Belle **Jardinière**," 1896.

K

Imprint of William Morris's **Kelmscott Press**, 1891.

Portrait of **Khnopff** by Alexandre, 1898.

Born in Eastern Flanders, of a family of magistrates, Khnopff grew up in Bruges. He enrolled at the Law School in Brussels which he soon abandoned for the Académie des Beaux-Arts. There he studied under Xavier Mellery who taught him to consider painting as an enquiry into the meaning hidden in the "soul of things." In 1877, on a visit to Paris, he discovered the work of Delacroix, Gustave Moreau (whose fertile imagination greatly impressed him), and the Pre-Raphaelites (particularly Rossetti and Burne-Jones). The influence of these painters was to be of vital importance. On his return to Belgium he was one of the founders, in 1883, of The Twenty ("Groupe des XX") and was much admired by both painters and poets. Emile Verhaeren wrote enthusiastically about him in *La Jeune Belgique* and at first the rest of the press joined in his praises, though they tended to prefer his child portraits and landscapes. In 1892 he exhibited in Paris at the first Salon de la Rose Croix, encouraged by his new friend, Sâr Péladan. However, this friendship brought him trouble within The Twenty, some members having little regard for the Rose Croix. He was a friend of the Belgian poets Georges Rodenbach and Grégoire Le Roy, some of whose books he illustrated. From this Symbolist poetry he took certain themes: silence, solitude, secretiveness and deserted towns. Already during his lifetime he was almost a cult figure, creating a personality for himself as a dandy much sought after in Society circles. He was given the Order of Leopold in recognition of his services to painting but despite this he was an exceptionally "private" artist. In about 1900 he had a house built to his own plans; it was like one of the structures in his pictures, a house out of a dream with false windows.

He did not limit himself to oils but experimented with pastels, watercolours and drawings heightened with colour. He also produced engravings, polychrome sculpture, decorative paintings (for the Hôtel de Ville of Saint-Gilles) and sets for the Théâtre de la Monnaie in Brussels.

"Fernand Khnopff possesses a rare gift... to have been able to show an interest in the various manifestations of the modern spirit, to have sipped of the dangerous cup of dilettantism, and yet to have remained a highly individual personality in whom strong ideals and an untiring will are united," so wrote Hippolyte Fierens-Gevaert in *Art et Décoration* in 1894.

As the son of a goldsmith Klimt was brought up in an artistic milieu and his taste was formed at an early age. His brother Georg also became a goldsmith, while Gustav and his brother Ernst entered the Kunstgewerbeschule in Vienna in 1876. There they studied under the painter-decorator F. Laufberger, and learned various skills, such as fresco painting and mosaic work. In 1883, together with one of their fellow pupils, F. Matsch, they decided to start a studio specializing in murals. They received numerous orders, in particular decorations for the theatres in Fiume (1883), Bucharest (1885), Carlsbad (1884-1886), and the Burgtheater in Vienna (1886-1888) for which Klimt made a special study of the art of antiquity. The most important of these orders was the decoration—begun by Makart—for the Kunsthistorisches Museum in Vienna (1890-1892). Here Klimt's task was to trace the history of art from Egyptian times to the Cinquecento. He made a sort of stylistic anthology, with eleven allegorical figures, each one conceived in the style of a great art period. At the death of his brother in 1892 Klimt gave up working with Matsch and started his own studio. He concentrated on easel paintings, in particular portraits of women, as well as on allegorical love themes: his world was ruled by sensuality. In 1893 he was made a member of the Künstlerhausgesellschaft in Vienna, a traditional academic club of Viennese artists which he left in 1897. With a group of like-minded artists, including J.M. Olbrich and Josef Hoffmann, who were also reacting against this traditionalist spirit, he founded the Vienna Secession that same year, and was its first President from 1897 to 1899. He was also an active contributor to the Secession journal *Ver Sacrum* (1898-1903). In 1905, together with the "Stylists," he withdrew from the Secession, as he did not agree with the new tendency towards Naturalism. Klimt was much criticized in his own country and recognition was to come firstly from abroad. In 1894 he received an order for three large paintings for the Hall of the University of Vienna: allegories of *Philosophy*, *Medicine* and *Jurisprudence*. When exhibited at the Secession in 1900, 1901 and 1902, they aroused a storm of protest because traditional iconography had been completely abandoned. As a result of this, Klimt was forced to resign the chair he had held at the Vienna Academy since 1901. In 1902, at the Secession exhibition, he showed his *Beethoven Frieze*, a liberal interpretation of the *Ninth Symphony* based on the theme of humanity's progression towards its own fulfilment. In 1903 he visited Ravenna, where the Byzantine mosaics had a profound influence on his future stylistic development. In 1905 he received a commission to paint a mural for the Palais Stoclet in Brussels which had been built by Josef Hoffmann. Klimt produced a mosaic frieze in collaboration with the Wiener Werkstätte which represented the theme of love: *Expectation* and *Fulfilment*. This decorative style with its profusion of gold, which was inspired by Byzantine mosaics, reached its zenith round 1907-1908: the abundance of symbolic ornamentation shows itself particularly well in the portrait of *Adèle Bloch-Bauer* (1907), or in *The Kiss* (1907-1908). From 1909, after a visit to Paris where he first saw the paintings of Bonnard, Vuillard and Vallotton, Klimt changed his style, the gold disappeared, the decoration became less ornate and the picture followed new rhythms. The portrait of *Baroness Bachofen Echt* (1912?) was one of the first of his pictures to show this new tendency. During this period, Klimt painted numerous landscapes though he did not give up his allegorical subjects, like *The Maiden* (1913), *Life and Death* (1911-1916), *Adam and Eve* (1917-1918), *The Bride* (1917-1918). Although Klimt was already famous abroad by 1900, as a result of international exhibitions in France, Germany and Italy, he was not given due recognition in Vienna until shortly before his death; in 1917 he was made honorary Professor at the Vienna Academy.

KLINGER Max (1857-1920) 36, 56-59, 69, 102, 106, 130, 136, 151, 154, 168, 183;
Deliverances of Sacrificial Victims in Ovid's Metamorphoses 151;
Fantasies on the Finding of a Glove 57-59;
Illustration for *Pan* 151;
Judgment of Paris 56, 57;
A Life 56, 58, 130;
On Death II 136.

Born in Leipzig, Klinger enrolled at the Academy of Fine Arts in Karlsruhe in 1874. He studied under Gussow and followed the latter to Berlin when he went to take up the post of Director of the Academy of Fine Arts there. From Gussow he learned how to observe reality and to transform it according to his own ideas. Realism reigned supreme at this time in Berlin, and Klinger found it hard to find a stimulus for his love of dreams, fantasy and imagination. Apart from Böcklin, whose work he had probably known since 1875 and with whom he felt a close affinity, he was interested mainly by the painters of the past, whether Menzel, Rembrandt or Goya; above all, he admired their engravings. Klinger made his name with his drawings, mostly in pen and ink; later, after having served an apprenticeship under the engraver Sagert, he took up etching. In 1878 his first two sets of etchings, *Thema Christus* and *Die Phantasie über einen gefundenen Handschuh*, came out and were very successful. He brought out further etchings later which were more sombre in tone: *Eva und die Zukunft* (1881), *Dramen* (1881-1883), *Ein Leben* (1881-1884), *Eine Liebe* (1879-1887) and two later series, *Vom Tode I* and *Vom Tode II*. In 1879, when his training was finished, Klinger spent some time in Brussels, then in 1880 he went to Munich from where he returned to Berlin. There, in 1882, he received an important commission for a monumental work, the decoration of the Villa Albers near Berlin. In 1883 Klinger produced his first sculpture, a bust of Schiller; it was an important moment in his career for he was to end up working almost exclusively on sculpture. He spent three years in Paris (1883-1886) where he undertook a series of works which were to be finished later; among them, his Beethoven statue. A long stay in Rome (1889-1893) enabled him to familiarize himself with fifteenth-century Italian painting; he also studied anatomy, the nude and the problems of conveying volume. His output during the years in Rome was impressive, both for its quantity and diversity. He returned from Italy with many paintings, several sets of etchings, a rough sketch of his last painting, *Christ in Olympus* (finished in 1897), studies, various projects, and even a treatise (1891), *Malerei und Zeichnung*. In 1894 his first one-man show was held in Leipzig and was very well received. After 1897 Klinger turned more and more towards sculpture, finishing his *Beethoven* which was triumphantly exhibited at the Vienna Secession in 1902. Shown together with a frieze by Klimt, it constituted a homage to Beethoven in the form of a *Gesamtkunstwerk*; it thus marked the consecration of Klinger as a "total artist."

KLOOS Willem (1859-1938) 113.
KOUSNETSOV Pavel (1878-1968) 186.
KRÄMER Johann (1861-1949) 167.
KRAUS Karl (1874-1936) 163.
KRIER L. 10.
KRISTEVA Julia 16, 77, 95.
KROPOTKIN Peter Alexeivich, Prince (1842-1921) 51, 78;
Paroles d'un révolté (1886) 78.
KUBIN Alfred (1877-1959) 12, 19, 138, 186-189;
Bat and Graveyard Wall 189;
Bride of Death 138;
Dancer 188;
Die andere Seite (The Other Side) 188;
Marsh Plants 186.

Born in Bohemia, Kubin spent his childhood and adolescence in Austria. From boyhood, he was fond of drawing scenes of fantasy which he dreamt up himself. From 1892-1896, after having spent a year at the School of Arts and Crafts in Salzburg, he was apprenticed to a relation who was a photographer in Klagenfurt. But he was not happy as a photographer, and in a fit of nervous depression tried to commit suicide on his mother's grave; psychically unstable, he was to suffer frequent bouts of neurosis throughout his life. In 1898 he left for Munich where he worked in Ludwig Schmid-Reutte's studio, while studying at the Academy of Fine Arts until 1901. Kubin was full of admiration for the "surreal" painters like Bosch, Goya, Munch, Ensor and Redon; he also discovered Klinger's work which was a revelation to him. He drew constantly, creating works of pure fantasy which seem like illustrations to some of Freud's contemporary theories. He freed himself from his phantasms by means of drawing, turning them into monstrous figures and grotesque characters. In 1902 he exhibited a number of pen-and-ink drawings (his favourite medium) for the first time in Berlin at Cassirer's. Here he had the luck to find people who appreciated his work. Later on, encouraged by Redon and Verkade, he tried his hand at tempera and watercolour, but did not persist and went back to his pen which better suited his nervous temperament. In 1906 Kubin left Munich and retired to a country house near Zwickledt, in Upper Austria, where, apart from a few trips, he lived in seclusion until his death. He remained, however, in contact with both the artistic life of Munich and the avant-garde artists. In 1908, after his father's death, Kubin wrote a fantastic novel entitled *Die andere Seite (The Other Side)*, the description of an imaginary nightmare-world where all the torments and anguish of the real world were to be found. He illustrated this book with a series of drawings. Kubin later illustrated the works of many authors of phantasy, among them Poe, Nerval, Hauff, Bierbaum, D'Aurevilly, Wilde and Strindberg. In 1909 he became a member of the Neue Künstlervereinigung founded in Munich by Kandinsky, and then in 1911 he joined the Blaue Reiter. He exhibited and worked with Kandinsky, Marc, Feininger and Klee, while retaining the highly personal style which he continued to develop throughout his career. Kubin was a "surrealist" who did not experiment with form; he rejected Cubism and abstraction. He never abandoned his fantastical vein, though it grew less morbid and pessimistic in later years. He liked to use legends, stories and allegories in his work, and after the Second World War he turned to prophetic visions.

KURZWEIL Max (1867-1916) 167.

Ll

Lévy-Dhurmer began to study drawing in Paris when still very young, then worked as a painter in a factory which produced fine china-ware in the South of France. When about thirty, he made the classic pilgrimage to Italy and throughout his life he travelled extensively in Spain, Holland, North Africa and Turkey. In 1896 he used, for the first time, the name by which he came to be known (his real name was Lévy); this was at his first one-man show organized at Georges Petit's which was extremely successful. He used pastels a great deal, this medium with its suggestive blurred effects lending itself to the magic of symbolism; several of his contemporaries, particularly Fantin-Latour and Khnopff, were equally attracted by the pastel technique. He was influenced by the ideas both of Khnopff and the Pre-Raphaelites (this latter influence can be seen particularly in his rather languid women and in his idealized figures). He exhibited frequently at the Salon des Artistes Français, then at the Salon de la Société Nationale des Beaux-Arts and much later at the Salon d'Automne. By the end of the century both critics and literary men began to admire his work: Mauclair, Soulier, De Miomandre praised him at great length and Léon Thévenin devoted his book *La Renaissance païenne* (1898) to him. His style, which played skilfully on the academic treatment of visionary subjects, delighted a society which flattered him, encouraged in this by the admiration which the well-known Belgian poet Georges Rodenbach had for him. The painter did a famous portrait bust of Rodenbach set against the background of the city of Bruges. He also did Pierre Loti's portrait, with the Bosporus as backdrop, in 1896: "In the twilight Stamboul of Loti's portrait, I have lit little lamps today, which are reflected in the Bosporus and which are the small trembling souls of Aziyadé and Achmet," he wrote. He also painted several portraits of the actress Marguerite Moreno, particularly an ambiguous one of her in the part of Sister Gudule in Rodenbach's play *The Veil. Autumn, The Squall, Silence* and *Salome* were some of his typical subjects. Music also fascinated him and he tried to turn Debussy's *The Afternoon of a Faun* and Gabriel Fauré's *Roses of Isphahan* into paintings. He never ceased to use symbolist inspiration even after the turn of the century, but this was never held against him as it was against others. In about 1910 he decorated the dining-room of a house on the Champs-de-Mars in Paris with a peacock motif; in general his landscapes were much sought after for many years.

Fourth Salon of "La **Libre Esthétique**," 1897.
Poster by Théo van Rysselberghe.

Born in Glasgow, where he went to the famous Allan Glen School, Mackintosh became interested in drawing when still very young and wished to become an architect. In 1884, while serving an apprenticeship, he went to night school at the Glasgow School of Art, where he won several prizes and a travelling scholarship to France and Italy. In 1889 he began work as a draughtsman in the office of the architects Honeyman and Keppie, where he was to stay for many years. At art school he met Herbert MacNair and the two Macdonald sisters, Frances and Margaret, and together they formed a small group, "The Four," which concentrated on drawing and the applied arts. In 1896 they exhibited in London, attracting the attention of the magazine *The Studio*. This family group (MacNair married Frances, and Mackintosh, Margaret) sought an art that would be valid for the whole environment and as their work was close to the spirit of European Art Nouveau, they were very successful at the international exhibitions (Munich and Vienna). In 1896 Mackintosh won the competition for the rebuilding of the Glasgow School of Art. The project,

begun in 1897, lasted until 1909 and was his most important architectural work. At the same time he received commissions to do the interior decoration of several tearooms (in 1898, 1900 and 1903), each one being more elegant and luxurious than the last. After 1900 he received commissions in ever-increasing numbers, but in 1913 he fell ill and was forced to leave the architects' office where he had worked so long. He went to live in the South of France and died in London in 1928 of cancer.

Though Maillol is best known as a sculptor, nonetheless at the beginning of his life he produced some very interesting pictures. He treated nature in a poetic, almost bucolic way, using harmonious lines and colour in a pointillist manner. Born in Banyuls (French Pyrenees), he remained very attached to this corner of France throughout his life; the rich quality of the Mediterranean light was an important element in his work. In 1882 he went to Paris; there, as he said later, Gauguin's painting came as a revelation to him. "The Ecole des Beaux-Arts, instead of opening my eyes, veiled them...I soon told myself that what I did would be good if Gauguin approved of it," and this is in fact what happened. Fascinated by the experiments of the latter artist, he turned more and more towards a decorative art stripped to essentials. Soon afterwards he devoted himself to tapestry-making and started a workshop at Banyuls, where, with the help of local women, he designed tapestries using natural unbleached wool spun specially for him, which he dyed himself choosing his own colours. In 1894 he showed a tapestry with The Twenty in Brussels which attracted Gauguin's attention, but as the workshop could not support him financially he began to think of giving up the entire project. At this stage, a group of friends in Paris managed to get him commissions, but eye trouble forced him to change direction and from now on he devoted himself almost exclusively to sculpture.

Marées began his career as pupil to the animal painter Steffeck, in Berlin in 1854, then in 1857 he went to Munich where he continued his studies under Lenbach. In 1866 Count A. F. Schack, a patron of the arts, commissioned him to paint copies of the Italian Renaissance masters and sent him to Rome to do so. He went there with Lenbach and met the German painter Hildebrand and also Konrad Fiedler, who was to be his patron later on. The copies he sent back to Count Schack did not please his patron, mainly because of a new way the painter had of using colour. Tones of brown and red and gleams of gold—imitated from Rembrandt, whose work he had studied with interest—were from now on to be characteristic of his paintings. His favourite subjects were taken from ancient mythology, as Böcklin and the majority of German artists liked to do. Thanks to Fiedler's help, Marées was able to work without financial hardship until the end of his life. He made frequent trips to Spain, Holland, France and Germany, but most of the time he lived in Italy, mainly in Rome, where after 1875 he settled for good. His most monumental work was the decoration of the Naples Zoological Station, commissioned from him in 1873 by its German director Anton Dohrn, and carried out with the help of Adolf von Hildebrand.

Octave **Maus** in 1885 by Théo van Rysselberghe.

Maxence was an official painter who was very successful in the Salons, where he was a regular contributor, as well as in the Salon de la Rose Croix where he exhibited from 1895 to 1897. A pupil of Elie Delaunay and Gustave Moreau, he was one of those *fin de siècle* painters who knew how to appeal to bourgeois taste by sprinkling their rather dry academic style with literary touches and nostalgic allusions. He took his subject-matter from medieval and legendary sources as the Pre-Raphaelites did, and the Early Italian Renaissance influenced him as well. This can be seen in his figures, often half-length portraits shown against a landscape background. The titles of his pictures, like *The Soul of the Forest* (1898) or *Serenity* (1912), are witness that, for him, as for many of his generation, painting was above all a question of charming, imaginative decoration. "Maxence's art is purposefully empty," wrote Henri Focillon in 1913; today we look at his painting with new eyes, it seems so close in time and yet so characteristic of a bygone era.

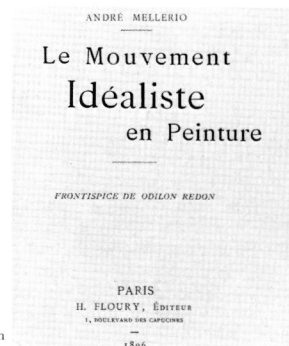

André **Mellerio:**
"Le Mouvement Idéaliste en Peinture," 1896.

Born in Brussels, the son of a gardener, Mellery studied art at the Académie des Beaux-Arts and also served an apprenticeship as a decorator. In 1870 he won the Prix de Rome and went to Italy. In Venice he fell under the spell of the Venetian masters, Carpaccio in particular, and in Rome was much taken by antique statuary and Renaissance art. Back in Belgium, he illustrated a book by Charles de Coster and then in 1880 he went to Holland to the island of Marken, where folk traditions were still very strong. His interest in the life of the people makes his vision close to that of Constantin Meunier.

After 1885 he tended to specialize in decorative and allegorical works which he designed to fill large spaces like some of Puvis de Chavannes's monumental compositions. The pictures often contained outsize figures, shown almost in bas-relief, set against a gold ground, the whole composition unfolding in strange rhythms. However, the painter never had a great success with these paintings and they were a source of bitterness and disillusionment to him. To study the techniques of fresco painting, he made several trips throughout Europe. He was a member of The Twenty and contributed to the Salon de la Rose Croix. He illustrated several books, notably *La Belgique* by Camille Lemonnier with whom he was intimate. "Very few people," the latter wrote to him in 1899, "have experienced as you have the despair of the searcher... you are, indeed, the *concentrated* hero that Baudelaire writes of." Mellery, who spoke of the spiritual life as "the soul of things," represented it in his drawings with an extraordinary intensity, where an anguished feeling of silence and suspended time hangs over everything.

Catulle **Mendès** in 1888 by Vallotton.

Born at Southampton, Millais began his artistic career as a mere boy, encouraged by his family. At the age of eleven he was accepted as a probationary student at the Royal Academy schools where he displayed a precocious talent and won prizes for his first works, which were large compositions done in an academic style. It was at the Academy that he made friends with Holman Hunt, who was less well-known than he within the school and whose rebellious and revolutionary nature encouraged Millais to examine his own views on art. Just then Ruskin was laying down the foundation of what was to become the new art, in his book *Modern Painters*. He exhorted the new generation of artists to return to a strict imitation of Nature and to the models of the Early Renaissance. In 1848 Millais and Holman Hunt, together with Rossetti, formed the Pre-Raphaelite Brotherhood with the aim of applying Ruskin's principles. When he was nineteen, Millais exhibited his first Pre-Raphaelite picture at the Academy, *Isabella*, which was hung next to Holman Hunt's *Rienzi*. The critics, surprised by the almost photographic realism of this painting, were divided in their opinions. The following year, when Millais showed his second Pre-Raphaelite painting, *Christ in the House of his Parents*, the majority were disapproving; they were mainly incensed by the fact that a religious picture was both so prosaic and so realistic. Ruskin had to come publicly to the defense of the group, though a change in public opinion occurred later on. The clamour was already beginning to die down when *Ophelia* (1852) was shown, a key picture for the Pre-Raphaelites. Millais attained a technical perfection in this work by the use of brilliant colours. The following year, *The Huguenot* was shown and received general critical acclaim. In 1853 Millais was made an Associate Member of the Royal Academy just at the time when the Pre-Raphaelite Brotherhood began to dissolve. In 1855 his friendship with Ruskin, which at one time had been very close (see his 1853 portrait of the latter), deteriorated when Millais married Effie Ruskin, his friend's ex-wife. Hoping to renew the success of *The Huguenot*, he painted another picture in the same style, *The Black Brunswicker*. He now began to abandon the minute attention to detail and the descriptive realism of his Pre-Raphaelite pictures, adopting a style which was less strict, more spontaneous and in which the details were treated in an impressionistic manner, painted in general in a thickish medium. Millais was by now held in great esteem and received numerous commissions, in particular portraits, a genre in which he excelled. He finally attained the glory after which he had been seeking, for in 1878 he exhibited at the Exposition Universelle in Paris; he was made an Associate Member of the Académie des Beaux-Arts in Paris and President of the Royal Academy in London just before his death.

Born in Ghent, Minne was the son of an architect and building contractor. From 1882 to 1884 he attended the local art school, then the Académie des Beaux-Arts in Brussels, where he met the leading Belgian poets and writers of his day. Possessed of an anxious nature veering towards mysticism, he was attracted to the symbolism of the poets Grégoire Le Roy, Emile Verhaeren (who greatly influenced him), and Maeterlinck; after 1888 he illustrated several of their works. In 1891 he was elected a member of The Twenty; he had exhibited his first sculptures under their auspices the previous year and was to exhibit frequently with them in the future as well as at the Salon de la Rose Croix in Paris. Minne did sculpture as well as engravings and drawings and between 1895 and 1898 he produced some important works, for example, *Kneeling Men* and *Man with a Goatskin Bottle*. In 1899 he settled in the Belgian village of Laethem Saint-Martin, where he formed an art group while pursuing his own work with intense concentration. He was professor at the Academy in Ghent both before and after the First World War.

In 1902 an important exhibition of Flemish Primitives was held in Bruges which was an eye-opener for many artists, including Minne, despite the fact that it only confirmed his search for an instantly perceptible way to express purity and truth. Minne conveyed in his work the sufferings and misery of humanity bowed down by the cares of life, in a tormented, though stylized form full of controlled passion. *Fountain with Kneeling Youths* at Essen remains his most famous work, while his drawings, which are intense and moving contrasts in black and white, show great sensitivity.

Jean **Moréas.**

Gustave **Moreau** by Puvis de Chavannes.

The Apparition 40-43;
Hercules and the Lernean Hydra 40, 42, 43;
Jupiter and Semele 15, 147;
Life of Mankind 53;
Notebooks 15, 42;
Oedipus and the Sphinx 38, 39, 179;
Persian Poet on a Unicorn 14, 15;
Rape of Deianira 42;
Salome before Herod 40, 42, 43;
Sketches of *Puvis de Chavannes* and *Elie Delaunay* 23;
Thracian Girl Carrying the Head of Orpheus 21-23;
Triumph of Alexander 178.

Born in Paris. His father was a city architect employed by the Ministry of the Interior. As a boy Moreau displayed a gift for drawing, and after a good classical schooling he entered the Ecole des Beaux-Arts, working in Picot's studio. He left several years later having failed twice to win the Prix de Rome. In 1852 he exhibited a *Pietà* at the Salon which was well received; it attracted the attention of the Goncourt brothers, even though Delacroix's influence shows strongly in the work (Moreau was a great admirer of the latter). He became a close friend of Chassériau who, though a pupil of Ingres, was also an admirer of Delacroix and tried to create a synthesis of these two very different styles. In the 1850s the two friends worked in neighbouring studios near the Place Pigalle and the influence of Chassériau (he died in 1856) as well as that of the Romantic movement were two important factors in the development of Moreau's rich, flamboyant style. The pure lines of Classicism can also be seen in his work; *Darius Fleeing After the Battle of Arbela*, which he exhibited at the 1853 Salon, is a typical example. In 1857 he set out for Italy as he felt the need for direct contact with the art of the past. He spent four years there travelling about the peninsula and going south as far as Naples. He fell in with several friends and got to know Degas, Léon Bonnat and the sculptor Chapu. He not only studied the art of antiquity, but also early and late Renaissance art; he made numerous copies in various techniques and brought back a quantity of beautiful landscape sketches in watercolour and pastel. This period abroad was extremely important for the development of his work. As soon as he returned he prepared to relaunch himself on the Parisian scene and after having done several studies (which were begun in 1861) he exhibited *Oedipus and the Sphinx* at the 1864 Salon. This masterly work created a sensation and the caricaturists, led by Daumier, let themselves go with a vengeance. Both allegorical and symbolic, the picture aroused an immense amount of comment and was bought by Prince Jérôme Bonaparte. Moreau exhibited at the 1865, 1866, and 1868 Salons and in 1869 he sent in *Prometheus*, another key picture; however, this time the critics were violently opposed and Moreau did not exhibit again until 1876. He sought a new style, though despite everything his inspiration was still at heart an allegorical one. His search for something new resulted in *Salome Dancing Before Herod* (1876 Salon) which received great acclaim. His last entry to the Salon was in 1880. In

1886 he exhibited a series of watercolours illustrating the *Fables* of La Fontaine at the Galerie Goupil which made a great impression on Rouault. This was to be one of his last public exhibits. Since his mother's death in 1884 he had been living a very quiet life, though not lacking in friends and admirers. In 1892 he succeeded his friend Elie Delaunay as professor at the Ecole des Beaux-Arts; among his pupils were the young Matisse, Rouault, Marquet and Evenepoel. He died in 1898 leaving his house and studio at 14 rue de La Rochefoucauld, which he had already arranged as a museum, to the Nation.

MORGENSTERN Christian (1871-1914) 151.
MORICE Charles (1861-1919) 12, 69, 70, 77, 80, 90, 95, 159, 160;
    La Littérature de tout à l'heure 70.
MORICE Madame Charles 160.
MORIN Edgar (1921) 7, 10;
    Le Paradigme perdu 10.
MORISOT Berthe (1841-1895) 148.
MORREN George (1868-1941) 107, 190;
    Cover of *L'Art Moderne* 107.
MORRIS Jane (née BURDEN, born 1839) 28, 29, 31, 32, 34, 35, 145, 146.
MORRIS William (1834-1896) 12, 27, 29-32, 34, 39, 131, 145-147, 149, 150, 152, 154, 159, 167;
    "Chaucer Type" 146;
    The Earthly Paradise 39;
    Life and Death of Jason 131;
    Queen Guinevere 29, 145;
    The Society of the Future 145, 146;
    The Works of Chaucer 146.

Born near London of well-to-do parents, Morris showed an early interest in literature. After a classical schooling at Marlborough College, he went up to Oxford, to Exeter College, to study theology as he intended to take orders; here, in 1852, he met Burne-Jones. A common interest in the arts drew them together and little by little they began to turn away from theology and towards literature and art. In 1856 they founded *The Oxford and Cambridge Magazine*. They were both strongly influenced by Ruskin's theories which were to play an important role in their future development. Unlike Burne-Jones, Morris completed his time at Oxford and obtained his degree. He then went to live in London and decided to become an architect, entering a firm of London architects as an apprentice in 1856. Even then he was beginning to develop his theory of a total art which should encompass all the applied arts concerned with everyday life. He was strongly opposed to mechanization and dreamed of a return to the craftsmanship of the Middle Ages. As a result he made himself proficient in many art and craft techniques. In 1857 he worked with Rossetti and Burne-Jones on the decoration of the walls of the Debating Hall of the Oxford Union. In 1858 he painted his only picture, *Queen Guinevere*; from now on he devoted himself to decorative arts, poetry and politics. His first work of total art was the house that he had built for himself and his wife, Jane, by the architect Philip Webb; this was the Red House on Bexley Heath in Kent, whose interior decoration and furniture were designed by himself and his friends. In 1861 he founded a business, Morris, Marshall, Faulkner and Co., whose purpose was to design everything that went into a house: furniture, china, stained glass, wallpaper, tapestries, *objets d'art*, etc. Morris set himself against the middle-class Victorian style of that time which was both pompous and decadent, and adopted a style based on ornamental naturalism which was to prepare the way for Art Nouveau. In 1891 he founded a publishing house, the Kelmscott Press, where the work was carried out according to his social ethic, that is to say, by hand, bypassing mechanization completely. At the Kelmscott Press he published some rare and beautiful books, for example *The Golden Legend* and *The Works of Geoffrey Chaucer*. Morris wrote a great deal of poetry, a series of prose romances, and many theoretical essays in favour of Socialism.

Moscow 40.

MOSER Koloman (1868-1918) 103, 164, 166, 167, 179;
    The Dancer Loie Fuller 179;
    Two Oriental Dancers 166.

Moser began his studies at the Vienna Academy and then went on to the Kunstgewerbeschule where he met Klimt and Matsch. From 1888 onwards, in order to earn his living, he drew illustrations for the *Allegorien* publications—which later became *Allegorien und Embleme*—as well as for the *Wiener Mode*. After a stay in Munich (1895-1896) he returned to Vienna (1897) where he was one of the founders of the Secession. The following year he was a founder member of the Secession magazine *Ver Sacrum* for which he produced a series of woodcuts in a linear decorative style. In 1900 he was made professor at the Kunstgewerbeschule in Vienna. He was also a founder member in 1903 of the Wiener Werkstätte and collaborated with these workshops of applied art until 1906. In 1904-1905 he designed the stained-glass windows and altar of the Kirche Am Steinhof in Vienna, designed by the architect Otto Wagner. From this time onwards he devoted himself chiefly to painting, a medium which was his particular passion. Encouraged by Hodler, he painted decorative works; roughed out sketches of frescoes for churches; and designed stamps and bank notes for the Austrian government (1909-1916).

MOUREY Gabriel (1865-1943) 34, 48.
MOXON Edward (1801-1858) 34.

Caricature of **Mucha** by D.O. Widhopff, in "La Plume," Paris, 1897.

MUCHA Alphonse (1860-1939) 12, 36, 148, 167, 168, 172, 173;
    Cover for *L'Image* 148; for *Ver Sacrum* 167;
    Design for a fan 168;
    Jewelry designs 168;
    Photographs 172, 173;
    Summer 172.

Born in Ivancice in Moravia, Mucha went to Vienna as a young man where he worked on decorative projects, before going to Munich. In 1887 he settled in Paris where he studied at the Académie Julian. He produced illustrations for various periodicals which soon brought him fame. In 1897 *La Plume*, a review to which he contributed, brought out a special edition devoted to his work. In 1894 he designed his first poster for the actress Sarah Bernhardt, who was so delighted by it that she signed a long-standing contract with him. The public also showed their enthusiasm for his sinuous linework which soon became one of the distinctive features of Art Nouveau. Mucha went on to design other posters which were as highly acclaimed and which brought him orders in other fields of decorative art. He designed calendars, stained-glass windows, decorative panels, jewellery (in particular some for the jeweller Georges Fouque), drew illustrations for children's books as well as for the book *Episodes from German History* which took up much of his time, and for *Ilsa, Princess of Tripoli*, for which he did 130 colour lithographs. He was intimate with the literary Symbolists as well as with fanatical esoteric circles. "His was the art of an Oriental transplanted to Paris, the golden, mosaic backgrounds of his posters, the richness of his ornamentation, the languid, hieratic poses of his women," all fascinated the Parisian public. Mucha decorated the Bosnian pavilion for the 1900 World's Fair in Paris and after a visit to New York he returned to his native Czechoslovakia and devoted himself to painting, which had always been his passion.

Son of a clergyman, his mother dying when he was a child. His father wanted him to become an engineer and so he went to Oslo Technical College. However, he was passionately interested in painting and in 1881 enrolled at the School of Arts and Crafts. At this time he painted interiors and realistic portraits in an academic style using sombre tones. On a three-week visit to Paris in 1885, he discovered Impressionism: it led him not only to think about colour but also to develop his ideas on art in general. On his return to Oslo he painted *The Sick Girl* (1885), which showed great freedom in its treatment of line and colour; the model for this picture was his sister Sophie. In 1889 he had a one-man show in Oslo where he exhibited about 100 works on the themes which were to haunt him throughout his life: solitude, illness and death. The same year, thanks to a grant, he returned to Paris and lived there until 1892. He worked for four months with the academic painter Bonnat, but was also in contact with the avant-garde milieu. During this time he painted *Rue de Rivoli, Rue Lafayette, Spring*, and *Karl Johans Gate* (1891). He then went to Italy and afterwards to Germany where he came into contact with a group of artists and critics: Dehmel, Bierbaum, Strindberg, Meier-Graefe and Przybyszewski. The paintings he exhibited at the Berlin Artists Association in 1892 caused a great scandal. On his return to Oslo, he joined the Bohemia group and in 1893 painted one of his most important works, *The Scream*, where he expressed his own inner despair by means of shrill colour and dramatization of form. Munch's art throughout was a series of revelations about his inner life which he exposed to the world without restraint. This manner of his, however, provoked violent reactions from the puritan elements of society,

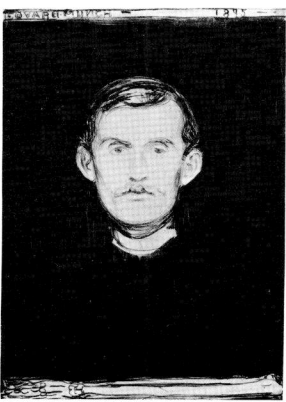

Munch self-portrait with skeleton hand, 1895.

particularly when he dealt with the theme of love in *Puberty* (1894); of the *femme fatale* in *The Vampire* (1895); and the mixture of mysticism and eroticism in his *Madonna* (1894-1895). In 1894 he began to do engravings which combined different techniques: etching, aquatints and lithography. A great number of his paintings he reinterpreted in the form of lithographs and woodcuts and they thus reached a large public. In 1895-1896 he stayed again in Paris, where now that he was known he exhibited several times. He became friends with Mallarmé and illustrated Baudelaire's *Fleurs du Mal*. He spent much of his time engraving, perfecting his technique more and more. In a sort of synthesis of all that he had done, he summed up his work from 1893 to 1902 in a cycle which he called *The Frieze of Life*, forming a general panorama of his themes: the birth of love, its development and its end; jealousy; anguish and death. He also painted many landscapes and portraits in which his powerful sense of colour was let loose. He had considerable influence on the birth of Expressionism in Germany where he often exhibited. In 1908 a nervous breakdown brought the development of his art to a virtual halt, but ironically it was at this time that he began to receive official honours; he was asked to paint murals for the University of Oslo and later on (1928-1944) for Oslo Town Hall.

The **Nabi** Paul Ranson in 1890 by Sérusier.

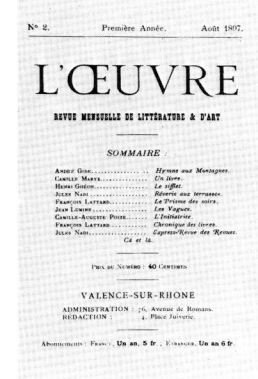

"L'Œuvre," Valence, 1897.

Olbrich began by studying architecture in Vienna with Otto Wagner. In 1897 he was one of the founding members of the Vienna Secession and it was he who, following Klimt's advice, designed the building to house the exhibitions held by the Secession. This is one of the major works of Art Nouveau architecture. He was a contributor to the magazine *Ver Sacrum*, doing illustrations, layouts and architectural designs for them. In 1899, he was invited to Darmstadt by Grand Duke Ernst Ludwig of Hesse to set up an artists' colony to stimulate creative life. Olbrich's work was important for the development of German taste; it revolutionized not only architecture, but also interior decoration and applied arts.

Born in Paris, Osbert studied at the Ecole des Beaux-Arts. His name is best known for the part he played in the Salons de la Rose Croix. His style tended towards a rather mannered idealism, often tinged with literary mysticism. At the Ecole des Beaux-Arts he became friends with Aman-Jean and Seurat, and under the latter's influence he undertook research into light and its influence on colour. He exhibited until the end of his life at the Société Nationale des Beaux-Arts and at the Salon des Indépendants. He also showed at major exhibitions in Milan, Brussels, Rome and Tokyo and was one of the founders of the Salon d'Automne in Paris.

Joséphin **Péladan**.

After studying at the Brera Academy in Milan, Pellizza da Volpedo went to Florence where he met Giovanni Fattori one of the most important of the *macchiaioli* painters. He made several visits to Paris, notably for the Exposition Universelle in 1900. He started out as a realist, but gave this up and turned towards Neo-Impressionism. *The Barn*, which he exhibited in Florence, Turin, and Milan, between 1895 and 1898, stirred up enormous controversy because of the divisionist style he used for the colour and brushwork. The debate that his pictures caused was very important for the later development of Italian painting, particularly in the North, and in fact Pellizza's experiments had far-reaching effects elsewhere. Intimate with the literary men of his time, he was interested in the theory of colour as well as being passionately concerned with socialist theories and the writings of Marx and Engels. The social problem is the subject of his painting *The Fourth Estate*, which when exhibited in 1902 at the Quadriennale in Turin did not have the success he had hoped for. *Love in Life*, the triptych that he painted between 1900 and 1904, deals on the contrary with a typically Symbolist subject which he treated by means of the chromatic division of colour. In 1907, very disturbed by several deaths, both of friends and family, he hanged himself in his studio at Volpedo.

Periodicals:

"La Plume," Paris, 1896.

Born in Ferrara, Previati went to the local Art School. He then spent some time in Florence before going to Milan where he won a prize with the painting *The Hostages of Crema*. In 1891 he painted *Maternity* in a style combining a pointillist technique with a symbolist inspiration. Exhibited at the Milan Triennale, this work aroused a violent controversy. In 1892 he exhibited at the Salon de la Rose Croix in Paris. Between 1891 and 1896 he spent a great deal of time working on the illustrations for Manzoni's classic novel *I Promessi Sposi*, for which he did more than 300 drawings. In 1902 he exhibited at the Berlin Secession and obtained a gold medal at the 1905 quadrennial exhibition in Munich. In 1907 he organized the *Dream Room* for the Venice Biennale which displayed an excessively sentimental and allegorical symbolism such as he and other Italian artists were fond of. Previati wrote several theoretical works: *The Scientific Principles of Divisionism* (1906) and *On Painting: Technique and Art* (1913). His art played an important part in the development of Futurism.

Born in Lyons of a bourgeois family long-established in the legal profession. His father was an engineer. He studied art in Paris in Henri Scheffer's studio and afterwards paid extended visits to Italy. He then worked in Couture's studio and, for a few days only, in Delacroix's. But it was with Chassériau's work that he felt the most affinity. In 1850 he made his début at the Salon with a *Pietà*; but he did not have anything accepted at the Salon again until 1859. In 1861 he received his first official commission for a decorative work (he had already tried his hand at this kind of painting with *The Four Seasons*, done for the drawing-room of his brother's country house). This time it was a series of decorations for the Amiens Museum, which he painted in various stages (he was still working on it in 1888 when alterations were made to the Museum). The many decorative

Puvis de Chavannes painting "St Genevieve Feeding Paris."

paintings for which he is best known and on which he spent most of his time, were not actually frescoes, but paintings done on canvas and then transferred to the walls. In each one, however, he tried by means of a unifying theme to create a work consonant with the building's essential function. In treating the space available to him, he refrained from opening up the wall by means of perspective recession and created surface rhythms unfolding like a frieze; this was often held against him. Contrary to a common assumption, he did relatively few real religious pictures. "Apart from frescoes, or something which resembles them, all other painting is to be deplored in a church. Frames hung on a stone wall are not right at all," so he said.

He did several decorative paintings for the houses of friends: for Madame Claude Vignon, who was a sculptor, writer and minister's wife (1866), and for the academic painter Léon Bonnat he painted his admirable *Pleasant Land* (1882).

However, the majority of his decorative works were done as official commissions: Marseilles Museum (1867-1869); the staircase of the Hôtel de Ville at Poitiers (1870-1875); the murals in the Panthéon in Paris (1874-1878 for the first series, 1893-1898 for the second); the staircase of the Lyons Museum (1884-1886) and that of the Rouen Museum (1888-1891); the Zodiac Room (1887-1892) and the Grand Staircase (1892-1894) of the Hôtel de Ville in Paris; and nine large panels for the Boston Public Library in the United States (1891-1896).

Despite his official commissions, his frequent exhibits at the Salons and his undoubted prestige, there were still critics of his work who were even quite savage at times. They criticized him as much for his use of pale, low-toned colours as for his over-literary manner. Castagnary wrote: "When one wishes to make philosophy out of painting one should at least do it correctly." Even the Salon juries were occasionally harsh and it was precisely in order to combat the narrow-minded attitude of the Société des Artistes Français that he founded a new Société des Beaux-Arts with Rodin and Meissonier. It was not until he had completed the decoration of the Church of Sainte-Geneviève in Paris (called the Panthéon since 1885) that he became the sort of mythical, official French genius that we think of today. However, this image of him is distorted. He was unquestionably a man of tradition, firmly entrenched in the bourgeois society for which he painted (for example, he was violently anti-Dreyfusard); but nonetheless he possessed a sort of elemental force (his enormous appetite, for example, was legendary), and like every great artist he was a prey to contradictory impulses which give an underlying power and fascination to his painting.

Born in Bordeaux, the son of an "explorer and pioneer"; his mother was a Creole from New Orleans. When he was fifteen, he met the botanist Clavaud, who interested him in biology, painting and contemporary literature; he also became a keen lover of music. A delicate boy, he was an introvert who liked taking long solitary walks in the countryside. In Bordeaux he became friends with Rodolphe Bresdin, which was important for his development as an artist, and at the same time he discovered Rembrandt. In 1867 he sent his first etching, *The Ford*, to the Paris Salon and wrote several articles on painters for the Bordeaux newspaper *La Gironde*.

After the Franco-Prussian war of 1870 he settled in Paris, where he met Corot, Courbet and Fantin-Latour; the latter initiated him into lithography and they studied the masters together in the Louvre. In 1879 he issued his first set of lithographs, *Dans le Rêve*. Later he produced other sets, notably *A Edgar Poe* (first published in the newspaper *Le Gaulois*, it excited the admiration of Huysmans), *Les Origines* (1883), *Hommage à Goya* (1885, described at length by Huysmans in *A Rebours*) and *La Tentation de saint Antoine* (two sets, 1888 and 1890).

In 1884 he exhibited at the first Salon des Indépendants of which he was a co-founder. In 1886 he was invited by The Twenty to exhibit at the Salon des XX in Brussels (he showed there a second time in 1890), but his works appeared to some people "extremely odd... like so many riddles, nightmares, morbid visions, hallucinations." He contributed to the *Revue Wagnérienne*. In 1886 he was profoundly upset by the death, at a few months old, of his first son (in 1880 he had married a young Creole). In 1889 he took part in the first exhibition of Peintres-Graveurs held at Durand-Ruel's gallery in Paris, where he met his future biographer, André Mellerio. He now became friends with Maurice Denis, Emile Bernard, Francis Jammes, Jean Moréas, Gide, Valéry, and particularly with Mallarmé. In 1890 he began to use colour in his first pastels and saw much of Gauguin. In 1894 he had his first one-man show at Durand-Ruel's and in The Hague. Soon afterwards, Ambroise Vollard published his *Temptation of St Anthony* (third series) and from 1898 on organized numerous exhibitions of his work. The following year Durand-Ruel held the "Homage to Odilon Redon" exhibition, which attracted the attention of many young artists, among them Bernard, Signac, Sérusier, Vuillard, Vallotton and Denis. Redon began to give up engraving and turned to painting; he was particularly interested in the use of pastels, conducting experiments with colour which enabled him to produce very deep tones. "What can I have put into my work to suggest so many shades of meaning? I only placed a little door there, opening on to the unknown. I invented a little. It is up to them to go further," he wrote in 1888. "They," in fact, *have* gone "further," for the admiration which the Surrealists had for Redon is still felt just as strongly by today's artists. In 1910 he decorated the library of the Abbey of Fontfroide (near Montpellier) where his friend, the art collector Fayet, lived. Despite his quiet, studious life Redon became well known abroad. After having exhibited at various important shows in London and St Petersburg, he had a room devoted to his work in the famous Armory Show in New York, Chicago and Boston (1913). He died on 6 July 1916. He had written: "The artist is born into this life to accomplish something of which we know nothing. He is an accident. He has nothing to expect from society."

Henri de **Régnier** in 1898
by Théo van Rysselberghe.

Riemerschmid began his career as a painter, turning later to the applied arts. In 1897 he was one of the co-founders of the Vereinigte Werkstätten in Munich. He was one of the first artists to be concerned, not only with the aesthetic aspect of the objects he designed, but also with their price and availability, hoping thereby to create an art accessible to all. He exhibited his mass-produced objects throughout Europe. Among his important commissions were the interior decoration of the Munich Theatre (1901) and a series of artists' studios at Hellerau (1910).

Born in Paris. His father came from Normandy, his mother from a family of humble origins in Lorraine. At fourteen he entered the Ecole de Dessin in Paris. After three years there (one summer of which he studied under the animal-painter Barye at the Muséum d'Histoire Naturelle), he applied to the Ecole des Beaux-Arts, but failed three times. He earned his living as a decorator, while carving his *Man with a Broken Nose*, which was refused by the 1864 Salon. He then began work at the Sèvres porcelain factory under Carrier-Belleuse who was famous for his bronzes. In 1866 he had a son by Rose Beuret (he and Rose finally married in 1917, the year they both died). In 1871 he moved to Brussels where he collaborated on the decorative sculpture of the Stock Exchange and the Palais des Académies. In 1875 he went to Italy where he studied antique and Renaissance art with great passion. On returning to Belgium he worked for eighteen months on *The Bronze Age* and exhibited the plaster at the 1877 Salon; he was at once accused of having made an exact cast of a man's head. An enquiry established that there was no basis for this accusation, and to make amends the State commissioned him to design a door for the Palais des Arts Décoratifs. He worked throughout his life on this project, *The Gate of Hell*, but without ever feeling that he had really finished it. In 1883 he met Camille Claudel, the sister of Paul Claudel the writer, and for about fifteen years he had a passionate affair with this talented woman. In 1889 the Georges Petit gallery exhibited the sculptural group *The Burghers of Calais*, commissioned in 1884 (though it was not set up in its appointed place until much later). The 1889 exhibition showed the works of Monet and Rodin together; Octave Mirbeau wrote the preface to the catalogue. From now on Rodin began to be very well known; in the eyes of the public he was the very incarnation of the creative spirit. "A restless, volcanic spirit, an imagination like a violent storm... the sculptor of sensuality," wrote Mirbeau. Rodin passionately sought to recreate "life," to record the fleeting gestures and movements of the human body. To achieve this he ordered his male and female nude models to move around in his studio, which naturally shocked the public. The attacks on his art continued unceasingly and when in 1896 he presented several models for the monument to *Victor Hugo* for the poet's tomb in the Panthéon—whom in an early version he had portrayed nude—the Art Commission demanded alterations. Then his monument to *Balzac*, for which he made more than forty models, also created an outcry and was finally refused in 1898. Rodin achieved world-wide recognition at the Paris World's Fair in 1900 where he showed a large number of works in his own personal pavilion. In 1902 he met Rainer Maria Rilke for the first time; the poet was fascinated by his personality and became his secretary in 1905. From now on he was admired and adulated by Parisian Society (he had been the Duchess of Choiseul's lover since 1904) and received visits at his studio of many eminent people, including Edward VII in 1908. In 1915 he went to Italy to work on the bust of Pope Benedict XV. He died in November 1917.

Roller studied art at the Vienna Academy and then travelled in Germany, England and France. He was a founder member of the Vienna Secession in 1897, and President in 1901-1902. He left the group at the same time as Klimt and the "Stylists" in 1905. For two years

he edited the Secession magazine *Ver Sacrum*, for which he did illustrations. His graphic work (engravings, posters, vignettes, etc.), both for the Secession and *Ver Sacrum*, was characterized by the ornamental linear tendency of Art Nouveau. In 1900 he was made Professor at the Kunstgewerbeschule in Vienna. But it was above all in the theatre that Roller showed his talent. He worked with Mahler in Vienna, then with Max Reinhardt in Berlin. His avant-garde projects revolutionized the world of stage scenery and production.

Letter from **Rops**, 1892.

Born in Namur, Belgium, Rops studied at the Brussels Academy, then enrolled in Brussels Law School, while simultaneously studying at the Academy of St Luke. In 1856 he founded a satirical paper, *Uylenspiegel*, where his characteristic verve and humour are already evident. He divided his time between Brussels and Paris where he studied etching techniques. In 1868 he became Vice-President of the Société Libre des Beaux-Arts of Brussels and then in 1870 founded the Society of Etchers and settled in Paris in 1874. He was a great success there and was much admired by artists such as Puvis de Chavannes and Gustave Moreau. He began doing illustrations and Barbey d'Aurevilly, Baudelaire and Huysmans enthused over his work for its caustic and erotic elements. His etchings for *Les Diaboliques* by Barbey d'Aurevilly are regarded as some of the best illustrative work ever done. Although he was not attracted by the metaphysical mumbo-jumbo of the Rose Croix, he was much admired by Péladan: "I have seen some of your masterly etchings, and find them so perverse that I, who am preparing a *Treatise on Perversity*, am overwhelmed by your exceptional talent," wrote Péladan. Despite the success of his etchings, for which he is mainly known today, he never gave up painting. From 1886 to 1893 he was a member of The Twenty in Brussels. At the Paris Salons, where he was a frequent exhibitor, his work never failed to create a sensation, for the licentious atmosphere which hung about his art and his life as well: by both the public was fascinated and shocked.

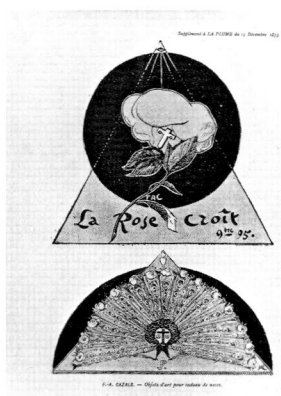

F. A. Cazals: "The **Rose** Grows. Objets d'art for wedding presents," 1895.

Born in London, son of an Italian emigrant, Rossetti showed an interest in the arts (drawing, poetry and literature) while still a boy. His childhood prepared him well for his double career as a painter and poet. When he was nine years old he went to King's College, London, and at eighteen to the Royal Academy Schools, to study art, but left without having finished the course. By the age of twenty he had already written some of his best poems, including *The Blessed Damozel* and *My Sister's Sleep*. Finding academic teaching too dull, he looked for inspiration elsewhere and found it in Ford Madox Brown's painting, *Wycliffe Reading his Translation of the Bible to John of Gaunt*, whose painstaking treatment heralded Pre-Raphaelitism. Rossetti worked as an apprentice for Madox Brown for several months. In 1848 he met Millais and Holman Hunt, whose latest work, *The Flight of Madeline and Porphyro*, he much admired, and with them he formed the Pre-Raphaelite Brotherhood (1848). Influenced by Ruskin, they took as their models the Italian Primitives and nature. The entire traditional method of painting was questioned; colours became clear and bright and the subject-matter was treated in great detail. Rossetti painted his first picture, *The Girlhood of Mary Virgin*, according to the new principles of the Pre-Raphaelite Brotherhood and it was well received in 1849. After a trip to France and Belgium in 1849 with Holman Hunt he started on a second picture, *Ecce Ancilla Domini (The Annunciation)*, which was taken to be an affront to religion by the critics. After 1853 the Brotherhood slowly began to break up as each member had different objectives in mind: Millais, for example, was looking for fame. From now on, Rossetti, unlike Holman Hunt, was no longer interested in true-to-life portrayal. He began to concentrate on drawing, illustrating Dante and his circle, Shakespeare, Browning and Malory (the Arthurian legends). In 1850 he met Elizabeth Siddal who became his model, then his muse, and finally, in 1860, his wife. In 1857 he undertook some murals for the Debating Hall of the Oxford Union, with the help of Burne-Jones and William Morris. The pictures of this period are tinged with a lyrical idealism and represent an idyllic vision of the Middle Ages. Between 1857 and 1860 his work gained in depth and took on a new tone. This was the beginning of his portraits of women which brought him both fame and fortune. The first painting in this long series was *Bocca Baciata* (1859), followed by other masterpieces: *Beata Beatrix* (1864), a homage to

Elizabeth Siddal who had committed suicide in 1862; *The Beloved* (1865-1866); *The Blue Bower* (1865); then those for which Jane Morris, William Morris's wife, was the model: *La Pia de' Tolomei* (1868-1880) and *Mariana* (1870). When his wife committed suicide, Rossetti buried all his unpublished poems in her coffin; but seven years later, in 1869, he dug them up and they were published the following year. The critics, apart from some who objected to a certain sensuality in the verses, were full of admiration. There is a definite link between Rossetti's art and his poetry: the themes, the form, the spirit are common to both. Though already a victim of paranoia, Rossetti did not cease to write poetry (a second collection came out in 1881) and paint pictures, even though some betray a certain mental disturbance. He died at Birchington-on-Sea in 1882.

Albert **Samain**.

Born in Altona, near Hamburg, Schwabe was brought up in Switzerland and adopted Swiss nationality when he was twenty-two. He studied under Mittey at the Ecole des Arts Industriels in Geneva and in 1890 he went to Paris, where, the following year, he exhibited at the Société Nationale. From 1892 to 1897 he exhibited at the Salons de la Rose Croix, organized by Sâr Péladan, first at Durand-Ruel's gallery, then at the Champ de Mars, and finally at the fashionable Georges Petit gallery. He designed a poster for the first Rose Croix Salon (at which Hodler and Vallotton also exhibited) which aroused much comment and stands as a landmark in the development of Art Nouveau. He designed wallpapers, full of stylized flower motifs, as well as illustrating several books; for Zola's *Le Rêve* he did a series of watercolours (it came out in 1892 with illustrations by Métivet as well). The preparatory sketches for this work were exhibited, together with sixteen pictures, at the first Salon de la Rose Croix. He also illustrated *L'Enfance de Notre Seigneur Jésus-Christ selon Saint Pierre* with watercolours and drawings; the Gospel text was rendered into French by Catulle Mendès. For the figure of Mary, Schwabe used his wife as model, whose maiden name, symbolically, was Ombra. He wrote about this book in 1895: "When I began these illustrations, I knew very little as I had studied for too short a time, having been obliged to earn my living since the age of eighteen. This work, therefore, is truly the work of a primitive, using that term with absolute sincerity. I did not know anything, but I loved with all my heart and soul."

In 1897 he produced coloured etchings for the poems of Baudelaire, and later illustrated *L'Effort* by Edmond Haraucourt, and poems by Maeterlinck and Samain. At the Paris World's Fair in 1900 he exhibited in the Swiss Pavilion. His art, decorative and over-refined, answered to a certain taste at that time. In his painting "the solemn heads are emaciatedly ascetic, the mouths tremble, the necks are bent, the hair is smooth or knotted, each figure is either in an attitude of humiliation or about to take flight, while their hands are twisted in mystical shudders," so wrote the critic Gustave Soulier in *Art et Décoration* in 1899.

Born in northern Italy, in the province of Trento, where his father was a carpenter. His mother died when he was very young and he was taken to Milan where, abandoned by his father, he spent a very unhappy childhood. After running away from Milan several times, he was placed in a reformatory (1870-1873), whose director enrolled him in the Brera Fine Arts Academy in Milan, where he did well and went on to give drawing lessons himself. In 1880 he met the picture dealer Vittore Grubicy, who was very knowledgeable about contemporary art, both Italian and European. Segantini signed a contract with him which, though it gave the artist financial security, gave the dealer exclusive rights over his work as well as over his personal possessions and the right to sign his canvases. This agreement, which lasted for many years, was the cause of violent recriminations between the two men. In 1883 Segantini settled in a village on the Lake of Lugano. He won a gold medal at the Amsterdam Exhibition in 1883 with his *Ave Maria*. From then on he exhibited regularly in Italy where his works were admired by both public and critics.

In 1886 he went to live with his large family at Savognino, a Swiss mountain village in the Grisons. The way of life of the local people provided him with an inexhaustible source of inspiration as well as supplying him with food for constant spiritual reflection. He read and studied a great deal and despite his isolation did not lose contact with the artistic and literary milieux (he kept up a long correspondence with Pellizza da Volpedo). Towards the end of his life he was much admired in Germany and Austria where he often exhibited. In 1896 the Munich Secession put on a one-man show of his work. He died in 1899 in a mountain hut on the Schafberg, while working on a great allegorical triptych on Nature, Life and Death for the Paris World's Fair of 1900.

Secession exhibition, Vienna.
1902. Poster by Alfred Roller.

"Serres chaudes" by Maeterlinck.
Tailpiece by George Minne.

Sérusier in his Paris flat photographed by Vuillard.

Born in Paris, Sérusier came of a well-to-do middle-class family; his father was head of the big perfumery firm of Houbigant. After a sound classical schooling, he studied art at the Académie Julian. A gifted musician as well as a painter, he was also passionately interested in philosophy and Oriental studies (he learned both Arab and Hebrew). In 1888, while staying in Brittany at Pont-Aven, he painted the famous *Talisman* under Gauguin's direction. Maurice Denis wrote: "It was in the autumn of 1888 that we first heard about Gauguin from Sérusier, who had just come back from Pont-Aven. After making a great mystery about it, Sérusier showed us the lid of a cigar box on which could be distinguished a landscape [*The Talisman*] which seemed formless because synthetically built up..." A year later the Nabi group (the word means prophet in Hebrew) was formed at his prompting and the meetings were held in a little restaurant in the Passage Brady. In 1889 and 1890 he worked in Brittany with Gauguin, and when the latter left for Tahiti he became friends with Verkade who interested him in theosophy. His art became more and more symbolic in expression, founded on the use of the golden number. He made a long stay in Brittany with Verkade and continued to see him at frequent intervals even when Verkade had entered the German abbey of Beuron as a monk. On one of these visits, in 1899, he met Father Desiderius Lenz, the founder of a school of religious art based on the theory of the "Holy Measurements"; in 1905 he translated Lenz's book on the subject into French as *Les Saintes Mesures*. He made frequent trips to Italy, twice with Maurice Denis, with whom in 1904 he visited Rome, Monte Cassino, Naples and Pompeii. "Don't talk to me about pictures, decorations are the only things that exist," he was fond of saying. In 1921 he published his *A.B.C. de la Peinture*, based on the aesthetic theories of Father Desiderius Lenz. After his marriage in 1922 he lived a more and more secluded life in Brittany and became passionately interested in Celtic poetry and medieval tapestries. He decorated his house and the church at Châteauneuf-du-Faou. In Brittany he found "his real homeland because he was born there in spirit."

A native of Düsseldorf, Strathmann studied art at the Academy there (1882-1886) before going to the School of Fine Arts in Weimar (1886-1889). He then did illustrations for *Fliegende Blätter* and *Jugend*. The themes he used in his painting, which was in a decorative linear style, were characteristically Symbolist ones: the *femme fatale*, lasciviousness, sin and the usual erotic subjects. Thus Salome, Cleopatra, Salammbó, and Judith were among the legendary female characters that he used. Some of his pictures, because of their ornamental character, are close to Byzantine mosaics, while others can be compared to sixteenth-century Netherlandish art for their minute attention to the details of landscapes and interiors. However, decoration for its own sake, which was so essentially a part of Art Nouveau, was always the most important aspect of his art.

Son of a peasant family from Lower Bavaria, Stuck began drawing as a boy, chiefly caricatures. He attended the Kunstgewerbeschule in Munich (1878-1881), then the Academy (1881-1885). To earn his living he did illustrations for commercial publications: *Allegorien und Embleme* (1882-1884), *Karten und Vignetten* (1886), *Fliegende Blätter* (1887-1892), *Die Zwölf Monate* (1888). In 1889 he exhibited a painting for the first time, *The Warden of Paradise*, which attracted attention. That same year he painted his *Wrestling Faun* and from then on, under the influence of Dietz, Lenbach and above all Böcklin, his work dealt more and more with fauns, tritons, mermaids, centaurs and all manner of legendary creatures. Stuck evolved from a naturalistic style, assimilated at the Academy, to a schematized, increasingly decorative idiom invaded by the unreal and supernatural. In 1892 he was one of the founders of the Munich Secession. From 1892 to 1895 he painted some large symbolic pictures in an ornamental style like *Sin*, exhibited in 1893. In 1894 he was made a member of the official purchasing commission for works of art and thus played an important part in the cultural life of Munich. That same year he exhibited one of his best pictures, *War*, a visionary work which shows a rider on a dark horse trampling humanity underfoot. In 1895 Stuck was made professor at the Munich Academy and was to influence a whole new generation of artists: among his pupils were Kandinsky, Klee and Albers. The picture he exhibited that year, *The Kiss of the Sphinx*, was characteristic of his work, the mythological subject being an excuse, as so often with him, to show human passion. In order that his erotic scenes should not be instantly seen as such, Stuck would set them in a legendary background and he continued to do this until the end of his life. He did illustrations for two magazines, *Pan* and *Jugend*, until 1901, when he gave up all such work. In 1897-1898 he created a "total" work of art. This was a villa that he had built for himself in Munich in which every detail was thought out and overseen by him. Stuck continued with his idealist pictures, refining his style and experimenting with decorative schematization. After the First World War he turned to sculpture and produced bronze statuettes of mythological subjects which he also took over in his painting.

As a child Thoma drew pictures of the Black Forest around his native village of Bernau. After primary school he worked in Basel for a lithographer, then in a lacquerer's shop. Returning to Bernau, he began doing small oil-paintings of the countryside. The landscapist J.W. Schirmer, director of the art school in Karlsruhe, encouraged him to study art, and in 1859 Thoma began working in Schirmer's studio where he stayed until 1866. During these years of training, he produced realistic studies, portraits and landscapes from nature. In Düsseldorf, where he next spent two years as assistant to a painter, his realistic art met with incomprehension, being contrary to the Biedermeier taste of that period. In 1868 he went to Paris with a painter from Frankfurt, Otto Scholderer, and this visit encouraged him to continue with his style, which was close to that of Courbet and the French Realists. On his return to Germany he painted a series of large naturalistic paintings. In 1870 he met Böcklin in Munich and from then on introduced strange, imaginative and fantastical themes into his art. In 1874 Thoma made the first of his five trips to Italy (1880, 1886, 1892, 1897), together with the painter A. Lang. The Italian landscape and contact with Italian art profoundly impressed him and brought him new sources of inspiration; on his return to Germany, nudes and mythological scenes made their appearance in his work. In 1876 he settled in Frankfurt where he married. He found few buyers for his work and success was late in coming. He executed a few monumental paintings for private patrons and produced a large number of canvases. In 1890 he had an exhibition of about sixty paintings, in Berlin and then in Munich which was well received. A change in public taste brought him honour and rewards, and he was appointed Director of the Kunsthalle in Karlsruhe and professor at the Academy there in 1899.

After having studied at the School of Fine Arts in The Hague, Thorn Prikker followed the example of Anton Breitner and painted in an impressionist and even neo-impressionist style. Then he discovered the work of Gauguin, Maurice Denis, and his fellow countryman Jan Toorop, which converted him to Symbolism (c. 1892): he now painted *The Bride*. Its linear style based on dynamic arabesques is similar to that of Toorop; the theme, the mystical union between a nun taking her vows and Christ, already reflects the religious preoccupations of his later work. Never accepted as a member of the Dutch Symbolist group, Thorn Prikker met with general incomprehension and he thus passed through a very difficult period, only sustained by the friendship of Henry van de Velde, who encouraged him to try his hand at the decorative arts, in particular batik and stained glass. But, mainly under the influence of Maurice Denis, he turned more and more to mysticism and religion. Working in a sober Art Nouveau style, often bordering on abstraction, he devoted himself to church art.

Born in Java of Dutch parents who were themselves of Chinese and Norwegian origin, Toorop went to Holland in 1873. In 1879 he began going to evening school at the Delft Polytechnic; in 1880-1882 he studied painting at the Academy of Fine Arts in Amsterdam, and in 1882-1883 at the Brussels Academy. There he met the Belgian Symbolist artists and writers: Ensor, Khnopff, Maeterlinck, Verhaeren, etc. He became a member of The Twenty, with whom he exhibited in Brussels until 1893, when the group broke up. In 1884, while on a trip to England with Verhaeren, he became intensely interested in the work of the Pre-Raphaelites as well as that of Blake; the style and linework of the latter artist was to particularly influence his work. Back in Holland for good in 1888, he lived in The Hague during the winters; the summers were spent on the islands in the North Sea. His first Symbolist works date from 1890, and are: *Venus of the Sea* (1890), then in 1893 *The Three Brides*, *Fate* and *Song of our Time*. His curvilinear style inspired perhaps by Javanese batik, which he himself described as "linear idealism," is not just mere decoration. By means of his drawing, the line acquires a symbolic force of expression which itself is capable of translating feelings and sensations. Toorop uses this very characteristic style in his oil paintings and also in his graphic work: drawings, woodcuts and lithographs for magazine illustrations, posters, etc. His themes—love, woman, lust, death—were similar to those used by contemporary Symbolist writers, and in fact he was part of the "Quatre-vingts" group. He was attracted to mysticism very early on and this search for a transcendental world, which became stronger as his life went on, ended up in his conversion to Catholicism in 1905. From then on he produced almost entirely religious works.

A native of Nidau, in the Canton of Berne, Switzerland, Trachsel was at the same time a painter, an architect and a writer. When he was still very young, he became a member of the *Humanistes* group in Geneva, then studied architecture and painting in Zurich and Paris. He paid extended visits to Spain, Italy and Germany and travelled the length and breadth of Switzerland on long walking tours. In 1892 he exhibited in Paris at the first Salon de la Rose Croix, at the same time as Hodler, with whom he became a close friend. Unlike other Swiss artists, Trachsel kept in touch all his life with his Swiss contemporaries as well as with his country. His name was never familiar to the general public. Like that of Hermann Obrist, his art tended towards abstraction and he liked using those linear rhythms which were characteristic of Art Nouveau.

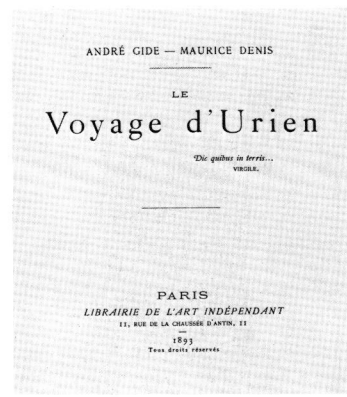

"Le Voyage d'Urien" by André Gide, 1893.

LIST OF ILLUSTRATIONS

Photographs and portraits

PRINTED BY
IMPRIMERIES RÉUNIES S.A., LAUSANNE

BINDING BY
GROSSBUCHBINDEREI H. + J. SCHUMACHER AG
SCHMITTEN (FRIBOURG)

Printed in Switzerland